MUZZLELOADER MAGAZINE'S

THE BOOK OF
BUCKSKINNING II

Edited by

WILLIAM H. SCURLOCK

SCURLOCK PUBLISHING COMPANY, INC./TEXARKANA, TEXAS

EDITORIAL STAFF

EDITOR:
William H. Scurlock

ASSOCIATE EDITOR:
Mary Frances Scurlock

GRAPHIC DESIGN:
William H. Scurlock

COVER PHOTOGRAPHY:
David Wright

PUBLISHER:
William H. Scurlock

ABOUT THE COVERS

American Mountain Man Rick Bauman and his wife Cathy grace our front and back covers. Buckskinners for several years, Rick and Cathy have made extensive studies into the clothing and equipment used by the mountain men. This knowledge is important to the customers they serve through Ne Shutsa Traders, in Haven, Kansas, which they own and operate.

First Printing: November, 1983
Second Printing: June, 1984
Third Printing: March, 1989
Fourth Printing: June, 1990
Fifth Printing: February, 1992
Sixth Printing: July, 1993
Seventh Printing: March, 1995

ISBN #0-9605666-2-7   Library of Congress Catalog Card #80-54597

Contents

DEDICATION

To the memory of Dave Schippers.
As a mountain man, buckskinner and family man,
he is missed. Dave's picture appeared on the front cover of
The Book of Buckskinning.

Why Buckskinners Create

by Dick "Beau Jacques" House

DICK "BEAU JACQUES" HOUSE has been a gun collector since childhood and a black powder shooter since early adulthood. He penned the keynote chapter for *The Book of Buckskinning.* His writings on black powder and buckskinning subjects have appeared in *Muzzleloader, Gun Digest, Black Powder Times, American Rendezvous Magazine, The Backwoodsman,* the *Dixie Gun Works Annual,* and the former *Trade Blanket.*

House has been a newsman and corporate public relations specialist for 35 years. A reporter-photographer-editor for Ohio and Arizona newspapers, he has also worked for Ford Motor Company and Occidental Life of California. For 14 years he has been an editor with the Jet Propulsion Lab in Pasadena, California, the nation's leading explorer of deep space and the planets, affiliated with NASA and Caltech.

"Beau Jacques" is a long-time member of the Western Writers of America, Inc., and served as membership chairman four years, two terms on the executive board, and is the current vice president. He serves as well on the executive board of the Cowboy Memorial and Library. He is a member of the Society for the Preservation and Encouragement of Barbershop Quartet Singing in America (SPEBSQSA), and the Huntington Corral of Westerners, International.

"But when it gets right down to the heart of the matter," says House, "give me a sweet shootin' smokepole, a horn of powder, patches and balls, and turn me loose to roam the High Lonesome. That's some, that is!"

1

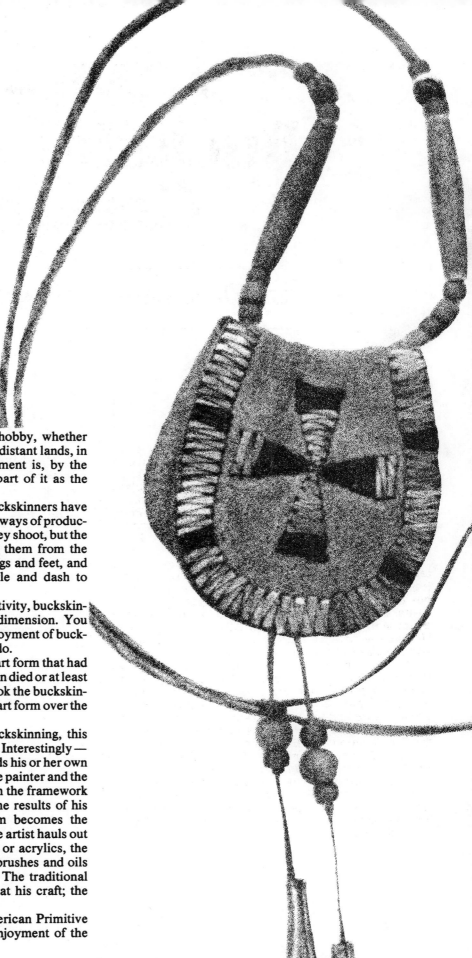

BUCKSKINNING is the only hobby, whether followed on American soil or in distant lands, in which making your own equipment is, by the very nature of the pastime, as much a part of it as the enjoyment of the hobby itself.

There, in a nub, is the reason that buckskinners have returned to the primitive crafts and simple ways of producing not only the vintage-styled weapons they shoot, but the utensils they use, the lodges that shield them from the elements, the coverings on their backs, legs and feet, and the foofurraw and finery that lends style and dash to their outfits.

Without its arts, its crafts and its creativity, buckskinning would be without a very essential dimension. You don't have to build your own, but your enjoyment of buckskinning is enhanced if you can . . . and do.

Underneath it all is an art. It was an art form that had flourished for centuries in America and then died or at least became seriously ill generations ago. It took the buckskinner movement to breathe new life into the art form over the past 20 or so years.

Let's face it, in the possibles of buckskinning, this truly American art form is emerging again. Interestingly — and uniquely — the buckskinner who builds his or her own gear is both the designer and the model, the painter and the canvas, the sculptor and the sculpture. On the framework of his own body, he drapes and hangs the results of his buckskinner art and craft. The medium becomes the message — I am a buckskinner. Where the artist hauls out canvas and brushes and the tubes of oils or acrylics, the buckskinner's canvas is himself and his brushes and oils are wood and metal, leather and beads. The traditional artist or sculptor stands back and looks at his craft; the buckskinner wears and uses his.

Buckskinner arts and crafts are American Primitive with definite function and purpose — enjoyment of the

rugged wilderness lifestyle; in many cases it serves to provide the means of survival.

Nowhere, absolutely nowhere, on the American scene, is there a hobby or interest to rival buckskinning in the creation of the tools, trappings and utensils for the enjoyment and pursuit of the interest. It would be unthinkable for the golfer to ever consider making his own clubs, or a skier to shape his own skis from hickory planks and a drawknife. (They used to, back in the days when mountain men and Indians were also making their own things. *They* never will again. By strong contrast, today's mountain men and followers of the Indian styles, the buckskinners, pride themselves on the creation of their own "possibles".)

Proper appreciation of every other sport, hobby, or recreational activity demands store-bought, mass-produced, or expensively custom-built implements. The proper clothing to appropriately take part in these other sports must come from the finest shops.

Contrast that with the buckskinner who can create the devices of his hobby from raw materials. With the possible exception of the guns, there is virtually nothing that cannot be created at home or for that matter, in the field. Whenever you step back in time, you simplify.

At the same time, the very attractive and interesting aspect of buckskinner crafts is that precision is not all that vital an ingredient. These modern-day mountain man artifacts retain a distinctive style and material for authenticity's sake. But from there, it's a case of every man — and woman — for himself, or herself.

Again, the significant exception is in black powder weaponry. For safety, accuracy and authenticity, these must conform to fairly rigid standards. However, the possible variation in design, finish and adornment — while not sacrificing safety, accuracy and authenticity — is just about as wide as the variations in human fingerprints. There is very little "look-alike" about 'skinning.

Going beyond that one narrow requirement in buckskinner weapons, the rest of the trappings are simple to create and a few flaws here and there only mark it as handhewn and more rustic than crude. And the ideas for creating authentic implements and clothing are equally broad — as the following pages of this book will show.

What is very special about buckskinner creativity is this ample margin for self-expression. You don't have to "color inside the lines"; it is not a paint-by-numbers craft. An individual, whether or not he or she has great artistic and creative talents, may study the designs, patterns and ideas, pull together the raw materials and parts and then, using imagination and even "by guess and by gosh", wing it for the development of a very satisfying and satisfactory outfit. Nowhere is it said "you must do it exactly this way". It does follow that authenticity is enhanced the closer you stick to some of the basic ideas, but authenticity can be preserved and even improved upon by improvising and calling forth your own innate creative juices.

For the most part, in outfitting yourself as a buckskinner, total authenticity is desirable and commendable and a goal to strive for. But when undue preoccupation over strict enforcement begins to dull the enjoyment of the hobby, it may have outlived its usefulness. Fortunately, the varieties in buckskinning are so vast and so broad that those who are numbered as purists when it comes to authenticity can come together and truly enjoy the precision and uniformity that attitude suggests, while those who take it just a bit more relaxed and easy can also find acceptance in buckskinner camps and rendezvous.

However, no matter where you go, synthetics and plastic in anything are out! As one buckskinner pointed out, he never wears naugahyde clothing because he's never been able to track, skin out and tan a "nauga". It's a simple truth in buckskinning that you can't get splinters from plastic!

Stemming directly from the post World War II interest in antique guns, the buckskinner movement — and its crafts — have undergone a generally gradual development over about the past 20 years. As it grew, research into the tools and trappings of the mountain man intensified. While the guns of the period held an ongoing fascination, whole new vistas opened up in the area of the "possibles" — the accessories that went along with life in the early and primitive wilds. As these items themselves were researched, surfacing with them were the ways in which they were made. Techniques that had lain dormant for 150 years came to life and people began to find enjoyment not only in having and using implements of the bygone era, but in savoring the sheer joy and pride in creating something useful from horn or bone or leather. The fun was in the making, by old-time techniques and skills, as much as in the owning and using.

4

Not only do buckskinners create items for themselves, they also make items for selling or trading at rendezvous. Many camps have a trade blanket which displays the owner's goods.

To get deeply philosophical, some of the terms that contributed to the death of the mountain man era — and coincidentally gave birth to its offspring buckskinner movement a century and a half later — were "Industrial Revolution", "standardization", "mass production", "automation", "planned obsolescence", "computerization", and "progressive or exponential technology".

If that last term sounds confusing, it simply states that new technologies and techniques are developed so fast that almost before they are perfected and put into use, they are rendered obsolete by other radical new technologies.

But notice that the order in which these are set out are just about the way these terms developed, historically. (Note also the growing harshness of the terms on the ear.) As the terms developed, they fostered increasing complexity and impersonality. Ultimately humans rebelled against such anonymity — just being a Social Security number or a driver's license number was insulting.

The Industrial Revolution, historically, has been a good thing for mankind, across the board. The successive developments have also lightened man's burden, made life easier and more abundant, and provided greater leisure time. Buckskinners enjoy the freedom today to pursue that hobby because of these great industrial and technological strides. Without them, we would still be virtually enslaved by a system that offers little or no relief from a humdrum and inexorable slogging in the rut of work merely to stay alive.

So, while there were benefits, there were also sacrifices. For each action, said a wise man, there is an equal and opposite reaction. The Industrial Revolution and all of its succeeding progressions took work out of small shops and turned it over to big shops. The artisan, instead of building the whole of a single product, was reduced to performing a small grinding or polishing operation on a vast multitude of small parts. He became the little frog in an awfully big and confusing pond. All around him were men doing the same thing, each of them performing a slightly different operation on the same vast multitude of parts. Somewhere, all of these component parts came together — maybe in another corner of the plant, or maybe in an assembly plant clear across the country or across an ocean. In his bewilderment with this turn of events, he sensed that his contribution as an individual was lost — and with it *identity*.

In the end came dimming of the light of personal achievement. The lofty glow that came with "This is my best" quickly slid down to the muck of disillusionment that comes with "I don't give a damn", and saw the rise of "TGIF" and "Take this job and shove it!" Gone was that essential ingredient to self-esteem — pride in a job well done . . . the satisfaction and joy of honest toil.

A small group of buckskinners enjoy the early morning solitude and prepare breakfast. Unlike other forms of camping, primitive camping allows the participants to make almost all of their own camp gear.

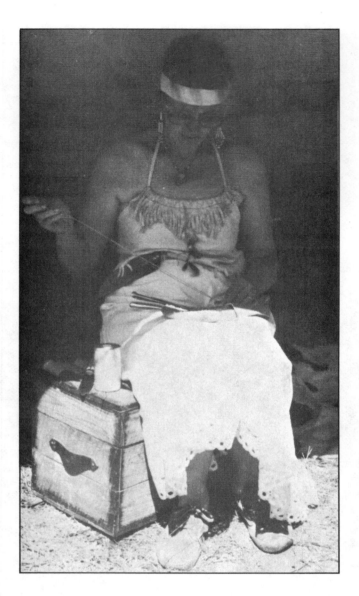

invading the High Lonesome. Names like Hawken and Leman gave way to Sharps and Spencer, and then to Colt and Winchester. Bulk powder and ball gave way to paper and linen cartridges, and then to brass casings and internal primers. "Factory loads" became the byword. By the mid 1890s, the frontier was declared conquered.

But it had all gone along marvelously, as though some great master hand was guiding the Industrial Revolution. Through it all and for a long, long time this matter of production still contained a degree of pride. Henry Ford with his Model T and Model A still harbored an illusion that he was building a car that would last a man a lifetime and could be repaired in the backyard. There was an oddly

Interestingly enough, night began to fall on the Dark Age of muzzleloading and the cabin crafts at about the same time gunmaker Eli Whitney kicked off the Industrial Revolution and the machine age with his invention of the cotton gin, and standardization and interchangeability of parts. Another gunmaker, Sam Colt, gave that movement a great shove with his manufacturing procedures. With these developments, a death knell was rung. No longer would the small gunsmith hammer and rifle his own barrels, form his own stocks with drawknife and rasp, and create lock sears and bridles and tumblers from tiny pieces of metal. The goods and services of life became easier to buy off the shelf.

The proximity in historical time of these events carries an irony all its own. The beaver felt hat went out of vogue within a few decades after the cotton gin, and the fur trade and the mountain man were doomed. The buffalo slaughter began with the rise of cartridge guns, and along with it the final repression of the American Indian. Meanwhile, a long line of white-canvas-topped wagons began snaking out of the east over the Great Plains and

Creating outfits for himself and his family gives the buckskinner the opportunity for self-expression which is lacking in most other hobbies.

Some things buckskinners love to make. Clockwise beginning at right: Music, Pouches, Knife Sheaths and Moccasins.

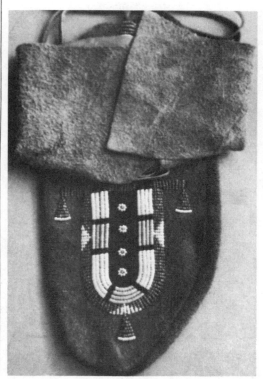

familiar ring in Ford's philosophy. We had last heard it most loudly proclaimed by men like Hawken and Leman.

But pride in craft continually suffered a watering down process. Metal got thinner. Less durable and incredibly brittle or incredibly limp plastic turned wood virtually into a product of the past, except for paper products and construction, in the main. The devices of day-to-day living began to carry warnings that only a certified service technician could properly maintain and repair household appliances. It got so bad that when something like that broke, you might just as well throw it out and go get a new one.

This led to new disillusionment. It is also interesting to note that when planned obsolescence and Space Age chagrin in sloppy manufactured products began to rub and to sting, the muzzleloader and the lifestyles and crafts associated with it began to reawaken. Buckskinning, except by a rare few, was not viewed as a substitution of, or an escape from, the 20th century. It was recreation in its finest sense: re-creation.

In the arts and the crafts and the creativity of the artifacts and the implements of buckskinning was simplicity, substance, and durability — if not nostalgia — for a few, at least, who had had it up to here with the transience and the "who-gives-a-damn" of a disposable society. The implements and the tools could be made well enough of rugged basic materials for a lifetime of use. They might even again be handed down from generation to generation. Great beauty is found in their simplicity. What rivals the clean, finely sculpted lines of a mountain rifle, is more pleasing to the eye than fine-print calico.?

Leather garments you have personally tailored and crafted for yourself soothe as they flow and conform to your movements; you realize there must be such a thing as "genetic memory" — the sensations are so fine and so familiar that you are certain that somehow, in another life, you wore buckskins before!

Beadwork, quillwork, weaving, scrimshaw — artistry that cannot be surpassed in the finest galleries! And what fits better in the hand than a fine and reliable old 'hawk or knife that you've made yourself and has been a trusted

You can even make your own tipi such as this one made of real buffalo hides. Photo was taken at an early American Mountain Men rendezvous held on Black's Fork of the Green River.

11

companion on a hundred adventures in the High Lonesome?

For every shrinking violet who protests, "But I don't have any talent for making things", there are a hundred buckskinners who felt the same way, but had the guts to take the bit in their teeth, studied the patterns and read the instructions of those who had researched and tried and come up with the techniques.

Every writer in this book whose contributions follow, started from the same base; nothing. They didn't know they could do it until they tried. Without exception, every one of them was once at the place the beginner is right now. They had to learn.

The best way to "get up to speed" with buckskinner crafts is to start simply. For some it may be a simple, inexpensive kit — a starting point. Sure with a kit most of the work is done for you. But it produces results with a bit of your sweat, elbow grease and midnight oil. A small leather project, perhaps, or a powder horn. So you wreck it or make a shambles of the venture. You've lost a few hours and a few dollars. But did you gain? Of course. Now you can say, I'll know what not to do the next time. This is the first glimmering that *you will know what to do next time*. So, you venture out and start again. This time the results are better; the next effort at building a buckskinner outfit will be even more of a success. Do you see what you are becoming? A buckskinner craftsman — or craftswoman.

In essence, the best advice to any beginner — at anything — is K.I.S.S. "Keep It Simple, Stupid". Take on a project easy enough to guarantee a reasonable expectation of success. When you've done that, hunt out another that has just a bit more challenge to it. Soon you'll find it fun, you'll be hooked, and going after the ones that really take some skill and technique. Then, before long, when you least expect it, somebody will come up to you and say, "Dogged if I don't wish I could make things like you do."

Remember that disillusioning loss of pride in a job well done we were talking about earlier? Well, hoss, you will have found it again!

Working With Leather

by Pat Tearney

PAT TEARNEY HAS BEEN IN THE business of American history since the early 1950s. For many years he specialized in the crafts and culture of the Indian peoples of the American plains, first as a hobbiest, and soon as a professional. He opened his first store in 1955 in Wichita, Kansas. After a stint in the U.S. Air Force, Pat moved to San Fernando Valley, California where he and three partners started the Buffalo Robe Trading Post of Canoga Park. It was here that Pat began to sharpen his historical knowledge and tailoring skills. He designed the clothing, made the patterns, and did most of the work related to historical and buckskin clothing. He was exposed to black powder and was immediately "hooked".

In the fall of 1971, Pat hitched up with Karalee, who soon turned out to be as avid an enthusiast for history and buckskinning as her husband. Two children, Heather, age eleven, and Conan Padric, age eight, are also fully involved in their parents' hobby/business.

After a short sojourn in Rollins, Montana, Pat and family moved down to southern Illinois and thence to Arrow Rock, Missouri. They have continued their business of providing fine historical clothing under the name of La Pelleterie.

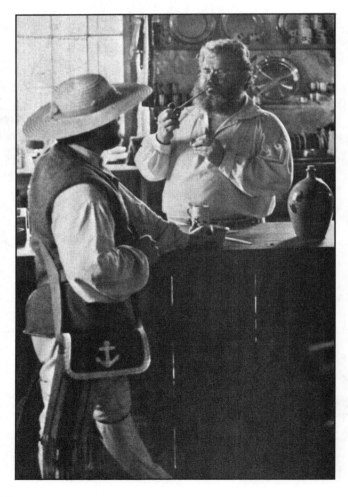

LEATHER has an interesting history. Items of leather have been found from as far back in time as the ancient Egyptians. Leather and furs were amongst the first body coverings. The earliest tents, blankets, and other such items were fur or leather, too.

Leather is versatile. It can be tanned as soft as velvet or as hard as a piece of copper. It can be as thin as cloth, or so thick it can be used as armor. For that matter, the Plains Indians made war shields of rawhide from the neck of the bison. It was shrunk, thickened, and hardened to the point that a shield of this sort has been known to actually turn a round ball from a heavy caliber rifle.

Leather comes in many forms depending upon the use to which it will be put. A few kinds of leather of use to the buckskinner and major uses to which we put them are following.

Buckskin needs very little introduction of itself. As we use the term it means the tanned hide from either a deer or an elk. Moose hides would fall into this general category but are too rare to bear much mention. Buckskin (deerskin)

is a soft tanned leather, sueded (brushed) on the flesh side to give a varying degree of velvet-like nap. Commercially tanned buckskin does not have the scarf skin on the hair side removed as a rule. It therefore has one "slick" or more or less smooth side.

Some commercial buckskin is split down. This is done by running it through a machine that slices through the thickness of the hide. The results are that you get one piece of top grain, with one smooth side and one sueded side; and one "hide" with two rough sides. This latter piece is called a split. Usually, the best side of this is then sueded.

Indian or hand tanned buckskin is the best kind of leather for frontier type of clothing. This is the kind of leather found in all existing leather garments of frontier origin. Also, we know that hundreds of thousands of processed deer hides were traded from the Indians during all periods of the fur trade. Far more deer hides were taken than those of any other animal. It is highly likely that many

14

Tanner and Currier: A wood engraving by John Trusler, 1791.

of them found their way to the tailors who then made breeches and other items of clothing and clothing accessories from them.

Hand tanned buckskin is made by first stretching it, either on a rack or by pegging it out on the ground, flesh side up and removing the flesh, fat, blood, and scarf skin with some sort of a scraper. A large butcher knife or a special fleshing tool may be used.

The second step was to remove the hair. To do this you first soaked the hide for a couple of days in a pond or the edge of a stream. Be sure to weight the hide down well with rocks if you do this. Then the hide was removed from the water and lots of ashes were worked well down into the roots of the hair. The hide was then folded hair in, rolled up and set away for a few days until the hair was loose and pulled out easily. It was checked daily to be sure it remained damp but did not rot. A more modern method is to soak the hide in a large container with a weak lye solution.

When the hair came loose easily, the hide was rinsed thoroughly, then laid over a log or stretched out on a frame and the hair was removed by scraping with a dull knife or a specially made hide tool. You now had rawhide.

After the hair was removed, the hide was checked to be sure that the hide was still thoroughly damp but not dripping wet. A mixture of the animal's brains, mashed thoroughly and mixed in a small amount of warm water, was made up. I have heard of this mixture being "cooked" but have not done this myself. A modern mix which I learned from an Indian friend consists of 1 pound of lard and a cup or two of flour or white cornmeal. The amounts are approximate. The flour or cornmeal merely "carries" the lard which takes the place of the animal's brains. The solution, whichever used, was then rubbed into the damp hide until it could absorb no more. The hide was then rolled up and set aside in a cool place for a day or two until the oils were absorbed. The hide was then checked occasionally to be sure it did not dry out. When the hide had absorbed the

oils, it was taken out and rinsed thoroughly 2 or 3 times, then squeezed dry. It was now ready for the final operations, beaming and smoking.

A hide was beamed to break down the fibers and make it dry soft. To do this it was rubbed, every square inch of it, over a sharp-edged stake, around a tree limb, or with a special paddle-like instrument of wood until it was dry and soft. Both sides were worked, the edges as well as the center. What was not worked would not be soft. This had to be done with great vigor and a lot of elbow grease *until the* hide was dry. If it dried hard in any spot, the hide had to be soaked down, wrung out and the process repeated.

When the hide was soft and dry, it was ready to use. It had only one drawback. It was not really "tanned", merely cured. If the hide became wet, it would become quite stiff unless worked dry as before. The answer to this was to smoke it.

Smoking a hide was done in this manner. First, the hide was stitched up one side to form a sleeve. Next, a small pit was dug in the ground deep enough to hold a small smudge fire. The fire was built in this and allowed to burn down to a few coals. Punk wood was placed on the coals to create a smudge (smoke). A tripod was erected over this to hold the hide. The hide was then placed inside the tripod and pegged down all around the lower edges.

The fire had to be a low smoky smudge with no flame. A flame or very much heat would destroy the hide. According to Elsworth Jaeger in his book *Wildwood Wisdom,* a good fuel for this is wood with dry rot that is itself quite dry. He says this will give off a thick bluish colored smoke. Different woods gave the hides different colors. (See what woods are available in your area and try them before attempting to do a hide yourself.) The hides were smoked for 10-20 minutes or longer. The longer a hide was "in the smoke" the darker it would become. When the hide was removed from the smoke, it was rolled up and set aside for several days to "cure". It was then ready to use.

As can be seen by the foregoing, hand tanned leather was quite a bit different from today's commercial leather and was even different from European style leather of the early period.

Early day garment leather was somewhat like today's commercial leather in that it was a vegetable chemical tan. Lime was often used to loosen the hair and break down the fibers. A solution of animal excretia and water was used to remove and to neutralize the lime. The hides had oil added, were washed, stretched, dried and were then ready for use. It might be interesting to note that very fine hides such as those used for fine gloves, kid shoes, and very fine garments were softened by use of solutions containing, among other things, egg yolks. These hides were generally worked by hand, even to a final polishing.

Oil tanned leather is a leather softened by the addition of oils such as that of cod. This makes a fine boot and bag leather. The black powder enthusiast will find this type of leather especially good for shooting bags. You can ask for it as "boot leather", or light-oil tanned leather.

Strap leather is another very versatile material for the buckskinner. It is oak tanned leather. It comes in varied weights and thicknesses. Very light weight, such as 2-3 ounce and 3-4 ounce are too light for most of our needs. 5-6 ounce and 6-7 ounce material is excellent for light weight straps. The 7-8 ounce weight makes good belts and 8-9 and 9-10 ounce is good for heavy tack belts, equipment belts,

knife sheaths, etc. Saddles and saddle equipment need 14-15 ounce weight strap. There is also a special saddle leather that is very thick and treated with a hot wax. For this sort of thing you should check with a good leather supplier such as S & T Leather Co. in Saint Louis.

Rawhide is an unfinished leather. The hide has been cleaned, dehaired, and in the case of Indian style (the best), softened slightly by pounding. It is the only material for Plains Indian parfleches and boxes as well as many other items.

As can be seen, there are many kinds of leather. We have touched on only a few. Like every material, it has its good points and its bad points. For some things though, even today, there is no really suitable substitute. Good leather is supple, water resistant to a limited degree, tough, does not turn brittle in extreme cold or soften in heat. It will mildew if closed in a damp area where it can't dry out; it is not as warm as wool or as cool as cotton or linen. But drawbacks and advantages both aside, there is a mystique to leather that cannot be denied.

Several uses of leather can be seen in this picture of Kirby Werner; buckskin for clothing, a buffalo robe (painted) for a bed, and rawhide for the parfleche bags hanging from the liner.

THE MOUNTAIN MAN:
What did he wear?

Remember that the mountain man was very many things. He was an adventurer, an explorer, a rugged individualist. He was a hunter, a trapper, a trader, a businessman. He was all of these and more; but still, he was a product of his environment and his society. He came from an 18th and early 19th century background. His clothing reflected this. The pattern of his clothing was that of the white settlers and citizens of his time or that of the Indians he met; or a combination thereof.

The mountain man's shirt, if of cloth, would have been of either cotton, linen, or wool. Probably solid colors such as natural (unbleached), off white, blue or red would have been used. Large print and striped calico (cottons) were popular, too.

The kind of shirt available would have been a simple pullover with large body and blousy sleeves. There seem to have been two basic types, based primarily on the neck opening. One, a colonial design that was worn up until the mid 19th century, had a deep slit in front with no placket and only one button at the top of the slit. The second style had a placket at the neck opening and several buttons in order to better close the front. This style seems to have come into use around the 1830s.

Trousers of the 1820s and 1830s were high waisted, full in the hips and seat with fall front. The legs were of three basic kinds: stove pipe cut (full and loose), tapered cut to a small ankle like our old "Ivy League" styles, or cut to fit closely to the leg, sometimes flaring from just above the knee toward the ankle in order to give room for boots. Oh, yes, and pockets are permissible in the side seams. No hip pockets.

Belt loops were unknown at this time. They don't seem to come into use until the late 1800s. Suspenders (galluses) were the thing. They were *not* the red fireman's suspenders we see today, but rather a pair of cotton, linen or even leather ribands with button holes at either end. A fancier and more complex design with adjustable tabs was in use by the 1830s, too. An adjustable ½ belt or a gusset and ties such as were found on 18th century breeches, served to "cinch up" the trousers.

A special note: The hidden button, center fly which we all know and love was not common until after 1840. Flys with the buttons exposed are to my knowledge incorrect. I have seen no references or sketches showing exposed button flys. The only possibility is that some one "may" have made a pair of pants this way because it was easier. However, most buckskins were tailor made or made by Indian women copying the white man's style. Otherwise, it would have probably been Indian clothes.

Footwear in the mountains was moccasins. Boots or brogans might be worn into the mountains by green horns and by gentlemen traders such as Henry, Ashly, Choteau, etc. The hivernants (ones who had survived a year in the

Chris Bartholemew in scout uniform, 1886. Much of this clothing is of Indian origin as was the clothing of the mountain men earlier in the century.

Modern frontiersmen David Wright, Bill Golden, and Don Wright. David and Don are outfitted in the eastern style and Bill is dressed as a western mountain man.

mountains) all seem to have chosen moccasins. I have even read comments by young men of the period who, when outfitting in St. Louis, traded their boots for moccasins. In studying any sketches and paintings of the period, one notices the absence of boots and the abundance of moccasins present.

Belts were basically weapons belts. They had to be heavy enough to carry a large knife, perhaps a tomahawk, have a pistol thrust through and so forth. Large sashes, such as the Hudson Bay Co.'s Assumption sash or a wide leather belt would do.

Hats often were wide, flat brimmed styles with a low crown. Fur hats might be used but don't forget, beaver was money. Would you make a hat out of five dollar bills? Miller, the artist, shows a form of wool hunting hood that is very nice.

Coats "of the period" are nearly always correct. I would not use a fancy dress coat under ordinary circumstances, of course. However, a frock coat such as the one displayed in the Jefferson Memorial by the Missouri Historical Society would be fine for an Ashley. Box coats and great-coats of wool, capotes, and the eastern style rifleman's coats are all good styles. The 18th century style linen wamus was still being worn by farmers and militia during the Black Hawk Wars.

TOOLS FOR WORKING LEATHER

The tools we are most interested in are, of course, those used in making garments. I shall, however, include a few very usable items that will help in the making of knife sheaths and things like that. They are, all in all, simple tools and easily come by.

1. soft lead pencil
2. soft chalk
3. tracing paper
4. pattern paper
5. gum eraser (to clean dirt and other mistakes)
6. hawkbill knife
7. flat blade knife
8. whet stone (med. Ark.)
9. scissors (10" and sharp)
10. fine awl (3 or 4 sided)
11. large awl (*very* sharp)
12. assorted glover's needles
13. sewing palm or leather finger cover (thimble)
14. yard stick
15. draw knife (stripper)
16. tape measure
17. thread (imitation sinew or waxed linen)

And as extras should you wish:

18. French curve
19. "triangle"
20. assorted punches
21. shoemaker's hammer or medium size ball peen hammer

With these tools you can lay out and sew most anything.

Stretching a Hide

To stretch a hide, just do this: Soak the hide in lukewarm water. Wring it out. Now, tack it to a wooden fence, the side of your garage, or what have you. Start by tacking the hocks first. Then stretch out and down for about ¼ of the hide. Now, pull the neck straight down and then pull out and down on each side of the neck. Keep pulling out and away from the center while stretching all around the hide. Let it dry and you are ready to go.

PLUGGING HOLES

Most deer hides have at least one or two holes in them. This is nothing to worry about. These holes, if neatly sewn up, can actually add a touch of "authenticity" to your garment. After all, the old timers, Indian or non-Indian, used what they had available. Hides with small holes were patched; hides with large holes were pieced. Everything was used.

Small holes or slits are simple to fix. You merely whip stitch them closed from the back side with a *fine* thread and a fine stitch. Pound the "bulge" gently and brush the rough side to raise the nap back up.

Holes larger than about a quarter of an inch in diameter should be trimmed and plugged. To do this, just trim the "rim" of the hole to form a smooth edge. Then cut a plug (circle) of the same size as the hole. Lay the plug into

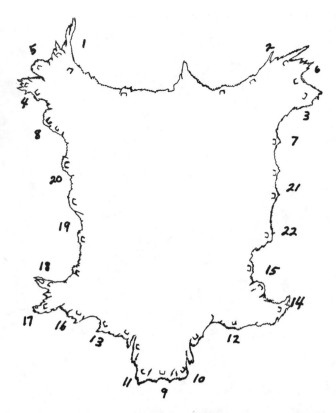

Stretch the hide by tacking or stapling according to the points numbered in the drawing then fill in between them as needed.

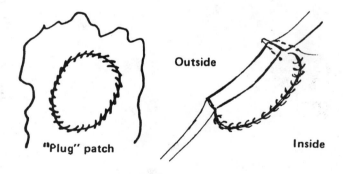

the hole and carefully sew it into place from the back side. Go all the way through the face of both pieces with each stitch. Use an overcast or whip stitch. Pound the ridge and brush. You'll have a neat looking piece of leather.

CUTTING & SEWING

The old saw about the first step in making a rabbit stew is very much true when applied to the making of any leather item, especially clothing. If you are not a tailor (and most are not) or a historian specializing in clothing and accoutrements (again, few are) then you must find or make a pattern. Green River Forge has some patterns that are pretty fair. They do not have everything, of course, but you can select from several eras of the fur trade and find a reasonable pattern for your needs. Folkwear Patterns have three very nice patterns: The Missouri River Boatman's

Shirt, The Kinsdale Cloak and The Empire Dress. *The Book of Buckskinning* (Volume 1) has a small section on how to adapt a modern pattern to 18th and 19th century styles. A good walk through your library art section should provide you with sketches and paintings of that period. Look especially for the works of Rudolph Kurz, Alfred Jacob Miller, Karl Bodmer and George Caleb Bingham.

After a particular item of clothing has been decided upon, the style and details chosen and the pattern made, we come to the cutting. We will, of course, assume you have already stretched the leather.

The best place to cut is on a large table: 4 feet by 6 feet is about perfect. An Old door or some planks up on saw horses will do. A "facing" for the table can be made from a large refrigerator box section. This could be secured from your local appliance salesman.

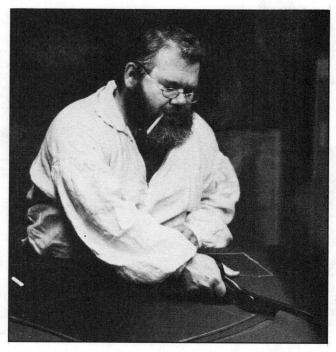
The easiest way to cut leather is on a large table, of the correct height, using large scissors or a sharp knife.

Lay the hide out on the table suede side up. Be sure the tail is either to your left or right. Lay the pattern on the hide so that the ends of the pattern are toward the ends of the hide. This way you will insure that the stretch goes around the garment, just as it does on the deer. Do this for each item you cut out. Be sure that you cut both rights and lefts where needed. It is very exasperating to end up with a coat which possesses two right but no left sleeve (or vice versa). In other ways, cutting leather is much like cutting cloth. Use sharp scissors. A very sharp knife may be used if you are cutting on a smooth table top such as masonite or an end grain cutting board. I would like to mention here. that if you are going to cut fringe, a sharp flat bladed knife and a cutting board make the job infinitely easier.

Once a garment is cut out, it must be put together. At this point, let me repeat myself for what seems the mil-

lionth time. "Sew it"! Don't lace it! I have never seen any old garment that was laced. They were all sewn using linen thread or sinew. Knives and scissors were abundant in old trade lists. Besides, punching holes and lacing weakens the hide and can be very uncomfortable. Talk to the man who wore his laced pants with the heavy seam crossings in the crotch while forking a saddle for several hours. A patch or other *emergency* sewing *might* get done using a very fine "whang". You can bet your Ligoniere moccasins that *that* particular repair was changed as soon as possible. The long hunters and mountain men were tough; they weren't stupid.

The most common stitch used was a simple overcast stitch. The close seconds would be the running stitch and the backstitch. The blind stitch (where the needle enters the material at the same point that it exits) and the saddle stitch were also used. The latter mostly on shooting bags and such. Stitches should be tight, 8-10 to the inch.

The thread used should be a fine thread. If you use imitation sinew, as I often do, strip it down and use it one strand singly, not doubled to the knot.

MEASURING FOR BREECHES, OVERALLS, TROUSERS & LEGGINGS

The best of tailors is helpless if he does not have correct and proper measurements from which to work. Without correct measurements, there can be no correct pattern. No correct pattern means you cannot properly cut the material. Should the cut of the material be too far off of correct, then the garment will fit poorly or not at all.

Measurements for trousers, etc., should be taken over Skivvies or fairly snug clothing. Do not ever take measurements over bulky clothing unless you intend to make outer garments that fit over them. Hold the tape so that it fits snugly but not tightly. Measure in the correct place. Here are the measurements you will need. Check the accompanying sketch before taking them.
1. True waist (at belly button level).
2. Hips at the bulge.
3. Thigh at the crotch.
4. Inseam A—from crotch to just below ankle bone.
5. Inseam—Knee breeches—from crotch to base of kneecap—then add 1½ inches.
6. Rise—from the true waist in front, under crotch, and back to true waist in rear. See the sketch.
7. Calf—measure at bulge.

MEASURING FOR COATS & SHIRTS

As I said before, measurements must be precise. Sloppy measurements will mean a sloppy fit.

First of all, measure the trunk, from neck to hips. Take each measurement over normal clothes and be sure to keep the tape snug but not tight.

Here are the places you must measure on the trunk:
1. Neck — at the base.
2. Chest — around at the breast — keep the tape horizontal.
3. The waist.

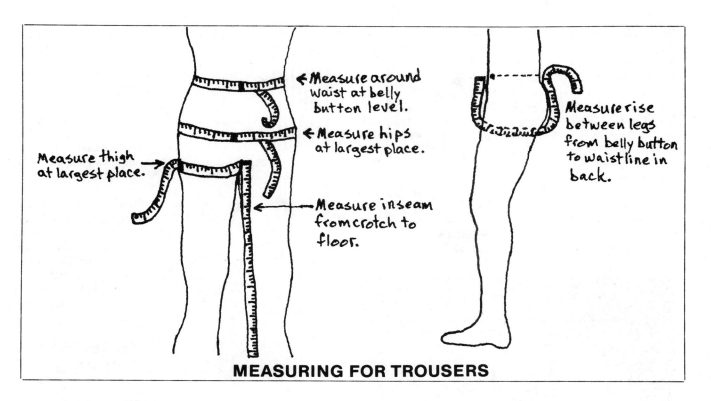

MEASURING FOR TROUSERS

4. Hips (at the bulge).
5. From the nape to the bulge of your hips.
6. From the nape of the neck to the waist.
7. Measure for the total length of the garment.

Now we measure for the arm. The first measurement is sleeve length. Raise the arm horizontal to the floor. Bend the forearm at the elbow 90°. Measure from the nape of the neck, around the elbow to the wrist. We also need a bicep measurement. Make a muscle and take your size. Measure the wrist.

From these measurements a pattern can be made or modified.

MEASURING FOR COATS & SHIRTS

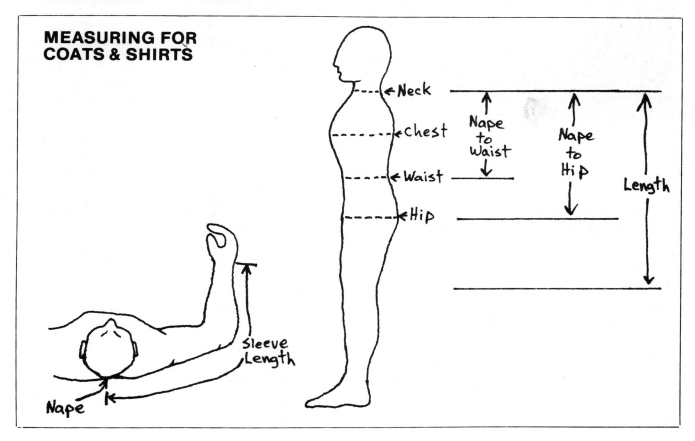

BROADFALL TROUSERS

This style of trouser was worn by the merchant, farmer, and other middle class folk as well as the lower classes. George Caleb Bingham shows us many details of these in his works of the 1830s and early 1840s. The material used as well as the quality of "cut" and "fit" varied with the wealth of the individual. Better classes used better materials as a rule.

As in the making of every garment, the first problem is the securing of a proper pattern. Since there are no such patterns available, you will have to make your own. To do this, look at the drawings and photographs accompanying this article.

For the general outline of the trousers, cut out and lay a modern pattern down over a large piece (or pieces) of heavy wrapping paper. Trace this with a pencil. This will give you a *general* outline of the front and back panels.

Now, alter this to fit the design of the drawings. Check the front rise. This is from your inseam at the crotch to your navel. This will allow for a seam on top.

Match up the front and back panels. They must match at the inseam and the outerseam. The rise (center back) of the rear panel should be approximately 3" higher than the front rise.

Cut out your waistband pattern. The front section of each half waistband is ¼ your waist measurement, plus ⅝" for overlap, plus a seam allowance (⅜" for leather, ⅝" for cloth). The back section is ½" shorter than the ¼ of your waist for leather. You leave this edge raw for leather. You add ⅝" seam allowance for cloth.

You now cut a pattern for the inner flaps. They should first match up with the waistband plus a seam allowance. Mark the line for your pocket.

Cut out your pocket patterns. It should be made so that when the pockets are sewn in place and folded down inside the pocket opening that they hang evenly and together. You will need a top and a bottom pattern.

Cut the gusset. This should be approximately 7" tall by 4½" wide at the widest part.

To be sure your pattern is correct, you should cut out a complete garment from an old sheet or other cloth. A heavier material would be even better. Be sure and allow the proper seam width (⅝" for cloth — ⅜" for leather). Baste the entire garment together. Put the garment on, seams out, and pin together in front as though it were buttoned. Check the fit *everywhere.* Have someone else mark where alterations must be made. Make those alterations and correct your pattern. Now you can cut out your garment.

Before cutting the trousers, stretch your hides. Then lay your hides, suede side up, on your cutting table. Lay the pattern for the fronts (on to one hide if possible) so that the stretch goes around the garment. Mark carefully with chalk. Cut out the front panels. Repeat with the back panels. If your hides are too short for your inseam length, then "section" the legs *below* the knees. Put a welt (a strip of material to cover the threads) sandwiched between the two pieces of the leg. See the sketch on extending the legs.

Now cut out your waistband, inner bands, and gusset.

The last things to cut are your pocket pieces, front lining, waistband lining, and flap lining. They are cut of linen or heavy cotton.

SEWING THE BROADFALL TROUSERS

1. Check your materials. You should have:

2 fronts
2 backs

23

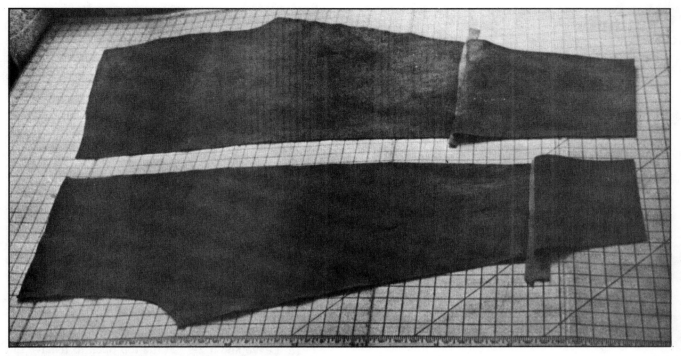

THE PARTS. Above: the front (top), and the back. Cut two each. Left: two piece waistband (top), inner flaps (right), gusset (center), and pocket (cut two).

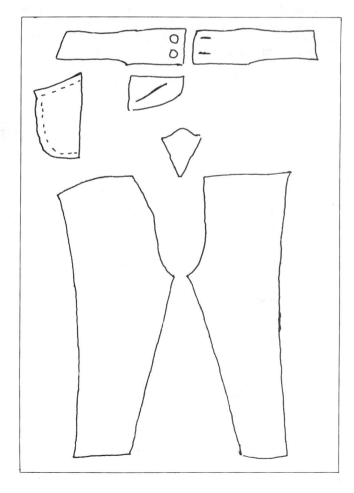

2 waistbands
2 waistband linings
2 inner flaps
2 inner flap linings
4 pocket pieces
1 gusset
(2 pieces for leg fringe if you wish)
1 instruction
1 needle
1 bobbin thread
1 thong
buttons

You will also need:
1 pair sharp scissors
1 hand stapler & staples
1 chalk
1 tape measure

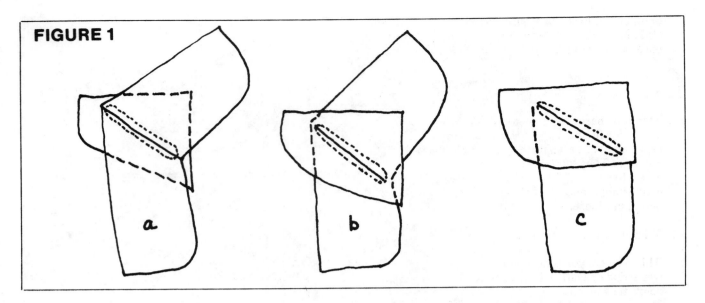

FIGURE 1

2. Lay the inner flap lining against the inner flap. Turn the lining under and sew to the inner flap with a running stitch.

3. Mark the pocket placement and sew the pockets onto the inner flap as shown in Figures 1a and 1b. First lay the pocket pieces against the leather side of the inner flap. Sew around it as in Figure 1c. Slit the opening. Push and work the pocket pieces through the slit. Straighten, smooth, and stitch around the pocket opening. Flatten the pocket so that it hangs down properly. Sew around the pocket. Trim. then zig-zag or bind the edge. Repeat for the second pocket.

4. Sew the inner flaps to the side edge of the back panels as shown in Figure 2a.

5. Sew the waistband on as in Figure 2b.

6. Sew the two back panels together as shown in Figure 2c. Leave about 2½" at the top open to receive the lower portion of the gusset.

7. Sew the gusset in place as in Figure 3. Punch three holes on each side. Insert a thong and close the gusset half way.

8. Sew the fronts of the trousers together. Sew the top 1½", leave ⅞" (or what is needed for a buttonhole) unsewn. Then sew the remainder.

9. Lay the fronts on the backs, face to face. Smooth them out from the crotch seams down each leg. Staple, glue,

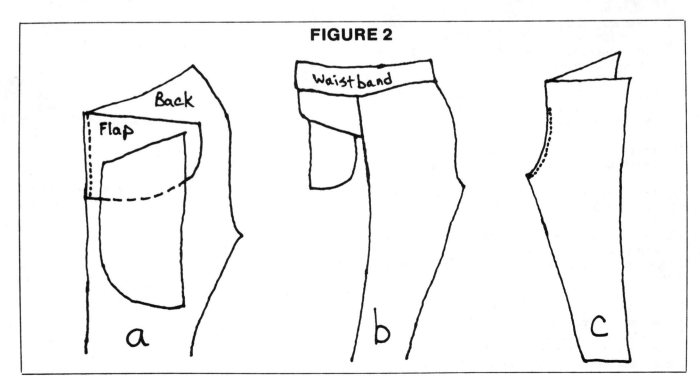

FIGURE 2

or otherwise baste the trousers together at the inseam. (If glue is used, use very little, and only at the very edge, about 1/32" wide.) Be careful; be accurate.

10. Sew the inseam. Use very tight, close stitches, about 8-10 stitches per inch.

11. Staple or baste the out seams. Try the trousers on. Check for fit and mark if you need to trim them. It is best if someone else fits the pants for you and does the marking. They should be snug in the waist with the gusset half closed. The seat should be loose, the thighs comfortable, and the balance of the leg slightly tapered, but loose.

12. Trim the trousers if needed.

13. This is where you put in your fringe if you wish it. Cut two strips of leather long enough to reach from just below the inner flap to 2" above the bottom of the cuff. The fringe should be about 5 to 8" wide at the top and 3 to 4" wide at the bottom. Cut the fringes about ⅛" wide. Lay the pants (inside out) face up, flat and smooth. Lay the fringe in with the face against the face of the *front* of the trousers. Baste or staple or glue in place, sandwiched between the fronts and backs.

14. Sew up the side seams.

15. Turn the pants right side out and try them on again. Pull the waistband together and mark the center, Figure 4. Mark for buttonholes and buttons. (Trim the ends of the waistband if needed.) You should have about 1½" extended beyond the center on each side.

16. Sew in your waistband.
    a. Sew around the front end and down the top edge of each.
    b. Put a small line of glue on the leather at the top. Now fold the waistband liner over so that the band is smooth and the seam is just "inside" the band. Pound the glued seams.

17. Cut and sew your buttonholes. You will have two in the waistband itself and one in the inner flap. This last is for the center hole of the flap.

18. Sew on your buttons in the center of the waistband and inner flap.

19. Try on the trousers again. Make any needed adjustments for fit.

20. Lay the trousers out flat with the front up. Button the waistband. Pull the fall up so that it lays flat with the rest of the pants. Make certain that the center buttonhole fits over the inner flap button.

21. Sew the lining into the drop front.
    a. Lay the lining face to face with the fall. Sew it in place with a running stitch.
    b. Trim the corners of the leather only.
    c. Fold the lining to its proper place inside the fall.

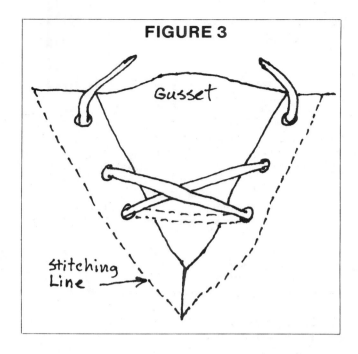

FIGURE 3

Gusset

Stitching Line →

d. If you wish, you may glue the seam down so it lies flat. Do not glue the cloth.
e. Top stitch if you wish. Fold the lower edges of the fall lining up, crease, and stitch.
f. Tack the center bottom of the lining (point) to the fall to hold it in place.

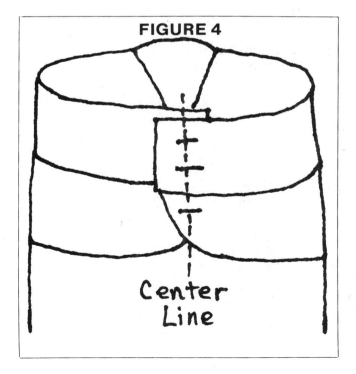

FIGURE 4

Center Line

NARROW FALL BREECHES, OVERALLS & TROUSERS

The differences between 18th century breeches, overalls, and trousers are in the legs. The knee breeches are cut to an inseam length of 1½" longer than the distance from the crotch to the bottom of the knee cap. They are snug in the leg. The bottom of the leg is finished off with either a casing for a drawstring or with a belt sewn on to which a buckle is attached. Also, a split is left at the outside leg seam. This split is closed with anywhere from two to six small (½" or ⅝") buttons depending upon the size and quality of the garment.

Overalls are a military style garment. They are merely shoe-length breeches. The legs are quite snug. They usually have a button closure side slit for the lower six to eight inches of the outer seam. Leather overalls such as those shown in period paintings seem to be just large enough to fit over the foot. They also have short fringe along the outer seams which are closed to the cuff line.

Trousers differ from overalls in that they are "stove pipe" legged. That is, they have very little taper from the thigh to the cuff. They were usually of a canvas type material or heavy linen in the 18th century although later on could be made from most materials.

To make your narrow falls you will first need to acquire a pattern. You can make your own pattern by following the steps given in the section on the broadfall trousers, or you can purchase a pattern such as that offered

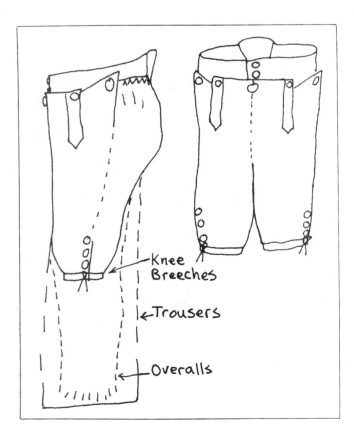

by Green River Forge, Ltd. of Roosevelt, Utah.

Once your pattern is made, cut out a cloth mock-up using an old sheet or other inexpensive material. Baste the mock-up together and fit it to your body. When the garment fits suitably, alter your pattern accordingly and cut out your narrow falls.

Be sure that you have allowed plenty of seat. If you don't, the pants will not fit correctly.

First check that you have everything you need.

SEWING THE NARROW FALL BREECHES

1. If necessary, sew on leg extensions (trousers and overalls only).

2. Sew crotch seams.

THE PARTS FOR NARROW FALL BREECHES

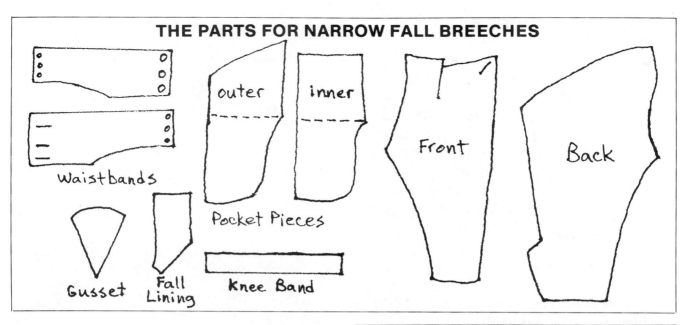

Waistbands

Gusset Fall Lining Knee Band

outer inner

Pocket Pieces

Front Back

3. Sew inner pocket pieces together to make one piece. Then sew them to the breeches backs. (Figure 1)

4. Gather the rear panels to fit the rear half of the waist band. Then sew them to the waist band. (Figure 2)

5. Sew the outer pocket to the fronts at the "flaps."

6. Sew the plackets to the side of the fall. Fold them over half all around and sew down to the fall itself. This is best done by hand. (Figure 3 & 4)

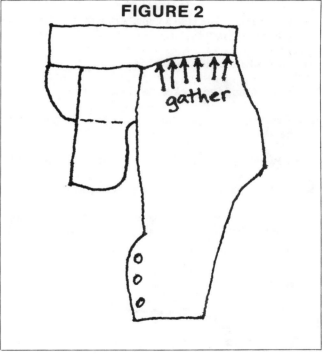

FIGURE 2

gather

FIGURE 1

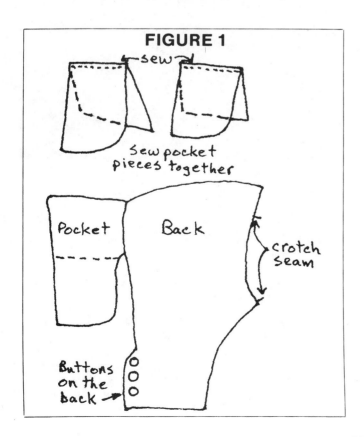

sew

Sew pocket pieces together

Pocket Back

crotch seam

Buttons on the back

FIGURE 3

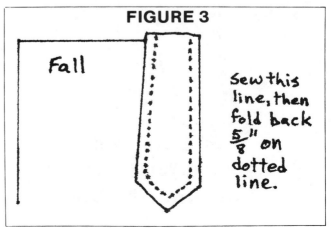

Fall

Sew this line, then fold back $\frac{5}{8}$" on dotted line.

FIGURE 4

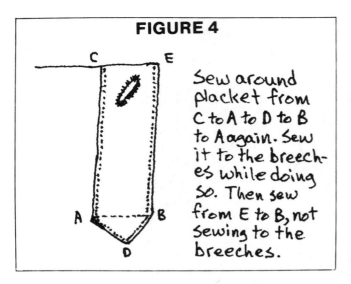

Sew around placket from C to A to D to B to A again. Sew it to the breeches while doing so. Then sew from E to B, not sewing to the breeches.

FIGURE 5

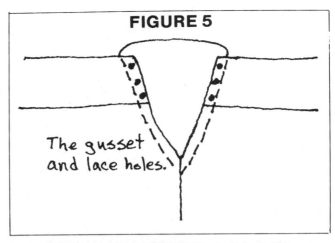

The gusset and lace holes.

Back view of breeches. A buckle can be used for the waistband as well as buckles at the knees. The baggy seat is correct for proper fit.

7. Join the front section to the back by sewing the inseam.

8. Pin or staple the side seams. Adjust to fit. Leave the seat be. It *must* be large.

9. Now sew the side seams.

10. Sew around the pockets to close them up.

11. Put a lining inside the waist band. Top stitch by hand.

12. Sew the triangular gusset in the back. (Figure 5)

13. Sew in the facing to the drop front (fall).

14. Put the breeches on. Adjust and mark the waistband and fall for buttons and buttonholes. Be sure the front fall lies flat. Mark the pockets for buttons and buttonholes.

15. Cut the buttonholes and bind with a buttonhole stitch. Sew on your buttons.

16. Punch and "buttonhole" three holes on each side of the gusset for lace holes. (Figure 5)

17. Adjust the length. If they are breeches, put the buttonholes and buttons on each leg. Sew a "tube" at the base of the leg and insert a lace to tie the knees, or use knee buckles.

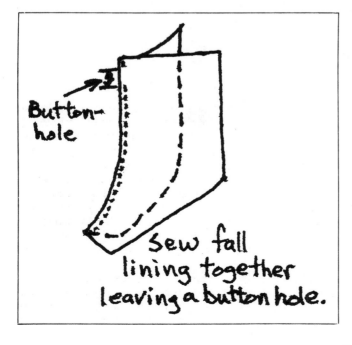

Button-hole

Sew fall lining together leaving a button hole.

I suppose the first question to answer would be: What do we mean by "mountain man trousers"? Of course, any trousers, pants, etc., worn in the mountains at that time would qualify. The real question then is, what did they wear?

For the most part, the trapper, trader, voyageur, etc., wore the clothing of the period for his station in life. Just as today, there are styles and fashions. When it came to trousers, regardless of the material from which they were made, there were three basic styles. Narrow falls were fashionable from the late 18th through the mid 19th centuries. Broadfalls were common through the same basic time period. However, the pants which we shall describe here are of the modern center fly variety. They were introduced at the end of the 18th century, but did not find general acceptance until the 1840s, at which time they pretty well superseded all other front opening styles with a few exceptions.

To make a pair of mountain man trousers, you must, of course, first make the pattern. Follow the previously given steps. You could even use a modern slacks or dress pants pattern if you wish and merely modify it to fit in the old style.

How should they fit? The waist should be high — about 2 fingers above the true waist. The seat should be roomy enough to sit, squat, jump (for you younger more athletic types), and to kneel. All of this should be possible without binding. I like to allow 3-5 inches over the hip size for a comfortable fit. This amount depends upon a person's size.

The legs can be a smooth taper to a narrow cuff, or they can be almost "stove piped" for those who like a comfortable looseness. The legs can also be made to fit very snug, (somewhat like Indian leggings) but be sure and leave lots of seat room or you'll not be able to sit down.

The fly should be the same as used on modern trousers except you'll use buttons, not zippers. You can also use an exposed button fly if you wish. This is not historically correct so far as I can find out, but I admit it does look "old timey".

Pockets are permissible in the side seams, but — *NO HIP POCKETS*. Suspender buttons are fine, but no belt loops, please. They seem to be past 1865.

Fringe is fine in the side seams as a welt and as short (½" to 1") around the bottom of the cuffs. I like to make my side fringe about 10" at the waist and taper to about 4" at the cuff.

Buttons should be of shell, bone, metal, or wood. Rough antler buttons are great for the exposed style fly.

PUTTING TOGETHER YOUR TROUSERS

1. This is the time to cut your fringe if you wish to do so. Cut the fringe about ⅛" wide and as long as possible. Leave about ¼" as a back for sewing. Figure 1a.

2. Sew the crotch on the fronts. Figure 1b.

3. Sew the back crotch. Figure 1c.

4. Sew the inseam. Start at the crotch and sew to the cuff on each leg, but leave about 1" for fringing.

5. Pin, baste, or staple the side seams. Try the pants on and measure and trim to fit the way *you* want them to fit.

6. Lay the trousers down (inside out), with the front panels up. Fold one front panel back. Lay a piece of fringe down face up (rough to rough against the fronts). Lay the front back so your edges are even. Figure 1d. Staple, glue, or otherwise secure the three pieces together. Sew the seam. Repeat this procedure for the other leg. *Note: If you wish to insert pockets,* leave 10" from the top of the waistband to the top of the fringe.

7. Fit the pants again. Adjust if needed. This is a time to place darts if you wish.

8. Put in the waistband.

   a. Cut a waistband of canvas or linen. It should fit the curve of the waist and must be cut from the pants pattern or it will not work. Figure 2a.

   b. Sew the tapered side seams of the waistband. Figure 2b.

   c. Sew the waistband into the pants.
      1. Staple the two sides in place and sew to the waist. Figure 2c.

      2. Put a thin coat of Barge cement on the leather side of this seam. Figure 2d. Let dry, then fold down. This step is optional, but it helps hold your material while you do the next step.

      3. Using a blind or "spot stitch", catch the top of

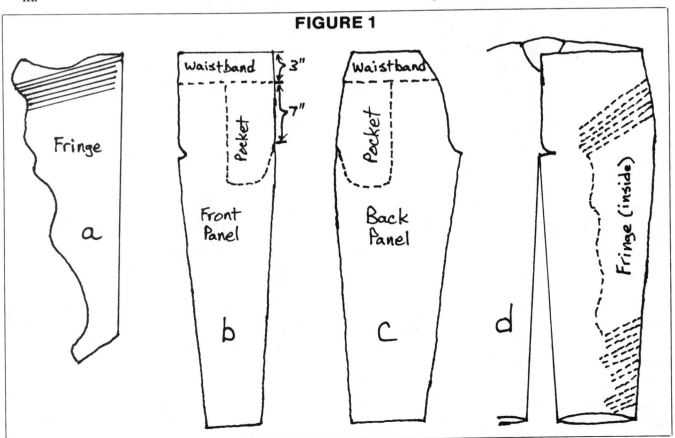

FIGURE 1

the waistband to the leather. Your stitch should not show through on the leather except for a dimpling or "spot" where you sew out, then back down (at an angle) in the same hole. Figure 3.

4. Repeat this method and sew the bottom of the waistband securely to the trousers.

5. Tuck the ends of the band in and sew them flat.

9. Put in the gusset. Figure 4. Note, the gusset is sewn in flat.

10. Fix the fly. The hidden fly would be the only thing a St. Louis tailor would do. Visible flys were considered vulgar and unseemly. They were basically unknown in this period. They (visible flys) would perhaps be done beyond the frontier by a man doing his own clothing or by his Indian woman. See Figure 5, concealed fly and visible button fly.

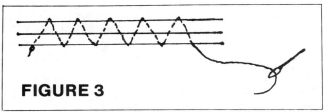

FIGURE 3

FIGURE 4

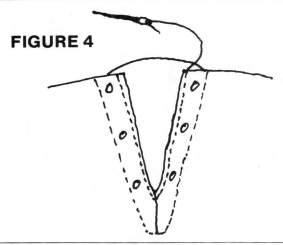

FIGURE 2

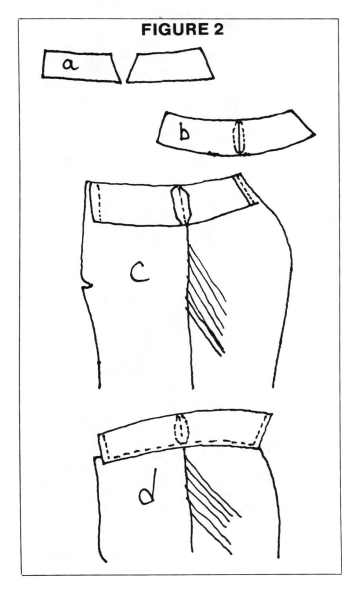

a

b

C

d

FIGURE 5

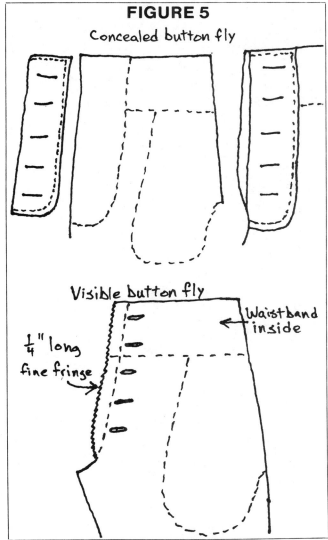

Concealed button fly

Visible button fly

¼" long fine fringe

Waistband inside

This center seam style legging is a very distinctive style of Early Woodland legging. The Iroquois and the Chippewa wore them. Many other tribes also seemed to have used them. They are simple to make, quite comfortable, and very useful. They are the style I would recommend to be worn with "Colonial" knee breeches or breech clouts.

In the very early days, these leggings seem to have been much shorter than we are used to. They often came no higher than a "hand" above the knee. In this case, they usually have no ties, but rather were held up by garters only. Even the hip high ones of the late 18th Century seem to have been worn with garters as a rule.

SEWING WOODLAND FRONTSEAM LEGGINGS

1) Lay out your pattern on a sheet of paper as in Figure 1.

2) Try the pattern on your leg. Adjust it if and where needed.

3) Lay the pattern out on your material. This should be either buckskin or wool. Be *SURE* to have a *LEFT* and a *RIGHT!* Figure 2.

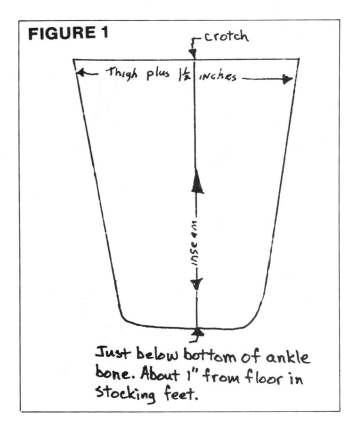

FIGURE 1

crotch

Thigh plus 1½ inches

inseam

Just below bottom of ankle bone. About 1" from floor in stocking feet.

Center seam leggings can also be made of wool as shown in this photo.

FIGURE 2

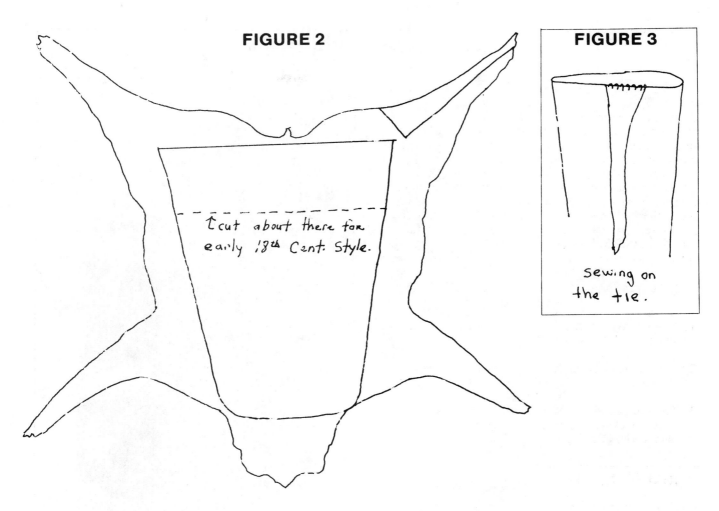

↑cut about there for early 18th Cent. Style.

FIGURE 3

sewing on the tie.

4) Cut the leggings out.

5) Cut out two long tabs, about 18" *long* by 1½" wide. These are for ties.

6) Sew the tabs to the inner top of each legging so that they will loop over your belt when the leggings are worn. Figure 3.

7) Fold the leggings inside out. Sew the front seam using a close, tight overcast stitch. Figure 4. Pound the stitch flat (pound lightly).

8) Turn the leggings inside out and they are ready to wear and to decorate should you wish.

Finished legging with garter (side view).

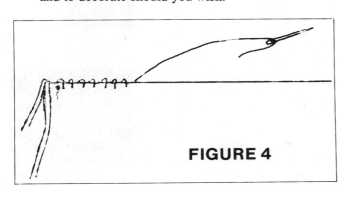

FIGURE 4

PLAINS INDIAN WAR SHIRT

The war shirt of the plains Indian is one of the most striking articles of clothing developed and worn by a people who were and are noted for their exceptionally beautiful wearing apparel. It was also a thing of importance. In the early days, not just anyone could have one. They were often considered "Medicine" and a "Shirt Wearer" was respected as a Big Man, a Chief.

The beaded or quilled strips which were so prominent a part of the war shirt were basically just decoration. The other "trim", however, such as painting, scalp or ermine fringes, and other small things, often had special meanings.

The shirt which I shall describe here is taken after one on display at the Plains Indian Museum, Whitney Gallery of Western Art in Cody, Wyoming. This is one of the most impressive and attractive museums for the buckskinner that I have had the pleasure of visiting. It is a perpetual must for me and my family anytime we are in the area. If you haven't been there, you should put it on your list of places to visit.

This shirt, by the way, is attributed to a Pawnee Arikaree Chief by the name of Sukhutel. The date is around 1800. This makes it one of the earliest shirts collected.

This shirt was made of two large hides. They were cut just behind the shoulders and the back or lower parts became the body of the garment. The neck, shoulders and fore-legs became the sleeves. The edges of the hides were left in their natural shape and the legs were left to dangle as decorations. Small cuts were made all around the edges of the garment so as to form a short thin fringe.

The shoulders of the shirt are whip stitched together, leaving a large enough slit for the head to go through. The edges of the shirt where the sleeves are to be sewn on appear to have been turned back, the sleeve layed up *under* the shirt and then the sleeve was whip stitched to the shirt. The neck of the shirt was bound with red wool.

The shirt is decorated with bead strips on the shoulder and sleeves. It also had blue pigment rubbed into the top half of the shirt while the lower half appears to have received a yellow color. There are several red lines drawn vertically at the shoulders near the neck opening. I count seven but there may have been another which I could not see. Long hair locks are attached profusely along outer edges of the shoulder strips and along the front of the arm strips. The locks have been rubbed with vermilion or red clay mixed with fat. The upper ends of the hair locks are wrapped.

MAKING A TWO HIDE WAR SHIRT

The first problem in making a shirt of two hides is that to do the shirt correctly, the hides must be large and com-

plete. That means they should be fifteen to eighteen square feet each and must have the legs. You will probably have to get some friends to skin out the full hides and save them for you. You can then take the hides to a custom tanner or do them yourself.

You can make the same shirt by using four hides instead of just two. Take two large hides and cut them to shape as in Figure 1 a. Then take either one very large hide, or two smaller hides and cut the sleeves as in Figure 1 b.

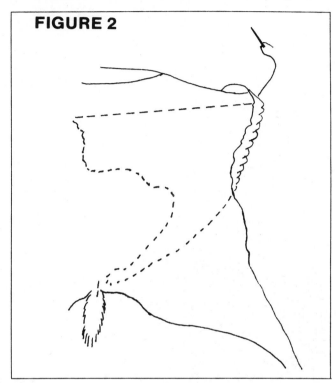

FIGURE 2

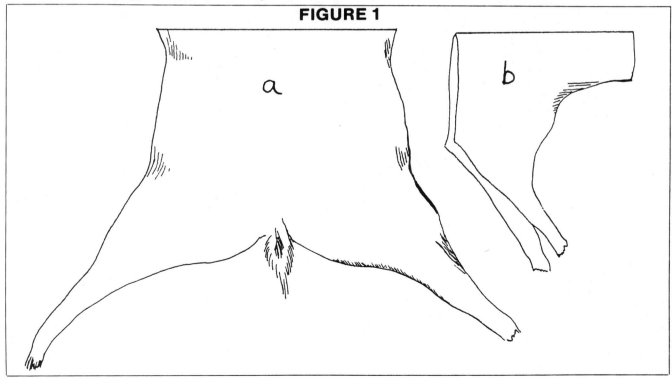

FIGURE 1

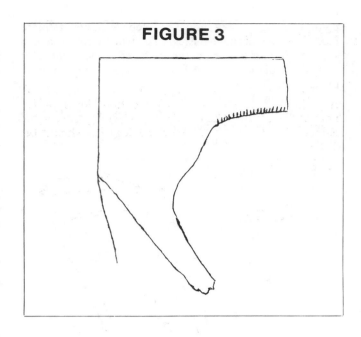

FIGURE 3

The next step is to cut the small fringes with a sharp knife. The cuts should be about ⅛" apart and ½" deep. Figure 5 shows where to cut the fringe.

Sew the shoulder seams together with a whip stitch.

Lay the shirt body out flat outside up. Turn back the shoulder edge. Lay the sleeve, outside down, on top of the body. Using a whip stitch, sew the first sleeve to the shirt body (Figure 2). Repeat this for the second sleeve.

Now fold the shirt together, outside in along the shoulder line. Sew the cuff end of the sleeves as in Figure 3.

Turn the shirt right side out. Sew two red cloth strips at the neck, one in front and one in back. See Figure 4.

Tie the sides together in 4 or 5 places with thin thongs. Tie the sleeve as shown in Figure 5.

To finish the shirt you will need about 100 hair locks and a set of beaded or quilled arm strips.

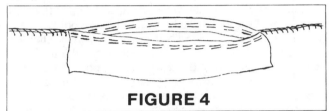

FIGURE 4

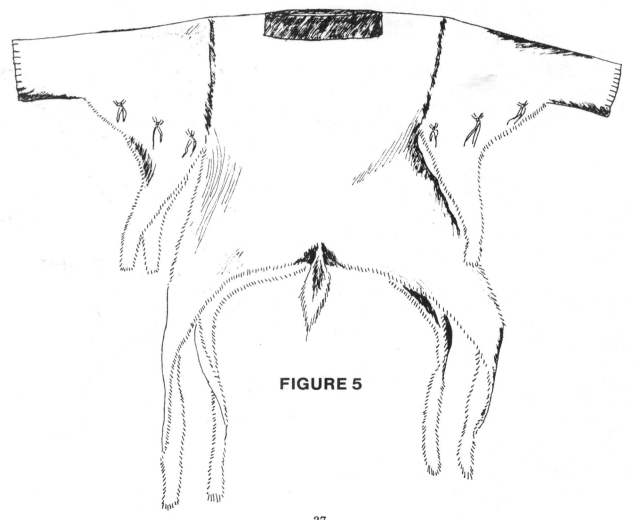

FIGURE 5

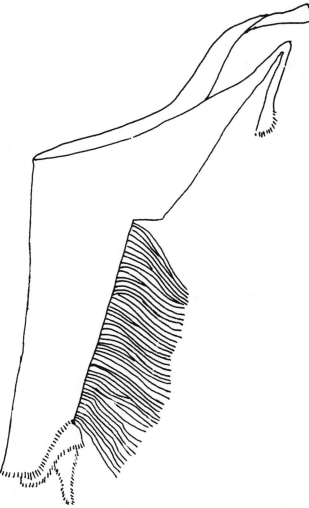

Next, fold the pattern lengthwise in the center. Fold the large hides lengthwise. Lay the pattern down on the hides and use it as a guide to draw the leggings out on the leather. See Figure 2 for how the leggings should be shaped.

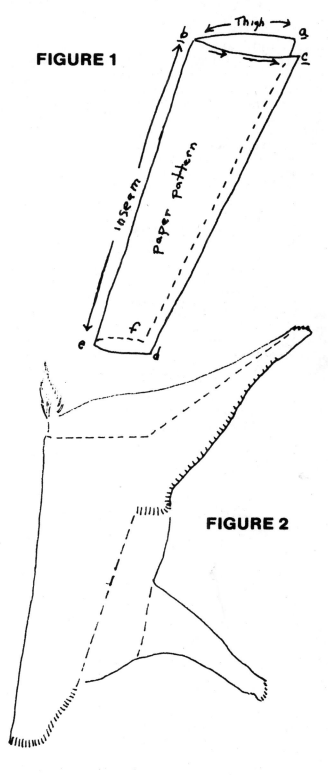

FIGURE 1

FIGURE 2

If you have a war shirt, you must have a pair of leggings. They should match in style and decoration, but it is not necessary. Here are instructions on how to make yourself a pair of early 19th century style plains leggings. As with the shirt, tribal designation and period are largely determined by the beadwork and other applied decoration.

The first thing you will need is a pair of large buckskin hides, preferably with the legs tanned on the hides. Indian brain tanned and smoked leather is best but also very expensive. You will probably want to settle for commercial tanned hides, at least for your first pair. Oh yes; should you wish long fringe, you will need two medium hides for cutting fringe.

Wet and stretch your hides, then let them dry. Keep the shape of the leggings in mind as you stretch them. The wet hides are quite pliable and can be shaped somewhat to your needs.

The first thing to do is to measure your inseam, your thigh, and your instep around your heel and up over the top of the arch. Transfer these to a large sheet and make a basic leg pattern. See Figure 1 for this.

Cut the leggings out. Cut the two tabs (Figure 3) from the fore-legs. Trim them to fit in as in Figure 4. After the side fringe is put in the leggings and they are turned right side out, these tabs are slid up just under the edge fringe and whip stitched in place as extensions to fill in the "hollow" created by the neck.

As soon as the leggings are cut out, plug any holes and stitch closed any cuts. Do this on the inside.

Now cut your side fringe. You will need 4 rectangles of leather the length of the legging side from the bottom of the flaps to the cuff (Figure 5, 1-2), and between 8-14 inches wide (the wider measure is preferred). Cut the fringe about ⅛" wide.

Lay your fringe together to form two sets of double fringe. The face (sueded) sides should be out. In the case of commercial modern hides, this puts the shiny or "hair" sides together. For Indian tan or split hides, the ragged sides go together. Fold the legging over as in Figure 6 and whip stitch.

Another way to put the fringe in place is to follow Figure 5. Lay the fringes face sides against the face side of the leggings, then fold the leggings as in Figure 6 and sew with a whip stitch. A very fine line of Barge Cement can be used to "baste" the pieces together for holding in place while sewing.

Turn the leggings right side out. Turn the flaps back over the outside of the leggings so as to continue the out-seam line. Using a very fine stitch, sew the legging flaps closed. Do *Not* let the stitches come through the leggings.

Your leggings are now ready to wear. To really be finished, however, you now need a pair of beaded or quilled strips. If beaded, use only light or dark blue and white beads. The best beads are the *small* size pony beads which can be purchased from such trading posts as La Pelleterie, Western Trading Post and Flathead Trading Post.

For beadwork patterns see paintings by Karl Bodmer and Catlin. You want the very simple designs from the first half of the 19th century.

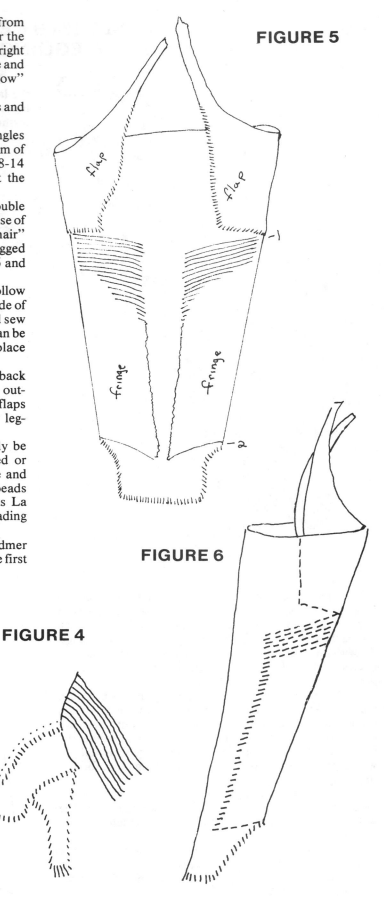

FIGURE 5

FIGURE 6

FIGURE 4

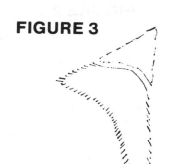

FIGURE 3

WOODLAND INDIAN
BUCKSKIN DRESS

The original of this dress is in the museum at Old Fort Wayne, Fort Wayne, Indiana. It is listed as being from the Miami Indians. The dress is not dated, but due to its construction, I feel the style could go back to the mid 18th century. It is a logical outgrowth of the one and two piece skirt of pre-contact with the white man.

This particular dress was made of three large hides which were trimmed to shape, fringed, and fastened together with long thongs which were allowed to dangle as extra fringe.

If you wish to make the dress, first secure and stretch three fairly large hides (depending on your size). Trim the largest one to fit as a yoke, Figure 1. Trim two hides to fit as a high-waisted skirt. They should fit fairly high under the bust so that you can fasten the yoke to them to form the dress. They should reach down to approximately mid-calf or a bit longer. See Figure 2.

When you have the yoke and skirt properly fitted,

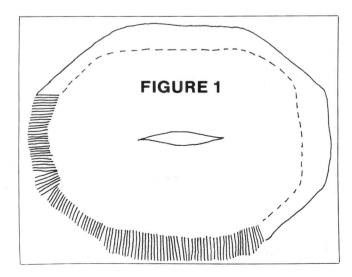

FIGURE 1

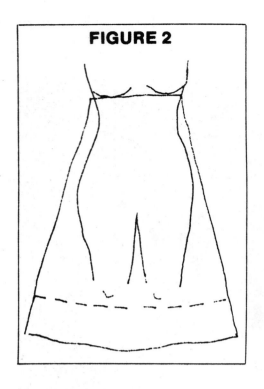

FIGURE 2

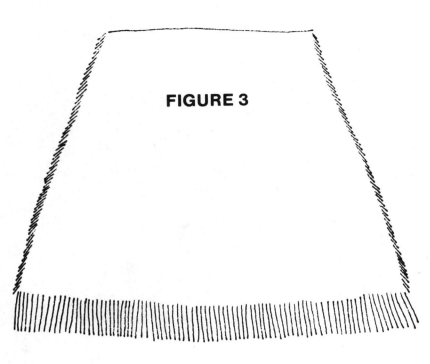

FIGURE 3

fringe them. The yoke is fringed with fairly long fringe all around. This can be from 3" to 6" depending upon how much hide you have. The skirt pieces are fringed about 1" on the sides and 3" to 6" along the bottom. See Figure 3.

Cut yourself about 32 thin thongs approximately 14" in length each. Be sure both ends are thinned and pointed.

To assemble the dress, first lay out the yoke — inside up. Mark the bodice part, front and back sides, with a chalk line showing where to lay the skirts. This line should be about ¾" up from the top of the fringe on each side. Lay the skirt pieces — front and back on their respective lines. You may wish to temporarily secure them in place with a *THIN* line of Barge cement. See Figure 4.

Take an awl and punch a series of double holes about ¼" below the top edge of the skirt pieces. Start at the center and make each pair of holes about 2½" apart. Each pair of holes should be vertical to the length of the dress. The top hole should be ¼" from the skirt top and the second hole ½" below that. Run a thong out to the outside of the dress at each pair of holes.

Turn the dress right side out. Punch a series of holes down each side of the skirt at 5" intervals. Insert a thong and tie at each set of holes. Tie the ends of each thong with a knot against the dress. Let the ends dangle as fringe. See photo.

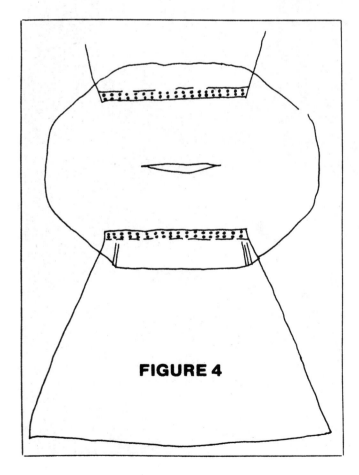

FIGURE 4

41

CHEYENNE DRESS

The following instructions will help you to make a buckskin dress of the mid to late 19th century. While the particular dresses that I have followed are labeled Cheyenne, this style seems to have been fairly widespread. I have seen similar dresses and photos of the same basic style labeled Crow, Arapaho, Kiowa, Nez Perce, etc. Each group had their own variations of course, but they were minor. The major variation in cut, to my eye, was the habit of the Cheyenne women of putting false legs on the yoke or leaving natural leg extensions on where possible. Otherwise, the style of beadwork was the real identifying mark.

We will not go into beading and beadwork techniques here, but should you wish to do so I would make a few suggestions. First of all, figure out the time period you wish to represent. Then get some books which show paintings or photos of women in your style of dress. If possible, visit a museum or two. Talk to someone who knows beadwork.

To make the Cheyenne dress you will need three very large hides for the body of the dress. The size needed will vary with the size of the individual, but I'd suggest the

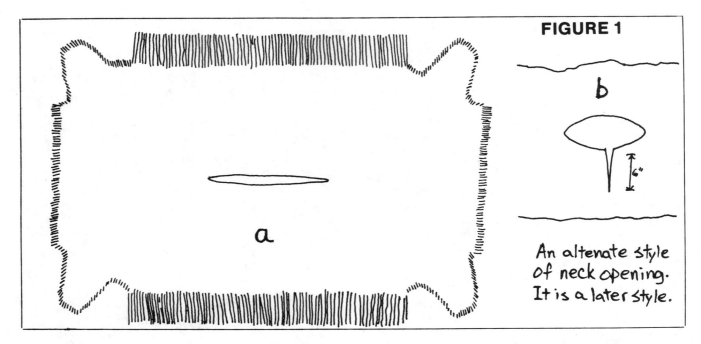

FIGURE 1

a

b

6"

An alternate style
of neck opening.
It is a later style.

largest hides available. Those for the average size woman (about 5'6", 135 lbs.) should be 14 feet or larger. You will also need two small 7-10 foot hides for the sleeve fringe if you wish to have any. The side fringe, which runs in a double row down each side of the skirt, can be made from trimmings.

The first thing after selecting the hides is to make yourself a cloth pattern. Baste this pattern together and try it on. Adjust the fit and make a new pattern that is correct. Be sure that there is plenty of room in the hips, etc. This should be a loose fit. The length should be about 3-5 inches up from the floor.

Lay the hides out. Choose two for the skirt and one for the yoke. Cut out the three pieces. Be sure you lay out and cut the pieces so the stretch goes around your body. Make any adjustments necessary. Lay the two small hides and cut out the sleeve fringe. Take scrap pieces from the dress and cut four pieces of leather, approximately 3¼" wide by the length of the skirt. This will be your side fringe. Now go ahead and follow the steps listed.

MAKING THE DRESS

1. First do the Yoke.
    a. Patch any hole or tear.
    b. Cut the sleeve fringe. The fringe will be cut the *short* distance, about 10-12 inches normally, and about 3/16" wide.
    c. Mark and cut the fringe at the bottom of the bodice. Figure 1a.
    d. Cut the short fringe around both sleeves of the yoke. Figure 1a.

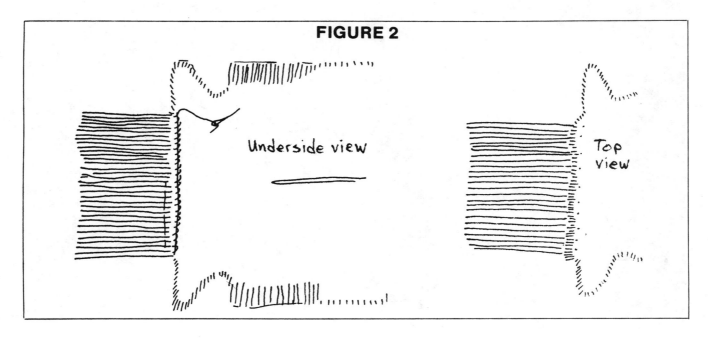

FIGURE 2

Underside view

Top
view

e. Fringe the "legs" that are either a part of or to be sewn to the yoke. If the legs are not an integral part of the yoke, then sew them to the yoke.

f. Make sure the neck opening is large enough to slip over your head. Make it either a straight slit 12" across (Figure 1a) or a rounded cut about 5½ to 6 inches across and with a 6" long slit down the center back of the yoke. Figure 1b.

g. Sew the arm fringe to the arms. Use an overcast (whip) stitch, but do *not* go through the sleeve surface. See Figure 2.

2. Doing the Skirt.
   a. Fit the skirt (Figure 3) around yourself (baste with a stapler) and check the fit. It should fit loosely from about 1" below the bust to the hips where you should have at least 6 inches or better on down to the ankle length bottom which should be very flaring. If the skirt is too loose at the chest line, take in as necessary, but be sure you have enough room to get it on and off. The balance of the "around" measurements really can't be too large.
   If it is too long — trim at the chest (top) not at the bottom. The skirt should reach from 1" below the bust (approximately) to the ankle line.
   b. Patch any holes.
   c. Fringe around the bottom of each skirt piece. See Figure 3. This bottom fringe is 3" long x 3/32" wide.

3. Assembling the Dress.
   a. Sew the skirts to the yoke. Use the overcast stitch as you did for the sleeve fringe. See Figure 4.
   b. Cut your "side seam" fringe. It should be cut in 2 pairs of "paired" strips and at an angle. Make it very thin.
   c. Glue the extreme edges of the 4 pieces of fringe. Then glue them together rough sides out (each separate pair).
   d. Fold dress inside out and tack the 2 pairs of seam fringes into the sides with as little glue as possible — *or* use staples.

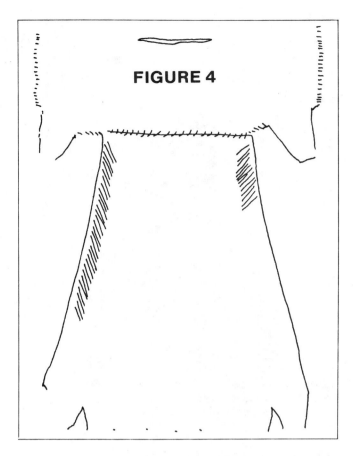

FIGURE 4

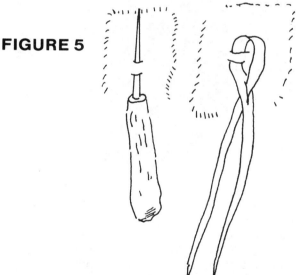

FIGURE 5

e. Sew down each side seam from bodice to "leg".
f. Turn the dress right side out. Lay smoothly and mark for the two rows of thong fringe. Start in the middle of the skirt each time and mark every 2½" towards the sides. The lower row should be about 12" above the top of the hem fringe. The second row should be 12" - 14" above that. Remember, the fringe is on *both* sides. See Figure 5 for attaching thong fringe. Use an awl, not a punch.

The basic dress is now complete, but you may wish to dress it up with elk's teeth or beading on the yoke.

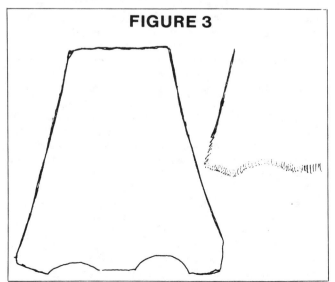

FIGURE 3

free and easy. In mild weather it can be worn over a light shirt, and yet it is large enough to be worn over several layers of winter clothing.

The capote dates back at least into the early 1700s. There are many period drawings showing French Canadians, British, and American soldiers wearing these garments. They were advertised in 1824. St. Louis newspapers advertised red blanket coats for sale. In 1834, John Townsend remarks that he purchased from an outfitter in St. Louis enormous overcoats made of green blankets and white wool hats with crowns fitting tightly to the head. The capote continued in popularity, one might say grew in popularity right through the period of the Indian Wars. Of course, today it is without doubt the most popular coat for our modern buckskinner/historian.

I often have persons come into my trading post and ask me how to make a capote. It is really very simple once one gets over the initial terror caused by knowledge that you have to rip a Hudson Bay blanket down the middle. A full blanket capote is made from a four point blanket. This will suffice for all but the very largest of human beings. Most Kodiaks and grizzlies take six pointers. A very small person can easily make one out of a three or three and one half point blanket. These were the most common blankets used in the 1800s. However, they do not allow for the full cut which is necessary for the best of fits. Should you have a three or three and one half point blanket which you wish to use, it is suggested that you make a slightly scaled-down pattern from an old sheet or other expendable material. When this is perfect, lay the pattern out on your blanket and cut out the capote. This method may be used for making a four point blanket into a coat, however, it is not necessary. The coat that we will discuss here is the later style western capote, the favorite of mountain men and Indians through the middle and late 19th century.

We will assume you are using a four point Hudson Bay blanket to construct your capote. Any full bed size blanket will do. It is suggested that it not be of reconstituted wool as this will often ravel when ripped. First, lay the blanket out foresquare on the floor or a large table. Now, before cutting the blanket, decide what length you would like your capote to be. For the average person 5'6" or taller, we recommend that the blanket be torn across at 52" up from the corner on which is sewn the Hudson Bay seal and along the edge where are found the four stripes indicating the blanket's size. This will give you 50" in length from the nape of your neck. Should you wish the capote to be shorter, merely measure up from that corner to the length you wish plus 2" for the neck fringe. The next step is to take all your measurements. Measure around your chest for your chest measurement. Take your sleeve measurement by measuring from the nape of your neck around the elbow of the raised, bent arm to the wrist. This gives you your sleeve length. A normal overcoat is cut approximately 4" larger than your chest size. We would suggest 4" is approximately correct for someone up to 42" chest size. Persons larger than this might wish to add an additional inch or two. This will allow room for winter garments. The measurements given in the drawings are for a

While the capote is not a leather garment, it is included here because it was worn by Indians and white men, from the east to the west, along the frontier. The capote couldn't be passed over in this discussion of clothing.

The capote, which mens a hooded overgarment or coat, is one of the most versatile of winter garments. When made out of a heavy, all wool blanket such as a Witney or a Hudson Bay, this capote will shed moisture in the form of light rain or snow. It can be used as both a coat and an extra blanket when camping in extra cold weather. It is good looking. It can be worn, as many people do, downtown. Even the civilized folks appreciate it. It is the ultimate garment for cold, snowy weather. It is light. It is warm. It is comfortable. The capote is a garment that if the weather is cold enough, you can wear while snow shoeing or skiing. It makes a fine shooting coat in the winter as movement is

BLANKET LAYOUT

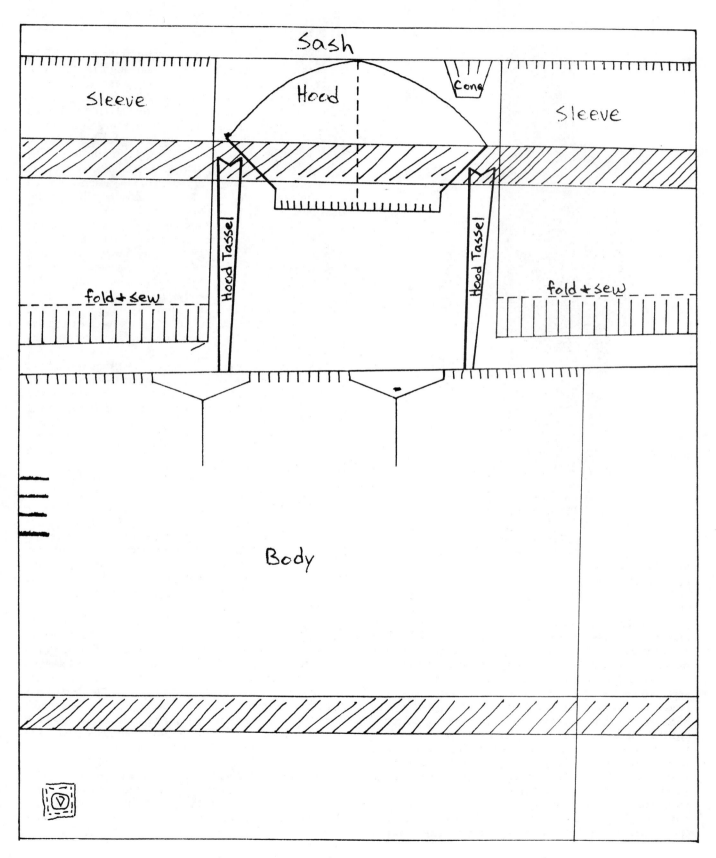

46

man of approximately 44" chest size and 5'10" in height. Take the lower part of the blanket (the end with the stripes and tag on it). Lay it out flat with the tag up. Fold the tag side towards the middle of the blanket so that the stripe lies perfectly square with itself. This flap is the front of the coat. It should measure ¼ of the coat's body (chest) measurement plus at least 4" for additional overlap. Now fold the other side of the blanket over in the same manner to form the other side of the front of the coat. The underlying part of the blanket is now the back. The two flaps form the front, one of which is much too large. Check your measurements at this time. Be sure that from fold to fold, the coat is at least 2" larger than ½ of your chest measurement. The under-flap should measure according to your size, between 15 to 18" from fold to edge. Measure the top fold and mark it so that it can be cut to the same size. Mark it with a piece of chalk. Double check your measurements. If all meets your approval, make a cut on the top flap (front) and then proceed to rip the blanket down the front so that both front flaps are the same size. Smooth out the blanket so that it lays straight and square. Measure the center across the top (towards the edge of your coat). Mark the center measurement out from the center on either side 5" of the mark. Mark down 1½" at either mark. This marks your neck opening which will be 10" across. Lay your yardstick along one folded edge from the top of the coat. Go down 3" and mark. Measure down an additional 9" for size 40 and under chest, 10" for size 42 and larger. Repeat on the other

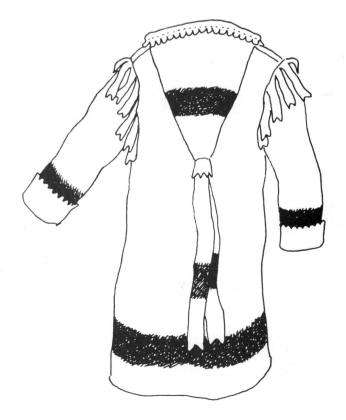

47

folded edge to measure the other side. Lay the yardstick on one side from the neck mark angle down to the top mark at the shoulder side marks. This measurement is the other shoulder. This will give you the shoulder seam. Take a pair of scissors and cut out the trapezoid at the shoulders to actually form your shoulder. Slip cut along the folded edge on each side to the second mark. This will form your arm hole. Cut a piece ¾"x12" of bright wool (I prefer red for most colors. Blue or green or black to go with a red blanket). Take one piece and fold it lengthwise and insert it in a shoulder seam with raw edges up. This forms a welt and will strengthen your shoulder seam. Sew this shoulder seam using a heavy, non-stretching waxed thread (not a heavy cord). If you use waxed linen or artificial sinew, be sure to strip it down to one strand only. Wax your thread heavily. Double it through the needle and knot it. Sew the shoulder seam using stitches approximately 3/16" deep and 6 to 9 stitches per inch. Be sure your thread is pulled tight so your seam doesn't open up. Check your work. The welt should just barely show in the seam. If all is well, do the same for the other shoulder. Take your scissors and fringe 1½" of flat material running across the neck opening. Make your fringe approximately 1" wide with 1¼" deep cuts. The body of the coat is finished.

Set the body of your coat aside. Take up the other end of the blanket. Fold this piece with the stripe on top lying parallel and perfectly square with the bottom part of the stripe. Make sure the entire piece of the blanket is square and smooth and flat. We are now ready to cut out the sleeve. The sleeve should be your sleeve length as taken previously less ½ of the back measurement of the coat plus 7" (6 to 8") for fringe plus 3" for turn-back cuff. The width of the sleeve as cut (when laid out flat as you are doing now) should equal the arm opening in the body of the coat. This will be 18" to 20". The average sleeve length as described, should be approximately 32". This, of course, will vary. Mark these dimensions on a laid out blanket with chalk or pencil going from the selvedge edge up towards the torn edge as shown in the drawings. If your blanket is perfectly square, you may wish to cut the sleeve out by making a cut with scissors and then ripping along the line or you may prefer to cut the entire sleeve out. The sleeve should be oriented so that the stripe will run around the lower forearm. Measure across the fringe end of the sleeve. Make cuts approximately 1" deep evenly spaced (approximately 1½" apart). This will allow you to tear your shoulder fringe when the time comes. If you wish the cuff end of the sleeve to be decorated, cut fringe approximately ½" wide by ½" long all around the cuff. Fold both sleeve pieces and carefully sew from the cuff fringe to the point designated as the beginning of the shoulder fringe. Repeat for the second sleeve.

Turn the sleeve right side out. Fold the fringe down. Set the sleeve into the body of the coat so that the bottom sleeve seam is at the bottom of the arm hole. The sleeve, of course, is inside the body of the coat. The body of the coat is still wrong side out. The sleeve is right side out. (You have right sides together.) Tack the sleeve in place. Whip stitch the sleeve to the arm hole. Repeat for the second sleeve. Turn the coat right side out. Rip all of the shoulder fringe up to the arm hole.

We are now ready to cut out the hood. Mark the hood on the remaining piece of material. Follow the diagram. The hood should be 11" from the fold down the face. Then cut squarely in 1½". Angle down as shown in the diagram 10" for the neck opening on the hood. Then cut up at an angle to form the back. Whip stitch along this back edge. Turn the hood right side out. If you wish to have fringe on the hood, you may cut 1½" fringe along the front edge of the hood. Fold it back to the outside. Tack it by using a running stitch or sewing it down with white pony beads or some other color beads. It will give it a finished look and be decorative.

Lay the body of the coat out with the front up. Fold the front back so that the coat is open. Turn the neck (collar) fringe back. It is to the outside of the coat. Measure across the neck opening and find the center. Mark it. Lay the hood as though it were folded back against the back of the coat. Tack the back seam to the center mark on the back of the capote. Tack the hood to the neck opening. Be sure that the hood is square with the capote. Place the folds of the hood forward and lay the front lower edge of the hood along the front edge of the coat. Tack the hood to the coat at the front corner of the hood. Be sure you have a 1¼" fringe running all along the neck from one lapel around the back and sides of the hood and back to the other lapel. If everything measures square, whip stitch the hood to the body of the capote. Now cut out two triangle tassels as shown in the sketch and one cone. Sew the cone together along the back edge (cut the top of the cone to form a fringe. Take the two tassels. Lay them with the narrow ends against the top center of the hood and sew them to the hood so that the tassels hang straight down the back of the coat. They will lay square along the center back seam on the back of the hood. Slip the cone over the tassels and slide it down to rest against the hood and cover the seam. The back seam of the hood should match the back seam of the cone. Whip stitch around the cone, gathering the cone as you go and sewing it to the hood.

Take the remaining long piece of blanketing which you should have left. Tear and trim as necessary to form a sash. Put on the capote. Pull up the hood. Wrap the sash around and tie. Happy cold weather. It's done!

HUNTER'S SHEATH

This is a very simple sheath to make. You will need a piece of heavy paper for the pattern, approximately one sq. foot of ⅛ ounce strap leather, and about 3 yards or so of harness thread. You will also need an awl and two needles as well as a bit of leather cement.

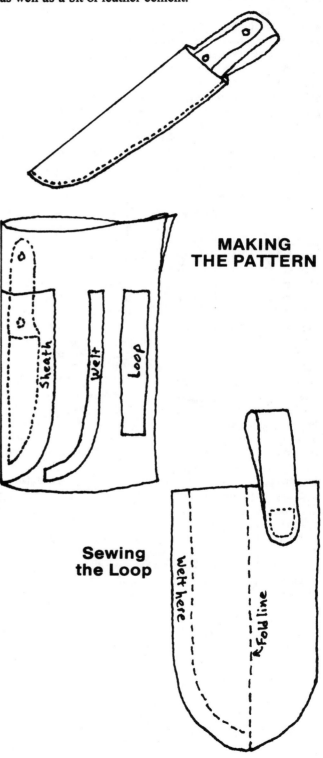

MAKING THE PATTERN

Sewing the Loop

49

Make the Pattern

Take a piece of heavy wrapping paper or thin shirt board and wrap it carefully around the knife. Trace around this with a pencil. Remove the knife and draw your pattern. Be sure to leave ample room for the knife to be drawn and returned with a snug fit. Allow about ⅜" to ½" at the edge for the welt and for sewing.

Cut out your pattern. Fasten it together with staples or rubber cement. Try the knife in it. Make sure it fits.

Cut out the leather. You will need the welt and the belt loop at once.

Fold the belt loop in half. Glue the bottom one inch of the loop together. Then glue the loop to the sheath. Be sure you make the sheath right or left according to the way you prefer it.

Sew the loop to the sheath. Use a saddle maker's stitch. (Figure eight stitch.)

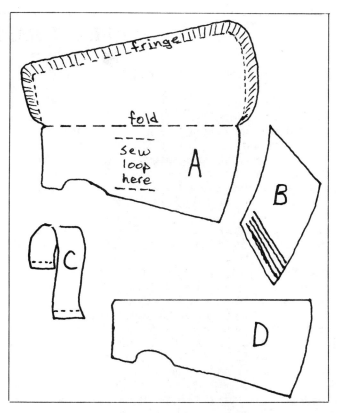

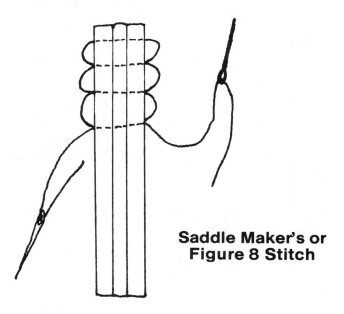

Saddle Maker's or Figure 8 Stitch

Glue the welt in place. Fold the sheath around it and cement it securely.

Saddle stitch the edge of the sheath closed. Sew about ¼" in from the edge. Make your stitches tight.

Trim the edges of the sheath. Dye the sheath if you wish. Rub the sheath down with a good top finish (even auto wax will do) and polish the edges with a hard surface. The sheath is ready to use.

TOMAHAWK SHEATH

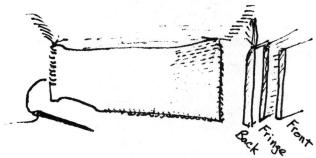

The Tomahawk sheath is very simple to assemble. Just go step by step.

1. Either trim off, or fringe the area shown by the dotted line on the sketch.

2. Fringe piece "B" leaving about ¼" for sewing. The fringes should be about ⅛" or less wide.

3. Sew the belt loop "C" to the back "A". Sew it as shown by dotted lines on "A".

4. Lay the front "D" on the back "A" so the sheath is inside out. Sew the back with a whip stitch a to b to x.

5. Lay the fringe in at c - d, so it is sandwiched between the front and the back.

6. Sew the front and bottom of the sheath.

7. Turn the sheath inside out. Attach a thong for closure and you're ready to go.

WOODLANDS SHOOTING BAG

This is just one style of a woodlands shooting bag. It is very simple to make, and when you have finished constructing it, you might even like to add a bit of beadwork to it. For design ideas check *Iroquois Crafts* by Carrie A. Lyford and old paintings of woodland warriors of the earliest period (circa 1750-1820). There is a picture of Robert Rogers, of Rogers' Rangers fame, on page 6 of *The American Provincial Corps - 1775-1784* by Phillip Thatcher. In this picture, Rogers is wearing a similar type bag. The strap shows the beadwork style quite clearly.

To make the bag, you must first make up a pattern. This is quite easy as everything is basically square or rectangular. The back should be 8"x12". The front is 8"x9". The fringe is 7½"x9" and the flap is 8" wide x 7" long at the point. The strap should be 2" wide by the length needed. The bag should rest on your hip with the opening at or slightly above your waist line.

Cut the pattern out of heavy paper or thin shirt board. Put the pieces together and make sure they match. Figure 1. Then cut out your bag. Be sure the stretch goes across (width wise) the parts. If you wish to put a wool flap on the bag, then cut *both* a leather flap and a wool one.

To assemble the bag, start with the flap. Lay the wool on top of the leather. Tack or staple to hold them. Then bind the flap around the edge with ribbon. Sew the ribbon down with a running stitch. Use 3 beads on the top of each stitch. See Figure 2.

Cut the fringe. Leave about ⅜ inch uncut for sewing. Make the fringe about 1/8" - 3/16" wide.

Lay the back of the bag out inside up. Place the fringe on top of this. Be sure that the bad side of the fringe is against the outside part of the back. Lay the front on top, face down. Sew the front to the back with the fringe sandwiched in between. Be sure and sew the fringe along the bottom only. Don't catch it on the sides. Figure 3.

Lay the flap in place and sew down. You can use white beads here too. Figure 4.

Cut the strap to length and sew to the top of the bag as

FIGURE 5

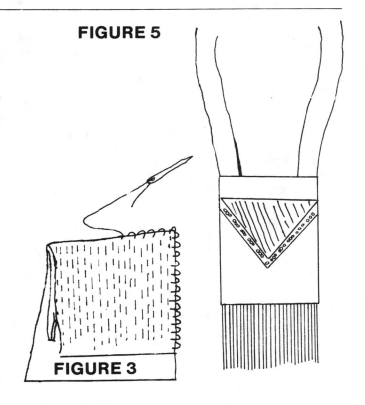

in Figure 4.

You can now bead the bag should you so desire. Otherwise, the bag is ready to use. Figure 5.

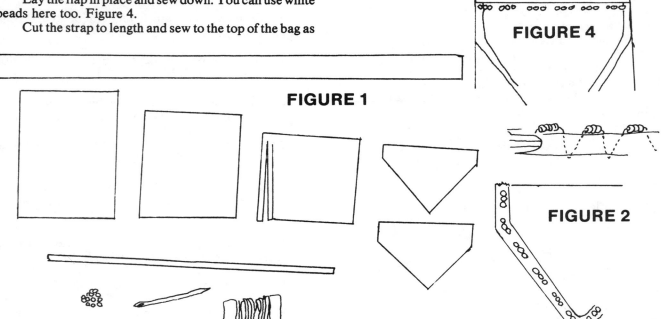

FIGURE 3

FIGURE 4

FIGURE 1

FIGURE 2

VOYAGEUR SHOOTING BAG

The voyageur bag is of a type used by Indians, long-hunters, and voyageurs of the late 18th century. The best leather to use for this shooting bag is full weight moose, elk or buffalo. You can also use very heavy deer or even moccasin weight glove tanned cowhide. The leather should be supple and yet heavy enough to hold its shape when the bag is in use. A stiff back was often used and is even preferable. This makes a very fine bag. For this you will need about 5 square feet of leather.

The strap should be of the same material as that from which you make the bag, about 2" wide by 52" long. You will also need: 10 yards linen or nylon thread, 1 - 1" button, knife — very sharp, scissors — carpet shears are best, awl, 2 needles, beeswax (for waxing thread), contact cement (optional — Barge Cement best)

Please read instructions over completely before embarking on this project. It will make construction of this bag simpler for you in the long run.

MAKING THE BAG

1. Cut out your pattern. Check it for accuracy.

2. Lay out the pattern on the leather before starting to cut.

3. Cut the parts out from the leather.

4. Cut the fringe. Make it very thin, about ⅛" thick. Use a very sharp knife and a cutting board.

5. Sew the inside accessories pocket to the back piece's smooth side. (See detail A for placement.)

6. Fold the strap tabs and sew together as in detail B.

7. Position the strap tabs as shown in detail C. Use a spot of glue to hold in place while sewing.

8. Lay the divider on the inside (smooth side to smooth side) of the back piece. Tack them together with a few *small* drops of glue — or — sew the divider to the back at each corner and about 4 or 5 places around the bottom and sides.

9. Put the fringe material on the *back* of the bag so that when it folds down the rough side will be toward the front of the bag. See detail D (i.e., with the bag back

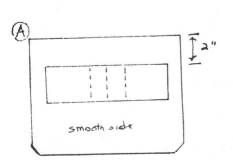

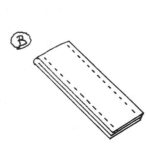

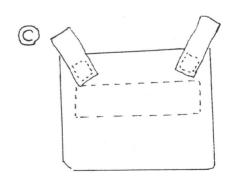

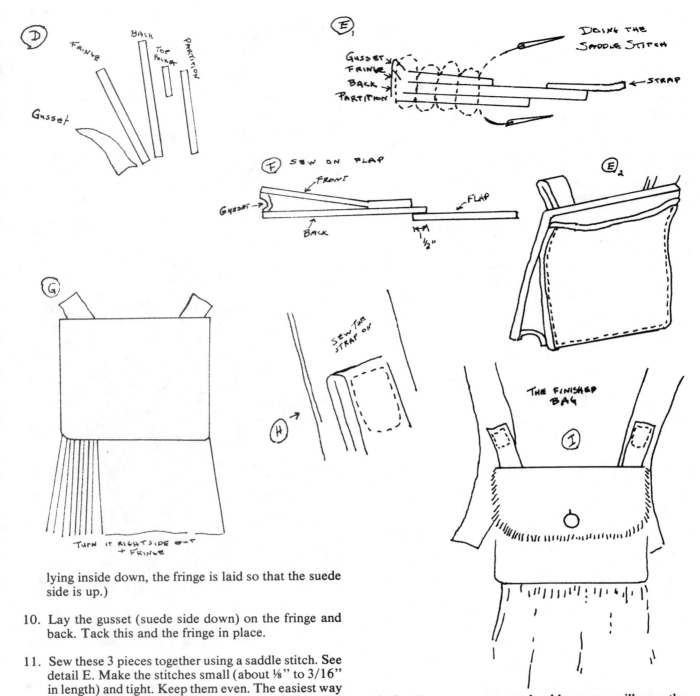

lying inside down, the fringe is laid so that the suede side is up.)

10. Lay the gusset (suede side down) on the fringe and back. Tack this and the fringe in place.

11. Sew these 3 pieces together using a saddle stitch. See detail E. Make the stitches small (about ⅛" to 3/16" in length) and tight. Keep them even. The easiest way to do this is start at the center bottom sewing up one side, then up the other side.

12. Sew the front to the bag, again using a saddle stitch. Remember — the bag is still *INSIDE OUT*.

13. Turn the bag right side out.

14. Sew the flap to the bag proper. Lay the flap onto the back of the bag so that the edges overlap by about ½". Sew them together using a saddle stitch. See detail F.

15. Fringe the flap all around. The fringe should be about ¾" long.

16. Put the strap over your shoulder as you will wear the bag. Hold the bag against your body and see where you will want it to ride. The bag should ride up under your arm and slightly forward on your body. It should hang high enough that it doesn't flop around and just low enough for you to get into it when you need to do so.

17. Measure the strap and mark it. Take it off and sew it to the bag tab (see detail H) or lace it.

18. Cut the buttonhole in the flap.

19. Fold the flap down and mark for the button. Then sew the button in place, and your bag is ready to use.

53

SMALL INDIAN SHOOTING BAG

This is taken from a small Indian made shooting bag which was on display in the museum at Jackson, Wyoming several years ago. It is made of white hand tanned leather, very nicely beaded.

The bag is approximately 8" high with the flap closed, and perhaps 6" wide. It is of envelope-style construction (no gusset). The back is higher than the front by about ¾ of an inch. The flap is separated and is attached to the back by way of a third piece of leather about 2" x 6", pinked by hand on the two long edges. The flap is also pinked. The pinking was done with a knife and is about ½ inch between points.

The bag is fringed all around the edge. The length of the fringe is about 4". The fringe is about ⅛" wide.

The strap is a heavy half-tanned thong about ¾" in width. It is attached to the bag with two thongs, one in each upper corner of the back.

The beading is of the floral style and looks as though it might have been Crow. I would guess the period to be late 19th century although the style of the bag is certainly older.

This would be a very nice and serviceable bag for hunting or out of the bag shooting. If you would like to construct one for yourself, just follow the accompanying drawings.

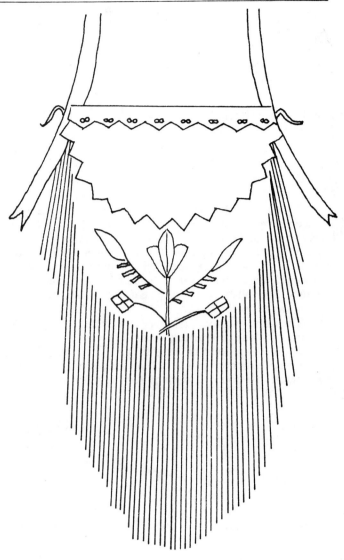

THE PARTS

MAKING THE BAG

1. Make a full-size drawing and decorate it with crayon or colored pencil.

2. When your drawing is the way you like it, make a pattern.

3. Cut the bag from heavy white tan deer or elk. Be sure the leather is *pre-stretched.*

4. Sew the flap to the bag.

5. Bead the front piece.

6. Sew the front of the bag to the back of the bag (inside out). Be sure the fringe is laid in correctly as a welt.

7. Turn the bag right-side out.

8. Attach the strap and you are all set.

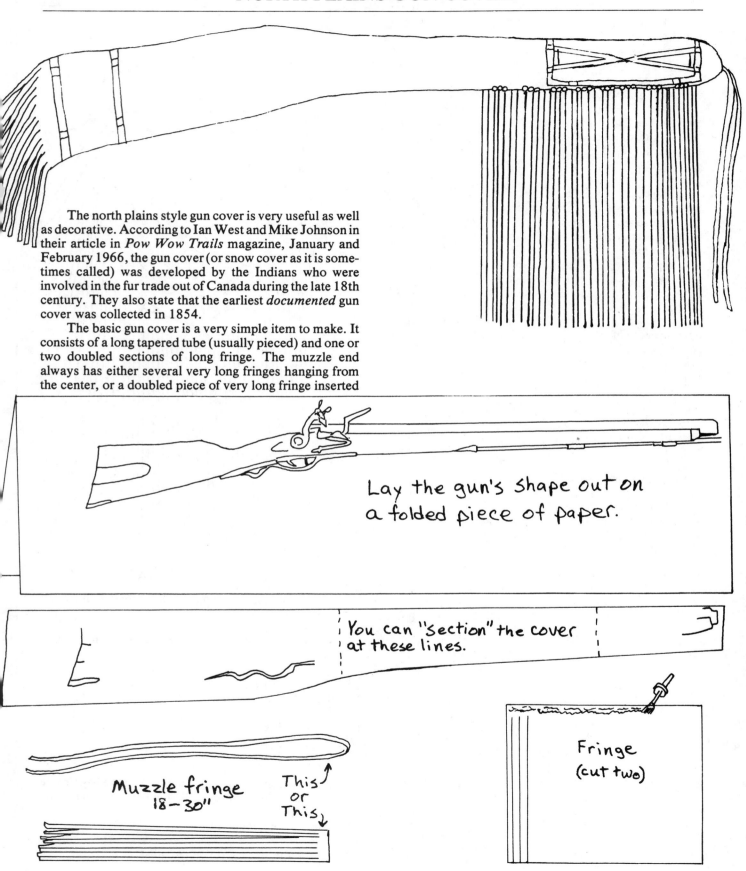

The north plains style gun cover is very useful as well as decorative. According to Ian West and Mike Johnson in their article in *Pow Wow Trails* magazine, January and February 1966, the gun cover (or snow cover as it is sometimes called) was developed by the Indians who were involved in the fur trade out of Canada during the late 18th century. They also state that the earliest *documented* gun cover was collected in 1854.

The basic gun cover is a very simple item to make. It consists of a long tapered tube (usually pieced) and one or two doubled sections of long fringe. The muzzle end always has either several very long fringes hanging from the center, or a doubled piece of very long fringe inserted

Lay the gun's shape out on a folded piece of paper.

You can "section" the cover at these lines.

Muzzle fringe 18-30"

This or This

Fringe (cut two)

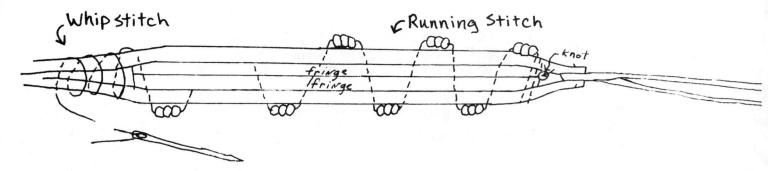

and sewn in as a welt. The butt end is usually fringed but sometimes is "pinked" instead. Very occasionally this end is left plain.

To make the typical north plains gun cover, you will need one good quality hide, about 12 feet in area and one thinner hide, the size of which will determine the amount of your fringe. Be sure and stretch your hides before using them. Look at the sketches. Then follow these simple steps.

Measure your gun from butt to muzzle. The cover should be about 1-2 inches greater than your rifle's overall length. The large (butt end) should be large enough around to contain your weapon with about 1-2 inches overall of play around it at any given point along its length. This will vary somewhat depending upon how you detail the shaping. Take measurements around the stock at butt, trigger, hammer area, center forearm, and muzzle at the sight. Take a piece of heavy butcher paper which is longer than your weapon. Fold it in half lengthwise. Mark the dimensions of the gun onto the paper. Draw a profile of the cover onto the paper. Cut this out and staple it along the bottom edge. Fit your rifle or musket into this sheath. Modify the pattern as needed. Remember that the paper does not "give" like leather. You can make a tighter fit with the leather. Make a pattern for your fringe. Lay the pattern out and trace it onto your hides. The casing can be in 2 or 3 pieces and then sewn together if need be. Cut out the gun cover. Cut the fringe pieces. Fringe should be about ¼" wide. Cut the fringe on the butt end if you are going to have any there.

If the case is in more than one piece, this is the time to sew it together. A thin welt sewn between the two pieces will hide the threads and make a neater, stronger joint. Trim the welt and pound the seam when you are finished. I would suggest an overcast stitch be used here.

Glue the two pieces of fringe together at the top to form a piece of double fringe. Fold the cover lengthwise, right side out. Insert the fringe up onto the gun case as shown in the sketch. I would recommend a thin line of Barge or some other good rubber base cement to hold the fringe in place while it is being sewn. This is not necessary, but it makes the job a lot easier.

An alternate way to sew your fringe is to fold the gun cover INSIDE OUT, insert the fringe, and whip stitch the entire length of the case, then turn it right side out.

The fringe is sewn in place with an even running stitch. I like to put pony beads on each stitch. Sew the balance of the length of the gun case using a whip (overcast) stitch. Insert the muzzle end fringe into the nose of the cover and sew it using a whip stitch if the fringe is merely a few long strands, a running stitch if you are using a welt style fringe.

The gun cover is now ready for you to bead, or you may use it as it is.

18th Century Clothing

by Beth Gilgun

BETH GILGUN HAS BEEN MAKING 18th century clothing for five years. What began as a natural outgrowth from an interest in history and the lifestyles of the 18th century has now become an occupation and obsession. She lives with her husband Chris in a 17th century house which is in the never-ending process of restoration. Weekends during the winter find them hosting 18th century style parties with food cooked in the brick oven and fireplace and drinks mixed according to recipes from colonial taverns.

Beth was first introduced to black powder in 1969 when she met her future husband, Chris. A life-long interest in camping and hiking has since been transferred to going primitive style. She combined college courses in fashion design, pattern making, and history, accented with her skill in needle arts and sewing, and began making period clothing.

Beth's clothing is field tested by her husband and friends who do primitive camping in all seasons. Usually the first question asked when they return home is, "Did anything rip?". She started a business in 1983 called Elegant Embellishments. Clothing of all types is made, with special emphasis on woolen fabrics for fall, winter and spring camping. To occupy the spare moments between sewing and travelling, Beth will also be writing for *Muzzleloader* magazine starting in 1984.

BEFORE starting to make your period clothing, there is a tool to help determine your clothes, accoutrements, gun and perhaps even speech. The tool is development of a character and there are four aspects to consider.

The first thing you need to do is pick a period of time. The loose constraint of "anything before 1840" does not help to give you a cohesive costume. You may want to pick a specific decade, year or period of struggle — such as the French and Indian War. You may pick a year because the town you live in was founded then. Or perhaps, you can trace a relative to that decade. There are many reasons for deciding upon a time frame — but the most important is that you feel comfortable within the constraints of that period.

You should also pick a place from which to hail. This can be as loosely defined as a region — mid-Atlantic, Northwest — or as definite as a town. Along with the place, picking a culture is important. Do you want to be an Indian, Frenchman, Englishman, or Colonial? Are you rich or poor? Perhaps you were the son of a wealthy landowner who was the black sheep of the family. Obviously, the quality of clothing you have in that case would be far different from that of a runaway indentured servant or of a backwoodsman.

This brings up the last point for consideration — having a personal history. You may want to go all out, find the name of a person, research his or her life and take on that identity. But you can also pick a type of person — a sailor who, after the war of 1812, goes west to the Rockies; a woman who was captured by the Indians and accepts their culture; a frontier boy who grows up being influenced by both white and Indian cultures.

These four aspects bracket the basic identity of an individual from which a mental picture can be formed. For example — you have decided that in 1756 you were a Dutch farm girl who was captured by the Seneca in central

58

New York. A little study into the Dutch and Iroquois cultures and into the trade goods available in the 1750s would provide an abundance of costume ideas. Variations in costume can be developed logically from variations in culture and personal history.

This is not to say that you can't portray a "typical" frontiersman, mountain man or soldier. Obviously, this is a good starting point, but it is doubtful that there was any such thing as a "typical mountain man". It is most likely that any one of them would have bristled at the label "typical". Your enjoyment should be the key factor as to how far you develop your character".

Logical non-uniformity should be the norm except for military organizations and strict, closed social or religious units. Even then, some form of individual identity or expression can be worked into personal items, or even speech.

There are many sources for ideas in developing a personality and clothing. Your local library may have books on period costume such as *Early American Costume* or *Rural Pennsylvania Clothing.* The library is also a possible source for first person accounts such as diaries and journals.

Period paintings help tremendously in suggesting colors and cut of clothing. They are especially helpful in portraying different Indian tribes. Of course, there are many magazines dealing with "buckskinning" and with specific ideas of American history. And, you will find many excellent books available through black powder catalogues.

Finally — use your own ideas. Minor modifications, using common sense, to your personal effects are appropriate even if not found in historical records. Please note that I used the terms "minor modifications" and "common sense." Eighteenth and nineteenth century people had to "make-do" and "modify" in order to exist in a time of poor supply and little or no cash. Your modifications should be a logical reflection of your "character's" needs, materials, imagination, knowledge, and experience.

Modifications which contain styles or improvisations from later periods should be avoided. Earlier period artifacts can almost always be used — old habits die hard. Many clothes and accoutrements were in use years after a new style had been introduced.

When your "character" has been decided upon, you are ready to design your clothing and begin sewing.

SEWING HINTS & TERMS

Seams are ⅝ inch unless specified.

Right side of fabric (as in right sides together) means the side which will be the outside of the garment.

Narrow hem means to turn under ⅛ inch on raw edge, and then turn under another ⅛ inch. Hem with either a slipstitch or running stitch, depending on the "look" you want.

Preshrink all fabric before cutting out the garment.

Cotton thread is ideal. If you plan to dye the finished garment it is a must — polyester thread will not take dye.

"Turn" — in most cases means to turn from inside out to right side out.

MAKING A SHIFT

The shift was the basic woman's undergarment and was also used as a nightdress. It was in use up through the 1850s. A shift can be made of fine, white linen, or of cotton (such as muslin). While linen is the more correct fabric, it is also much more expensive. I would suggest making a cotton shift first — if for no other reason than to make sure you like the fit.

No pattern is necessary to make the shift—just a yardstick or tape measure. You need about 3-1/2 yards of fabric, thread, and about 4 yards of 1/4-inch tape, ribbon or cord for drawstrings. I sew all my inside seams by machine for two reasons. One is because I can do it so much faster. The other reason is that I do not sew 22 stitches to the inch by hand, which is what a good seamstress was expected to do "back then." I do try to stay away from machine stitching on the outside of my garments where stitching will show. Wash your fabric before you cut so that the finished garment will not shrink.

1) Measure the distance from your shoulder to mid-calf. Double this measurement, and you have the length of the main pattern piece of the shift. The width should be 30 inches.

2) Cut two pieces 15" X 15" for the sleeves and two squares 6" X 6" for the underarm gussets. Fold the main body of the shift in half so that you can cut the neck opening and the triangular gussets that will go onto the bottom sides.

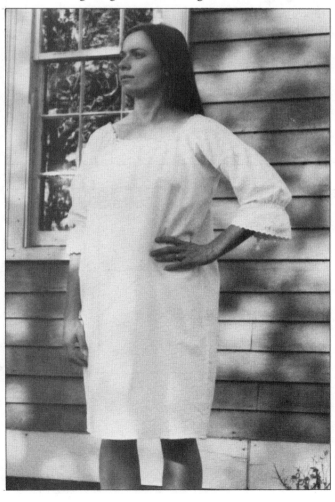

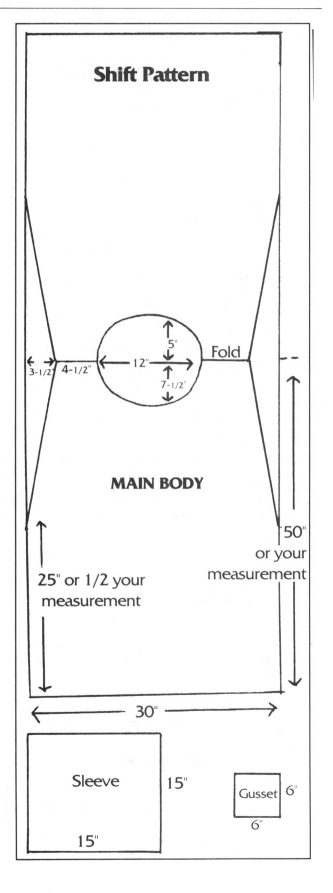

3) Shifts should be sewn using flat-felled seams, although you might find it easier to just overcast the raw edges. The first step in sewing the chemise is to sew on the triangular pieces cut from the side tops of the main piece onto the side bottoms. Make sure to match the straight grain of the fabric.

4) Assemble the sleeves. The six-inch square gussets will be under your arm in a diamond shape when the shift is put together. Fold the sleeve pieces in half and sew the seam, leaving a six-inch opening at one end. Insert the gusset into this opening and sew.

5) Fold the main body of the shift in half and mark the shoulder lines either by pressing or with a pin. Mark the center of the top of the sleeve and match the center of the sleeve to the shoulder. Be sure to put the right sides of the fabric together.

6) Measure down the side of the main body six inches from the shoulder line on both the front and the back. Pin the bottom of the sleeve to this point (not the bottom of the gusset) and make tiny tucks or gather the sleeves to take in the fullness to match the shift. Sew the sleeves to the shift and then sew the side seams.

7) The neckline can be finished in two different ways. The first is with a drawstring. Measure the neckline and cut a piece of wide twill tape the length of the neck measurement plus two inches. Fold the ends of the tape over twice and stitch to prevent the tape from ravelling.

8) Place one end of the tape at the center front of the neckline on the right side of the shift and stitch the tape to the shift about 1/4 inch from the edge all the way around the neckline. Turn the tape to the inside of the shift and sew the bottom of the tape to the shift. There will be an opening at the center front of the shift where the two ends of the tape meet. Run a piece of narrow tape throught the casing you have just made and have the ends come out at the center front. You can then gather the neckline in to fit.

9) An alternate neckline finish is made by turning the edge under in a narrow hem and not gathering it at all. If you want a rufffle on the neckline, it is added to the finished neck edge.

10) To make a ruffle, you need a piece of very fine linen 1-1/2 inches wide and 45 inches long. Join the two ends of the strip with a small, flat-felled seam and then make a very fine rolled hem on both sides of the ruffle. The ruffle is sewn onto the neck edge using a whip stitch over the rolled hem of the ruffle and into the top edge of the neckline hem. You will need to space the ruffle evenly around the neck and take tiny gathers or tucks to ease it to fit the neck.

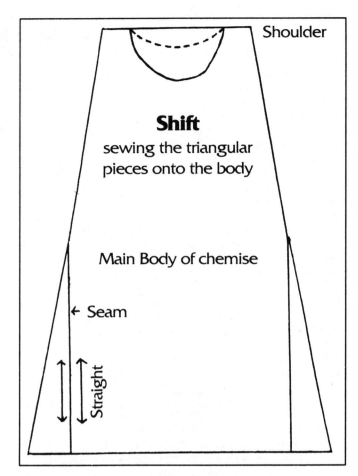

Shift
sewing the triangular pieces onto the body

Main Body of chemise

← Seam

Straight

Shoulder

11) Make a 1/2-inch hem on the bottoms of the sleeves and the shift, and it is ready to wear. If you like, you can form a casing at the bottom of the sleeves and run a drawstring through to gather them in. The sleeves can also be finished with ruffles or narrow cuffs.

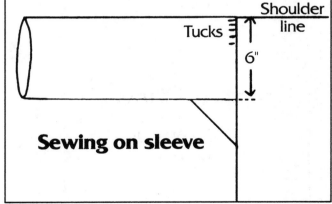

Tucks

Shoulder line

6"

Sewing on sleeve

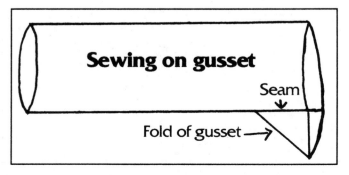

Sewing on gusset

Seam

Fold of gusset →

MAKING A PETTICOAT

Over her shift, a woman wears her stays[1] and some sort of jacket or waistcoat and a petticoat. In the winter you might want to wear several petticoats to keep warm. I like to wear a linen or cotton one underneath and a woolen one as my outer. You do not need to limit yourself to just two petticoats, either. Many women wear as many as seven quite routinely, and I have heard of one who wore 16 in the dead of winter! Petticoats can be made from the plainest linen or cotton to the fanciest silk. Most working women do not wear the length of their petticoats overlong, as they get in the way. I have seen some nice striped ones and must admit a preference for them myself. I also prefer my petticoats quite full at the hem—usually 90 to 108 inches. Narrower petticoats cause me much distress when trying to move quickly.

The easiest way to make a petticoat is with a drawstring waist. This is also a good idea if you are likely to be pregnant or if your weight fluctuates a lot. You will need 2-1/2 to four yards of fabric, depending on your height and the width you plan to make the petticoat. A circumference anywhere from 80 to 144 inches is fine. Thinner fabrics make nicer petticoats if they are quite full. If you are using a heavy wool, you will want to make it narrower. The length can be anywhere from mid-calf to the top of your feet.

1) After pre-washing, cut as many panels of the fabric as you need for the width. Cut the panels the length you want your finished petticoat to be plus two inches. For example if your fabric is 45 inches wide, and you want the finished petticoat to be 36 inches long and about 90 inches wide, you will cut two pieces 45 inches wide and 38 inches long.

2) Sew the panels together, leaving the top of each side seam open eight inches for your pocket slits. Make a narrow rolled hem on the sides of these openings.

[1]Stays were a boned undergarment worn to give the body support and the proper shape.

Carol Neville is wearing the dark kerchief common to the people of rural Quebec. She is also wearing a cap, jumps without sleeves, a tan apron and a striped petticoat of linen. The jumps are not a short, waist-length garment. They have skirts that come over the hips.

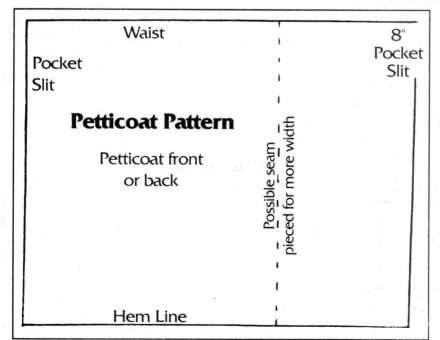

Waist   8" Pocket Slit

Pocket Slit

Petticoat Pattern

Petticoat front or back

Possible seam pieced for more width

Hem Line

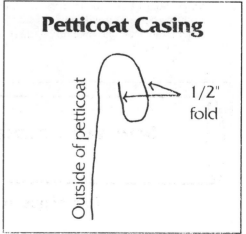

Petticoat Casing

Outside of petticoat

1/2" fold

3) To make a casing along the top edge of the petticoat, fold the edges over 1/2 inch twice. If you are using a very heavy fabric, you will want to fold the edge over only once and finish the raw edge by whipstitching. Sew the folded edge to the wrong side of the petticoat to form a casing for the drawstring, being sure to leave the ends of the casings open.

4) Hem the bottom by folding the edge over 1/2 inch twice and hemstitching.

5) Run two lengths of twill tape through the top casings and your petticoat will be finished. The tapes should be about one yard long, and they are tied at each hip.

The author is wearing her shift, petticoat, stays and apron.

MAKING AN APRON

This apron is a simple apron with no pinafore. Made of fine linen or muslin, aprons were often white, but could also be gray, blue, tan, striped, or checked. Length is to personal taste — I make mine rather long. Aprons are indispensable for use as towels, hot mitts when cooking and as sacks for carrying.

You will need about 2 yards of 45 inch fabric.

1) Decide length of your apron.
2) Measure waist. You will cut your waistband 3½ times this measurement, by 5 inches wide. This makes long ties in back. You will probably need to divide the total length in half and piece the waistband in the middle. Figure 1.
3) Cut a length of fabric 2 yards wide by your chosen length. Figure 1.
4) Either narrow hem the bottom edge or use selvedge as finish. Narrow hem the two sides. Figure 1.
5) Use your waist measurement minus 6 to 8 inches and mark the length on the waistband.
6) Gather apron to fit between the marks and sew to waistband using ⅝ inch seam.
7) Fold waistband in half, turning under ⅝ inch on all sides.
8) By hand, stitch waistband all around open edges using small back stitches, and double thread.

This apron will cover all your front and part of your back.

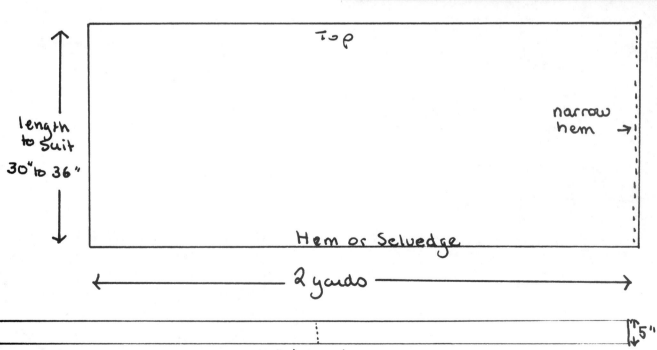

length to suit 30" to 36"

Top

narrow hem →

Hem or Selvedge

← 2 yards →

waist band
3½ times waist measurement

5"

MAKING A POCKET

Pockets were an eighteenth century answer to a pocketbook. Worn under or over the skirt, they were useful for carrying many items. Pockets were made either singly or in pairs and were tied around the waist with hand loomed tape. Made of linen, canvas or cotton, they were sometimes beautifully embroidered.

You will need ½ yard of fabric, and enough tape to tie around your waist. If you do not know of a source of hand-loomed tape, cotton twill tape ¼ to ½ inch wide is a good substitute.

Follow the diagram for measurements (Figure 1). If you plan to embroider the front, outline the pocket, transfer your design, and embroider before you cut it out. Diagram includes ½ inch seams. Cut two pieces per pocket. Add slit to front.

To finish edge of slit you have three options. Figure 2.
1) If Front is embroidered, line the front. Sew around the slit with right sides together and turn right side out. Press.
2) Narrow hem the edges of slit.
3) Bind edges of slit with tape.

Once the slit edges are finished, put right sides of front and back of pocket together. Sew around all edges. Either overcast or bind seams. Turn right side out through slit. Attach tape ties and you are finished.

There are three methods of attaching the tape ties. Figure 3.
1) Fold tape over top edge of pocket and sew.
2) Cut ties into two lengths. Whipstitch ends to either corner of the pockets.
3) Insert the tape through the top of the pocket as you are sewing the front and back together.

Pockets are tied around your waist and accessed through slits in your skirt or may be worn on top of your skirt. If you are making a pair, measure the distance across the front of your waist, divide in half, and position pockets that distance from the middle of your tape ties. Pockets should be directly over the hips.

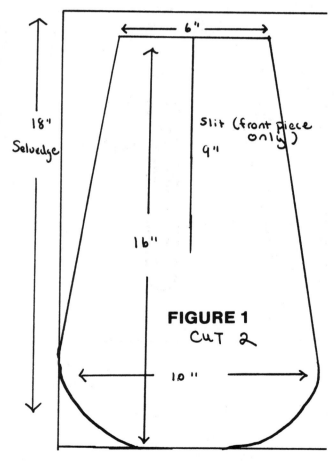

FIGURE 1
CUT 2

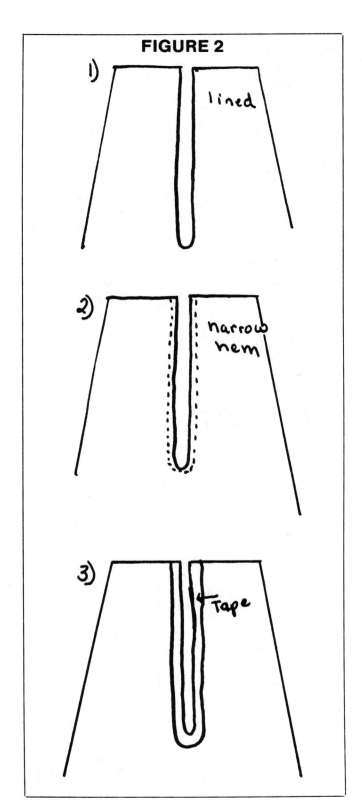

FIGURE 2

1) lined

2) narrow hem

3) Tape

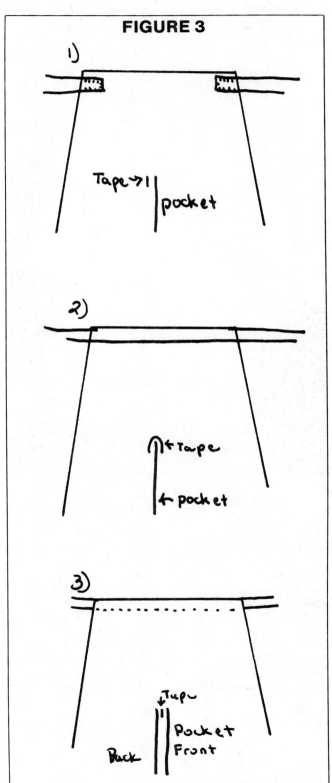

FIGURE 3

1) Tape→| |pocket

2) ↑←Tape
   ←pocket

3) ↓Tape
   Pocket
   Front
   Back

66

MAKING A WOMAN'S WAISTCOAT

According to Anne Buck in *Dress in Eighteenth Century England,* "...women's bodices or waistcoats...either covered the stays or were worn in their place, beneath the woolen gowns."[2] Extant examples of these garments are all quilted, which leads us to believe they were worn for added warmth. It is most likely that these were not worn as outer garments. They are a valuable addition to your wardrobe for cold weather wear.

To make your waistcoat, you will need one yard of outer fabric, one yard of lining and two yards of twill tape or cording for the front lacing. Waistcoat and lining may be made from the same fabric.

Cut the pattern pieces according to Figure 1. These measurements are for a size 10. To adjust larger or smaller, add or subtract 1/4 inch to the side and shoulder edges. Also add 1/4 inch to the waist length.

Sewing the Waistcoat

1) Sew center back seam from neck to waist.
2) Sew shoulder seams, matching notches, then sew front to back, from waist to armhole, on side seams.
3) Press open all seams.
4) Construct the lining as you did the waistcoat.
5) Pin waistcoat and lining together starting at one shoulder seam.
6) Sew the waistcoat and lining together starting at one shoulder seam. Sew down the front, across the hem line, up to the side seam and so on. You are creating four separate flaps from the waistline to the hem. Continue sewing up to the opposite shoulder seam. Leave the back neck open to allow you to turn the waistcoat right side out.
7) Turn right side out and press. Turn in 5/8 inch on the back neck edge. Slipstitch edges together.
8) Turn under 5/8 inch on armhole edges, pressing and clipping curves to lay flat. Slipstitch together.
9) Make eyelets on the front edges. Depending upon the look you want to achieve, as few as four and as many as nine eyelets may be used.
10) Lace the front with twill tape or cording and your waistcoat is complete.

[2]Buck, Anne. *Dress in Eighteenth Century England.* New York: Holmes & Meier, 1979: 197.

Diane Tidy, of Tidy's Storehouse, models her quilted waistcoat. What we once called a bodice should probably be called a waistcoat. They were most likely not outer garments but were quilted and worn as an extra layer in cold weather.

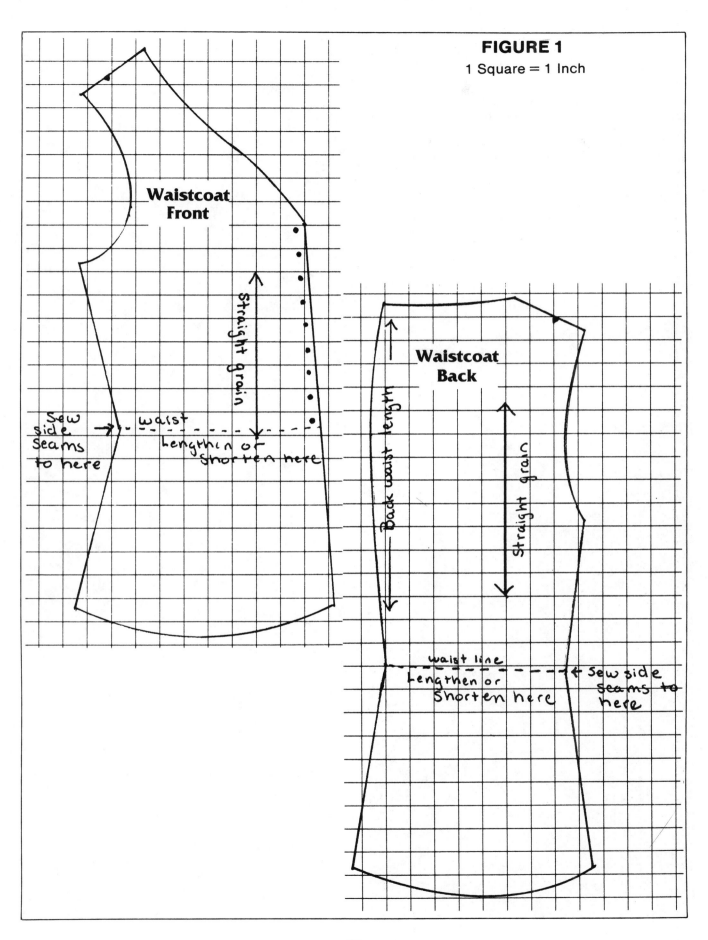

FIGURE 1

1 Square = 1 Inch

Waistcoat
Front

Straight grain

Sew side seams to here

waist

Lengthen or shorten here

Waistcoat
Back

Back waist length

Straight grain

waist line

Lengthen or shorten here

Sew side seams to here

MAKING A CAPE

A long cape will keep you warm on cold nights and chilly days. You will even find it handy as an extra blanket, if needed. This cape should be made from wool, and can be lined with wool, cotton, linen, or satin, or can be made unlined. A word of caution — if you line the cape with wool, be prepared to handle a lot of bulk.

You will need 4 yards of fabric and the same amount of lining.

1) Measure from the nape of your neck to the length you want the cape to be. Add 2 inches for a hem.
2) Cut fabric according to the Figure 1 — 2 lengths for the cape and one each of the hood and neck binding.

3) Cut lining according to diagram except for the neck binding.
4) Sew the 2 lengths of fabric together, right sides together, along one edge. This is your center back seam.
5) Sew center back of lining together.
6) Cut 2 inch strips of interfacing the length of your cape. Attach to the front edges of the cape fabric.
7) Put cape and lining right sides together. Sew along front edges.
8) Turn right sides out and press.
9) Sew the center back seams of hood and lining.
10) Place hood and lining right sides together. Sew along front edge. Turn right side out and press.
11) You have two options for creating fullness at the neck: gathers or pleats. If your fabric is not very bulky, run

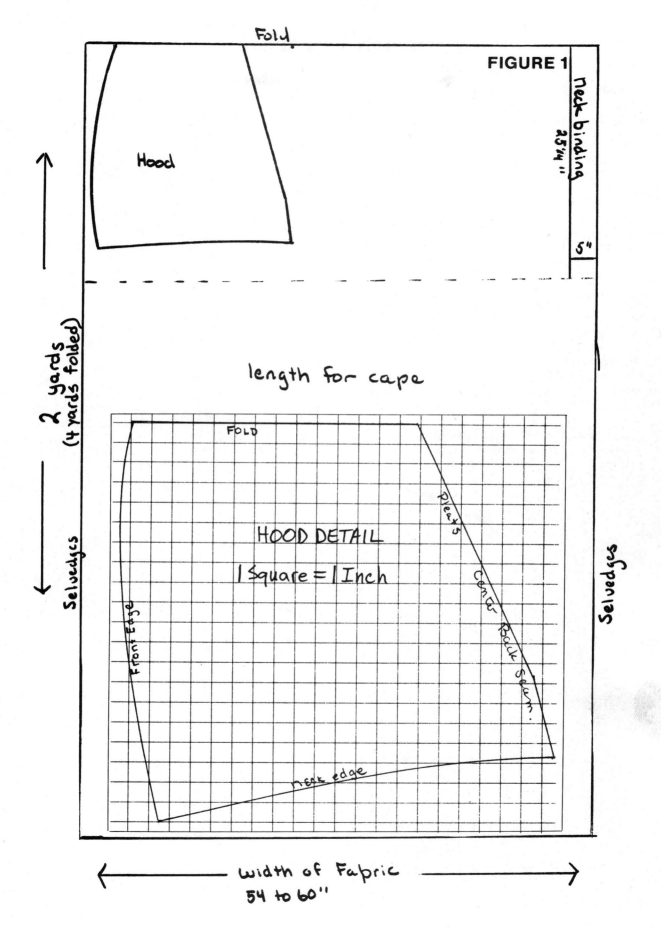

Fold

FIGURE 1

Neck binding
2.5¼"

5"

Hood

length for cape

2 yards
(4 yards folded)

Selvedges

Selvedges

FOLD

Pleats

Center Back Seam.

HOOD DETAIL

1 Square = 1 Inch

Front Edge

neck edge

width of Fabric
54 to 60"

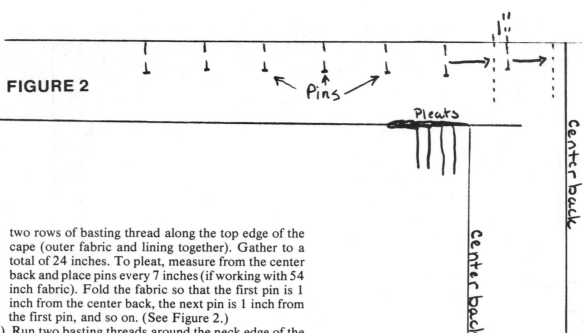

FIGURE 2

Pins

Pleats

Center back

Center back

1"

two rows of basting thread along the top edge of the cape (outer fabric and lining together). Gather to a total of 24 inches. To pleat, measure from the center back and place pins every 7 inches (if working with 54 inch fabric). Fold the fabric so that the first pin is 1 inch from the center back, the next pin is 1 inch from the first pin, and so on. (See Figure 2.)

12) Run two basting threads around the neck edge of the hood. Gather to fit 24 inches.

13) With right sides together, sew hood to cape through all thicknesses of fabric.

14) Fold neck binding in half the long way with right sides together. Sew along the front edge. Turn right side out and press.

15) Mark the center of the neck binding and match one edge to the cape. Sew along this edge.

16) Fold under the other long edge of binding, and slip-stitch to cover the neck seam on inside of cape.

17) Mark hem of cape and lining, fold and press. The lining is best if it is 1 inch shorter than the cape. Sew.

18) On the center back seam of hood, take four tucks 1 inch each. Tack down by hand. (See Figure 3.)

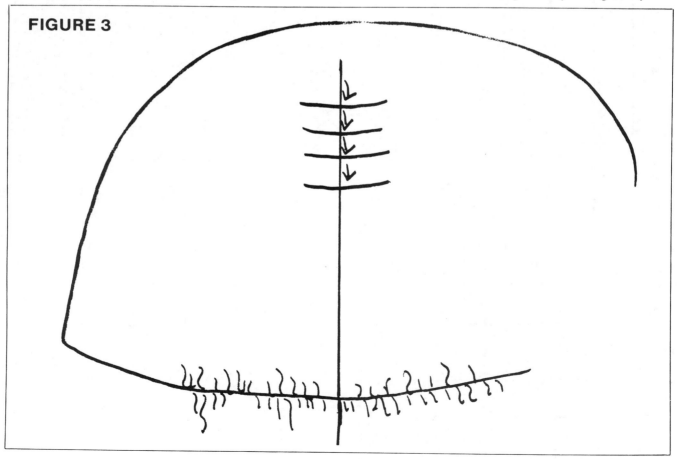

FIGURE 3

Straw hats were popular for summer wear in the 18th century. They were worn over linen caps and could be tied under the chin with ribbon or secured with a hat pin (left).

MAKING A CAP

This cap is made to look like the woman's cap in the accompanying plate from Diederot. It is not taken from an existing cap. Cut one of the cap back from medium to light-weight, white fabric. Cut two cap ears from very fine fabric. They do not hang correctly when made from a fabric that is too stiff. Cut two lengths of cotton string or narrow tape and anchor them on the cap back at B. Turn under a narrow hem forming a casing over the strings. Have the free ends of the strings come out of the casing at the center back. They will be used as drawstrings to gather the cap back. Narrow hem the curved edges of the cap ears. Run a gathering stitch from A to B on both the cap back and the cap ears. Gather the cap and the ears so that the measurement from A to B is 9 inches. Sew

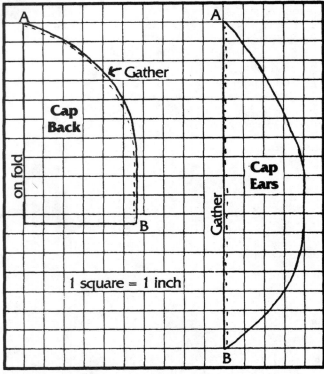

the ears to the cap using a narrow, flat-felled seam. Make sure that the ears are attached to the cap so that A is in the center front. Pull up the drawstrings so that the cap fits your head and, if you wish, put a ribbon over the seam. This is a small cap, and you might want to try it from scrap fabric before cutting your fine linen. The caps of the middle of the 18th century were small and hugged the head.

FABRIC MITTENS

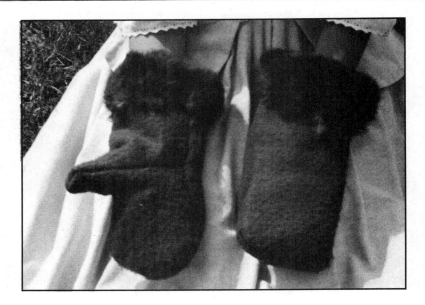

If you are doing any winter camping, you will want to have mittens. Of course, knitted mittens are authentic, but if you want to keep your hands warmer, make some from blanket scraps or heavy woolen fabric. These mittens can be lined or made from fur, also.

1) Cut two of each pattern piece. See diagram.
2) Pin piece 2 (palm) to piece 1 across seam line A.
3) Sew in a ¼ inch seam from point C to point B.
4) Fold along Fold Line, matching points D.
5) Sew from point D to point B with a ¼ inch seam.

Seams can either be made on the inside or outside of the mittens. Mittens can also be lengthened at the bottom edge to suit your needs.

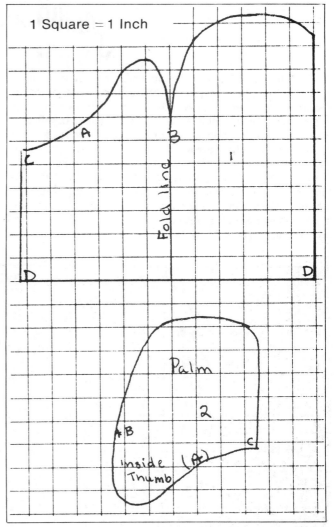

1 Square = 1 Inch

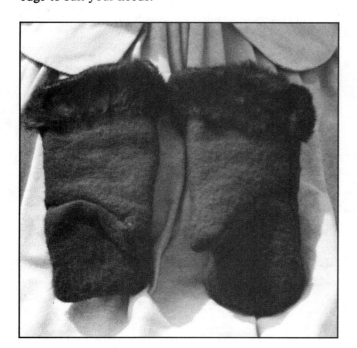

74

MAKING BREECHES

Breeches were common attire for men in all walks of life. The cut was the same, but fabrics were different. Breeches are comfortable and practical. They can be coupled with over the knee socks, or with leggings of fabric or leather. Suitable fabrics for breeches are wool, linen or heavy cotton. There are accounts of canvas being used, but you will find it a very hot and unbreathing choice.

You need 2 yards of breeches fabric and ½ yard of lining fabric. Cut your pattern pieces according to Figure 1. Adjust the inseam length to reach 2 to 3 inches below the knee. This gives ample room for movement. This pattern will fit waist sizes 34 to 38.

1) Sew center front seams of breeches and front facing. Clip the curve and press.
2) Sew side seams from waist to side opening. Press.
3) Sew center back seam from point A to crotch. Press.
4) With right sides together, sew around the edges of the inside flap. Turn right side out and press.
5) Place inside flap on breeches, right sides together, and sew through the top layer of the flap and breeches. Turn and press seam toward the inside of the flap. Turn under seam allowance of the lining of the flap and sew by hand to the inside of the breeches.
6) With right sides together, sew the front facing to the

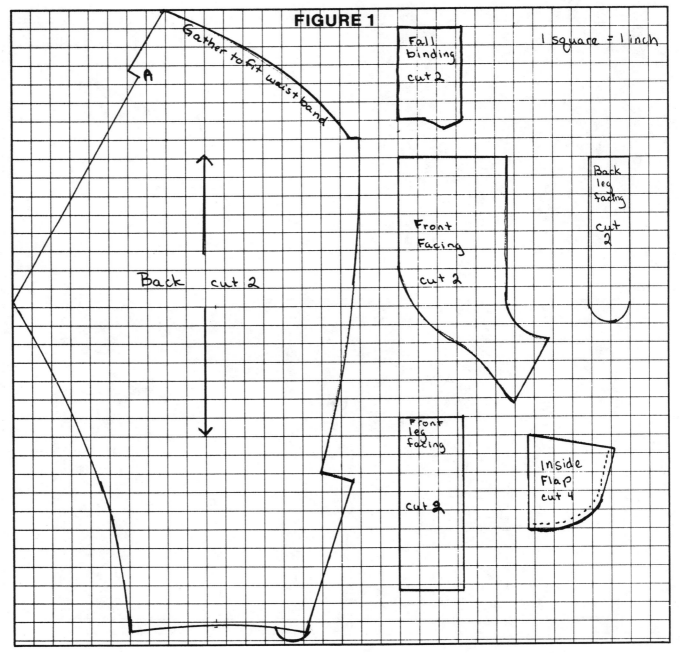

FIGURE 1

75

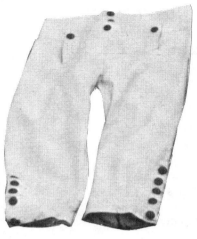

breeches front along the top edge. Turn and press.

7) Pin the fall binding to the breeches front along the raw edges through the breeches and the facing. (Figure 2) The binding will extend ⅝ inch above the top of the breeches. Sew with a ¼ inch seam, turn and press. Turn under the inside edge and sew by hand to the seam line.

8) Press under ¼ inch on the point. Pin to breeches and sew through all thicknesses, including the inside facings. (Figure 3)

9) Sew waistband and lining together along front, back, and top edges. Turn right side out and press.

10) Run two rows of basting stitches along the top edges of the breeches back.

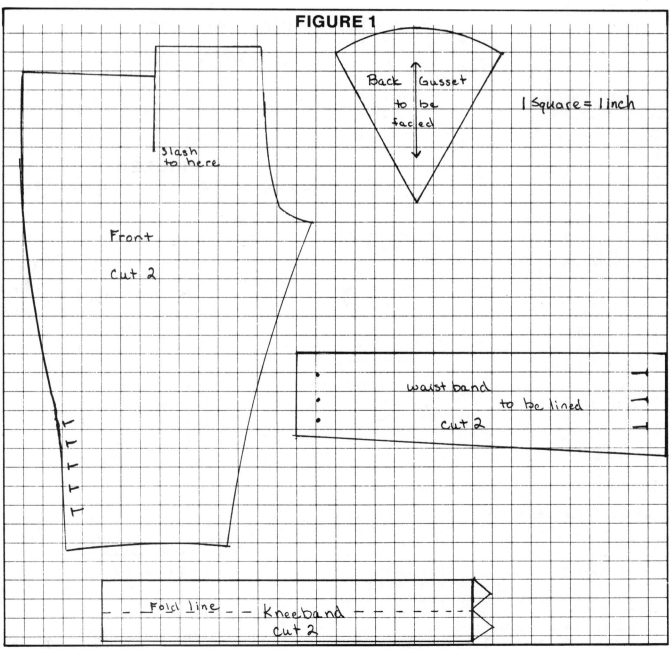

FIGURE 1

Back Gusset to be faced

1 Square = 1 inch

Slash to here

Front

Cut 2

waist band

to be lined

cut 2

Fold line — — Kneeband

cut 2

76

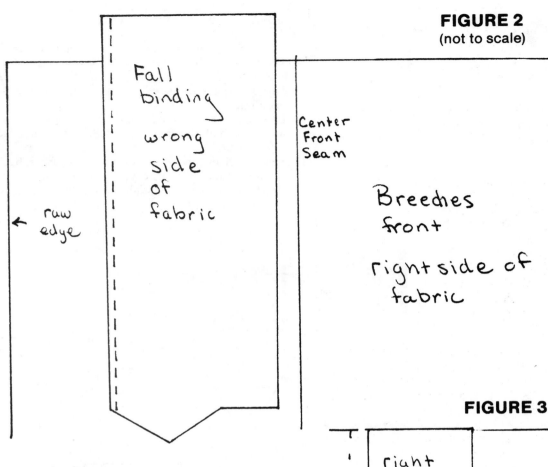

FIGURE 2
(not to scale)

Fall binding wrong side of fabric

← raw edge

Center Front Seam

Breeches front right side of fabric

FIGURE 3

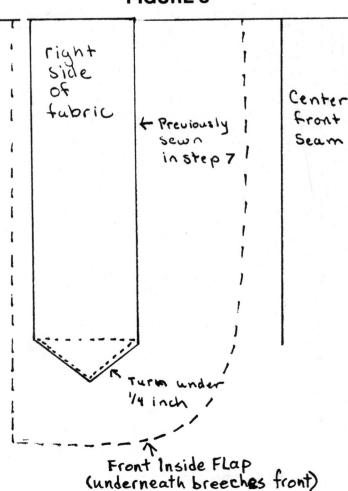

right side of fabric

← Previously sewn in step 7

Center Front Seam

Turn under ¼ inch

Front Inside Flap (underneath breeches front)

11) Pin waistband to breeches, gathering in the breeches to fit. Sew in place. Press seam toward waistband, and slipstitch the waistband lining to the inside of the breeches.

12) Sew front knee facing on the breeches front along the side and lower edge. Turn. Finish the remaining raw edges with a ¼ inch seam.

13) Sew the back knee facing along the side and around circular edge. Hem remaining edges.

14) Fold knee band lengthwise and sew pointed ends to form a tab. Trim seam allowances, turn and press.

15) Measure 1½ inches from the edge of the front knee opening. With right sides together, pin knee band to breeches. Continue around the leg until the edge of the circular tab is reached. Sew to breeches and turn and press.

16) Turn under seam allowance of the inside of the knee band, and sew to the breeches.

17) Turn under seam allowances of the back tab and top-stitch.

18) Make buttonholes in the Fall, Waistband, and Knee openings. The knee bindings can be either buttoned or buckled. Make 2 or 3 eyelets in the back waistband to accommodate lacing.

19) Stitch along the top edge of the back gusset and facing. Turn and press. Overcast the raw edges of the gusset sides. Sew the gusset to the waistband and breeches back through all layers of fabric.

20) Lace back with cording or rawhide.
    These breeches sit low on your hips and the lacings in the back hold them tight so that they stay up.

MAKING A MAN'S SHIRT

A man's shirt, like a woman's shift, is his underwear. It is rarely worn without a waistcoat or jacket over it. Shirts are quite long. They come to mid-thigh or knee length, depending on the man's preference. Because of the straight cut, the shirt is made quite wide and full, so that the wearer has freedom of movement. This shirt is a pullover style with one button at the neck. In general, the cut of the shirt up through 1840 remained unchanged from the shirt made in the early 1700s.

The first step to making a shirt is to obtain the fabric. Most shirts are 36 to 40 inches long. The way an 18th and 19th century shirt is cut, you will need fabric twice the length you choose, if you are using fabric that is 60 inches wide. Add to this length five to six inches for shrinkage. Once you get your fabric, overcast the two cut edges and wash it. If you are using linen, wash it two or three times with hot water and soap. (If you are going to dry the garment in a dryer once it is made, dry the fabric in a dryer to pre-shrink it. Even if you are going to dry clean wool, it is a good idea to have it dry cleaned and steam pressed before you sew it.)

To determine the length of the shirt, measure the person from the shoulder to where he wants it to end. This measurement (usually 36 to 40 inches) is doubled. The width of the shirt will be from 27 to 36 inches depending upon the man's size and also the fineness of the fabric. A very fine handkerchief linen shirt can be wider than a heavy wool one. One way to determine the width is to measure from six to seven inches below the natural shoulder line of the man's left arm, across the shoulders and back of the neck to six to seven inches below the natural shoulder of the right arm. In general, the width of the shirt will be from 27 to 30 inches. The body of the shirt is generally cut as one piece—there are no shoulder seams. However, if your fabric cuts to better advantage by using the crosswise grain rather than the lengthwise grain, it is acceptable to cut it that way and have a seam at the shoulder.

Sleeves are 20 to 25 inches wide and 19 to 23 inches long. Personal preference and fabric weight will make the difference in how full you want the sleeve. The length varies according to arm length. If you are using inexpensive fabric (and for your first shirt that is probably wise), I recommend cutting the sleeve pieces the longer length and adjusting them by trying the shirt on the man before the cuffs are put on. The fullness of the sleeves is regulated by the width that you cut them and by using different size gussets under the arm. The collar is cut 2-1/2 to three inches longer than the person's neck measurement and anywhere from two to ten inches wide. Some

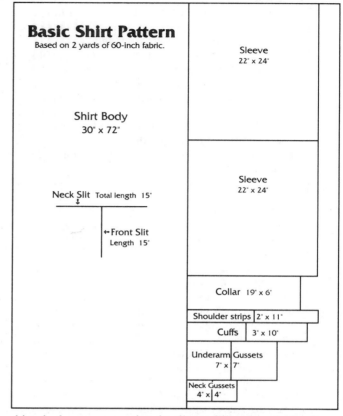

shirts had very narrow band collars while others had collars high enough to fold over the neck stock. The cuffs also can be very narrow or quite wide. In general cuffs are one to 2-1/2 inches wide when finished, so they should be cut three to six inches wide. The length of the cuff should be the wearer's wrist measurement plus 2-1/2 inches—usually about ten inches.

Since these shirts are cut in rectangles and bodies are generally rounded, gussets are used to give shaping to the neck and room in the armholes. The neck gussets are two 3-1/2" to 4-1/2" squares. I generally use four-inch squares. The underarm gussets range from five to nine inches square. I use seven-inch squares in my instructions and in the accompanying diagram. Optional are two small triangular pieces used to reinforce the bottom of the side seams. These are cut as two pieces about three inches square and folded into triangles. Not all shirts have these reinforcements. Two other types of reinforcement that are optional are found at the shoulder area, and sometimes both are used on the same shirt. The first is a shoulder reinforcement, a narrow strip that covers the neck gussets and runs across the top of the shoulder. This is necessary if you have used a shoulder seam. The second type is an armhole reinforcement. A piece of fabric about seven inches wide is sewn on the inside of the shirt from the bottom of the sleeve gusset in the front, up across the shoulder and down the back to the bottom of the sleeve gusset (30 inches approximately). There is one last possible piece, which is the facing for the front slit. During the 18th century, shirts had a narrow rolled hem on the front slit, not a facing. However, as the 19th century progressed, the front slit acquired a facing and sometimes buttons.

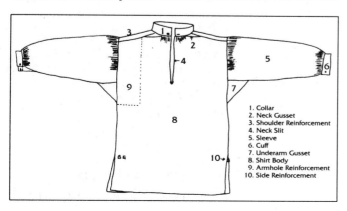

1. Collar
2. Neck Gusset
3. Shoulder Reinforcement
4. Neck Slit
5. Sleeve
6. Cuff
7. Underarm Gusset
8. Shirt Body
9. Armhole Reinforcement
10. Side Reinforcement

1) Cut out all your pieces on the straight of the grain. Fold the body of the shirt in half crosswise (this will be the shoulder) and then fold it in half lengthwise. Press the shoulder folds and press down the fold that will be the center front and the center back for about nine inches. These pressing lines serve as an easy way to mark the shoulder line and the center front and back.

2) On either side of the center front fold, cut a slit along the shoulder line 7-1/2 inches. A 28-inch wide shirt will have shoulders of only 6-1/2 inches, or you can adjust the neck slit to be smaller. Down the center front, cut a slit of eight to ten inches. Be sure to cut this slit in only the front of the shirt, not through both the front and the back.

3) Sew a narrow rolled hem on the front slit. This should be rolled to the inside and stitched with a whip stitch. The bottom of the slit should be reinforced so that the shirt doesn't rip down the front. Doing a buttonhole stitch around the bottom and about 1/2 inch up the sides is a good way. I like to make a bar of stitching across the opening from side to side, too. A small heart cut from the shirt fabric will also serve. Turn the edges under 1/8 inch and sew to the shirt with buttonhole or whip stitches.

4) Cut the four-inch-square neck gussets in half diagonally to make a total of four triangles. (You do not have to cut the diagonal. The squares can be folded instead.) Press under 1/4 inch on the four-inch sides of the triangles. Place one triangle on the underside of the end of the neck slit and sew it into place. The other triangle is placed on top and sewn down, thus enclosing the raw edges. Do this again on the other end of the shoulder slit.

5) If you choose to put strips across the shoulder for reinforcement, they go on next. Press under 1/4 inch on the long sides of the strips. Place the strips across the shoulders and continue them over the points of the triangular gussets up to the neck edge. Having pressed a crease along the shoulder makes it easy to center these reinforcing strips along the shoulder now.

6) If you have chosen to put in a reinforcement along the armhole, turn under 1/4 inch of the raw edge on the two seven-inch ends and on one of the 30-inch sides. Placing the reinforcement on the inside of the shirt, match the long raw edge to the side seam and the middle of the reinforcement to the shoulder crease. Baste the side seam edges together and sew the other three sides using a fine back stitch.

7) Fold the collar in half lengthwise with the right sides

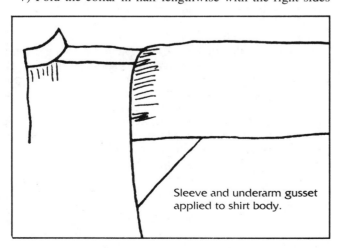

Sleeve and underarm gusset applied to shirt body.

together. Sew the ends together with 1/4-inch seams, turn right side out and press. Place two rows of gathering or basting stitches across the back of the shirt and the two sides of the front. However, if you are using very heavy fabric, you will want to make little pleats instead of gathers, so that the collar will lay flatter.

8) Mark the middle and quarter points on one long edge of the collar. Pinning the right side of the collar to the wrong side of the shirt, match the ends of the collar to the edges of the front slit, the middle of the collar in the middle back of the shirt, and the two quarter marks to the middles of the triangular neck gussets. This will insure that your gathers are even around the collar. Pull the gathering stitches up so that the shirt fits the collar.

9) Sew the collar to the shirt. Turn under the raw edge of the other long edge of the collar and sew to the outside of the shirt using either a whip stitch or back stitch.

10) I sew the sleeves to the shirt before putting in the underarm gussets, but the sleeves can also be made as a unit first. If you are unsure about the sleeve length, it is easier to attach the sleeve to the body before it is finished so that you can shorten them if necessary. Measure down from the shoulder line eight inches on both front and back side seams and mark. Find the middle of the width of the sleeve and match it to the shoulder line, pinning the pieces with the right sides together. Pin the two edges of the sleeve to the marks on the side seams. Gather or make tiny pleats in the sleeve to fit the body and sew with a 1/4-inch to 3/8-inch seam.

11) Place one underarm gusset on one sleeve, right sides together. Sew the gusset to the sleeve edge (not the shirt) using a narrow seam. Take the edge of the gusset that is perpendicular to the stitching and sew it to the other sleeve edge. The gusset is forming a diamond shape under the arm.

12) Sew the underarm sleeve seam from the point of the gusset to five inches from the end of the sleeve. Now sew the remaining gusset edges to the side seams of the shirt. Finally sew the side seam of the shirt from the gusset point to within five to ten inches from the bottom of the shirt. Repeat with the other sleeve. Make a narrow hem along the openings in the sleeves and along the bottom and side slits of the shirt. If you wish, reinforce the tops of the side slits with 3-inch squares folded in half to form triangles. These triangles are sewn on the inside of the shirt with the point of the triangle toward the shoulder.

13) Sew the cuffs in the same manner as the collar. Gather the sleeves into the cuffs or, if you are using very heavy fabric, make pleats.

14) Buttons can be horn, bone, wood, covered or thread. Cuffs can be buttoned or you may use linked sleeve buttons (cuff links). Buttons should be small, 1/2 inch to 5/8 inch. Make buttonholes on the back side of each cuff, centered on the cuff and about 1/2 inch from the edge. The collar has one button. The buttonhole is placed on the left side of the collar about 3/8 inch from the front edge and close to the seam where the collar attaches to the body. Sew the buttons on, and the shirt is finished.

MAKING A WAISTCOAT

A waistcoat, or vest, is worn by most men as a normal part of their everyday clothing in both summer and winter. To have a sleeved waistcoat for winter is much preferred, for it is certainly warmer. The sleeved waistcoat and sleeveless waistcoat can be cut from the same pattern. The length of the waistcoat can be adjusted to suit the wearer, although it is generally cut to be finished at mid-thigh.(The waistcoat gets shorter as the century progresses. This pattern is suitable for the mid-1700s.)

Although a fine gentleman's waistcoat would probably have the back cut from cheaper cloth, as it would never be seen under the frock coat, a commoner usually has a waistcoat made from all one fabric. Linen, fustian and wool are suitable fabrics and they might be checked, printed or striped. I particularly like vertical stripes. While many waistcoats are cut to fit the wearer snugly and fashionably, others are made with lacing or ties on the back to draw the waistcoat snug. Lacing or ties are very practical if the wearer gains and looses weight regularly. I must add here that these ties and lacing are used only on sleeveless waistcoats.

To enlarge this pattern, treat each square as one square inch. On paper large enough for the pattern, draw a grid of parallel lines horizontally and vertically (at right angles) one inch apart. Copy the pattern on your grid, one square at a time. Once the pattern is enlarged, you may want to construct the waistcoat from waste fabric to check the fit before cutting the good fabric. This pattern uses 5/8-inch plain seams unless otherwise stated.

1) Cut the waistcoat pieces from both good fabric and lining. The pocket can be cut from lining fabric or pocketing material. Cut interfacing strips two inches wide and the length of the front of the waistcoat. Also cut interfacing for the pocket flaps using the pocket flap pattern. Mark all the pattern pieces.

2) Pockets are placed on the fronts of the waistcoat with the top line of the pocket flaps at roughly waist level. With right sides together, pin the pockets to the waistcoat fronts, matching the stitching lines. Stitch along the lines, pivoting at the corners. Slash along the line between the stitching, clipping diagonally to the corners. Turn the pocket to the inside and press.

3) Stitch around the opening, making sure to reinforce the short sides well. Sew the edges of the pocket together and either overcast the raw edges or stitch around twice. This is to make the pockets strong and to keep them from raveling and creating a hole. On the right side of the waistcoat front, stitch the sides and top edge of the pocket opening through all thicknesses. Carefully reinforce the short side edges.

4) Place the pocket flaps right sides together and sew around using 1/2-inch seams. Leave two to three inches open along the top edge to allow you to turn the flaps right side out. If you are using linen or cotton, overcast the edges of the seam to prevent raveling. Turn the flaps right sides out so they are ready for pressing.

5) With right sides together, pin the back seams of the

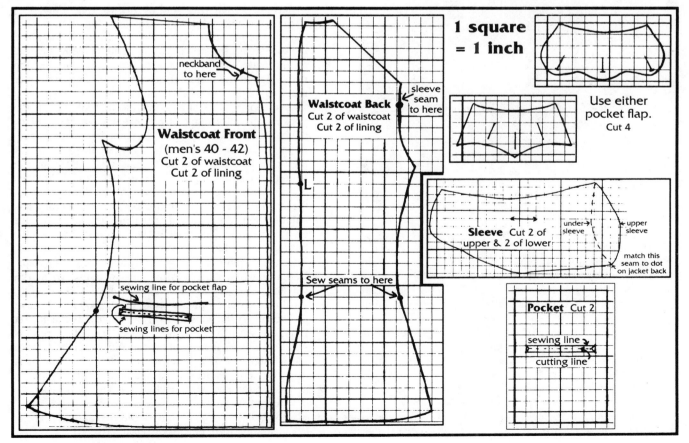

Chris Gilgun wearing a linen cap, a shirt, a striped waistcoat, breeches, stockings and shoes of the mid-18th century

pieces together. Be sure that you have a left and a right sleeve, especially if the right and wrong sides of the waistcoat fabric look alike. Stitch the front sleeve seam from top to bottom. The back sleeve seam is stitched from the top to the dot (four inches from the bottom). Repeat the steps with the lining. Press all the seams open, clipping the seam allowances when necessary.

8) Turn the sleeves right sides out. Hold the waistcoat wrong side out with the armhole toward you. With right sides together, pin the sleeve to the armhole edge, matching the sleeve seams to the dots on the armhole. Stitch the sleeve into the waistcoat, and then stitch again 1/8 inch from the first stitching (into the seam allowance). Cut away the extra seam allowance. Repeat with the lining. (Please note that an 18th century coat does *not* have shoulder pads and, in fact, fits quite closely in the shoulder. The look should be very rounded.)

9) Place the lining and waistcoat with right sides together. Pin around the neck edge, down the fronts and around the bottom and side and back vents. Sew the lining to the waistcoat around all edges, leaving the back vent open on one side so that you can turn the waistcoat right side out. Do not sew around the armholes if you are making a sleeveless waistcoat. Turn the garment right side out and make sure all of the points are sharp and neat. Press all the edges, making sure to press under the seam allowances on the armholes or sleeve bottoms, and on the rear vent that was left open. Slip-stitch these openings closed.

10) Before working the button holes, you should add the binding around the neck edge. This binding gives the neck a great deal of stability. Cut a bias strip of waistcoat material 3/4-inch wide and 20 inches long. Place this strip on the neck edge with right sides together. Fold in the ends of the strip so that they are finished and place the strip so that the strip begins and ends at the Xs marked on the pattern. Stitch in place. Fold the strip over the neck edge to the inside of the waistcoat and turn under the long edge. Slip-stitch in place.

11) I have found it easier to work the buttonholes on the pocket flaps before attaching them to the waistcoat. Mark the buttonholes on the waistcoat front and on the pocket flaps. Make sure the buttonholes are on the *left* front of the waistcoat. They should be spaced about 1/2 inch in from the edge and anywhere from 1-1/2 to 2-1/2 inches apart, depending upon the size of the buttons used. Generally, a waistcoat out of more expensive fabric has smaller and more buttons than one made of a more common fabric. The pocket flaps do not always have buttonholes or buttons.

12) Once the buttonholes are worked, attach the pocket flaps. Lay the waistcoat out flat and measure from the waistcoat's bottom edge and from the front edges to position the pocket flaps evenly. It is a good idea to have the wearer try the waistcoat on and make sure the pocket flaps are visually even. Sometimes "visually even" is not the same as "measured even." Slip-stitch the flaps to the waistcoat, making sure not to catch the lining. It is often a good idea to start at one end of the flap, work across the top and work back again. This will make the attachment sturdier.

13) Add the buttons and you a have a finished garment. These are generally horn, pewter or fabric-covered.

waistcoat. Sew together from the dot to the neck edges. Repeat with the lining. If you are planning to lace up the back, stitch only from the neck edge to the letter "L" on both the lining and the outer fabric.

6) Pin the sides and shoulder seams of both the lining and the outer fabric. Sew the shoulder seams of both the lining and waistcoat. Stitch the side seams from the dot to the armhole. You should now have the lining together in one piece and the waistcoat together. Press the seams open and also press the pocket flaps. Attach the interfacing along the front edge of the waistcoat leaving about 5/8 inch along the edge. You do not want the interfacing in the seam if you can help it, as it will be too bulky,

7) If you are making a sleeved waistcoat, now is the time to sew the sleeves. With right sides together, pin the sleeve

A CANADIAN CAP

A Canadian cap is a wool cap sewn from four to six triangular pieces. It has a fur band and fur top knot. Canadian caps were so popular that Ben Franklin even wore one in Paris. Old fur collars can be found at flea markets for reasonable prices and most of them have ample fur to make more than one cap.

You will need 26 inches of fur, 1½ to 2 inches wide, ¼ yard wool fabric, thread, and a small piece of fur for a topknot.

Cut 4 wedges of wool fabric according to the diagram.

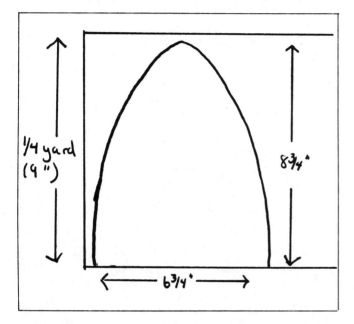

Use ¼ inch seams. Sew the 4 wedges together. Turn a hem of ¾ inch around bottom edge and sew in place.

Sew the fur around the cap with bottom edge of the fur even with the bottom edge of the cap. The fur will overlap the wool. You can either sew along the top edge of the fur, attaching it to the cap, or you can leave it loose to pull over your ears in case of very cold weather.

Attach a small piece of fur to the apex of the wedges as a top knot. You could also add feet or part of a tail to the back of the fur band.

Horseback Travel

by Jeff Hengesbaugh

PERHAPS IT WAS ZEBULON PIKE'S "celestrial" influence on his distant relative or exposure to Fess Parker's Davy Crockett, but Jeff Hengesbaugh had his first brigade at the age of ten. It led not to the mountains but to an official ultimatum to hang up the coon skin caps, (or else), for capgunning up a saloon, theater and the local post office.

He was raised with a Spanish 28 gauge percussion shotgun and grew up thinking all barrels were supposed to jump off the stock and that gasses exited through the breech.

After high school, Jeff robbed stage coaches at Knott's Berry Farm in California, until he set aside his Colt one day and used a .69 caliber Tower flintlock pistol on an overbearing shotgun rider, nearly overturning the coach.

Jeff earned a Bachelor of Science degree and fought a war. He made a sincere effort to become a member of society with several promising careers, but walked away from them to put another brigade together.

He started from scratch and studied Remington and Russell drawings to make leathers, then coerced two friends to do the same. And, with a dog, Jedediah Growler Smith (Duke for short) left from Phoenix, Arizona on a open end journey that went as far north as Banff, Canada.

A letter awaited upon return, from the American Mountain Men and an invitation to rendezvous on the Henry's Fork of the Green. His friends after a magnificent first effort, retired from the trade. Another three man brigade was formed and they fought their way through starvation, blizzards, dysentery, lightning strikes, tick fever and a genuine raid by the Navahos on the horses. After thirteen hundred miles and three months on the trail, they skidded down a hill to the creek bottom and into Rendezvous.

There have been other rides but Jeff's real pleasure has been to participate in three full-sized (eighteen to twenty men), fully outfitted brigades filled from the ranks of the A.M.M., and dead-reckon through the Rockies, in the tradition of the mountain man of old.

Jeff has recently completed a ride to Santa Fe from Arizona and is writing a book entitled *Once Upon a Mountain Man,* about the ride to Canada and other adventures.

The 1820s would see a departure from the Missouri River as a pathway to the Rocky Mountains. It had been a demon. If the mighty current wasn't smashing keelboats to pulp, then it was the everpresent gauntlet available to any Indian hostile to upriver travelers.

Trappers and traders now entered the Great Plains. The encounter was met on the backs of horses and mules; an occupational answer to demands of vast distances, exploration and survival.

History is short on the "between the lines", day to day, maintenance of this alliance. There were plenty of accounts of how it came to a conclusion. Animals abandoned or destroyed at a moment's notice; "Ya don't name somethin' ya might eat", depicts the severity of alternatives that were common to the mountain men.

If I strike a somber note, it's intended. The man on foot or in a canoe had inherent problems with wilderness survival but in neither case did they have to feed or water those problems. This was just the beginning of a complex, mobile relationship that gave the mountain man his historic dimensions.

For buckskinners interested in putting their "tools and trappings" in the saddle, the challenge is awesome. Not only in learning the numerous skills and responsibilities surrounding the use of animals, but knowing, like the trappers of old, that they will take them through horizons "where deserts still don't care if you're out of water, or mountains, if you're lost or starvin'."

"A little knowledge is a dangerous thing." I offer just a glimpse into this equestrial partnership. That "chance favors the prepared mind" is equally true. In either case, adventure awaits. Long range, cross-country travel, like the mountain man, has been a lost experience in American culture, at least until now.

One more thing . . . "forgive the author's foibles and imperfections, considering as you pass along, that he has been chiefly educated in nature's school . . . Also bear in mind, the author does not hold himself responsible for the correctness of statements made otherwise from observation".[1]

HORSES

Hold on mule skinner! The debate between the attributes of horse and mule, favor by far, the mule. Good saddle broke mules are expensive and not as readily available as their country cousins. Though I'll talk about horses, much of the information will pertain to both.

The U.S. Cavalry created a set of standards for an acceptable mount. It's of interest to us because their animals faced similar conditions and the same terrain as the fur trapper.

It starts . . . "Horses must be sound, well bred, gentle under saddle, free from vicious habits, without blemish or defect, of kind disposition" . . . I stopped there. I ain't never seen such a horse! If there is one, it must be chiseled in stone and standing in the front yard of *Western Horseman*

headquarters. And, at today's prices, beyond reach.

The Cavalry did prefer a gelding of uniform and hardy color, in good condition, from 15¼ to 16 hands high. Weight not less than 950 nor more than 1150 lbs. That he be from four to eight years of age (a younger horse was occasionally used if fine and well developed).

They had tried a lot of different animals, including the tough Texas cowpony (700-850 lbs.). A soldier's basic weight was 160 lbs. and fully equipped with saddle, weighed 225. It was too much for the animal's frame. The Cavalry came up with a weight ratio of four to one. Thus, a 225 lb. payload, requires a 900 lb. horse. Also of note, the few horses that exceeded their height and weight allowances, were found to be unwieldy, cumbersome and slow in performance.

Trapped by economics, ignorance, or both, I've fallen

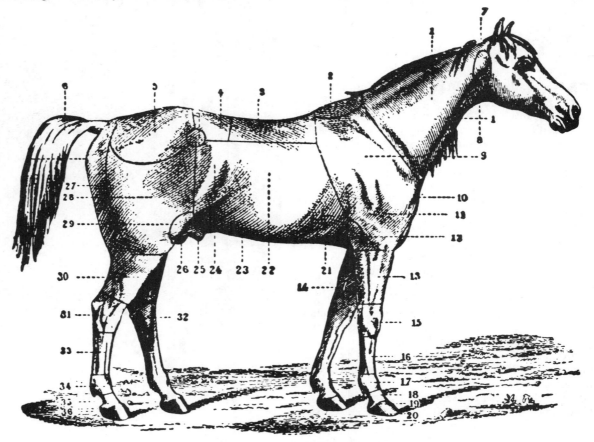

POINTS OF THE HORSE

1. Neck	13. Forearm	25. Sheath
2, Withers	14. Chestnut	26. Testicles
3. Back	15. Knee	27. Point of Buttock
4. Loin	16. Cannon	28. Buttock
5. Point of croup	17. Fetlock	29. Stifle
6. Tail	18. Coronet	30. Leg
7. Poll	19. Heel	31. Hock
8. Throat	20. Foot	32. Spavin-place
9. Shoulder	21. Chest	33. Cannon
10. Point of shoulder	22. Ribs	34. Fetlock tuft
11. Arm	23. Belly	35. Coronet
12. Elbow	24. Flank	36. Heel

A good all-around horse for the trail can make the difference between an enjoyable ride and one filled with anxieties, tension, and downright danger.

off either end of what the Cavalry considers ideal. Most of the horses worked, but those within their limits worked obviously better.

EXAMPLE: A small horse, with all the guts in the world, has difficulty staying with a longer strided, indifferent animal. One person constantly restrains his horse, while the other pushes to stay up. Strain makes for pain especially when the environment is hostile. People can adjust, but in the long run, the smaller horse will falter.

A few tips on purchasing: Read Ben Green's books *Horse Trading* and *More Horse Trading,* popular in any library. Thus armed, I suggest a private individual with a horse for sale. It has usually been a family pet complete with health records and a history of ownership. Still beware! I buy horses for extended adventures and sell them at the other end. For shorter ranged sojourns, leasing may be the way to go. Be sure all terms are mutually agreed on. Injury, death, return obligations; get an exact dollar value.

Putting together a brigade, no matter the size, is a complicated affair (it was back then too). None are alike. My first attempt included building a corral, then scheduling the purchase of horses to put in it, so that most were fed the least amount of time. Animals were wormed and stitched (wounds inflicted by a growing remuda), sprayed for a mite epidemic, cured of coughs and colds (it was a wet, cold, winter), shots and shod, vets and papers and much more. We looked forward to the hardships of the trail.

In conclusion, spirit is one thing, size and weight another. "Roman nosed" horses seem to bear ill-will. Buckskins, as a breed, consistently hold their own. The most infirm horse can kill a healthy human in a heart beat.

HORSE BACKS & HORSE TACK

THE WITHERS: The part of a horse between the back and the shoulder blades that materially affect the fit of a saddle. They cover large, strong muscles that demand free action. It is important that they are well-formed. Too high, and the saddle is apt to pinch them. Too low, the saddle will slip forward and chafe them. Too broad, the saddle will be held too high and press into the back at the cantle. The withers should be moderately elevated. Beware of a high withered horse with hollows behind the shoulder blades. A saddle will not work on this animal.

SADDLING: Saddling starts with the saddle blankets. Wool seems to be an all time favorite, preferably clean and soft. Throw the blanket well forward, then bring it back to smooth the hair in its natural direction. Leave three or four inches in front of the saddle to head off the tendency to slide back. *ABSOLUTELY NO WRINKLES!!!* Let the CENTER of the saddle be placed over the CENTER of the back.

CINCHING: Cinching is probably the most important task in saddling. Cinches should be of soft material (and kept that way), and at least four inches in width. Take care the skin is not caught, pinched or hair pulled. Cinch moderately tight, enough to keep the saddle in place. A finger should be able to slip between it and the horse. This method can be used to check the tightness on the trail. Cinch sores, raw spots or boils are hard to cure and can disable a horse. Another common abuse is placing the saddle too far forward and bearing down on the cinch. It stops the action of the lungs causing the horse to stumble, and at times drop like a rock.

Saddling is a fine art. But few horses can carry rider or saddle without needing readjustment every few hours. No one has ever figured out the perfect saddle tree. If the tree fits when the horse is fat, it galls when he looses flesh and vice versa. At no point should a saddle press into a horse's back with a greater force than any other. Sore backs are from bad saddling or using ill-fitting equipment to begin with. A horse can knock a saddle out of alignment with one roll on the ground. A dog circles and a horse starts pawing before they go down . . . sometimes.

A well outfitted horse. All gear is kept to a minimum and placed for balance. Tied in front of the saddle is a capote and bag (black bear fur) with picket rope on off side to balance bear bag. The rifle will be slung on rider's back. An epishimore is thrown over saddle (will double as a warm wrap on a cold night) with blanket under saddle (for sleeping) and another rolled tight in canvas tied behind saddle.

Left: The author shows three guns that have proven good for horse back travel. All three are smooth bores, weigh between four and six pounds and can be fired with one hand. The light weight and short barrels make them easy to move around on a horse. The small pistol makes a nice backup. The larger knife takes the place of a small ax. Below: A canteen made of leather holds up well under a beating. The author admits that water stored in it leaves something to be desired for taste. Bottom left: A collection of quirts. Left to right: moose tine, Indian style; Mexican; Indian, also used to count "coup"; rawhide. Quirts are used mostly to collect the horse or provide inspiration at appropriate times. They are easy to lose; keep on wrist. Bottom right: A comfortable way to carry a smokepole. Remember to remove before going through trees. This type of sling is versatile and can be tied to the saddle several ways.

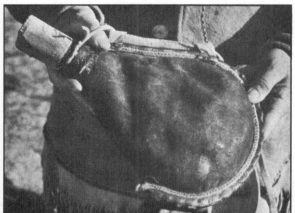

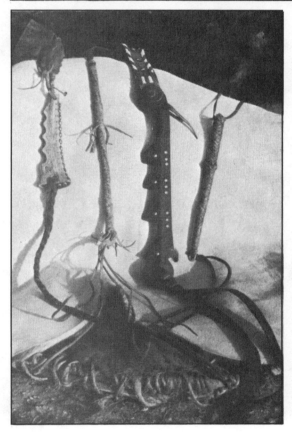

OLD WEST SADDLES

The problem remains: a saddle for a horse or a horse for a saddle? This is further complicated by wanting to use period gear. There are few examples today that can be certified as having been used in the fur trade. The next best approach for a credible saddle would be to use the tools of the historian, such as visual records from the past, references from journals and artists' renditions.

That the mountain man used saddles is unquestioned. It is also safe to assume they used whatever was in reach. The following material, drawn mostly from *Man Made Mobile²*, offers a serious insight to saddles known to be available the first half of the 19th century.

At the end of the Colonial conquest of Mexico, saddles began to diversify into more practical styles designed to manage herds of cattle drifting north into the vast grass lands of present day Texas, New Mexico and Southern California. Though there were regional differences, they shared common characteristics.

Four wooden parts made up the whole. The fork and horn were fashioned out of a solid Y-shaped crotch of a tree and became the *pommel.* The other three parts were two lateral supports called *side boards* and the back bridge or *cantle.* They were joined together by mortising, wooden pegs and glue. The entire tree was covered with rawhide, applied wet and stitched fast with rawhide thongs. This bound the saddle as it dried, giving it overall solidarity.

This model of simplicity was built to take it. Its rigging was exposed, coming down the fork or wrapped around the horn and braced by another rigging strap that came from behind the cantle. The open trees were unpadded, adorned by little more than short skirts, *el acion* (the leather strap that suspends the stirrup) and *tapaderos* (leather stirrup covers).³ This tree was the foundation of all Mexican stock saddles from late Colonial times to this day.

Known as the Mexican vaquero saddle or Spanish tree, the Americans were well aware of it by the 1820s.

The earliest known drawing of a "vaquero" saddle done by Ignacio Tirsch, a Bohemian Jesuit missionary in 1765. It shows a "grapefruit" type horn and a possible swelled pommel.

89

Lewis and Clark describe a Spanish saddle in their travels across present day Montana being ridden by a Shoshone. Zebulon Pike saw it in Sante Fe in 1807. It became common knowledge with the establishment of the Sante Fe trade in 1821. Sibley, the man who surveyed the trail, outfitted his homeward bound crew with vaquero saddles. Trans-Taos trappers, not to mention the boys pilfering Mexicana beaver between New Mexico and California, were familiar with vaquero saddles.

According to the record, the Western Department of the American Fur Company, at the height of the trade (1830s), had three classes of saddles available: Spanish, English and Indian. Spanish was by far the favorite. Thorton Grimsley, leading saddlemaker in St. Louis, made a saddle patterned after the Spanish tree.

The earliest known illustration of the Mexican vaquero saddle (1760s), has a horn comparable to a grapefruit set on a short, forward slanting stem. It's not clear if the pommel shoulders swell, but shadowy lines, apparently stitching, suggest a configuration other than a "slick" slope. Another artist, Tapia (1827-1831), depicts the vaquero saddle with tapaderos and a pommel horn resembling a hemisphere. Horn development had been different in California and amounted to a slender horn on a sloping pommel. Both horns, in their many variations, were in evidence in the fur trade. However, a significant change came over the horn by mid-century. It would spread out like a pie plate after 1860 and would continue to exaggerate into the 70s.

If a relic tree is found and more than a few exist, check the gullet (the inverted V shaped junction of the pommel). Remember, most of them were designed for the horse of yesterday. If a decision is made to obliterate the relic value, there are commercial outfits that can rebuild and re-rawhide the trees. They also offer reproduction trees of good quality. Pursuing a proper saddle is a worthy endeavor. I've found Rick and Cathy Bauman of Ne Shutsa Traders to be a good source for supplying old horse gear.

The author holding an original saddle tree that has been rebuilt and rerawhided, circa 1840s. On the saddle rack is a very early gourd horn, *vaquero norteno* saddle (circa 1800-1840 probable). On ground at right is an early Ute or Navajo saddle of four piece wood construction and covered with rawhide. To its left stands a handmade pack saddle reinforced with hand forged iron. This one had also been used for riding. Saddle trees such as these can still be found and resurrected.

A closeup view of the early Vaquero saddle (gourd horn) seen on preceding page. It is of basic four piece construction, Spanish rigged with tapaderos and horse hair cinch. The Mexican coin inlaid into the horn is dated 1829.

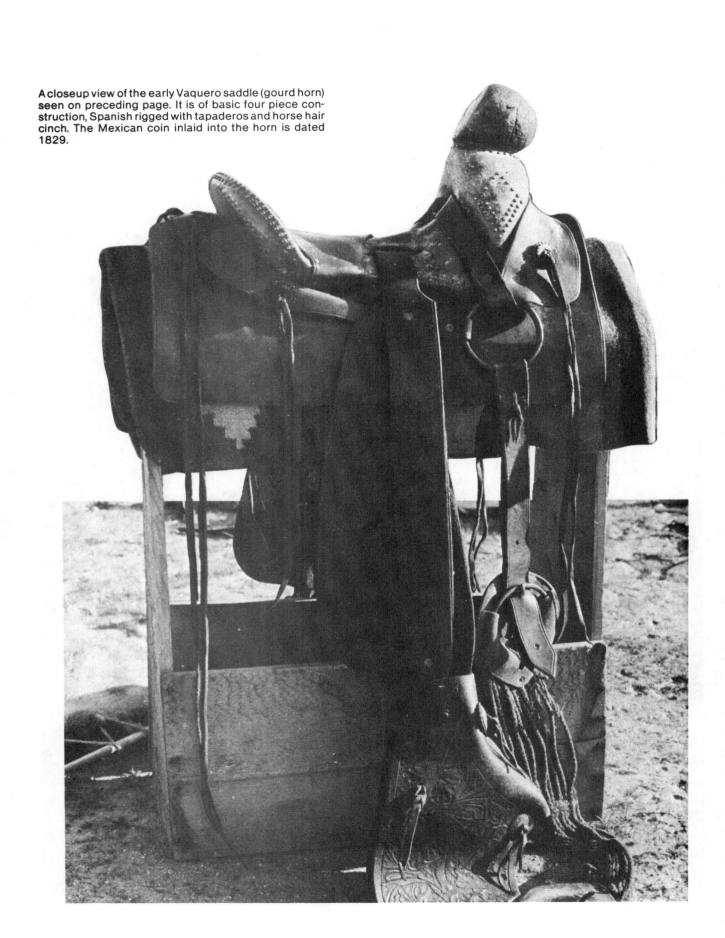

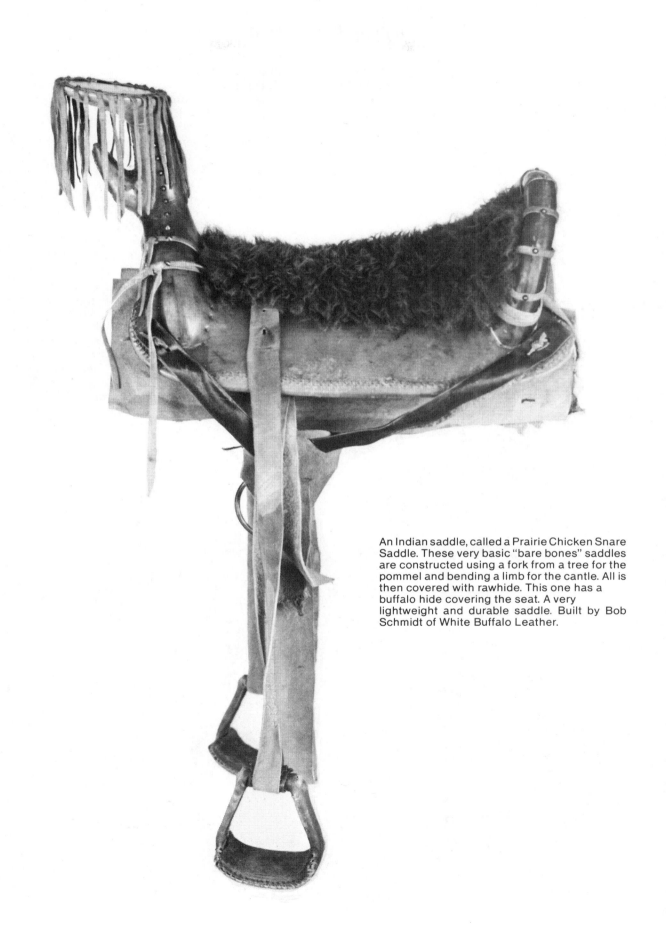

An Indian saddle, called a Prairie Chicken Snare Saddle. These very basic "bare bones" saddles are constructed using a fork from a tree for the pommel and bending a limb for the cantle. All is then covered with rawhide. This one has a buffalo hide covering the seat. A very lightweight and durable saddle. Built by Bob Schmidt of White Buffalo Leather.

Snaffle bit

Port curb bit

Spanish spade bit

Hackamore bit

BRIDLES & BITS

The devices used to manage a horse haven't changed much down through the centuries. The Romans made extensive use of the "curb" bit, popular today. The idea is to CONTROL WITH THE LEAST POSSIBLE PAIN. There is a progression of control. The hackamore with bosal and the hackamore bit place nothing in the mouth. But most riding is done with a bridle and bridles are designed to carry bits.

A bridle generally consists of a noseband, cheek pieces, a headstall (the strap that goes over the head, behind the ears) and another strap across the forehead above the eyes (browband), plus a throat latch (a strap that goes under the throat from the junction of the cheek piece and browband).

For our purposes, the bridle could have wide straps or narrow, home crafted or commercial (handstitched), decorated with conchos, tacks, plain, fancy, braided, or horse hair, as long as it is functional.

Traditional bits available in the old west were the Spanish spade and the Chileno ring bit. Notoriously brutal in the hands of the unskilled, but exacting with a top horseman. The curb and bar bit, snaffle too, were well represented. There's lots of handsome, period curb bits in a variety of ports, the curved part of the mouthpiece that determines severity of control. Bits come in sizes as do mouths. Study the properties of any bit used. Warm up any bit on a cold day before placing it in a horse's mouth. Remove a bit at every available chance.

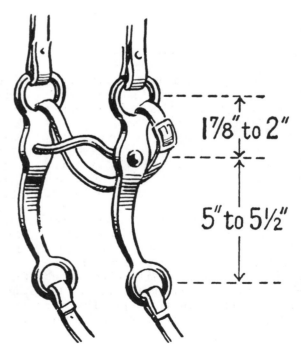

Simple Curb Bit

HOOVES

Spend some time with a ferrier. He can give tips about the structure of a horse's foot, and foot care along with a real respect for the tasks they perform. It should be explained that the mission of the shoe is to prevent undue wear of the hoof walls. That an ounce at the toe means a pound at the withers (amazingly, a heavier shoe doesn't necessarily outlast a lighter one). That there is only one way to shoe a horse: the right way (nowadays, people call it custom). Ask about a hoof pick and how to use it. And maybe some of the injuries a hoof may sustain such as punctures of the sole or frog and hoof cracks. It may end up with a demonstration of tightening a loose shoe, or letting you pull one off. Bring the beer!

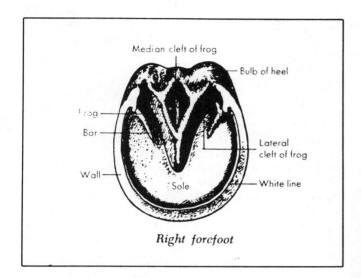

Right forefoot

SKILLS

No matter how good the horse, how fine the equipment, a rider must pull it all together. Contrary to what most think, a horse is a fragile critter. The reason the saddle is placed in the middle of the back and designed to keep the backbone untouched is that the spine must flex and muscles fore and aft must be free to work. The front legs bear the weight and the hind legs provide the thrust. The rider is in the balance spot, and anything done other than sit erect has to be taken into account. Upright in the saddle, the front legs receive a little over half the rider's weight. Lean back and it's a little less than half, but lean forward and fore limbs receive two thirds of the entire weight. Either action often repeated or held, throws an uneven pressure on the saddle and it digs in accordingly ruining skin, muscle and tendons.

Riding properly is a combination of balance, friction provided by the thighs and the stirrups. The pommel, cantle and reins each have a job. They don't include holding up a rider. Watch a parade and see what I mean.

ENROUTE

Neither humans nor animals are created equal, each being different in their capacities to endure. Maintain a position of strength; never expend it carelessly. The restful hours for both seem to be from midnight to dawn. There is

A time for reflection. Nearing the end of a 3000 mile ride to Canada that took six months to make, the author and companions take a break.

Top: As with the mountain men of the 1800s there's almost always snow to cross when traveling high in the mountains. Some snow patches can create quite formidable obstacles. Bottom: Part of a nineteen man brigade that traveled more than 100 miles up the Gros Venture from Jackson to the Wind River in 1980.

Coming down a street in Santa Fe at the end of a 21 day, 590 mile ride from Arizona.

96

no use leaving camp before that unless conditions justify the loss of rest.

Breakfast is optional. This came as a result of having little to eat, at least nothing that couldn't be chewed in the saddle. It also avoided the inconsistencies of morning temperament of hard pressed men. No thought required; gather and make fast the bedroll, find and water the horses, pack and saddle, check the fire, circle the camp once for wayward belongings and depart. In large brigades, short range travel, morning repast is more compatible. But even then, tensions arise from "them" that guard their coffee cups and those who want to make miles.

Start from camp at an easy walk. If it was hard mileage the day before, lead them out and loosen them up. Ride for an hour then call a brief halt for a complete check of saddle, blankets, cinch, bridle and bit. Be sure of gear tied to the saddle and give the pack animal the same consideration. If necessary, rebalance the load.

Establish a pace and keep it. Choose the terrain that offers the least resistance. Avoid all unnecessary detours and hills. Stay straight in the saddle; rest the back by getting out of the saddle and walking. Lead the animals in climbing and descending steep, broken country. Besides relieving the weight and pounding, air is allowed to circulate under the saddle and blanket. Water at every opportunity, but water together to know that every horse has had its fill.

With mileage gained, break down for noon. Strip the animals of their equipment and pull the packs leaving the pack frame and blankets in place. When pulling the saddle, be sure the horse is as cool as possible. Blankets pulled from hot, sweaty backs cause rapid evaporation and result in tender skin, blisters, lumps and swellings. Leave the blanket on for half an hour. The back of a pack horse by the nature of his load, always runs hot. Put them to graze.

One day in six or seven should be put aside for rest and repair. Camp by water if possible; extend travel to do so. An experiment was performed in Europe (1850) to determine the endurance of horses. A horse will live on water alone for twenty-five days. Seventeen days without eating or drinking. And *FIVE* days if fed but not watered. A horse kept without water for three days drank 104 lbs. of water in three minutes.

The horses were kept in a controlled environment; figures would change drastically under varied conditions. The five days of feed with no water is significant to humans also. If there's no water, don't eat! One mouthful of food or twenty, makes the same demands of the body's water reserves. Control the access of a thirsty horse to water.

PACK ANIMALS

It's hard to do better than an illustrated copy of Joe Back's *Horses, Hitches and Rocky Trails* on the subject of packing and related skills. I'll provide a few words of advice.

A pack animal carries dead weight and is not relieved of it until it's removed. Inspiration for moving forward is limited to the fear of being left behind. Even fear submits to exhaustion.

Minimize the necessities; dried food, small shovel, gun powder, a couple of horse shoes and nails, tack hammer and pliers, a small, well thought out medicine kit for horse and human, rope, a stash of tinder and whiskey. Be sure it's evenly distributed and packed low to help the horse keep his equilibrium. Adjust to fit snugly being careful to protect the animal's side from sharp projections and prevent interference with the action of the horse.

While on the subject, fight the tendency to crowd the pommel of the saddle with useless odds and ends. A rolled blanket or capote, a coiled catch rope and canteen. Behind the cantle, small saddle bags and another blanket rolled in a light tarp. Another good place to put a sleeping blanket is under the saddle. Hobbles should be tied to the saddle. In every case, balance the load. Put the rifle on your back, across the lap or in a scabbard under the leg. A heavy rifle, swaying back and forth on a horn mount, is hard on the withers.

One of the rewards of any horseback trip is being able to see country usually inaccessible by automobile. The slow pace allows more time to take in the little things — as well as the big things — like the San Juan Mountains in Colorado.

Left: At the end of the ride from Arizona to Santa Fe, the author prepares to receive congratulations from the governor of New Mexico. Below: As pretty as it looks, when at a spot like this, always be on the lookout for bogs and soft places.

SECURITY

"Better to count ribs than tracks", is an adage that echos out of the old wild west. Whoever spoke it first was out to limit their worldly frustrations. Security then, as it is now, was a compromise between allowing animals to feed and never seeing them again.

To hobble a horse is to hamper its movement by tying two feet together. This is accomplished with rope, rawhide, connected cuffs or an assortment of other devices. Hobbling the front legs together hampers next to nothing. It's useful when space is unlimited and vegetation scarce. Tying a front leg to a back one, on the same side (sidelining) is considerably more effective for keeping them close. The graze must support this proximity.

Picketing ties a horse up and allows him to feed at the same time. The rope can be attached to a front fetlock (only if it has had previous experience with it), or tied in a fairly snug bowline around the neck. The picket, a live green stake (as opposed to one that might snap), must be driven deep. In soil unable to hold a picket pin, a "deadman" is used. A rock, bundle of sticks, bag of sand, is tied with a rope and buried at least 18" deep. Place him within earshot of camp. To hear a horse is a good sign. If you hear a horse in trouble with the picket line, be ready to move.

Hobbles should be soft and supple and easy to undo. If for any number of reasons a horse makes a break, circle the camp to find the outbound tracks. They usually head for ground traveled the day before. In the woods, take the precaution of belling a couple of animals.

The largest brigade in the mountains. Twenty-two men at the beginning of a ride across the Uintas in 1978.

101

AN OLD TIME MOUNTAIN MAN

Left: Enroute from Cody to Henry's Fork in '77 the author is trying to thaw out after being forced into a cottonwood grove by a storm and freezing temperatures. Below: The brigade on the move. The Uintas — 1978.

Crossing the Mohave Desert on the trip to Canada in '73. This was only one of the many hardships encountered on this ride. Makes you appreciate those shining mountains — and crystal cold streams of water.

Water crossings can be hazardous, no matter the width or the depth. Try to pick the best spot to ford.

CROSSING WATER

Crossing water, no matter how wide or deep, is potential trouble. Looking for a ford is time well spent. Test it on foot and mark it with stakes if necessary. If it is deep enough to swim and the span less than twenty feet, take it in the saddle. Water the horse first, don't crowd the crossing and make sure there is access out on the far bank. Use extreme caution.

A wide, swift river, with no other place to cross, is a formidable adversary. Guns, clothing and packs must be floated across. Leave saddle and bridle in place. Cross the stirrups, knot the reins behind the neck to prevent entanglement with the legs. As a horse begins to swim, the rider should float off on the downstream side. Hold onto the pommel with one hand, reins with the other, use them very gently, only to guide the horse, never to stop it. The landing place should be well thought out, somewhere downstream, to allow for the drift. If the grip is lost on the saddle, grasp the horse's tail and let it pull you to shore. Splash water in the horse's face to direct the course. Consider this type of crossing a very dangerous undertaking and only resorted to when no other means is available. *BOGS:* Most bogs are hard to detect. Long, sloping meadows in mountainous country should be suspect. It happens fast. A horse plunges in to its chest, leaving the rider standing. Get clear! . . . or the first lunge will do it for you. Give the animal immediate encouragement to free itself. Some horses will give up in a couple of hops.

105

DISTANCE & DIRECTION

Horse travel is limited travel. It is determined by destination and dependent on geography and season. Time is at the mercy of all three.

My ride to Canada lasted over half a year. Though there were many long, hard rides, the average distance covered was 22 miles per day at a pace of three miles per hour. That amounted to seven or eight hours in the saddle. The Cavalry maintained 20-25 miles for a day's march. They did it at a walk and found "both man and horse improved under these conditions". They were also supported with a supply train, though the horses (for the most part) lived off the land.

There is no rule that can govern the length of a day's ride or how it will be made. Wake up in the morning and see what it brings.

To figure the time to reach an objective, map the easiest geographical approach. Take that figure and divide

On the 1300 mile ride from Arizona to Wyoming in '75, the party was forced into the aspens by a hail and lightening storm. This hastily improvised shelter protected them for the night.

Crossing South Pass at sunset. Another one of those spectacular events that nature has to offer up.

it by a low average; in our case 20 or even 15 miles a day. Four hundred miles, excluding disaster, should take 20 days with the former mileage and 26 days with the latter. (Don't forget the days of rest.) As men and horses harden to the task, push to reach the halfway mark. Then set the pace for the rest of the journey accordingly.

Geography and Season: Prior to the first effort, there was no experience thinking in horse time. Arizona's high country was choked with snow. So we headed west through the deserts. Hospitable when we started, it was the biggest kind of trap. Rising temperatures chased us across 2000 miles of badlands including the Arizona-Sonora, Mohave, Great Basin and the alkali flats of southeastern Oregon until it let up.

There was no haggling over maps however. It was west until stopped by the Sierra Nevadas, then right until we hit Hudson Bay country. We were never lost because we never knew where we were going.

WATER?
WATER?
WHAT WATER?

There were and always will be times when water comes dearly, as shown by these photos of the ride from Arizona to Wyoming that took three months to complete. Time to make camps and no water in sight. When crossing vast expanses of land such as this it pays to know where the water holes are. Makes you appreciate the little things in life.

At the end of a long and great trip. On the trail for six months that covered 3000 miles from Arizona to Canada, this small party of mountain men had a chance to sample some of the rigors the mountain men of the 1800s shared. Left to right: Bill Hamilton, Jeff Hengesbaugh, and Steve Johnson with Duke.

CONCLUSION

Most of us have a great capacity to ignore the basics. I had to make the effort, consider it done. I can honestly say I've made every mistake described herein, and a lot more that are not. None were intentional and most were from just not knowing.

Inexperience, became knowledge with careful observation and a willingness to do what was necessary. When saddles were pulled, hands went over every inch of contact feeling for lumps and abrasions. Adjustments were made and a lot of "stuff" was buried by the wayside. Horses were packed and unpacked until they were right.

Sleep was destroyed night after night until it was understood what to expect from a hobbled horse. If desert travel offered no water by dusk, horses were led by moonlight in a desperate bid to be nearer water by morning.

Disasters are an accumulation of small mistakes. Don't get me wrong, there are a few straight up ones like walking up on a sleeping horse in the noonday sun. But Murphy's law, coupled with the inconsistency of Nature, will call a weak hand. Make a decision or one will be made for you. Remember, there are no problems, just changes of plans.

[1] Taken from the author's preface of Osborn Russell's *Journal of a Trapper,* University of Nebraska Press.

[2] *Man Made Mobile, Early Saddles of Western North America,* Smithsonian Institution Press, 1980.

[3] The *mochila,* a loose, tanned leather covering for the saddletree, with openings for pommel and cantle, was concurrently used.

Design & Construction of Powder Horns

by Don Wright

DON WRIGHT LIVES THE PART. His home in Gallatin, Tennessee was built in 1795 when Indian wars still threatened and Tennessee was not yet a state. The house is of stone with walls fully two feet thick.

When Don was seven, "Our parents gave my younger brother Dave and me coonskin caps for Christmas and our love for the frontier was born. We still have those caps."

Wright is a charter member of the Tennessee Longhunters, a member of the NMLRA, and is presently working toward admission in the AMM.

His powder horns grace not only the hunting bags of buckskinners and black powder shooters nationwide, but have been featured in numerous publications, including the book, *SCRIMSHAW CONNECTION*, which depicts the nation's leading scrimshaw artists.

"When I first started building powder horns, I thought I was good at it. And, I suppose I would have gone right on thinking that if it hadn't been for a friend of mine and something he said: 'That's a nice horn, Don, but if you're going to put that much time into building a powder horn, why don't you build it right?'

"What he meant by right, was to build a horn that adhered closely to traditional and historical design. I was also handed several books that contained pictures of original horns. After letting them lay for several weeks, curiosity got the better of me and I flipped one open and studied colored photographs of original 'Golden Age Horns'. I read and studied that book and all the rest I could lay my hands on. Then I tried to build something comparable to the horns that were pictured. It was a long, drawn out process to figure out how they did certain neat little tricks, like engrailing, fluting, etc., and I'm not sure to this day that I have figured it out — but I can (and you can) duplicate the procedure to look authentic.

"So, I hope that you, the reader, can benefit from the knowledge which I gleaned during months of research, study and experimentation, and be able to hand craft a keepsake you can be proud of."

I N THE BOOK OF BUCKSKINNING (Volume One) the history of the American powder horn was covered by David Wright. Therefore, I shall only refer to the historical significance of the horns portrayed in this chapter for reference as to a particular period or time in history which the builder might wish to recreate.

I will say, however, that the cow horn played a significant role in the evolution of colonial America — providing the settlers with such items as powder horns, rum horns, salt and pepper horns, blowing (Fox) horns, water (canteen) horns, grease horns, snuff horns, message horns, tinder (fire starting kits) horns, shot horns, and other sundry articles such as ink wells, cups, combs, spoons, knife handles, and windows for lanthorns.

Our primary interest in this text is the building of powder horns. Without further delay let us commence this adventure into the unheralded American folk art of "Horn Building".

For the sake of simplicity I shall divide the horns into categories, beginning with the more simple Fur Trade or Mountain Man Horn and eventually progress to the difficult "Golden Age" horns.

There are certain standards that will apply to any horn you choose to build, such as selecting the correct horn for the period of history which holds your interest.

SELECTING THE HORN

Decide beforehand on the style of horn you intend to build. If possible, study an original horn, paying particular attention to such details as the length, color, and shape of the horn; the type of plug it has; whether it is pegged or tacked; whether the spout is plain or fancy; and the type of pouring spout plug it has.

If an original horn cannot be obtained, the next best thing is the use of photographs. There are several good powder horn books on the market that depict original horns and studies of engraving that are worth obtaining — AMERICAN ENGRAVED POWDER HORNS by John S. Dumont, ENGRAVED POWDER HORNS by Nathan L. Swayze, The Magazine ANTIQUES (August 1968 issue), THE KENTUCKY RIFLE HUNTING POUCH by Madison Grant, THE PENNSYLVANIA-KENTUCKY RIFLE by Henry J. Kauffman, and AMERICAN POWDER HORNS by Stephen V. Grancsay.

After you have decided on a particular style horn, the work begins. Searching out a horn that is in keeping with the type you intend to build can be a frustrating experience, especially to a city dweller. But several sources are available to one who is willing to investigate. I have found some fine horns at garage sales, auctions, and junk shops. There are also veterinarians, packing houses, and farmers. But the easiest way to procure a horn is at a rendezvous, rifle frolic, or of course at the many muzzle loading supply houses across the country (such as K-W Cap and Ball Horns, Dixie Gun Works, and others).

Another thing to take into consideration when you select your horn is against which side of your body the horn will lay. Most horns have either a left hand or right hand twist, and it is important to choose the correct one for your particular need. If you wear your horn on your right side, you would most likely prefer a left hand twist. This would insure that the spout tip lays firmly against your side and would be free from limbs, brush, and other obstacles.

Most of the horn builders with whom I have become acquainted share a mutual opinion concerning the texture of a horn. We agree that dairy cattle horns have not only the best color, but also the finest texture; whereas beef cattle are characteristic of possessing heavy, thick, coarse-grained horns that are usually grey or green in color.

As you study a prospective horn, it is most important to be aware of weight, thickness, and texture.

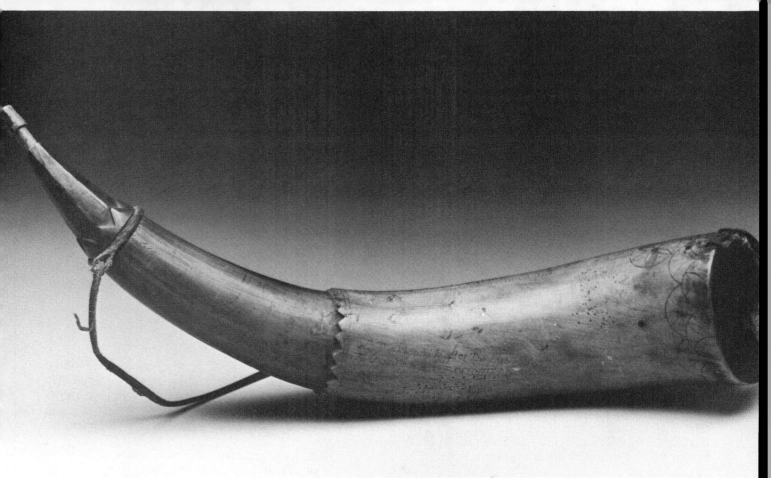

An original horn from the French and Indian War period that exhibits a nice twist and curve. 16½" in length and lightly engraved pictorially with trees, ship, dog, deer, house and circles. It reads THOMAS GOWING :: HIS HORN MADE AT READING, BY JOSIAH DODGE :: Januy 12, 1776.

I prefer working with a rough horn, one that has had no refining and is as natural as if it had just come from the cow. However, I am not implying that I prefer to work with a green horn, a horn fresh from the head of a cow, for a horn should be allowed to cure for a few months or longer before being worked. I am merely stating that I would rather work with a natural horn than a pre-finished one.

The advantage of working a natural horn is that the builder can take the surface down to whatever thickness and texture he or she desires; whereas most of the commercially-finished horns, especially the ones imported from Mexico, are highly polished to the point of having a plastic appearance. Most of the original horns I have examined have a warm, hand-rubbed glow, as opposed to a highly-polished finish. Rough horns are also usually less expensive than finished horns.

COLOR

Color is especially important if you intend to build a horn that will be engraved. Many dark horns were engraved, including the black buffalo horn; as a rule, the engraved horn had a light body and a dark throat and spout. The same is true of the "York County" horn.

The color of a horn cannot be judged by its exterior surface. Most professional horn builders study the inside of the horn to obtain a general idea of what the outside appearance will be when the horn has been rasped or sanded smooth.

The rough outer surface may appear to be just what you are looking for — white, or cream color — but if the inside is black, or striped, or spotted, chances are that when you finish the surface by taking off the outside layer, you will be disappointed to find that what remains looks exactly like the inside. I have been fooled several times.

Study the horn carefully from the *inside out* before making your final choice.

SHAPE AND SIZE

Horns vary greatly in shape, size, and length. I have taken the liberty to measure the length of forty-eight original "Golden Age" horns. All were measured around the curve. My findings are as follows:

Twenty inches in length	3
Nineteen inches in length	4
Eighteen inches in length	2
Seventeen inches in length	11
Sixteen inches in length	8
Fifteen inches in length	10
Fourteen inches in length	6
Thirteen inches in length	1
Twelve inches in length	1
Eleven inches in length	2
Ten inches in length	0

The results of my evaluation show that of the forty-eight horns measured, forty-two per cent were seventeen inches or longer. Ninety-two per cent were fourteen inches or longer and only eight per cent were less than fourteen inches long. Therefore, it would be a safe assumption to think that the length of a horn (especially Golden Age) would fall somewhere between fourteen and twenty inches with seventeen inches being a good solid average.

The width across the base of the horns measured averaged between two and three inches. Most of the horns had a graceful double curve (or twist) that added a touch of elegance to the overall shape.

THE BASICS OF HORN BUILDING

Regardless of the style of horn you intend to build, the basic steps are the same for all horns.

1) You will have to shape and fit the base (or large) plug.
2) You will have to shape the spout and drill or burn the spout hole and fit the plug (or stopper).
3) It might also be noted that although I have listed an extraordinary amount of tools and machinery, one can build a functional powder horn with nothing more than a pocket knife. Do not be distressed when you see the tools I have listed; for, in truth, they are the ultimate in a horn builder's dream and are *not* absolutely necessary for your task.

TOOLS

In any endeavor, the more appropriate the tool, the easier the task. The same is true of horn building. A powder horn can be built with a pocket knife, or one can invest a considerable sum of money in fine machinery.

I have acquired many various files, rasps, and other small tools; but when I need a lathe, belt sander, band saw, etc., it certainly helps to have a friend like Glen Sheppard who has a really fine work shop.

I will set down a list of tools that would make horn building a more simple profession. While I am not advising you to purchase these tools, I am indicating to you those tools I have had occasion to personally use.

1. hacksaw
2. coping saw
3. hand saw
4. half round bastard file (10-inch)
5. ½ inch rat tail file (round)
6. ¼ inch rat tail file (round)
7. 10 inch single cut mill file
8. wood rasp (8 inch four in hand)
9. tri-corner file
10. assortment of needle files
11. vise
12. Dremel tool set
13. Exacto knife set (woodworking)
14. lathe
15. band saw
16. drill press
17. ¼ - ½ inch drill motor
18. rubber or leather mallet

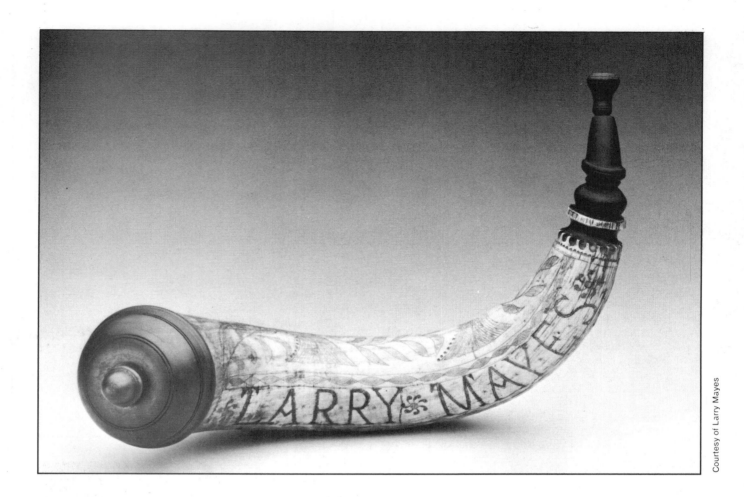

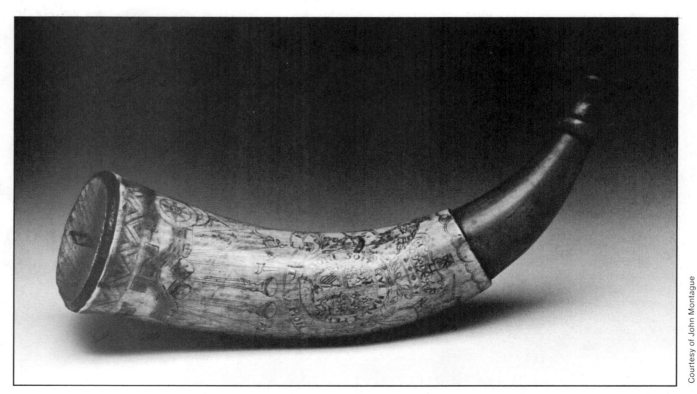

Top: "Golden Age" horn with floral design. This horn has an exceptionally quick twist. Bottom: An original horn, undated. It is beautifully engraved with animals and the British Royal coat of arms. The plug is slightly concave and made of pine.

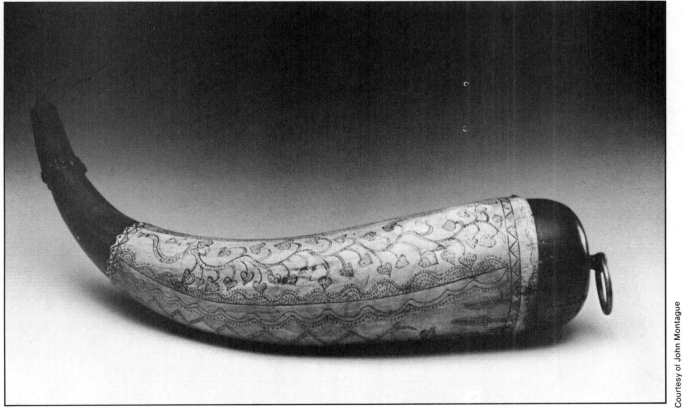

Courtesy of John Montague

Two views of an original horn of the Revolutionary War period. It is a warm ivory color with a brownish green throat. It measures 15⅜" in length and the plug is of cherry. The engraving includes geometric designs, animals, birds and running vines. It is also engraved with the name SAMUEL STAPLES 1775 F * O * 1776

THE FUR TRADE HORN

Trade horns (or commercially-made horns) were produced by the thousands. They were inexpensive; and, although there were a few that could be termed "fancy", for the most part they were just plain, serviceable horns.

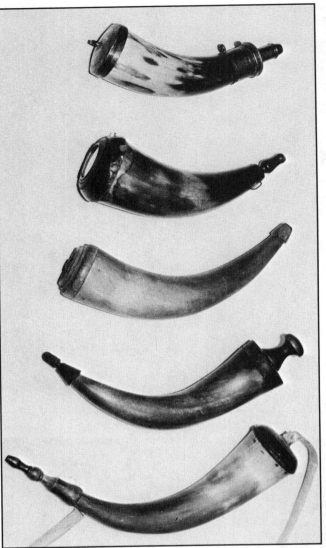

Five commercially produced powder horns during the fur trade period. The top horn has a brass adjustable spout. The second has a mirror in the base plug. The third from the top is traditional, with the fourth having a removable finial on the plug. The bottom horn has a screw tip to facilitate filling the horn.

An original fur trade period powder horn and pouch. The horn is made from a buffalo horn.

CUTTING OFF THE TIP

The first step after acquiring a suitable horn is to gauge the depth of the hollow body. Take a piece of wire (a straightened coat hanger works well) and bend it to match the curvature of the horn. Insert the wire into the horn until it reaches the solid core of the spout end. Remove the wire and lay it parallel to the horn, or directly above the inside section you have just measured. Mark the outside of the spout approximately one-half inch *below* the end of the wire. This will insure that your mark is over the hollow portion of the body. (See Figure 1).

After you have marked the horn, lay your drill bit along side the spout so that the tip of the bit is on line with the mark. (See Figure 1). Check the bit from all directions along the spout to insure that the spout is straight enough to receive the length of the bit. (Remember, a steel drill bit does not bend).

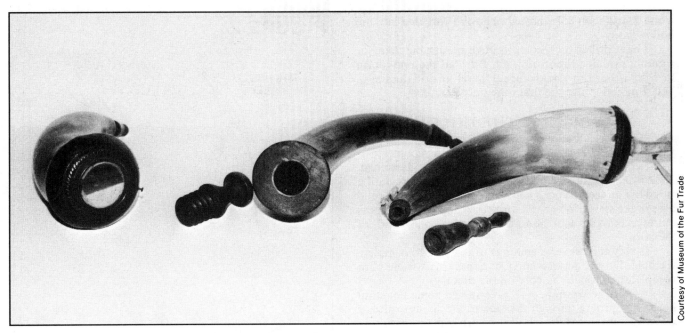

Another view of three of the horns on the preceding page.

If the spout is straight enough to allow the bit to drill into the hollow body without coming out of the side of the horn, mark the spout at the face of the drill chuck. (See Figure 1).

Using a hacksaw, handsaw, coping saw, etc., cut off the excess tip. Do not discard the tip for you may find a future use for it — a powder measure, a spout stopper, a button, etc.

DRILLING THE SPOUT HOLE

Place the horn in a vise (do not attempt to hold the horn in your hand) and secure the horn firmly, being careful not to crack the hollow body. I usually wrap the horn in an old towel to act as a buffer, for the steel jaws of the vise could damage the surface of the horn.

Staying close to the center of the spout, carefully drill

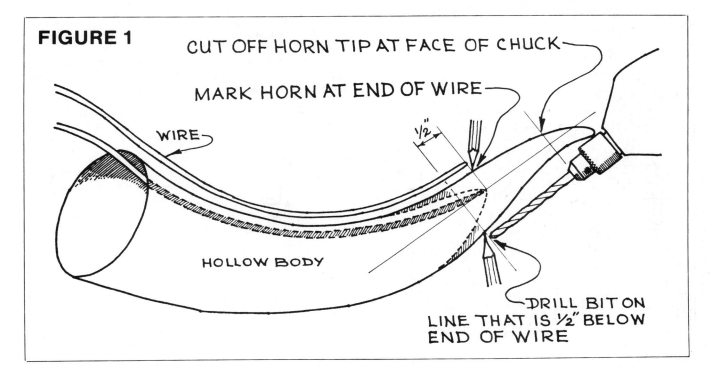

FIGURE 1

CUT OFF HORN TIP AT FACE OF CHUCK

MARK HORN AT END OF WIRE

WIRE

½"

HOLLOW BODY

DRILL BIT ON LINE THAT IS ½" BELOW END OF WIRE

a one-fourth inch hole through the solid core and into the hollow body.

I have drilled pilot holes through spouts; but then, for some unexplained reason, when I drilled the one-fourth inch hole, the horn would crack. I therefore drill the size of hole I intend to use the first time out.

BURNING THE HOLE

If you are a die-hard purist, you may prefer the hot-wire method of burning the hole through the spout.

Secure the horn in a vise as previously described. Heat a one-eighth inch or three-sixteenth inch wire until it is red hot on the tip end. Then, force the wire into the solid core of the spout. When the wire cools, repeat the process until you burn through the core and into the hollow body of the horn.

It may take several heatings of the wire to complete the hole. Do not get in a hurry or expect the wire to burn completely through the core on the first try.

A word of warning — I have ruined some beautiful horns by burning through the side of the spout or throat when attempting to burn a hole in a horn with a particularly quick twist.

Also, unlike a drill bit that cuts a hole the size of the bit, a wire will burn an over-size hole. Do not use a one-fourth inch rod and expect a one-fourth inch hole.

One concluding thought — work outside. Horn smoke can be harmful to your health — (when your wife gets a whiff, she'll probably kill you).

SQUARING THE TIP

Squaring the spout tip in order that the plug (or stopper) will set square and continue the unbroken line of the contour of the horn can be accomplished by rasping, filing or sanding the face of the spout tip until it is at a 90-degree plane with the center line of the spout. This is a very important part of horn building; for should the plug set out of line with the horn, it can ruin an otherwise beautiful specimen. (See Figure 2).

FIGURE 2

RIGHT

WRONG

THE SPOUT PLUG (OR STOPPER)

The spout plug can be made from almost any type of hard wood. I have used dowel rods, broken ram rods, excess wood from gunstocks, limbs from trees, and other sources.

A plug is simple to make—or extremely difficult—depending on how intricate you wish the plug to be. If you want a plug that will simply seal the pouring spout, then one made with a knife or file will suffice. But if you desire a beautifully turned plug, a lathe is required.

There are straight-stem plugs and split-stem plugs, depending on your preference. Both work well. Should you decide to try a split-stem, be sure to saw the split. *Do not attempt to split a stem with a knife or chisel.*

If you have made a stem that is slightly over-sized, take a single-edged razor blade and gently scrape the stem. Do not file or sand the stem because it is very easy, without

FIGURE 3

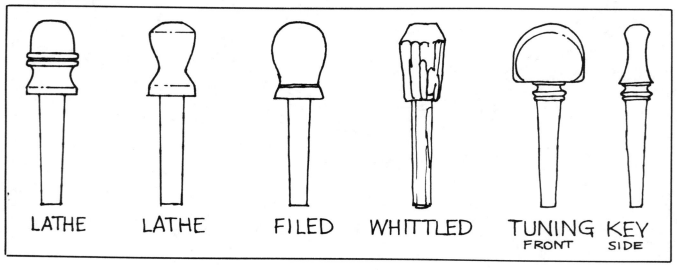

LATHE LATHE FILED WHITTLED TUNING KEY
                                 FRONT   SIDE

realizing it, to remove more wood than you intend. An under-sized stem is useless.

The knob end of the plug can vary in size and design, depending on the desire of the builder. Most originals, however, appear to be dome-shaped, or flat like the tuning key of a violin The builder is free to use his own ideas as far as size and styling are concerned. (See Figure 3).

PREPARING THE BASE END

Secure the horn in a vise as previously described. Study the rough opening of the base itself, being careful to mark the place where you intend to cut off the horn behind the deepest indent or crack. In order to insure a straight line for the cut, I wrap masking tape around the horn at the mark I have made behind the deepest indent. (See Figure 4). The edge of the tape acts as a straight edge or guide for the saw blade.

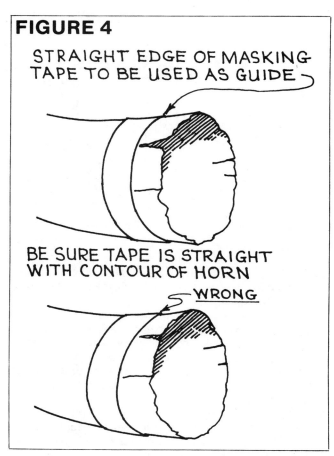

FIGURE 4

STRAIGHT EDGE OF MASKING TAPE TO BE USED AS GUIDE

BE SURE TAPE IS STRAIGHT WITH CONTOUR OF HORN

WRONG

After the rough end has been eliminated, sand-paper or emory cloth the end of the horn to remove any burrs or flakes caused by the saw.

You are ready to work the inside of the horn at this time. Grind or rasp away excess interior that is not needed. It only adds weight to the finished product. Many original horns were worked down until they were paper-thin.

You will also find that a thin horn is far more pliable when it is boiled, making the job of inserting the base plug much easier.

When the inside is worked down to your satisfaction, submerge the first two or three inches of the horn in boiling water, leaving it for thirty or forty minutes. The horn

should become pliable and will have a certain amount of elasticity that will allow the base plug to slip in easily.

I have a conical-shaped piece of wood that I refer to as a sizer. Because most horns are not round, I find it necessary to round the base opening myself — hence, the sizer. If you wish to fit a plug to an oval or flat-sided opening (natural opening), then the boiling of the horn and the use of a sizer will not be necessary. Assuming, however, that you wish to use a round plug, boil the horn until it is pliable and drive the sizer into the opening until the mouth of the horn is round. Lay the horn aside to cool. As the horn cools, it will return to its natural hard texture. When the sizer is removed, you will find a nicely rounded opening. (See Figure 5).

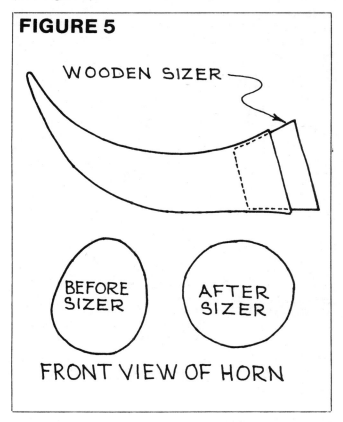

FIGURE 5

WOODEN SIZER

BEFORE SIZER

AFTER SIZER

FRONT VIEW OF HORN

THE BASE PLUG

Most novice horn builders have the mistaken idea that all powder horns were plugged with such hard woods as walnut, cherry, and maple. This simply was not the case. Hard woods were used occasionally, especially on such horns as the "York County Horn", but on most of the originals I have studied the plugs were made of pine or poplar or some other type of softer wood. Soft wood is easier to work and lighter in weight.

The plug should fit the opening snugly and, hopefully, be air tight. (The use of a sizer makes fitting the plug *almost* easy.)

Step Number One is to determine the actual size of the opening. Take a tape measure that is pliable — one made of fabric is best — and measure the circumference or distance around the horn at the opening. (See Figure 6A.) Divide that measurement by 3.14 or pi. The answer will be the true outside diameter of the horn. (See Figure 6A.)

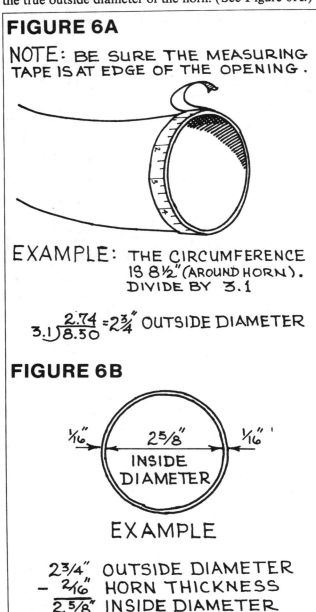

FIGURE 6A

NOTE: BE SURE THE MEASURING TAPE IS AT EDGE OF THE OPENING.

EXAMPLE: THE CIRCUMFERENCE IS 8½" (AROUND HORN). DIVIDE BY 3.1

$$3.1\overline{)8.50} = \frac{2.74}{} = 2\tfrac{3}{4}"\ \text{OUTSIDE DIAMETER}$$

FIGURE 6B

2 5/8" INSIDE DIAMETER

1/16"   1/16"

EXAMPLE

2¾" OUTSIDE DIAMETER
− 2/16" HORN THICKNESS
2 5/8" INSIDE DIAMETER (PLUG DIAMETER)

You are probably asking yourself, "Why doesn't he just measure straight across the opening?" Even when using the sizer, the horn may not be perfectly round; and a turned plug is made to fit a round opening of an exact size.

If the outside diameter of the horn is 2¾ inches, when you build the plug, subtract twice the thickness of the horn. The answer, after you subtract the thickness, will be the *inside* diameter or the actual size of the intended plug. (See example with Figure 6B.)

The exposed portion of the plug can vary in size and style according to the builder's preference as can the portion that will be inside the horn. One-half inch is sufficient for the portion that fits inside the horn. (See Figure 6C.)

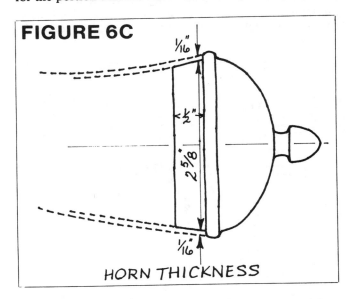

FIGURE 6C

1/16"

½"

2 5/8"

1/16"

HORN THICKNESS

SHAPES OF BASE PLUGS

The shape, size, and style of the plug is almost entirely the builder's choice.

Plugs were flat, dome-shaped, pointed, fluted, engraved, relief-carved, and just about any other way the human mind could conceive. The carrying strap connector was the same way — from square nails, staples, screws, and eyelets to finely carved finials and even brass drawer pulls from an ornate piece of furniture. For basic plug shapes — (See Figure 7.)

After you have selected a style of plug and finished it to your satisfaction and feel that it is ready to inset into the horn, boil the horn again until it becomes pliable. Then, using a rubber hammer or leather mallet, etc., carefully drive the plug into the opening until it is seated firmly against the face of the horn or flush with the face, depending on which type plug you build. (See Figure 8.)

Be extremely careful while driving the plug into the horn; for even though the horn is pliable, it will only stretch a certain amount before splitting.

After the plug is seated, the horn should be laid aside and allowed to cool. **NOTE:** *Be careful not to drive the plug too far into the opening, an act which might accidently split the horn. If the plug does not drive in easily, remove it and carefully rasp the portion that fits inside the horn until you can almost fit it by hand. Then boil the horn again and seat the plug.*

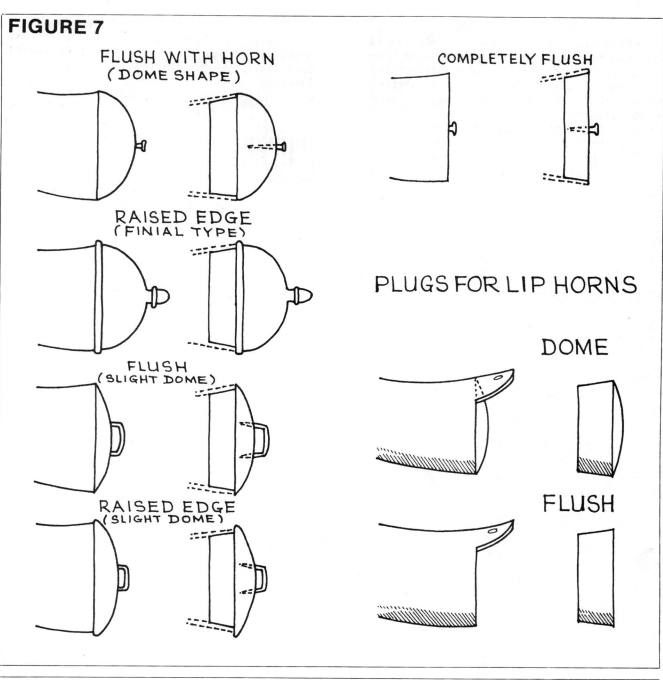

FIGURE 7

FLUSH WITH HORN
(DOME SHAPE)

COMPLETELY FLUSH

RAISED EDGE
(FINIAL TYPE)

PLUGS FOR LIP HORNS

DOME

FLUSH
(SLIGHT DOME)

RAISED EDGE
(SLIGHT DOME)

FLUSH

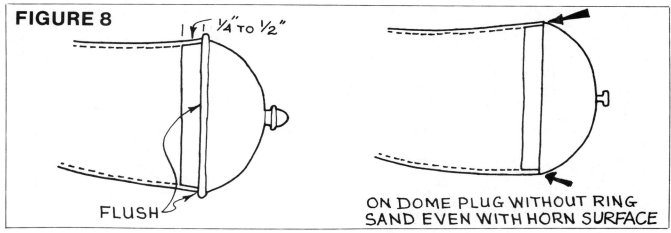

FIGURE 8

¼" TO ½"

FLUSH

ON DOME PLUG WITHOUT RING
SAND EVEN WITH HORN SURFACE

THE PEGS

For years I whittled, worked, and cursed the peg, until in major frustration I sat down, considered possible alternatives, and came up with an easier method.

The thorns from a Black Locust or any thorn-bearing tree, work fine. But those round, pointed-end, toothpicks work best. They are made of hard wood and are already neatly pointed. All that is required is for the builder to cut them to the length he desires and drive them into a predrilled hole in the horn. (See Figure 9A.)

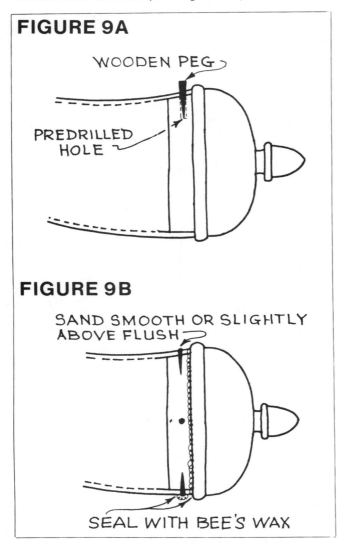

FIGURE 9A

WOODEN PEG

PREDRILLED HOLE

FIGURE 9B

SAND SMOOTH OR SLIGHTLY ABOVE FLUSH

SEAL WITH BEE'S WAX

I prefer a peg that is approximately 5/16 inch in length and I use anywhere from four to eight to secure the base plug. After the pegs are inserted, sand the exposed portion until it is flush or slightly above the surface of the horn. See Figure 9B.) You may stain or leave them natural.

When the pegs are finished to your satisfaction, heat a small portion of bee's wax and seal each peg and also the crack where the base plug and horn meet.

Sealing in bee's wax is an added precaution which helps to prevent leaks. It evidently works, for many of the original horns were sealed this same way.

I use a small stick to scrape away unwanted wax and hand rub the remaining excess wax into the wood and horn.

SHAPING THE HORN

Shaping the horn is the part of horn building that gives the finished product "character". The builder can allow his creative nature and imagination to take the upper hand. Variations of styles are virtually unlimited, although I might point out or remind you that the fur trade horn was usually rather plain in design. (See Figure 10.)

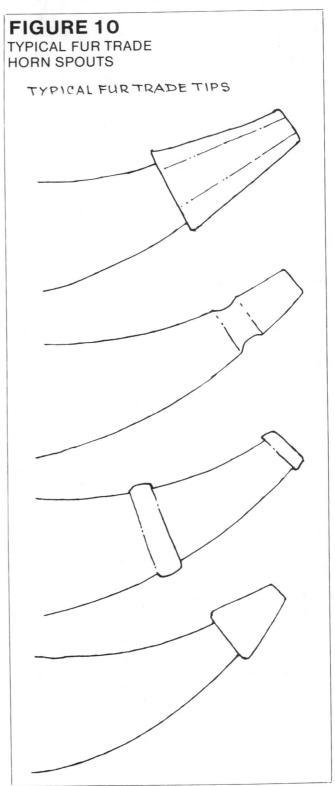

FIGURE 10
TYPICAL FUR TRADE HORN SPOUTS

TYPICAL FUR TRADE TIPS

123

Most horns are laid out and finished in either two or three sections — the body and spout; or the body, throat, and spout.

The body length can vary according to the preference of the builder, but it usually runs approximately two-thirds or sometimes three-fourths the length of the entire horn. The body can be finely finished or left in the rough state. If you intend to engrave it, however, the body should be finished smooth.

Decide the length of the body and draw a line around the horn. (See Figure 11.)

Next, decide where you want the raised rings for the carrying strap and lay them out. (See Figure 11.)

Using a small file, make guide lines (grooves) where the pencil lines are drawn. Then file or rasp the unwanted portion of the horn until you have a rough version of the intended design. (See Figure 12.) **NOTE:** *Be careful to pay particular attention to the spout hole that runs the length of the throat. Do not file or rasp completely through the horn. If you listen closely, you can usually tell how thin the horn is by the sound of the file. You can also periodically hold the horn up to the light and look down the spout hole while running your fingers across the throat and gauge the thickness accordingly.*

When the rings, recesses, etc. are as you want them, fine sand, using fine emory cloth or sandpaper until the body (if you desire a fine finished body), throat, and spout are smooth and even. Then buff with a piece of triple aught steel wool.

The final touch after the horn has been finished to your satisfaction is to give it a good coat of paste wax. The horn should have a soft luster, plus have an added protective wax coating that will help turn moisture should you be caught in the rain.

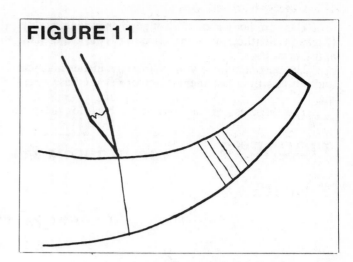

FIGURE 11

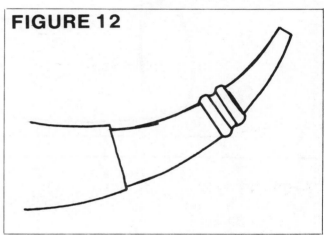

FIGURE 12

FRENCH & INDIAN AND REVOLUTIONARY WAR HORNS
(GOLDEN AGE OF HORNS)

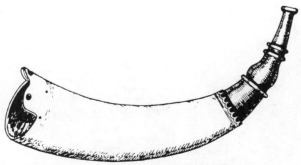

The "Golden Age of Horns" was relatively a short span of time, ranging from approximately 1753 to 1784. The horns produced during that twenty-year period are considered by collectors to be the ultimate in style, grace, and elegance.

Engraving peaked during this time span, leaving in its wake beautiful map horns, rhyming horns, name and date horns, and pictorial horns.

The body, throat, and spout on many "Golden Age" horns are expertly worked into recesses, raised rings, knobs, flutes, and octagonal flats which are extremely pleasing to the eye.

The lobe, or protruding lip that attaches the carrying strap was much used by the builders of that fine era and polycrome (artificial coloring) was a common practice.

The selection of a horn is important for there are qualities the builder must take into consideration while working a "Golden Age" horn.

The horn body should be of good engraving quality. (Light in color that runs at least two-thirds the length of the entire horn.)

The horn should be at least fourteen inches in length and not less than two inches in width at the base opening.

The thickness of the horn at the base for the pro-truding lip type should not be less than ⅛ inch, for the lip will be fragile even if it is ¼ inch thick.

The spout should be solid for three inches or more to allow the builder flexibility in design. (See Figure 13.)

Be certain the horn has the correct twist, as mentioned earlier.

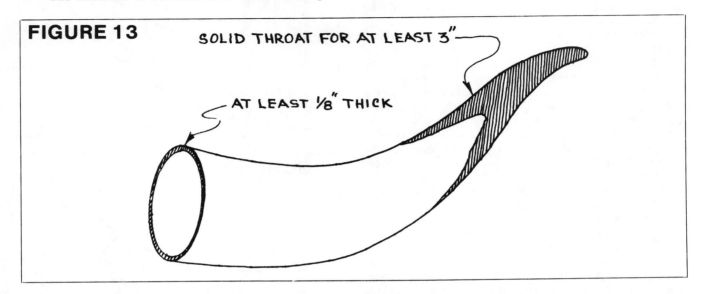

FIGURE 13

SOLID THROAT FOR AT LEAST 3"

AT LEAST ⅛" THICK

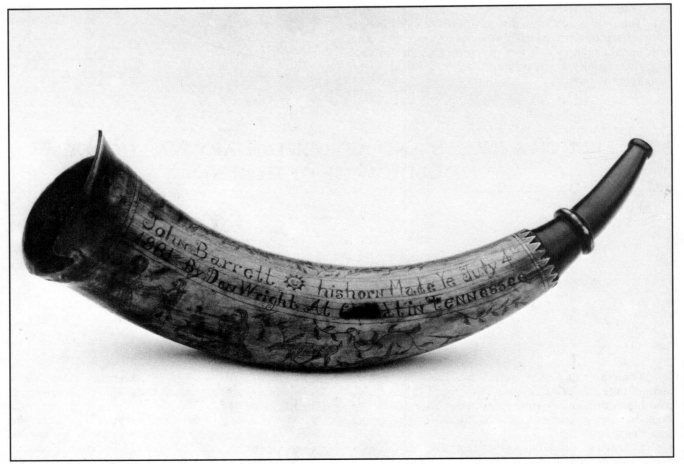

"Golden Age" horn, early style with primitive engraving. The body is orange to gold; the throat and spout are black. The base plug is poplar.

BUILDING THE "GOLDEN AGE" LIP HORN

Lay the horn against your side or hang the horn from temporary strings to determine how the finished product will hang. (See Figure 14.) Mark the rough base with pencil where the center of the lip should be (Figure 14).

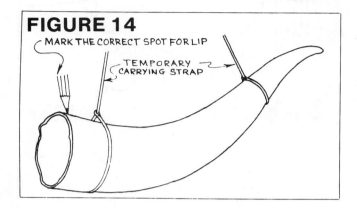

FIGURE 14

MARK THE CORRECT SPOT FOR LIP

TEMPORARY CARRYING STRAP

Draw a rough outline of the intended lip, centering the pencil mark between the outside lines of the lip. (See Figure 15.)

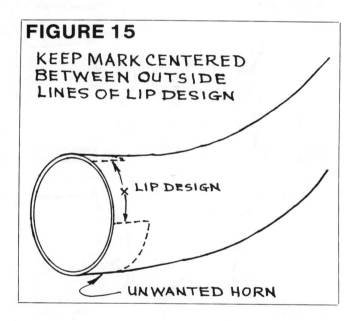

FIGURE 15

KEEP MARK CENTERED BETWEEN OUTSIDE LINES OF LIP DESIGN

LIP DESIGN

UNWANTED HORN

Place the horn in a vise and, using a hacksaw, coping saw, etc., saw directly into the horn the depth of the intended lip. (See Figures 16 A and B.) Then saw sideways through the horn until you cut away the rough base and the lip is left exposed. (See Figures 17 A and B.)

Draw the finished design on the roughed out lip and carefully file out the desired shape. (See Figures 18A and B on the following page.)

Rasp, file, and sand the horn body until it is free of scales, cuts, scratches, etc.

Using the method mentioned earlier, measure the depth of the hollow body, cut the tip; and drill or burn the spout hole.

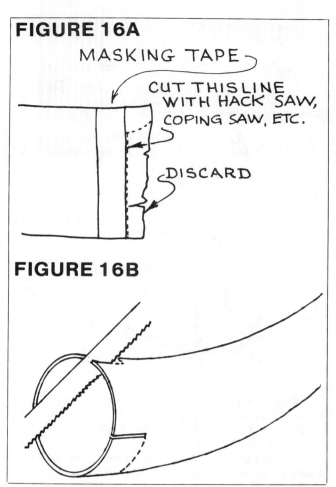

FIGURE 16A

MASKING TAPE

CUT THIS LINE WITH HACK SAW, COPING SAW, ETC.

DISCARD

FIGURE 16B

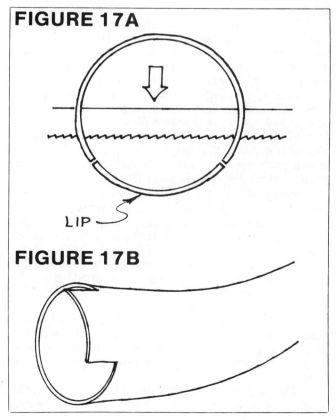

FIGURE 17A

LIP

FIGURE 17B

FIGURE 18A

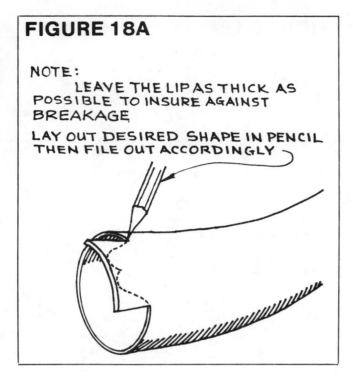

NOTE:
     LEAVE THE LIP AS THICK AS POSSIBLE TO INSURE AGAINST BREAKAGE.

LAY OUT DESIRED SHAPE IN PENCIL THEN FILE OUT ACCORDINGLY

FIGURE 18B

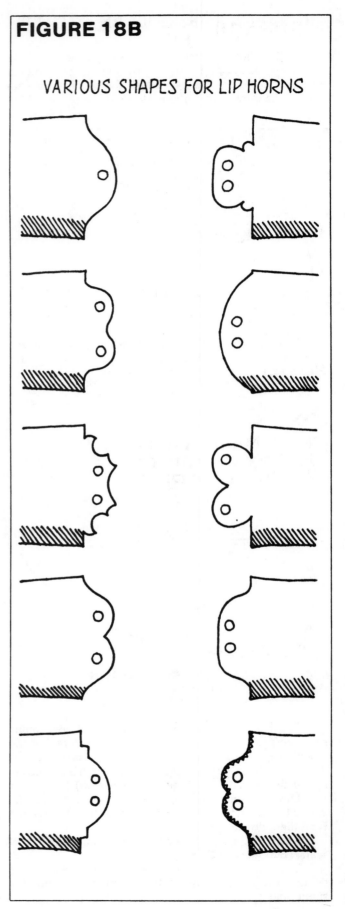

VARIOUS SHAPES FOR LIP HORNS

Build the spout plug and fit it to the horn, considering again the natural contour of the body lines. Using fine sandpaper, emory cloth, and steel wool, work the body down to a smooth finish.

When I work the horn body, I place the throat in a padded vise and fine sand the horn with a length of emory cloth used much the same way as if I were polishing a pair of shoes.

When the horn is smooth (engraving smooth), you are ready to lay out the throat and spout. There are so many variations of throats and spouts, the builder almost has a free hand to design his own combinations and still be authentic. The more intricate the design of the throat and spout, the more essential the correct tools are for a neat job. You might wish to purchase or borrow a round (rat tail) file and, if possible, a set of needle files.

Study photographs of original horns and decide which design or portions of a design are personally appealing or which you would like to recreate. Lay out the throat and spout accordingly. (See Figures 19 and 20.)

When the horn is roughed out to your specifications, sand and polish the knobs, flutes, raised rings, etc. until you have removed the file marks; then polish with triple aught steel wool until the horn achieves a soft glow. Do not hurry!

The base of the horn demands special attention. The only place you require thickness is the actual lip, or lobe, itself. The remainder of the base should be filed or ground out as stated earlier. (See Figure 21.)

When the base (except for the lip) is thinned to your satisfaction, boil the base until it is pliable and insert your sizer. Allow the horn to set for a day or two before removing the sizer. The base should retain the round shape.

The plug can be of the builder's choosing. Most of the original plugs, however, were of pine or poplar. Measure

127

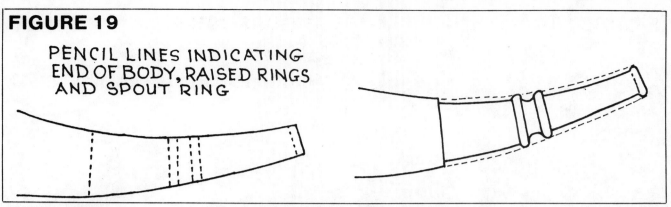

FIGURE 19

PENCIL LINES INDICATING
END OF BODY, RAISED RINGS
AND SPOUT RING

FIGURE 20

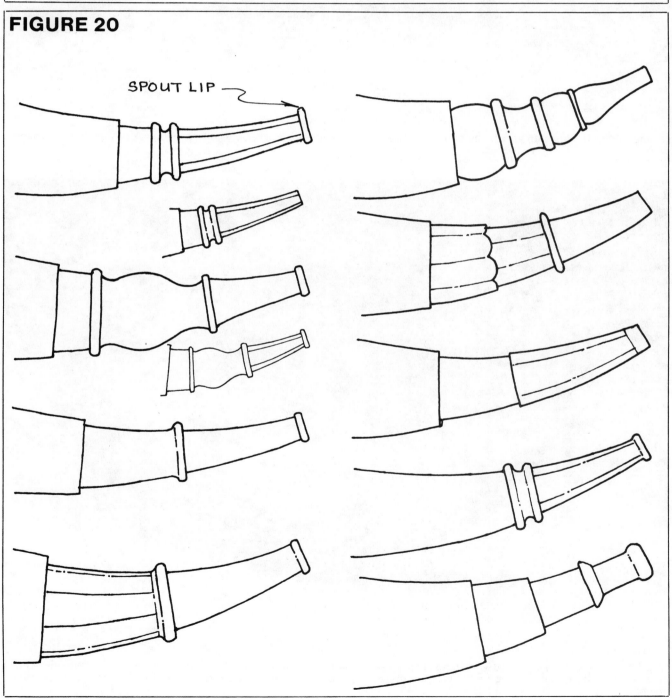

SPOUT LIP

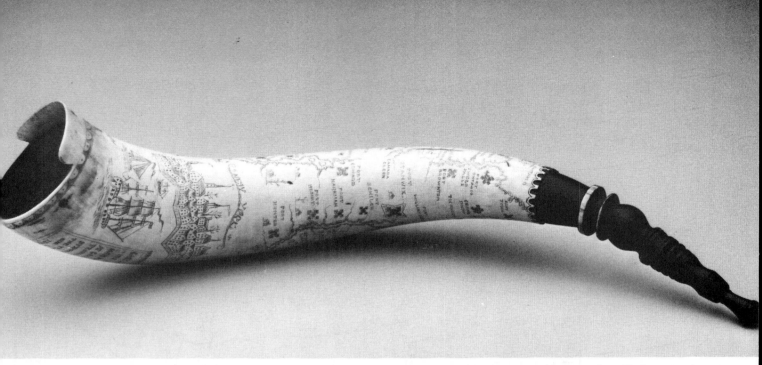

"Golden Age" lip horn with very fancy engrailing, multiple raised rings and knobs. The large plug is poplar with four wooden pegs.

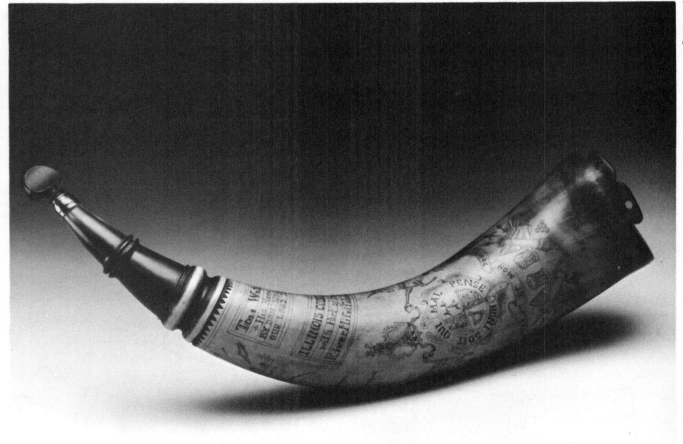

"Golden Age" map horn engraved with a map of the Illinois country, the owner's name and date in cartouche, and the British coat of arms. The body is golden orange with a brown throat and spout. Note the engraved brass band around the spout tip to prevent splitting.

FIGURE 21

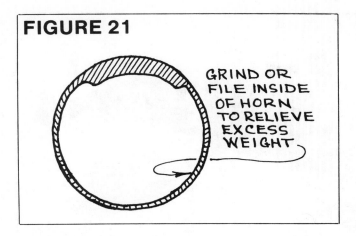

GRIND OR FILE INSIDE OF HORN TO RELIEVE EXCESS WEIGHT

the base as was stated earlier and saw out the plug accordingly. (See Figures 6A and B.)

Boil the horn again and carefully set the plug and pegs. Seal with bee's wax.

Mark and drill the carrying strap holes; 3/16 inch holes are large enough. (See Figure 22.)

FIGURE 22

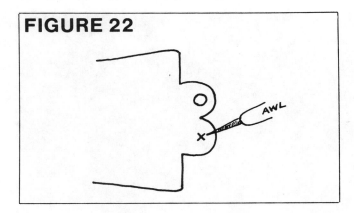

AWL

Sand the rough edges of the holes until they are rounded and smooth as if the horn had been well-used.

Move your attention once again to the throat and spout. On many originals, the recessed edge that separates the body from the throat (See Figure 23) is engrailed. Engrailing is easy to accomplish and adds a nice touch to the overall elegance of the horn. (See Figure 24.)

I have boiled a horn until it is soft and engrailed the edge with a U-shaped gouge, but the Dremel tool with a small ball-shaped cutter is much faster and simpler to use. Whichever method you decide to use, there are guidelines you may wish to follow. (See Figures 25 and 26.)

FIGURE 23

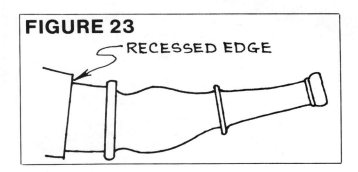

RECESSED EDGE

FIGURE 24

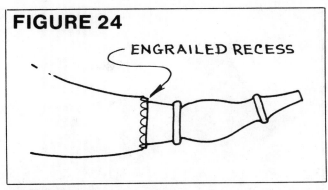

ENGRAILED RECESS

FIGURE 25

DRAW A LINE AROUND THE BODY OF THE HORN AT WHATEVER THE LENGTH OF ENGRAIL YOU SHOULD DESIRE

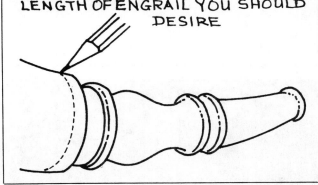

FIGURE 26

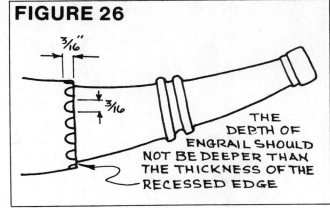

3/16"

3/16

THE DEPTH OF ENGRAIL SHOULD NOT BE DEEPER THAN THE THICKNESS OF THE RECESSED EDGE

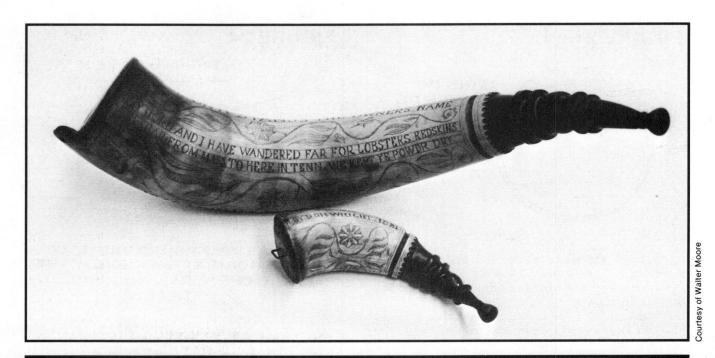

Top: "Golden Age" horn with matching priming horn. Rhyme horns were popular during the Revolutionary War. Bottom: An original Revolutionary War horn. 15" in length. It has a lip drilled with three holes and a brass staple for attaching strap. It is engraved with geometric designs and CHA^S GOODRICH HIS HORN PITT^{S}FIELD TO FORT TYCONDROGA ye 16 DEC^r 1776.

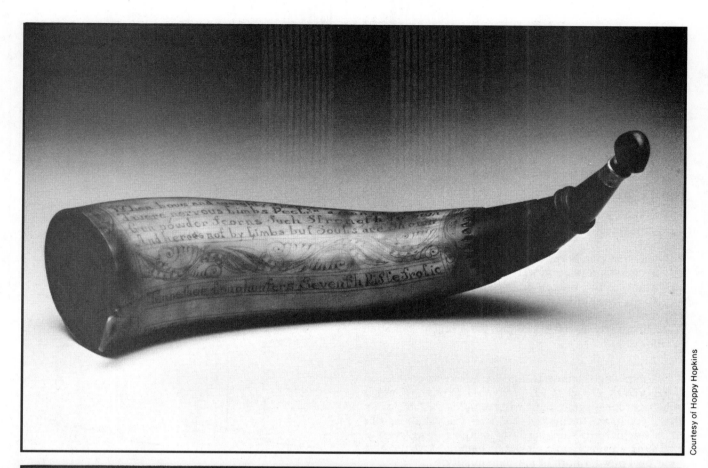

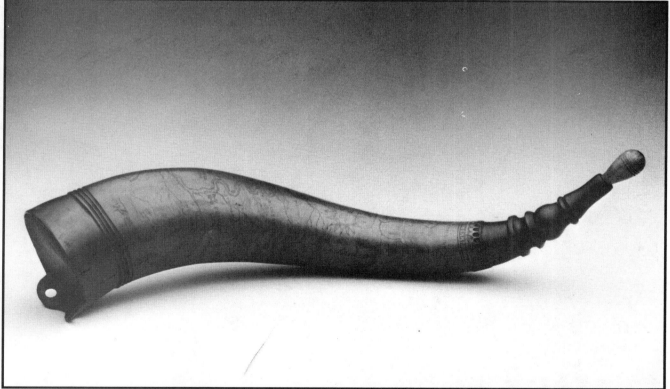

Top: "Golden Age" lip horn showing engrailing, fluted octagonal throat, and raised ring spout. Brass cover on pouring spout prevents splitting. Bottom: "Golden Age" horn showing nice gentle curve and twist, engrailing, knobs and raised rings at throat and spout. This is the author's personal horn.

Study pictures of originals and decide which style of engrailing you prefer. (See Figure 27.)

If you intend to engrave your horn, there are a few rules you might wish to remember should you desire to be reasonably consistent with the originals. (I am not implying that all originals followed these guidelines; only that most of the ones I have studied seemed to follow the same pattern.)

(1) If not in a cartouche (box), the owner's name usually was displayed lengthwise of the horn.
(2) The name was normally followed by the words: "His Horn".
(3) Maps were displayed lengthwise of the horn, while the names of cities, rivers, lakes, forts, etc., ran around the body.
(4) On most map horns the name of the owner and other personal information were set in a cartouche (box).
(5) Many of the French & Indian War horns had the "Great Seal of England" engraved on them.
(6) The Revolutionary War horns did not have the lip or lobe nearly as often as did the French & Indian horns.

Engraving (scrimshawing) the horn was covered in *THE BOOK OF BUCKSKINNING* (Volume One). I shall not repeat again; but I will reemphasize once again that if you intend to engrave your horn, study photographs of the originals. By studying the techniques of engravers of two hundred years ago, you will be better able to recreate your own powder horn of museum quality.

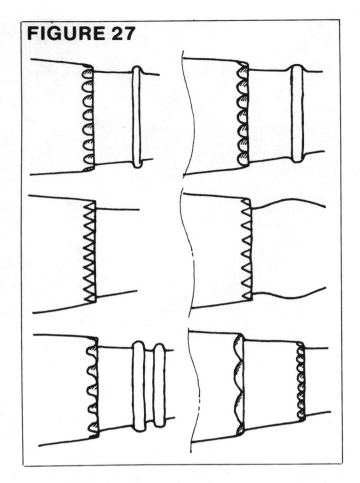

FIGURE 27

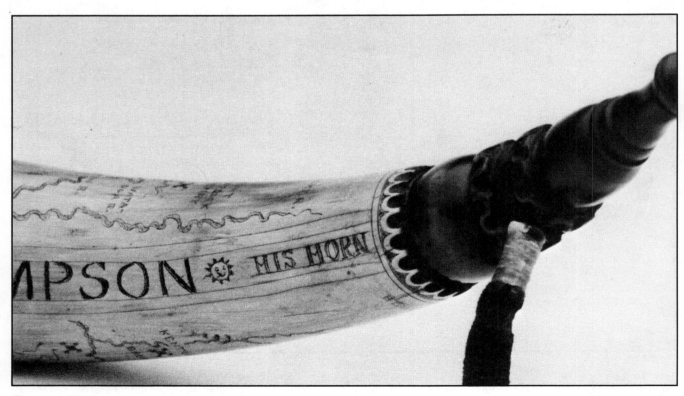

Close up showing one style of engrailing popular during the "Golden Age" of horns.

133

THE MINUTE-MAN HORN
(GLASS COVERED PLUG)

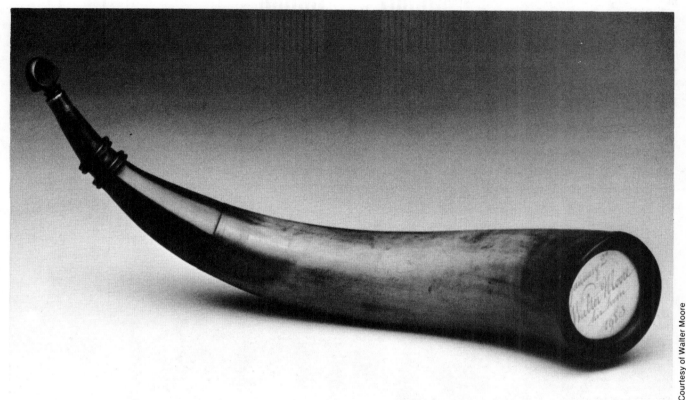

"Minute Man, or Glass Fronted" horn. The base plug is covered with a piece of paper and protected by glass which is held in place by a wooden ring.

The glass covered plug horn is very rare; and very few builders attempt to recreate them. They are difficult to build; and the end result is a fragile piece of workmanship that one would almost be afraid to carry or show rough usage.

The original horns I have studied have been large horns, running from sixteen to nineteen inches in length and between three to four inches across the base. They had very little twist, and the body and throat were rather plain in design.

I have seen one that was engraved. The engraving was very primitive, suggesting that the engraving was done at a later date by someone other than the builder.

The unique thing about the "Minute Man Horn" is the glass cover over the plug. Theory has it that the glass was used for signaling purposes, but I am inclined to disagree. I believe the glass was a horn builder's scheme to build something characteristically different from the standard wooden plug. Whatever the reason, the "Minute Man Horn" definitely has a style all its own.

Select a large horn that has a medium twist and is naturally round at the base. The horn should be fairly thick at the base because the carrying strap will be attached to the horn by means of a protruding lip. The lip or lobe should be thick enough to support the weight of the horn plus the amount of powder it will contain.

The color of the horn is not important, unless you intend to engrave it. If this is the case, choose a horn with a light-colored body.

Repeat the same procedure for working the horn as you did in the section on the "Fur Trade Horn" *except* that when you lay out and cut off the base end, be sure to leave a protruding lip for the carrying strap.

Decide which body, throat, and spout you desire and finish the horn accordingly.

The reason for finishing the horn body, etc., before inserting the base plug is because of the chance of breaking the glass while filing, sanding, or working the body.

When you are ready to start work on the base plug, a sizer is almost a necessity. The opening needs to be as round as possible for the glass and locking ring to fit evenly.

Once you have sized the horn, take a measurement approximately 5/16 inch back from the opening. (See Figure 28.)

Figure the inside diameter as previously shown. Saw out a backing plate from a piece of hard wood. (See Figure 29.) The plate should have a tapered edge that will fit the natural contour of the horn as it diminishes in size.

Insert the backing plate 5/16 inch inside the horn. It should fit snugly and seal the opening. (Elmer's Glue around the edge is an extra safeguard.)

Find an old piece of paper or parchment (old books are a good source) and write the owner's name and date or whatever you feel appropriate in old script. Then cut the paper to fit in front of the backing plate.

Locate an old window pane or piece of glass (old

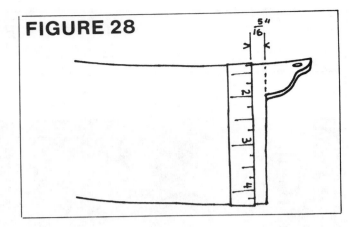

FIGURE 28

Close up of glass front showing hand written date and name. The author utilized original handmade paper made in the 1700s on which to write the owner's name.

Courtesy of Walter Moore

135

FIGURE 29

¼" HARDWOOD WITH TAPERED EDGE, (WALNUT, CHERRY, ETC.)

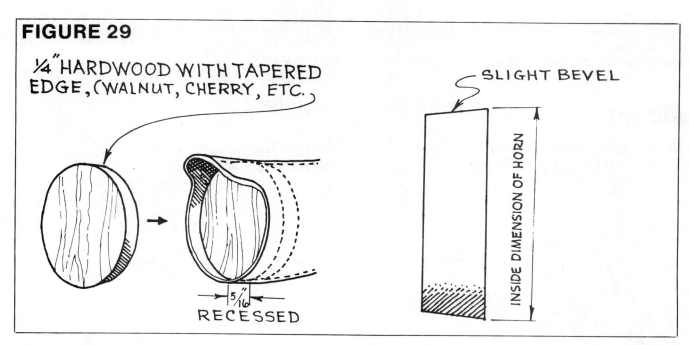

5/16"
RECESSED

SLIGHT BEVEL

INSIDE DIMENSION OF HORN

FIGURE 30

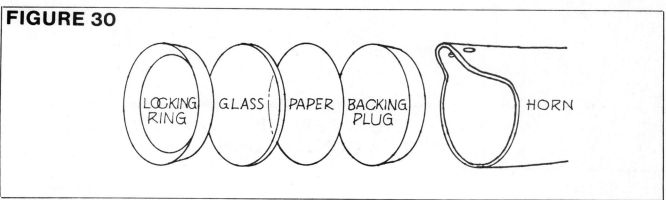

LOCKING RING   GLASS   PAPER   BACKING PLUG   HORN

FIGURE 31

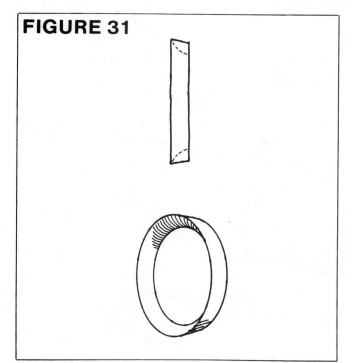

abandoned buildings are a good source) that contains waves or lines or bubbles and have a glass cutter cut a circle that will cover the paper and hopefully fit closely against the inside of the horn. It does not have to fit tightly, only closely. (See Figure 30.)

The difficult part comes last — the building of the locking ring. Measure the distance from the glass to the outside edge of the opening of the horn. It should be no less than one-fourth of an inch.

The next step is to go to a friend that has a lathe and ask him to cut a ring that is one-fourth inch in depth and rolled at the front. (See Figure 31.) It is not an easy task to accomplish. Glen Sheppard cut mine while I stood by and watched. It was no simple matter. He made the ring out of walnut and held his breath each time he made a cut. It turned out to our satisfaction, much to his surprise — and mine.

Slip the locking ring into the horn and secure it with a

piece of masking tape to hold the ring in place while you drill the peg holes, being careful not to drill completely through the locking ring. (Peg as you go.) (See Figure 32.)

The final step is to seal the ring with hot bee's wax, as stated earlier, and put a good coat of paste wax over the entire horn.

FIGURE 32

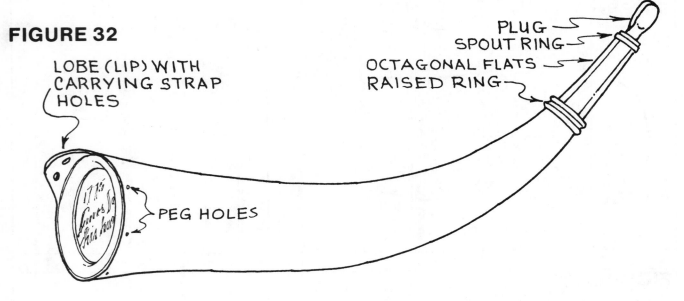

LOBE (LIP) WITH CARRYING STRAP HOLES

PLUG
SPOUT RING
OCTAGONAL FLATS
RAISED RING

PEG HOLES

THE SCREW TIP
(YORK COUNTY) HORN

These are referred to as "York County" horns because the majority of the screw tip horns that are in collections today were found in or known to have been built in York County, Pennsylvania.

The screw tip horn is extremely difficult to build, but the finished product is worth the effort. They vary in size and color. However, a light body with a dark tip is preferable to attain the most beautiful result. Very few were engraved, but I have seen one original that was very lightly done. It was the exception, however, rather than the rule.

Even without engraving, I class the screw tip horn among the best for elegance, style, and grace for it is truly a superb piece of craftsmanship.

The screw tip itself is made from a solid core horn tip approximately three inches in length. The tip should be as straight as you can find. (See Figure 33.) Cut the tip end of

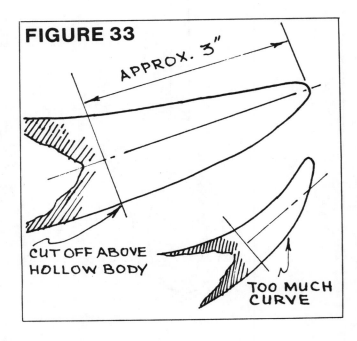

FIGURE 33

APPROX. 3"

CUT OFF ABOVE HOLLOW BODY

TOO MUCH CURVE

the three-inch piece as square as possible. (See Figure 34.) Then, rasp the sides of the future screw tip until it is roughly the shape of a cone that is 2½ to 3 inches in length and one inch to 1¼ inch in diameter. (See Figure 35.)

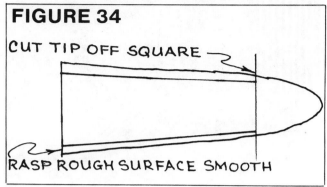

FIGURE 34

CUT TIP OFF SQUARE

RASP ROUGH SURFACE SMOOTH

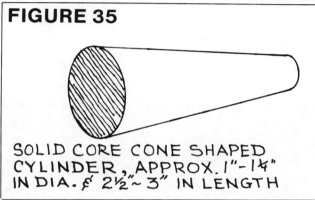

FIGURE 35

SOLID CORE CONE SHAPED CYLINDER, APPROX. 1"-1¼" IN DIA. & 2½"~3" IN LENGTH

When you have completed roughing out the tip, secure it in a drill press or vise and carefully drill a 9/16 inch hole, ½ inch deep in the center of the tip. (See Figure 36.)

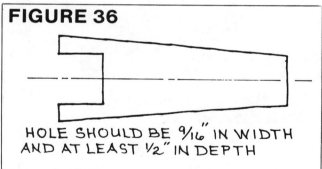

FIGURE 36

HOLE SHOULD BE 9/16" IN WIDTH AND AT LEAST ½" IN DEPTH

Using a ⅝ inch bottoming tap, carefully tap (thread) the 9/16 inch hole, backing up and going forward very slowly, thus cleaning the threads as you work. I stress caution, because cutting threads on horn is a delicate process. (See Figure 37.)

When you have tapped the hole, cutting the threads completely to the bottom, lay the tap aside and select a horn for the body of your "screw tip" horn.

Depending on the color of the screw tip, choose a horn with a light body that tends to run to the same color at its tip. In other words, if the tip that you just tapped is black, brown, or grey, be sure to choose a body that runs to that particular color so that the body will match when screwed together.

FIGURE 37

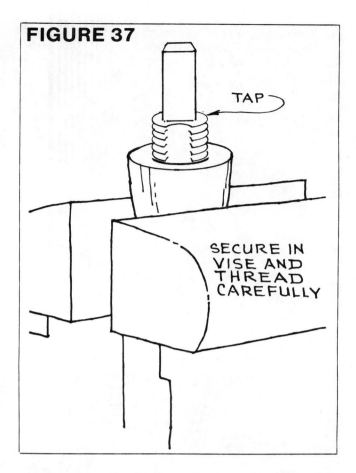

TAP

SECURE IN VISE AND THREAD CAREFULLY

Secure the horn in a vise and gauge the depth of the hollow using the same method as described earlier in Figure 1. Cut the horn off above the hollow, where the solid core is at least one inch in diameter. (See Figure 38.) **NOTE:** *Be sure to cut the horn off far enough above the hollow to insure room for the male threads.*

FIGURE 38

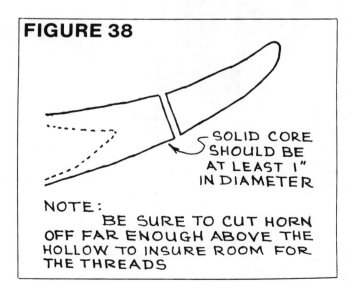

SOLID CORE SHOULD BE AT LEAST 1" IN DIAMETER

NOTE:
BE SURE TO CUT HORN OFF FAR ENOUGH ABOVE THE HOLLOW TO INSURE ROOM FOR THE THREADS

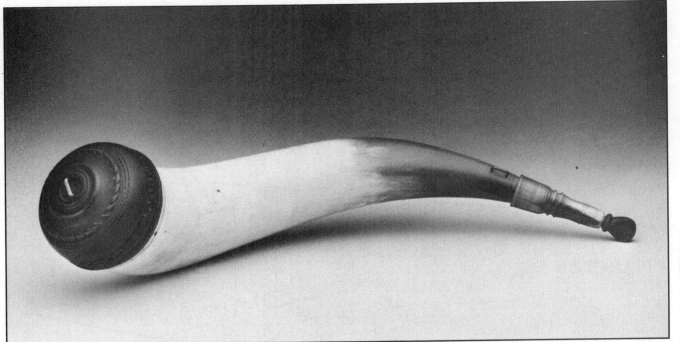

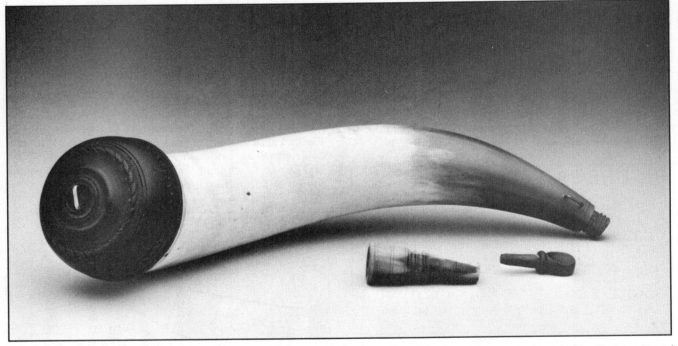

Top: "York County or Screw Tip" horn. The body is white to grey with two black incise lines on both ends. The tip is grey and matches the body. The base plug is walnut as is the spout stopper. Bottom: "York County" horn showing screw tip and spout stopper removed.

Leave the horn in the vise and borrow or purchase a three-quarter inch hole saw. (The inside diameter of a three-quarter inch hole saw is approximately ⅝ inches.) Making sure you are in the center of the horn, drill (saw) straight into the horn the depth of the saw, which should be ½ to ⅝ inches. (See Figure 39.)

FIGURE 39

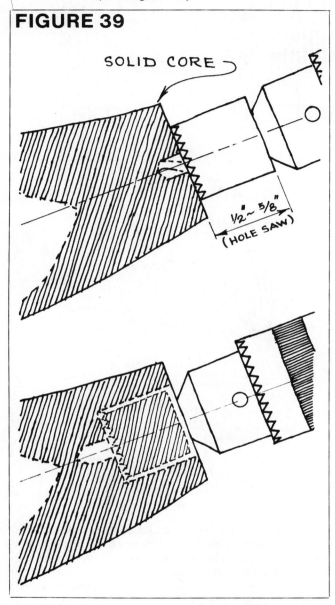

SOLID CORE

½" ~ ⅝"
(HOLE SAW)

FIGURE 40

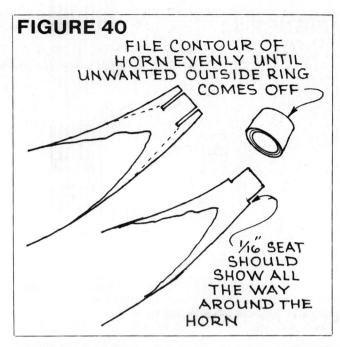

FILE CONTOUR OF HORN EVENLY UNTIL UNWANTED OUTSIDE RING COMES OFF

1/16" SEAT SHOULD SHOW ALL THE WAY AROUND THE HORN

FIGURE 41

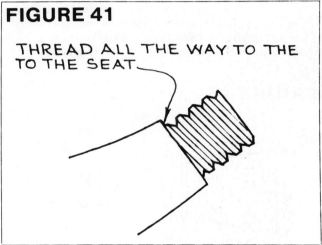

THREAD ALL THE WAY TO THE TO THE SEAT

Screw the female threaded tip on to the male thread of the horn proper. It should screw on easily until it seats against the 1/16 inch lip seat on the horn body. It may be necessary to screw the tip off and on a few times to loosen the threads.

Remove the saw and carefully file away the excess body of the horn, bringing the contour of the body down evenly all the way around until the unwanted outside ring caused by the hole saw is removed. (See Figure 40.)

Take a ⅝ inch x 11 threads to the inch die; and gently, but firmly, start the thread. *Be sure the die is started squarely.*

Work slowly, cleaning the die as you progress by backing up and going forward. Take your time, working gently and carefully until the die bottoms out against the 1/16 inch seat of the horn proper. (See Figure 41.) Turn the die over and repeat the process. By doing this, you should be able to insure thread all the way to the 1/16 inch seat.

FIGURE 42

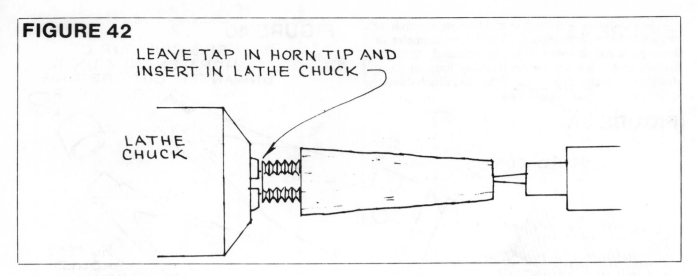

LEAVE TAP IN HORN TIP AND INSERT IN LATHE CHUCK

LATHE CHUCK

You are now ready for the more delicate work. Screw the tap back into the tip. Place the tap in a lathe chuck and carefully turn the rough screw tip down until you have a smooth, round, cone-shaped cylinder. (See Figure 42.)

Study or, if possible, draw a picture of the tip you wish to build — noting each recess, line, and ring. (See Figure 43.) Keep the picture close for reference and turn the tip to your specifications. (See Figure 44.) When the tip is finished, the next step is to drill the pouring hole.

FIGURE 44

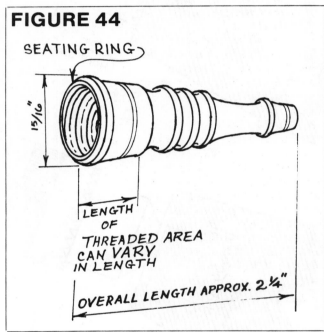

SEATING RING

15/16"

LENGTH OF THREADED AREA CAN VARY IN LENGTH

OVERALL LENGTH APPROX. 2¼"

FIGURE 43

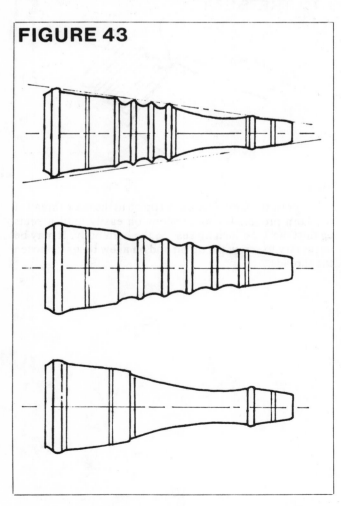

Leave the tip in the lathe chuck and place a ¼ inch drill bit in the tail stock chuck. The hole you drill should be centered perfectly, as shown in Figure 45. If you attempt to drill the hole with a drill press or hand-held drill motor, you chance drilling the hole off center. Should this occur, you have ruined the screw tip.

With the tap still in the lathe chuck, buff the screw tip lightly with triple aught steel wool to remove sharp edges and burrs. Also, while the tap is in the chuck, check the seating ring on the screw tip to be sure it is perfectly flat. It should seat squarely with the seat on the horn body.

141

FIGURE 45

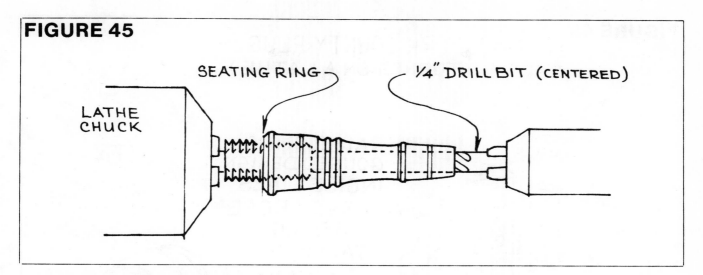

LATHE CHUCK

SEATING RING

¼" DRILL BIT (CENTERED)

The next step is to work the horn body. (Be sure to screw the die (or a nut) tightly over the threads for protection's sake.) The contour of the body should flow smoothly and evenly from the base opening to the 1/16 inch lip seat. (See Figure 46.) Take special precaution while rasping away the unwanted horn body that you do not disturb or file away the lip seat. It must be at least 1/16 inch in depth.

After the body is shaped and smoothed and the contour flows evenly, you are ready to shape the base end. Using the sizer, round the base as described earlier; then square the end. This can be accomplished with a disc sander or belt sander; or, if you are fortunate, by simply cutting off the rough end with a hack saw. However, due to the necessity of an exact fit, I suggest using a sander. (See Figure 47.)

Rasp or grind the interior of the horn until it is thin and light. Then sand the exterior until it is smooth enough to engrave. Using a small tri-corner file, file two thin lines

FIGURE 46

LINES OF HORN SHOULD FLOW WITH AN EVEN TAPER

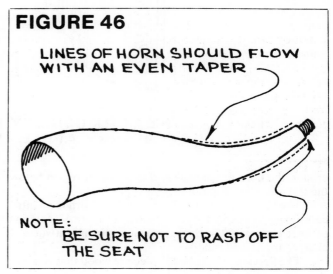

NOTE:
BE SURE NOT TO RASP OFF THE SEAT

FIGURE 47

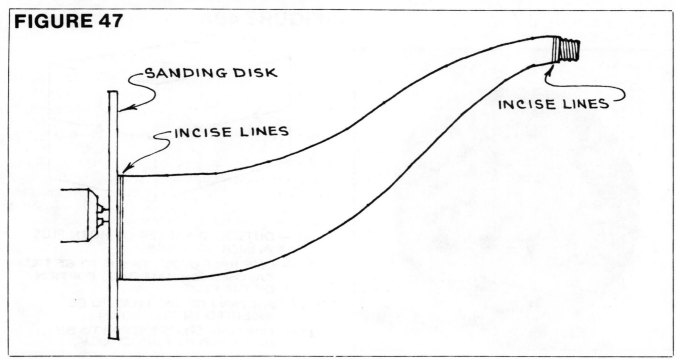

SANDING DISK

INCISE LINES

INCISE LINES

FIGURE 48

YORK COUNTY PLUG
(TURNED ON A LATHE)

RAISED RING
GOUGED DESIGN
INCISE LINES
CARVED ROPE
RAISED LIP
STAPLE

NOTE: THE YORK COUNTY PLUG IS MADE OF HARDWOOD
(CHERRY - APPLE - WALNUT - ECT.)

---

around the horn at the base end and two more just below the threads. (See Figure 47.)

The base plug of the "York County" horn is an intricate piece of workmanship, as shown in Figure 48. It is one of the few plugs that were made exclusively of fruitwood — cherry, apple, and others.

The first step is to select a piece of wood that is larger in width than the outside diameter of the horn opening and at least as long as it is wide plus the portion that you insert into the chuck. (If the horn opening is 3" in diameter — select a piece of wood at least 3¼" in diameter, 3¼" or more in length plus the portion that inserts into the chuck. See Figure 49A.)

Close up of York County plug showing the carved rope design, double incise lines and Greek or Georgian design.

FIGURE 49A

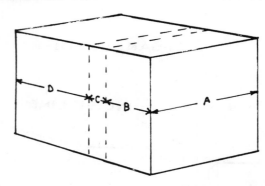

A — OUTSIDE DIAMETER OF HORN PLUS ¼ INCH OR MORE.

B — ONE HALF OF 'A'. THIS IS TO BE THE EXPOSED (OR HALF BALL) PORTION OF THE PLUG.

C — PORTION OF THE PLUG TO BE INSERTED IN THE HORN.

D — PORTION (PLUS EXTRA) TO BE INSERTED IN THE CHUCK.

The *finished* diameter of the cylindrical block should be the outside diameter of the horn plus ⅛". (If the outside of the horn opening is 3", then the diameter of the finished plug should be 3⅛". See Figure 49B.)

FIGURE 49B

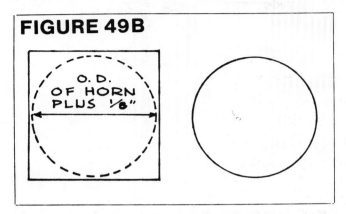

O. D.
OF HORN
PLUS ⅛"

Measure the base of the horn as described earlier and lathe turn the plug to the correct outside diameter. Glen's lathe has a four-inch jaw chuck that is ideal for turning "York County" plugs because the block of wood that will eventually become the plug is chucked up without the aid of a tail stock which would hamper the builder's progress when the front of the plug needed to be worked.

Take the diameter of the opening at the base, and divide the diameter in half. (If the diameter is three inches, half the diameter (or radius) will be 1½ inches.) Measure back on the block the proper distance and mark with a pencil. That mark represents the raised ring near the back of the plug. (See Figure 49C.)

FIGURE 49C

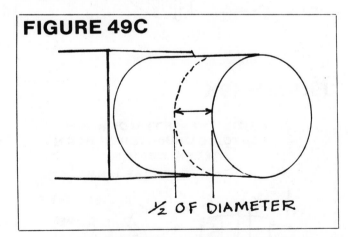

½ OF DIAMETER

Starting at the line, cut the block into a half ball, leaving the line raised approximately 1/16 inch. (See Figure 49D).

Next, to determine the position of the rope, measure back approximately ½" (or ⅓ of the distance) and mark with a pencil. (Figure 49 E.) Gently take off the surface of the incline until the rope is exposed 1/16" (Figure 49 F).

Concave the front of the ball just below the rope, being sure to leave the center of the ball raised. (See Figure 49G.)

Another raised surface can be cut on the raised center if the builder should desire. (See Figure 49G.) Face off the

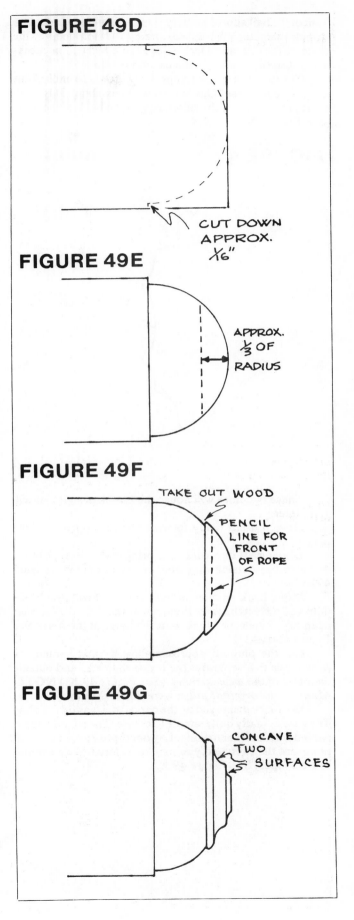

FIGURE 49D

CUT DOWN
APPROX.
1/16"

FIGURE 49E

APPROX.
⅓ OF
RADIUS

FIGURE 49F

TAKE OUT WOOD

PENCIL
LINE FOR
FRONT
OF ROPE

FIGURE 49G

CONCAVE
TWO
SURFACES

front of the ball approximately ¾ inch diameter. Concave a ½ inch diameter hole approximately ⅛ inch deep in the center of the last raised face. (See Figure 49 H.) The recess will house the staple for the carrying strap.

Cut two incise lines approximately 1/16 inch apart just above the rope. Cut two incise lines about 3/16 inch apart just in front of the raised ring at the back of the plug. (See Figure 49I.)

FIGURE 49H

TAKE OUT TIL ABOUT ⅛" DEEP

These two lines will house the Greek design that will go in later.

Now you are ready to work the rear portion of the plug.

Leaving a ⅛ inch wide ring, bring the back of the block down to the outside diameter of the horn. (See Figure 49J.)

Move back another ⅛ inch and cut away the block until you have it the same diameter as the inside of the base opening. (Taper the block to fit the taper of the horn. See Figure 49 K.)

Cut the plug off approximately ¼ inch behind the raised face that separates the inside diameter and outside diameter of the base opening. (See Figure 49 K.) **NOTE:** *Many of the original plugs were hollow inside.*

Do not be dismayed by the carved designs on the plug. They are actually quite simple to create. The rope design is carved with an Exacto knife. Lay out the lines in pencil that represent the twists so you can be assured of an evenly-spaced rope. (See Figure 49 L.)

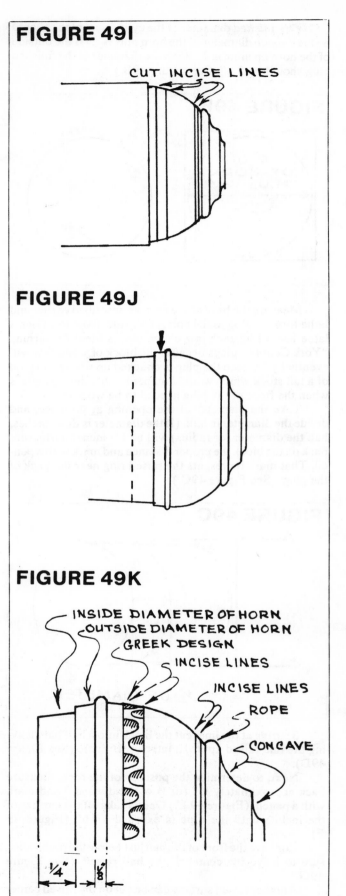

FIGURE 49I

CUT INCISE LINES

FIGURE 49J

FIGURE 49K

INSIDE DIAMETER OF HORN
OUTSIDE DIAMETER OF HORN
GREEK DESIGN
INCISE LINES
INCISE LINES
ROPE
CONCAVE

¼"   ⅛"

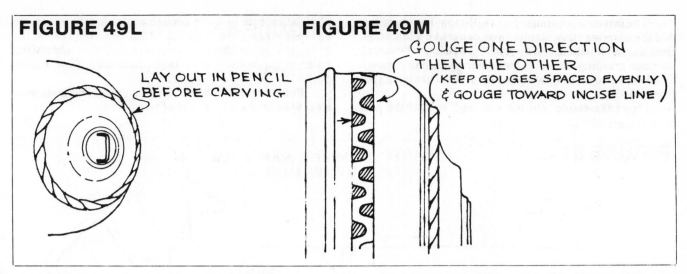

FIGURE 49L
LAY OUT IN PENCIL BEFORE CARVING

FIGURE 49M
GOUGE ONE DIRECTION THEN THE OTHER
(KEEP GOUGES SPACED EVENLY & GOUGE TOWARD INCISE LINE)

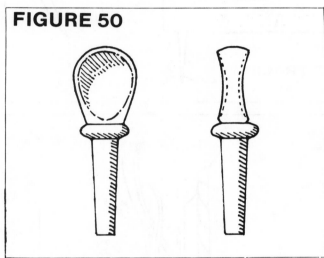

FIGURE 50

Carve the pencil line away, leaving a small valley with a slightly deeper groove at each side. The finished product will be worth the effort.

The Greek, or Georgian, design near the back of the plug is done with a small U-shaped gouge. An inexpensive wood-carving kit with several interchangeable blades will work well. Gouging out the design is simple and fast. Cut toward the incise lines from one direction, then the other, being sure to keep the cuts evenly spaced. (See Figure 49 M.) When the carving is finished, buff the entire plug with steel wool to remove any burrs or sharp edges.

Fit the plug into the base, making sure that the horn and plug fit flush all the way around. Then peg the horn as described earlier.

Many of the original spout plugs (stoppers) were the tuning-key style. Glen made one for me in about ten minutes, using his lathe to turn the plug and a Dremel tool to disk out the sides. (See Figure 50.)

The last step in completing the "Screw Tip" horn is to add the carrying strap staples. You can make a fine staple from a small finishing nail by grinding a point on both ends and then grasping the nail in the center with a pair of pliers. Bend the nail over the jaw of the pliers with a hammer. (See Figure 51.)

Drive the staple into the recessed area in the base plug, being sure to leave enough protruding to attach the carrying strap. (See Figure 52.) Move to the rear of the body just below the screw tip and drill two undersized holes in the body. Set a staple there also. (See Figure 53.)

Polish the entire horn, screw tip, plug, and body with steel wool and apply a coat of paste wax.

FIGURE 51

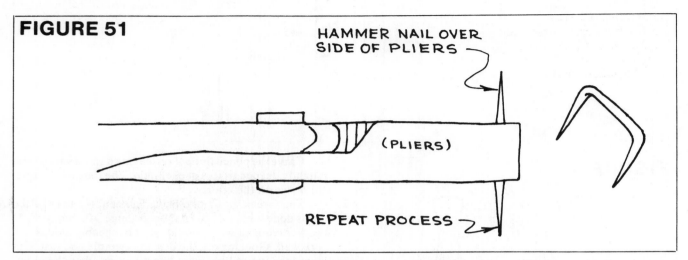

HAMMER NAIL OVER SIDE OF PLIERS

(PLIERS)

REPEAT PROCESS

FIGURE 52

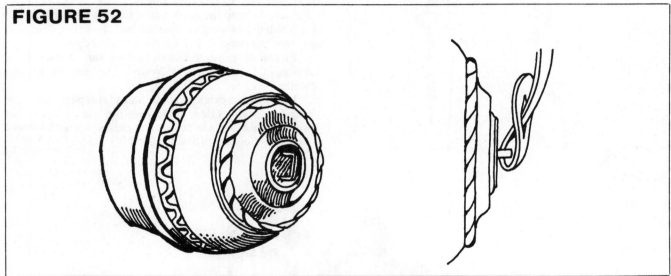

FIGURE 53

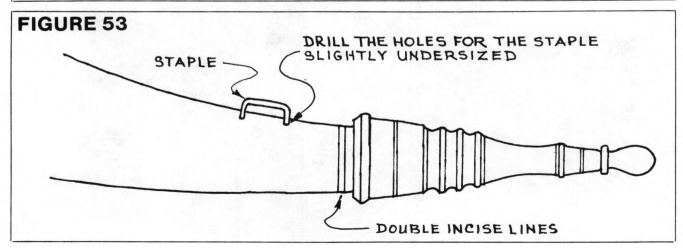

STAPLE

DRILL THE HOLES FOR THE STAPLE SLIGHTLY UNDERSIZED

DOUBLE INCISE LINES

THE RUM HORN

This fine example of a rum horn was built by David Wright. He used a portion of a discarded horn that was not up to the standards we require for a powder horn. (I believe the horn was straight, without much curve at all.)

The rum horn is built exactly like a powder horn except that both ends are plugged. A hole is drilled in the top of the horn for an air vent and a hole is drilled in the plug for a drain. Both holes are sealed with wooden plugs that are removable.

The horn can be engraved , as this beautiful specimen is, or they can be left plain. They make an authentic addition to a buckskinner's accoutrements.

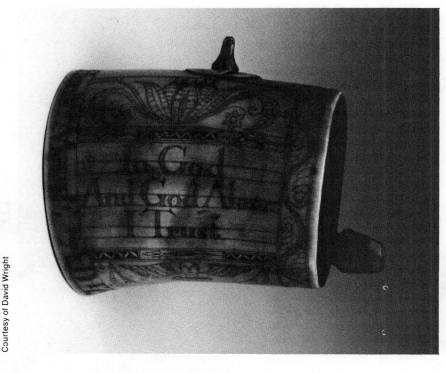

Courtesy of David Wright

Rum horn of about one pint capacity. A fairly straight horn was utilized and plugged at both ends with pine. The two spouts allow one to be an air vent while pouring from the other. Rum horns were popular during the war years.

CONCLUSION

I sincerely hope these pages will be of some assistance to those of you who wish to try the art of horn building. I have tried, I hope successfully, to cover each individual step with line drawings, explanations, and photographs.

The procedures which I have set down in this chapter are very possibly not the easiest, nor in many instances the best, way to build a horn — but it is the only way I know. I appreciate the opportunity to pass this knowledge along to you.

Firemaking

by Warren "Hawk" Boughton

WOODCRAFT AND SURVIVAL SKILLS have been principal interests of Hawk Boughton's since childhood. He has taken particular pains to learn the uses of trees and plants of our eastern and western states. Other consuming interests include the history and life styles of the frontiersmen, mountain men, and Indians. With this background, Boughton initiated and managed the semi-annual survival classes which, for six years, operated out of the Tennessee Valley Authority's facility at Golden Pond, Kentucky, in Land-Between-the-Lakes.

As part of the Illinois Sesquicentennial celebration in 1968, Hawk organized a group of 23 buckskinners to duplicate, as faithfully as possible the overland march made by George Rogers Clark and 125 men during the Revolutionary War to secure the Illinois country by capturing Fort Kaskaskia on the Mississippi River. Leaving Fort Massac on the Ohio River, near present day Metropolis, Illinois, they made the 125 mile march to Fort Kaskaskia in the same time and on the same days of the month that Clark and his frontiersmen performed the original feat in 1778.

Boughton has been a member of the American Mountain Men since March, 1972, the year this association was formed. From 1974 to 1980 he served as the Eastern Territory Segundo in charge of the eastern section of the A.M.M. During this time, Hawk was active in building a strong organization in the eastern states and in promoting muzzle loader shooting, hunting, canoeing, hiking, and camping. In 1983, he was elected to the office of El Capitan of the A.M.M.

I was told that my great-grandfather Orris Horatio Boughton performed such homely duties as holding me on his lap and sometimes, when his arthritis wasn't hurting too much, giving me a "horseback" ride on his knee. As you may already have guessed, this occurred when my saddle was the three-cornered cotton type cinched at the waist with safety pins. At one year of age I had not yet developed a bent for early American history and mountain man doin's, and Orris Horatio died the year after I was born so I didn't get to ask him the many things I wish I could have. He was an outdoorsman in the truest sense of the word and many great stories were passed down in the family about his boyhood on the site of the Seneca Indian village of Gannagaro on what came to be known as Boughton Hill near the town of Victor in western New York. But the tales I liked best were those of his western travels with his brothers during the Gold Rush of '49.

Of the many questions great-grandpa could have answered, one concerns the various ways of making fire without matches. We know that matches did not become commonplace until the last half of the nineteenth century. Have you ever felt a twinge of desire to know the ways used a hundred and fifty years ago for producing fire? Today it is too late to ask our distant ancestors, but fortunately a few of them — a very few indeed — left written records that detail fire making techniques.

For many years now I have had nothing to do with matches and lighters in the woods, preferring instead, the primitive methods of making fire. This shunning of modern fire starting methods has not been without its benefits. It has caused me to take a greater interest in learning alternative materials and techniques which, in turn, has led me to research first-hand accounts and personal narratives of

PHOTO BY KATHRYN GOBLE

"Buckskin" Russ Sidebottom blows a spark into a fire. If you hold the spark and tinder at or below face level, you will probably inhale smoke and get it in your eyes.

A friction-top can used for making charred cloth. The small hole in the top allows the gases formed by the process to escape. When smoke quits coming out of the hole, it is done. Let the can cool before opening it or the cloth may catch fire.

the early explorers, frontiersmen, and trappers to discover, whenever possible, their methods of fire starting. I believe that these methods, together with a few modest discoveries — or re-discoveries — that I have made, are worthy of recording here where they can be read and put to use by today's mountain men and other like-minded travellers in the wilderness. Try as you may, you will not find a more comprehensive collection of fire making techniques in any other publication.

Finding reliable documentation of various fire making methods proved a difficult and time consuming task, for if we accept observations without testing them we tend to perpetuate misconceptions that long ago left the realm of folklore and are downright fallacies. Ken Carsten, head of the Archaeology Department of Kentucky's Murray State University, assisted me in locating reliable reference material. Even here, such material was scanty. On one of my forays into the ivy clad halls he said, "You know, I am amazed at the lack of reliable documentation of primitive fire making methods in archaeological literature." And that is true. To be sure, you will find references to fire mak-

151

ing techniques but you will not find specifics as to the physical dimensions of the implements, nor reliable information on the species of wood used in their construction.

But why should anyone want to know these things? — for various reasons: maybe you like to actually get the feel of history; or you may wonder whether or not you can do some of the things your ancestors did; or you may be a collector of esoteric knowledge. In all likelihood, however, you have in mind the more practical aspect of survival. Sometime, somewhere, a combination of circumstances may arise when an alternate method of making a fire could save your life and possibly the lives of others. At the very least, you may be spared an uncomfortable night in the woods.

One of the most effective ways to catch sparks struck from flint and steel involves the use of charred organic material. Today, almost without exception, the material used is cotton cloth but 200 years ago, linen, a product of flax, was the preeminent material used both for gun patches and for making charred cloth — it was less expensive and more suitable for both jobs than cotton. The fringes of civilization were, of necessity, forced to discover and rely upon other materials for fire starting.

In early literature no distinction is made between charred cloth and other types of tinder. We will hold to that same principle which was defined in the first edition of Noah Webster's dictionary published in 1806, the same year Captains Lewis and Clark and their "company of adventurers" returned from the far west. The complete definition given in this first American dictionary is: "Tin'der, n. burnt linen, what easily catches fire."[1] By definition then, the term "tinder" may be properly applied not only to charred cloth, but to many other combustibles such as dry grass, shredded bark, cattail down, fungus, etc., which may or may not catch and hold a spark struck from flint and steel.

In the first *Book of Buckskinning* I wrote a detailed description of how to make good charred cloth, but for those who haven't read it, the method very briefly stated is this: Use a tin can of one - or two-pound capacity with a pressure-type lid; punch a 1/16" hole in the lid and another in the bottom of the can. Use 100-percent pure cotton cloth; synthetics will not work. Cut the cloth into 4"x6" pieces and drop them into the can. Press on the lid. Twist an iron wire around the body of the can leaving a double three-foot length of wire for use as a handle. Place the can in a campfire. Smoke will start to blow from the holes. Using the wire extension, frequently change position of the can on the fire so the cloth will burn evenly. Continue changing positions of the can until little or no smoke is evident. Remove the can from the fire and allow it to cool before taking off the lid. If the cloth is not totally dark black throughout its mass, return it to the fire for more heating. Caution: Do not over-burn the cloth or it will disintegrate when handled.

"Hawk" talks about making charred cloth during his fire making demonstration at the 1983 Mid-America Rendezvous.

Satisfactory substitutes for charred cloth are so few in number as to be almost nonexistent. The natural materials listed as tinder in most wilderness survival books will not really do the job they receive credit for doing. While not wishing to dissuade anyone from searching for natural tinders, I caution you to avoid wasting precious time in an emergency trying to catch sparks in materials such as mice and bird nests, the hair-like fibers of Florida's cabbage palm, decayed punky wood, the powder left by wood boring insects, dead Spanish moss, the down of thistle, milkweed, cattail, and cottonwood, the dry flower heads and leaves of goldenrod, pulverized birch and cedar bark, the mature heads of cottongrass and feathergrass, the pith from elderberry and poke plants, powdered evergreen needles, and dry moss. They won't work. All of these things, when bone-dry, make excellent "small" kindling, but to lead readers to believe that they are capable of catching and holding a spark struck from flint and steel is merely to continue a dangerous myth.

No one disputes the fact that charred linen and cotton cloth makes the most convenient spark catcher we can carry. We can pack enough charred cloth in a 4" x 3" x ½" tin box to light dozens of fires, pipes, and cigars. To set it glowing we don't have to use up powder and caps or wear out gun flints. But there must have been a natural material growing almost everywhere that mountain men and pioneers used when they ran out of charred cloth. What was it? Nowhere did they leave fainter tracks than when they approached this subject. Charles Goodnight left the only documented trace I could find when he said, "If we had none of these cloth materials, we would char a soft cottonwood root, which would catch like punk, from which we would light our kindling rag, cedar bark, rotten wood or grass."[2] I have tried punk wood in its natural state from many species of trees and have yet to find any that would catch and hold a spark. If, however, the punk wood is first charred, it holds a spark very well. From this I have to conclude that the punk so often mentioned in early literature was charred before it was used in fire starting. The kind of wood used is not as critical as is the condition of the wood used. That is, most species of wood make good charring material if they are thoroughly decayed and porous and weigh only a fraction of what they did as solid dead timber.

Punk wood can be charred in a tin can the same way cotton or linen cloth is charred. In camp, punk wood is charred without a can by burning it in the campfire. After it

Chief Charles Towne, a Chippewa Indian of the Turtle Clan, collects the hair-like fibers from a cabbage palm tree in Florida. These fibers make great tinder but will not catch and hold a spark from flint and steel.

is well burned and is totally black, remove it from the fire and bury it in warm ashes. Leave it covered until all its fire has been completely smothered; this may require as long as ten minutes. You will find that a piece of well charred punk catches and holds sparks struck from flint and steel every bit as well as good charred cloth. Once set glowing, it can only be extinguished with water — a moistened fingertip will do — but it may take several applications before it is completely quenched.

Another myth that finds its way into print from time to time is that in the absence of a steel fire striker all one need do is strike two pieces of flint or chert together to obtain the same hot sparks one gets when one of these is struck with carbon steel. A single trial will convince you that this is not so; the sparks struck from two pieces of flint or chert are too weak to ignite even the most carefully prepared charred cloth. Iron pyrite, however, is another matter. An archaeological dig in a cave occupied by Cro-Magnon people 10,000 years ago in Belgium turned up a grooved fist-sized chunk of pyrite that was determined to be a fire striker. On this continent, the journals of early 18th century explorers in Canada further document the fact that some primitive peoples had discovered the fire making capabilities of flint and pyrite.[3] Lacking the cotton and linen material we use for making charred cloth, primitive people could have gotten similar results with other types of charred vegetable matter obtained from a campfire or from a burned-over area of forest or grassland.

Natural organic material that will catch and hold sparks can sometimes be found in the wild and sometimes it can't. This is made clear by the story of the Sammons brothers.[4] The Sammons family farmed land in the Mohawk River valley of New York near the large estate of Sir William Johnson, the British appointed colonial superintendent of Indian affairs. Sir William died in 1774 at the outbreak of troubles just prior to the Revolutionary War and his son, Sir John Johnson, inherited his father's estate, which included not only vast land holdings, but slaves, tenant farmers, the family home on the Mohawk River named Johnson Hall, and all its furnishings. At the outbreak of war, Sir John Johnson, who had declared himself loyal to the British crown, buried the family silver in the basement of the home and fled to Canada.

In May 1780, Sir John at the head of several hundred soldiers, Tories and Indians, slipped through the woods from Lake Champlain and suddenly appeared in the neighborhood of Johnson Hall. The main object of this expedition was to take possession of the estate and recover his silver plate. The inhabitants of the area were so taken by surprise that he was able to dig up the silver and spend several hours in his old home. Then, to avoid the local militia, he parceled out his booty to the care of twenty or more of his former slaves, rounded up the prisoners who had fallen into his hands, and set out for the canoes he had cached at the lower end of Lake Champlain.

Among the prisoners were Jacob and Frederick Sammons who in a few days were brought to Fort Chambly on the Richelieu River, a water route connecting Lake Champlain with the St. Lawrence River. The brothers immediately started planning their escape. One day they made a break for freedom and dashed off barefoot through the woods hotly pursued by British soldiers. Jacob fell into a ditch and sprained his ankle. At his insistence, Frederick

left his brother and continued his flight toward the friendly New York settlements. After Jacob heard the soldiers returning to the fort he rested his swollen ankle a short time then, barefoot and without food and with no equipment except a pocket knife, he continued his journey as best he could.

In the course of the next few days, his only food consisted of the inner bark of birch trees and twigs, small fish caught by hand in a creek, and a black duck caught on her nest. (He could not force himself to eat the eggs when he saw that they were almost ready to hatch.) All the food he found, of course, was eaten raw because he was unable to make a fire.

On the tenth day of his escape attempt he was bitten in the calf by a rattlesnake. After incising the wound with his knife and squeezing out as much of the venom as he could, he skinned the reptile and ate its heart and body fat. He decided to remain for several days in the area where he had been bitten in order to recover his strength and recuperate from the effects of the snakebite. While scouting around nearby for food, he came upon some dry fungus on a maple tree and with this he was enabled to catch a spark and make a fire. We already know that a pocket knife was his only equipment on this trip so we must assume that he used it for striking sparks. It would have been a simple task to find a piece of stone that would have enabled him to strike sparks from either the carbon steel blade or the back of his knife. This, of course, he could not have done had his knife been made of non-ferrous metal such as many that are made today of nickel and chromium alloys. Only a steel of fairly high carbon content will work properly as a fire striker.

The fire enabled him to cook the remaining snake meat but he could not continue his journey before wrapping his coat around one of his cut and bruised feet and tieing his hat around the other. Two days later he dragged himself up to the door of a house of friendly settlers and a few days after that he travelled on to Schenectady where he had a joyful reunion with his family. As the Sammons home had been destroyed in the attack that led to the brothers' capture they decided to move to another part of the area.

Turning our attention to Frederick Sammons we see that he did not fare as well as Jacob. After leaving his brother in hiding with a sprained ankle, Frederick struck out for home. He, like Jacob, appears to have been barefoot, but unlike his brother he carried with him his box of "fireworks," as the settlers in their area called fire making equipment. For the first seven days all went well. On one occasion he killed a farmer' steer and took a hind quarter. On another he was able to catch and kill a fawn. By his calculations, in another day or two of travel he should reach the first of the friendly settlements. The eighth morning, however, began with a severe attack of pleuresy, and further aggravating his condition, was a downpour of rain that continued for three days, during which he lay in pain on the ground, wet, cold, without food, fire, or shelter. On the fourth day when he tried to eat some of the steer meat he carried he found that it had spoiled and was inedible. Intense thirst drove him to drink from a small stagnant pond of water and here he caught a few frogs which he ate raw because he could no longer make a fire. In all probability he was either out of tinder, or what he carried had become wet in the drenching rains of the past three days.

Lying sick and desperate on a bluff overlooking the eastern shore of Lake Champlain, Frederick decided to hoist his hat on a pole where it would be seen by a passing vessel, be it friend or foe. His signal was seen and he was carried on board a boat senseless and speechless only to awake to find himself once again on his way to prison in Canada.

This time, Frederick was interred with other prisoners of war in a camp on an island surrounded by rapids of the St. Lawrence River. It ws two years before he and another prisoner named MacMullen attempted escape by leaping into the raging rapids surrounding the prison and swimming downstream until they were safely out of gunshot range. Their entire equipment on this trip consisted of one pocket knife each, and one tinder box each, without charred tinder. Their first concern was to provide themselves with a short stout club which could be used for a defensive weapon and for hunting.

For twelve days they struggled southward through the wild Adirondack region east of Lake Champlain. They were hot during the day, cold and sometimes wet at night, plagued by mosquitoes and gnats, and always hungry. A haunting fear was that they would be recaptured by a British patrol, or worse, by an Indian war party. Without trousers or shoes, which they had apparently abandoned in order to swim the streams and rapids they encountered, the pair finally reached the town of Schenectady. United at last with his family, Frederick, bearded and gaunt, with cut and swollen feet and wearing the remnants of his tattered clothing, was not recognized by former friends; one lady who approached to grasp his hand was reported to have fainted dead away.

This true story of events that occurred a little over 200 years ago is recounted here to stress how vital to the wilderness traveller is the capability of making fire. It will also serve to warn those who are not familiar with the problems involved that only in rare cases can they expect to have the benefits of fire unless they have basic fire making materials, including dry spark-catching tinder, with them. Both of the Sammons brothers were experienced woodsmen who had been raised on the border during troubled times. Yet, for want of fire, Frederick was recaptured on his first escape attempt, and if Jacob had not been fortunate in finding a dry spark-catching fungus on the trunk of a maple tree he would have, in all probability, died before reaching the friendly settlements.

It was February and we were having our annual late winter rendezvous in the Daniel Boone National Forest of eastern Kentucky. There were, perhaps, forty of us there; I remember it well. The frozen ground was covered with snow and it lay heavily in the branches of pine trees surrounding our camp. On the hot coals of the fire a coffee pot hummed contentedly to itself as its temperature neared the boiling point. The conversation between a young pilgrim and myself had slipped easily from one subject to another when finally we touched on fires and fire making.

"If you were a hundred miles from nowhere, in the dead of winter, and you had nothing but your primitive gear with you, how would you make a fire?" I asked the pilgrim.

"With my flint and steel," he replied.

"Show me how you'd do it."

"Sure," he said, and proceeded to make a fire in the usual manner. Taking a handful of dry cedar bark from a pouch on his belt he arranged it bird nest fashion on the ground. In the center of the tinder he placed a piece of charred cloth and holding his flint a few inches above the black cloth, struck it several glancing blows with his fire steel. Two or three sparks glowed on the cloth. On hands and knees he knelt in the snow and blew into the cloth and bark until it burst into flame.

"That was good," I said, glancing down at the wet knees of the pilgrim's buckskins, "but you could have held everything in your hands and avoided kneeling in the snow. If you were lighting your pipe or cigar I'm sure you wouldn't do it that way. You would hold the flint in your hand, wrap charred cloth around it and strike one of its sharp edges through the cloth."

"By the way," I said as a sudden thought struck me, "how would you start a fire if you couldn't use charred cloth? Say, for example, you have used all of it; or it got wet in a rainstorm, or while you were crossing a stream. What would you do then?"

"I don't know," the young man replied. "Are there other ways?"

Obviously, the pilgrim had a lot to learn. Grandpa would have told him, "There's more than one way to skin a cat," and let it go at that, but my ego cropped out and I showed him two or three different ways he could make a fire without using charred cloth for tinder. In the following pages I will explain alternative methods of fire starting. Some of them you will learn involves the use of gunpowder with, and without, a firearm. I feel this is warranted here because the mountain man of today usually has black powder near at hand, just as did the frontiersman and mountain man of yesterday. Finally, no comprehensive study of primitive fire making methods would be complete without a description of the ancient friction method. "Difficult?" you ask. Yes, but if you can start a fire with just the materials picked up in the forest or desert, you need never fear being for long without a fire. To become proficient you must actually practice and use these various methods. A serious stumbling block for most persons trying to make a fire when their survival is at stake is that they have never done it before and they are desperately trying to remember exactly what to do. The thing to do now, of course, is to practice at home every method you know so if you are faced with an emergency you will know which one offers the best chance of success considering the materials available.

Before starting on their long journey west the Lewis and Clark party camped on the eastern bank of the Mississippi River near the mouth of the Dubois River in the present state of Illinois. While awaiting the arrival of spring and the breakup of ice in the river they attempted to train their men and to inculcate in them the principles of military discipline and, at the same time, to instill in everyone concerned the importance of their mission. Here, too, they waterproofed and packed their stores and equipment. Black powder was put in specially designed lead cannisters then stoppered and sealed with wax. Each flask contained enough powder to fire the lead containing it. Much of the goods was placed in boxes lined with oiled linen cloth and in bags manufactured by a contractor of oiled "Russia Sheeting". Among the items that required no waterproofing for the river voyage but which were made ready at the Dubois River camp were one 70-pound box of candles, one 50-pound box of candles, and one bag containing eight pounds of candlewick.[5] This last item could be used by the party in making candles of tallow cut from the carcasses of large game animals they would encounter farther west.

A candle may sometime prove to be one of the most useful items in your pack, and not necessarily because of the light it can provide. Under adverse weather conditions a lighted candle, even a one-inch stub, will sustain heat long enough to ignite small kindling when it is damp and would ordinarily be difficult to light. To illustrate the point, suppose the woods are soggy with rain or fresh snow and you have no dry kindling — no dry grass, or shredded cedar bark, or leaves, nothing. But you do have flint, steel, and charred cloth tinder in your fireworks kit. Looks like you may as well settle in for a long cheerless night because charred cloth, by itself, will not blaze and you want a flame to light the damp twigs. Then you remember the candle in your pack! Defeated? Not by a long shot! You can resort to a little trick I learned from my old friend John Cramer at a mountain man rendezvous in the Uncompaghre country of southwestern Colorado. Did I call John "old?" Actually

Chaz Rauch demonstrates lighting a candle with charred cloth. A candle is an important asset when you're in the wilderness.

156

he is considerably younger than me. No offense meant. After all, coon hunters call their favorite hounds "old" using such terms as "ole' Jack," or "ole' Sam," regardless of how old their dogs actually are, so old John won't mind.

No matter. Right now the problem is to light the candle and you have nothing that will burn except charred cloth. Here's how to do it: Place the candle within easy reach, then select a piece of charred cloth that is about 3" long and 2" wide. Roll it end to end to obtain a tight roll 2 inches long and about the diameter of a lead pencil. Hold the flint and the roll of charred cloth in the fingers of your left hand with the upper end of the roll positioned next to a sharp edge of the flint. With the fire steel in your right hand, strike sparks to cause them to fall onto the end of the roll of charred cloth. When they catch and ignite the cloth, drop the flint and steel, pick up the candle and place the roll alongside it. Blow hard into the smoldering end of the cloth. The entire end of the cloth roll will immediately glow orange-red and reach the combustion point of cotton but it cannot burst into flame because all its burnable gasses have been driven off during the charring process. It will, however, melt some of the wax on the side of the candle, absorb some of it, and after a few seconds of continuous blowing, burst into flame. Using the blazing roll of charred cloth, you can now light the candle and, with it, the kindling.

Often during the candle lighting process, some of the charred cotton adheres to melted wax of the candle. Unless you need an extremely large flame and a lot of heat, it is best to remove this adhering cloth. If you don't, your candle may be consumed within a few minutes.

Anyone who spends much time in the outdoors learns to accept rainy weather and wet woods as part of the natural order of things. But it is then, when you have no dry kindling, that a simple piece of rope becomes a handy thing to have. I recall a late afternoon in autumn when I got to a rendezvous in Missouri. Although it was past time to cook supper, only one or two fires were to be seen among the twenty-odd lean-tos occupying high ground at the edge of the forest. Rains that had continued off and on for the better part of four days and stopped only that morning had turned what should have been bone-dry woods into sodden masses of greenery. I knew that getting a fire going under these conditions might be difficult but I walked into the woods looking for the best materials available. From the low branches of an oak tree I broke off a double handful of dead twigs, mostly match stick sizes up to those of a quarter-inch in diameter. They were still somewhat damp but because they were small in diameter they came closer to being dry than the larger limbs and it wouldn't take much heat to make them burn. Going a few yards farther I spied a large black oak tree lying horizontally and about two-feet off the ground where it had fallen in its last battle with the wind. Wood on the underside of a dead tree is always comparatively dry if it is not lying directly on the ground. With my tomahawk it was the work of only a few minutes before I had an armload of wood split from the tree and I returned with it to camp.

Now for the tricky business of getting this damp stuff to burn. Although I usually carry dry grass or cedar bark in my fire kit I had neglected to bring any on this trip and dry tinder would be hard to find in these woods where it was getting noticeably darker by the minute. Remembering a method I had used before, I placed the smaller diameter sticks in the familiar cone shape of a tepee about five-inches high. I then cut five inches off the end of one of my leanto ropes and carefully unwound the twisted fibers. After laying out my flint and steel I compressed the now bushy rope end as tightly as possible and wrapped it with a two-inch strip of charred cloth. Taking up the flint, I placed the end of the cloth-covered rope against one of its sharp edges and held both the flint and the rope in position with the fingers of my left hand. With the fire steel in my right hand I struck the flint one or two glancing blows and a spark caught and glowed in the blackened cloth at the end of the rope. By blowing through the glowing cloth the frayed end of the rope soon ignited and burst into a hot flame. This was quickly placed under the small sticks and they readily caught fire.

After the small kindling had burned a few minutes I started laying on progressively larger pieces of wood and while it burned to a bed of hot coals I had enough time to cut three five-foot long saplings. Arranging these as a tripod over the fire I tied them with rope well above the heat and from the rope hung a forked stick in such manner that my small cooking pot was suspended directly over the fire. Supper was assured and after that a bright fire would welcome brothers to sit and smoke and yarn until bedtime.

Seldom did the pioneer or the mountain man waste quill, ink, and paper by writing a detailed description of fire making. Why should he? No reader of the time would be interested in an account of a chore that he either did, or saw done, every day. We may tie our shoes every day, but where would you go to find an account of how to do it? Morris Birkbeck was an exception. A wealthy English landowner and gentleman farmer, he had servants who performed the menial chore of fire lighting, but in 1817, in the backwoods of the United States, Morris Birkbeck used his skill to light a fire which, because of the circumstances, he later deemed noteworthy.

Morris Birkbeck emigrated to the United States in 1817, the same year the Seminole Indians stormed out of the swamps in Spanish East Florida and invaded Georgia. Birkbeck was searching for cheap farm land. Landing in Norfolk, Virginia, he and his party, which included women, children, servants and occasionally a guide or hunter, made their way by horseback, in carriages, and afoot, from Norfolk to the vicinity of Princeton in Gibson County, Indiana. (Indiana had been admitted to the Union the previous year.) Here in the southern end of the state, in the area just north of the Ohio River and east of the Wabash River, he found conditions to his liking and bought 1,500 acres of good black land.

"Hawk" prepares to start a fire with cloth and touch-paper. The touch-paper is placed in the middle of the cloth and powder is sprinkled over both before sparks are stuck on it with flint and steel.

In a book written by Birkbeck to encourage emigration to this country, he made two revealing statements about fire starting.[6] During their journey, Birkbeck and his party usually stayed at taverns and inns along the way. One dark and rainy night, however, he and a lady and a servant boy "in consequence of accidental detention" were "benighted" and forced for the first time on the trip to camp out. Because the tinder and combustible fire making materials were in the baggage of the party ahead, they were forced to make do with his flint and steel, and powder from a flask he carried in a saddle bag. As no mention is made of a firearm, I assume it also was with the division ahead.

Birkbeck first made what he called "touch-paper" by moistening a piece of paper and rubbing gunpowder into it. He then placed the touch-paper on an old cambric handkerchief (cambric may be made of either cotton or linen, both of which are readily combustible). On this he scattered gunpowder "copiously" as he termed it. Sparks struck with the flint and steel ignited the powder and this

set fire to the handkerchief and touch-paper. A collection of kindling and dry wood from the forest enabled the travelers to make a "noble" fire for the night.

If you find it necessary to resort to this method of fire starting, cut a piece of paper about three inches square. Moisten it and rub gunpowder into both sides until they are uniformly dark black. Allow the paper to dry for a few minutes. Cut an eight-inch square piece of cotton cloth; dress shirt material, undershirt material, calico, or cotton flannel is satisfactory provided it has no synthetics in it. Position the prepared piece of touch-paper in the center of the cloth. Sprinkle 40 grains of black powder as evenly as possible onto both the paper and the cloth. Strike the flint with your steel using a horizontal slashing motion so you are simultaneously moving both hands from above the cloth and paper to prevent scorching your fingers when the powder flashes. (Powder does not flash vertically more than about one-inch if it is not heavily concentrated.) Ignition of the powder causes the cloth to ignite and smolder and the paper to burst into flame.

Birkbeck advised his English readers, and I cannot fault him, that anyone travelling alone in the backwoods of America, as would a hunter, should always carry a tomahawk, a good blanket, a half-pint of liquor, a few biscuits, and "the means for lighting a fire." He further recommended that the woodsman carry tinder and made the comment that tow rubbed with gunpowder is good tinder. This last bit of advice regarding tinder I found would not work, that is, the tinder would not ignite directly from a spark, even when the gunpowder was further pulverized with a hammer and then pounded into the tow. It is possible, however, to make a fire almost every time by proceeding as follows: Prepare a small handful of good flammable tinder such as dry bark, grass, or shredded leaves. Cover the thumb and fingers of your left hand with thin flexible leather. A leather glove or a piece of scrap leather is satisfactory. Position the flint, sharp edge out, on top of the tinder you have prepared and compress both the flint and the tinder with the protected thumb and fingers of your left hand. Pour 15 grains of powder onto the tinder directly below the sharp edge of the flint. Holding this combination out away from your face, strike the flint with the steel in your right hand. Follow through after each stroke so your right hand will be well out of the way when the powder ignites.

Whenever you use this method to start a fire, always observe these four precautions:

1. Pour only a small amount of powder on top of the tinder — never more than 15 grains. Use a graduated powder measure if you have one. (By kitchen measure, 15 grains is slightly less than one-half teaspoonful.)
2. Always replace the stopper in the powderhorn and place it safely to one side.
3. Use a piece of thin flexible leather to protect the fingers of the hand holding the flint, tinder, and powder.
4. To prevent scorching the fingers of the hand holding the fire steel, move it out of the way each time you strike the flint.

This is a good easy way to start a fire without charred cloth but if you find that the shock and vibration caused by striking steel on flint scatters the powder so thoroughly that it will not ignite, shake the remaining powder from the tinder, pour another charge of powder onto it and try again. You may discover that you get better results by placing the tinder and powder on the ground, but always protect the hand holding the flint with a piece of leather.

The English adventurer and author, George Frederick Ruxton, is undoubtedly the most beloved and respected writer of the Fur Trade era. He was admired and respected in his own time by the mountain men with whom he came in contact, and through his writing, which is still available, he is a favorite of today's mountain men.

Ruxton's books provide us with a first-hand verbal portraiture of how they talked. He knew all the quaint expressions and special terms used by the trappers that set them apart from the flatland pilgrims more certainly than had they carried membership cards proclaiming, "I am a mountain man."

George Frederick Ruxton was unique in another re-

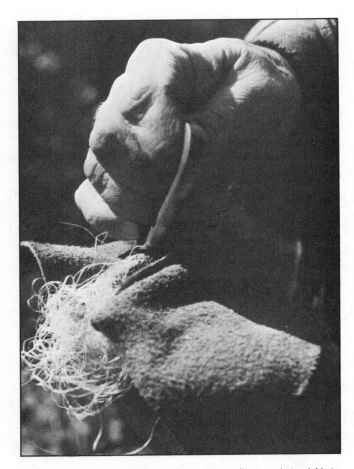

Starting fire with gun powder, frayed rope, flint, and steel. Note the leather piece protecting hand. After striking sparks and setting off the powder, the tinder should be smoldering (bottom photo). It's time to blow the spark into a flame.

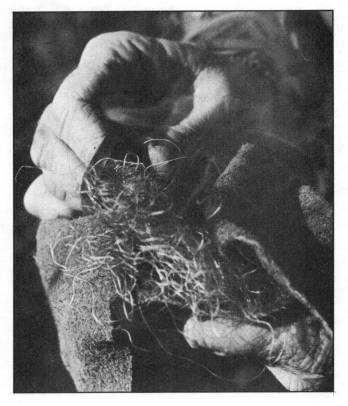

spect. Unlike most other writers of his time, he carefully recorded how the beaver trappers did many of their ordinary day-to-day tasks, such as setting traps, making camp, butchering buffalo, cooking, mule packing, etc. He made the following statement concerning how they made fires: "Fire-making is a simple process with the mountaineers. Their bullet-pouches always contain a flint, and steel, and sundry pieces of 'punk' (a pithy substance found in dead pine-trees), or tinder; and pulling a handful of dry grass, which they screw into a nest, they place the lighted punk in this, and, closing the grass over it, wave it in the air, when it soon ignites, and readily kindles the dry sticks forming the foundation of the fire."[7]

We cannot doubt the veracity of Ruxton's statement. He clearly wants us to understand that he and the trappers he observed struck sparks into tinder composed of punk obtained from dead pine trees. John Lawson writing of Indians in the wilderness of Carolina says punk ". . . is a sort of soft, corky substance, generally of a cinnamon colour, and grows in the concave part of an oak, hickory, and several other woods, being dug out with an ax and always kept by the Indians, instead of tinder or touchwood, both of which it exceeds."[8]

Dumont de Montigny, an early visitor among the Indians of Louisiana, furnishes us with an additional note relative to tinder: "Mulberries, as I have remarked, are very common in this province, and along the trunks of the largest specimens knobs or swellings form. It is from these swellings that the savages obtain a soft, dry, and light wood, which takes fire like true touch-wood, and it is this which is called tinder."[9]

Should you find yourself in a situation where a fire is absolutely necessary, don't stake your life on being able to find a supply of fungus or punk wood that will catch and hold a spark. When Indians, frontiersmen, and mountain men were fortunate enough to discover a source of good tinder, they took as much as they could handily carry and kept it dry in a parfleche, a horn, or a waterproof metal box. If you have dry punky wood that will not catch and hold a spark, you can overcome this difficulty by rubbing black powder into it and sprinkling its surface with a few additional grains. You can either place the piece of treated wood on the ground or hold it and the flint in one hand and strike a sharp edge of the flint with the steel held in your other hand. Do not use more than 15 grains of powder and observe the other precautions detailed for starting a fire with hand-held tinder.

Most European and American Colonial homes were equipped with a flintlock fire starter or, as it was called by some, a "strike-a-light".[10] This instrument, which usually sat upon the fireplace mantle, resembled a pistol without a barrel but its function was strictly utilitarian. Like a pistol, it had a trigger, cock, and frizzen, but in place of a powder pan, a small container of greater capacity than the usual pan, was located beneath the frizzen. Fire was produced by placing a small piece of charred cloth in the container, lowering the frizzen, cocking the lighter, and pulling the trigger. Sparks showered directly onto the tinder. The lighted tinder could then be placed in a handful of flammable material and blown or fanned into a blaze.

If one placed a bit of tow or other flammable tinder in the container and poured a small amount of powder on top of it and sent a shower of sparks into it, presto, a blaze was created immediately. This could then be inserted under kindling to produce a fire.

The flintlock fire starter was a direct descendant of the

Left photo: The arrangement of powder and tinder in the flintlock pan. It's easy to see how the trade gun lock ignites the tinder in the pan (right photo).

flintlock firearm; hunters had learned long ago that they could easily produce a fire with a flintlock pistol, rifle, or musket merely by placing charred linen or cotton under the frizzen and sparking it. The faster method, of course, was to roll a small ball of tinder, place it in the lock pan, pour a few grains of powder over it, lower the frizzen and spark the powder. Should the firearm already be loaded with powder and ball it was only necessary to block the touch hole of the piece with a tight fitting twig before putting tinder and powder in the pan. Captain John G. W. Dillin has pointed out that accidental discharge of firearms occurred when guns that were thought to be empty contained a charge. Old log houses near his home in Pennsylvania showed unmistakable evidence of this form of accident where a load of shot or a bullet had accidentally gone into the ceiling or the fireplace mantel.[11]

Shooting at a candle flame on a dark night is fun and at the same time, exasperating. For me, it is more a test of judgment than of marksmanship because I can only catch fleeting glimpses of my rifle sights; and when I do see them it is so briefly that by the time it takes to bring them in line with the small yellow flame they have disappeared again and become part of the surrounding darkness. Finally, in desperation, as I imagine that my friends are wondering why I don't shoot, I squeeze the trigger. A six-foot long envelope of smoke, sparks, and yellow fire belches from the gun's muzzle lighting the features of the other shooters for an instant, then it is dark again and I notice with chagrin that the candle is still burning. All too often, that's what happens when I try to snuff the elusive candle flame.

There is no doubt about it. A lot of fire is generated when the trigger is squeezed on a black powder gun. Can this fire-making capability be put to use to make a campfire in an emergency? Indeed it can! Try it yourself. Pour about 10 grains of powder down the barrel. Shape some good tinder into a ball and ram it down on top of the powder. Prime the pan if you are using a flintlock, or cap the nipple on a percussion gun, and fire the piece straight overhead. The tinder should be blazing when it falls back to earth. If a brisk wind is blowing, allow for it by shooting into it. Don't use too much powder or you will blow the tinder all to pieces.

Should fate ever be so cruel as to leave you with no fire making apparatus except one of those strange newfangled cartridge guns that became popular after 1850, you can still make a fire — but not as quickly — by proceeding as follows: In the side of a cliff or earth bank, dig out the dirt to form a pocket about one foot in diameter and six inches deep. Place some good flammable dry leaves and kindling in the hole thus formed. Remove the bullets from two or three cartridges. This can best be done by holding the unloaded rifle horizontally and inserting the tip of the bullet into the end of the barrel. Downward pressure on the cartridge will cause bending and distortion of the neck of

the brass cartridge and allow the loosened bullet to be removed. Pour the powder from each of the cartridges onto a piece of cloth. Remove a bullet from another cartridge. Leaving about one-half of the powder in this cartridge, add the remaining one-half to that already accumulated on the cloth. Seat a small bit of cloth down on top of the powder in the cartridge to prevent it from spilling. Make a small bundle of the powder on the cloth and tie a string around it to keep it from spilling. Place the bundle of powder under the leaves and kindling in the fire hole. From a distance of about four feet, fire the cartridge containing the reduced powder charge into the bundle of powder. With the small kindling burning well you can either make the fire larger by adding more wood or move it to a more favorable location.

Unlike black powder, modern smokeless powder, when it is unconfined, burns slowly and with little pressure buildup. Black powder, on the other hand, always burns rapidly. In the fire making method just described, if we were to substitute black powder for smokeless powder the kindling in the fire hole would be scattered to the four winds.

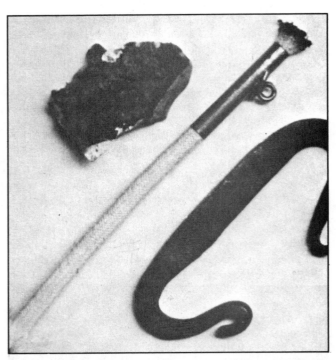

A reproduction of the "New Mexican tinder tube" as seen in the *Mountain Man's Sketchbook, Volume Two* by James Hanson and Kathryn Wilson. The brass tube with a ring soldered on top holds a cotton wick.

Mountain man Fred Floth of Wheatridge, Colorado gave me a fire tube "on the prairie," as the old timers used to say when giving something free and with no strings attached. We were camped at a July rendezvous in the Rocky Mountains of Colorado. The thing he gave me was just a brass tube about three inches long by 5/16" in diameter and had a small ring soldered to it on the side near one end. I had never seen one exactly like it before but at

Chaz Rauch displays the author's fire tube, flint, and steel. This tube is made of cane with a cotton wick.

home I had a larger more functional type made from a half-inch section of cane. Its use as a fire starter goes way back in history but just how far back, I don't know. On the morning of December 12, 1929, a famous old lawman, rancher, and veteran Texas Ranger died in bed at his home west of Clarendon, Texas. His description of the fire tube he used in Texas is virtually the same as the one described above.[12] A few years ago a friend showed me a tube he had brought back from India. They are still used in the back country there, as they are in parts of Africa, South America, and Mexico where matches are either a luxury or are unobtainable.

This simple device is, undoubtedly, the forerunner of the modern cigarette lighter. In use, the tube contains a cotton wick, one end of which has been charred. To light a cigar or pipe it takes but a few seconds to force the charred wick end out of the tube and start it smoldering with sparks struck from flint and steel. After each use the wick is snuffed out by pulling the lower end of the wick until its lighted upper end is back inside the tube. Lack of oxygen causes the smoldering wick to smother and go out.

The fire tube I now carry in my pack, although larger, is similar to the one given me by Fred. One important dif-

ference, however, is the wick and this will be described later on. The tube body is a section cut from a dipper gourd handle. It is four inches long and has an inside diameter of ⅝". An 18" length of sinew tied through a small hole at one end of the tube connects the tube and firesteel together.

The wicks in most fire tubes are composed of cotton cloth. It is inserted into the bottom of the tube, then twisted and forced upward until one end projects from the upper end. Before the fire tube is used the first time the cloth must be burned at one end then pulled back into the tube to extinguish the fire, after which it can be used repeatedly for fire making.

The inherent weakness of the fire tube is the fragile charred end of the wick. To catch a spark in the wick the charred end must be positioned and held close to the flint, and both must be held together with the same hand. In wielding the steel with the other hand it often inadventently brushes the end of the charred wick, thereby knocking off small bits of this very delicate material. It takes but a few badly directed blows with the steel to render the wick useless until it has been charred again. A cloth wick that is less fragile and at the same time a more effective spark catcher can be made as follows: Select three pieces of well charred cloth, each of which is six inches long and three inches wide. Align them evenly on a flat surface and roll them tightly to form a six-inch long roll. Cut a piece of unburned cotton cloth — cotton flannel works very well — to a measurement of six by three inches. Again on a flat surface, place the roll of charred cloth on the unburned cotton piece and roll it to wrap the clean cotton piece around the charred cloth. Using cotton or linen thread, make snug ties around the roll about ¾" apart the entire length of the bundle. Complete the job by inserting the wick into the tube. The core of this improved wick is good charred cloth inside a shell of tough cotton material that chars as it is used.

Charles Goodnight was a young boy when his family moved to Texas in 1845, the same year it became the 28th member of the Union. This was only nine years after the siege of the Alamo in San Antonio and the new state was a raw and lawless frontier and would remain so for many years. While still in his teens, Goodnight became an Indian fighter and in his early twenties he became a scout for the Texas Rangers during the first years of that famous organization when defense from raiding Apache and Comanche Indians was more the order of business than the pursuit of horse thieves and cattle rustlers. While much of Texas was still wild frontier he turned to ranching and when he died at the age of 93 he was one of the most famous of the old-time cattle ranchers.

Goodnight's mind remained sharp throughout his 93 years and when he told the story of his life to an admiring author he recalled past events as clearly as if they had occurred just yesterday. Like all frontiersmen, the rangers had more than one way of making fire.[13 Ibid] The most common method involved the use of punk and steel but in the prairie country where there was no punk they would "burn red corncobs to ashes, put them in a tin plate and make them into a thin mush with water." Into this mush they would put colored calico cloth, which was preferred over white cloth, and thoroughly saturated the material. When dry, Goodnight explained, it could be readily ignited with flint and steel, and the frontiersmen carried a supply of these "kindling rags" with them.

I made kindling rags using both white and red (Indian) corn cobs and white flannel cloth. I succeeded in igniting the flannel rag that had been impregnated with charred red cobs, but for some reason, the rag saturated with charred white cobs did not catch and hold sparks. I subsequently found that a cloth soaked in a solution of water and 4-F black powder and thoroughly dried, ignited, but no more readily than the red cob rags. I concluded that charred cotton cloth or punk wood makes the most effective tinder and, like Goodnight, I would reserve the kindling rag for times and circumstances when the better materials were not available.

Apparently, it was customary for most men to carry a fire tube, which has already been described in this chapter. From the glowing cloth in the tube he could light a cigar or pipe, or one of the kindling rags kept dry in a saddle bag.

Like trappers, hunters, soldiers, and other men on the frontier, the rangers were often forced to ride all day in cold wet weather, crossing streams and ploughing through snow before making a wet camp. It was then that a hot fire was most urgently needed and could be least expected from the wet tinder in their packs and saddle bags. The ranger was now forced to rely on another bit of strategy. Taking a scrap of wet cloth, he poured gun powder into the palm of his hand and rubbed it into the cloth. While in a sitting or kneeling position, the powder saturated cloth was wrapped around the shank of his Mexican style spurs and a percussion cap placed on one of the points of the big "sunburst" rowels. With the back of his Bowie knife or revolver butt he then "busted the cap" and it shot fire into the cloth, setting it afire.

When we were young, who of us never held a magnifying glass between the sun and our hand and focused the bright spot of light to a small dot, then jumped with surprise as it burned the skin: And later, perhaps, we learned that this same glass could be used to burn a hole in a piece of paper or to start a dried tree leaf smoldering. This ability of the magnifying glass to produce heat by refracting or "bending" sun rays and concentrating them in a small spot has been used for several centuries and can still be used to start a fire in an emergency. The objective lens from a pair of binoculars, a telescope, or from any other optical type instrument can also be used.

The list of articles purchased by Israel Whelen, Purveyor of Public Supplies for the Lewis and Clark expedition in 1803, includes eight dozen (96) "burning glasses."[14] One or two of these, along with various other gifts, were presented to each group of Indians with whom they came in contact. They were also used on occasion to purchase goods, especially food, when their supplies ran low.

Glass, however, is not the only material that will bend and concentrate sun rays. The interesting circumstance under which a mountain man friend, Charles "Chaz" Rauch, learned this fact bears recounting. Chaz knew that his girlfriend was an outdoor person but he didn't think she knew anything about outdoor survival that he didn't know. He had good reason for thinking as he did. For several years he has made a living as an instructor in the Project Apollo Program teaching basic outdoor survival skills to teen-agers and in that time just about every conceivable situation, routine as well as emergency, has occurred. But Chaz had to revise his opinion of his girl's abilities. They were hiking one bright cold winter day when she asked him if he could make a fire with ice. "No," he replied, "and neither can you." She promptly accepted this implied challenge and broke a large clear icicle from a rock overhead and commenced to melt and shape a piece of it with her bare hands. When her hands became too cold, Chaz took over, then alternately using their hands and a knife they soon had a clear magnifying lens of solid ice. With the improvised lens completed it took but a minute to focus the sun's rays on a piece of punky wood until it smoldered, then using it and a handful of good tinder, to blow it into

Ted Belue starting fire with a magnifying glass.

a flame.

As a medium for concentrating the sun's rays, the advantage of optical glass over clear ice is negligible. Even water held in a clear watch crystal or a clock glass is effective when kept level. Unfortunately, in the winter of northern latitudes, a crystal or a clock glass cannot be turned toward the sun without spilling the water.

Opaque or cloudy ice will not work as a lens material; neither will ice that has cracks and fracture lines in it. As far as size is concerned, a diameter of two inches or more is alright but sizes larger than, say, four inches take more time to complete and are no more efficient that the smaller sizes. Roughly shape the lens with the cutting edge of a knife or tomahawk, or by rubbing it on the face of a large rock. As it nears completion, give it a smooth bright surface by melting it with your hands.

You may have read the story of Ishi, the last so-called "wild" Indian who was captured in 1911 near Oroville, California.[15] For those who haven't read the story, Ishi was the last surviving member of the Yahi tribe, one of the "Digger" bands which, in its isolation, had been living in the Stone Age. Fortunately for Ishi, the Oroville Sheriff released him in the custody of two anthropologists, Professors Kroeber and Waterman of the University of California. Ishi was taken by them to San Francisco where the University's Museum of Anthropology was then located. He was treated well by the professors and he, in return, showed them how all the everyday tasks of Stone Age man were done. Professor Waterman was especially interested in fire making and with Ishi's coaching, he succeeded in making a fire with the hand fire drill. Enthusiastic as always, Waterman promptly announced to his class in Berkeley that to get a passing grade all students would have to repeat his success and "make fire" as he had done. After delivering his announcement, Waterman tried to show his students what he wanted them to do. This time, however, Ishi was not there and with all his huffing and puffing the only trace of fire he could get was a thin wisp of smoke no matter how hard he tried. As might be expected, "The new course requirement died as did the unborn spark at the bottom of Ishi's fire drill."[16]

Seldom is anyone successful in making a fire by friction the very first time. However, you can be successful if you use well made equipment and can either follow these printed directions or are coached by someone skilled in this ancient fire making technique. Under survival conditions, unless you are experienced in making fire by friction, you should not attempt it until after you have exhausted all your other options — only if you have no flint, steel, and charred cloth or charred punk; if you have no firearm and/or gunpowder; no burning glass or other means of concentrating the sun's rays.

No one can deny that the wood used in creating a fire

by friction is important, both as to the species used and its condition, that is, whether or not it is gummy or resinous, hard or soft, dry or damp, solid or decayed. Why are these things critical? Because gummy and resinous woods develop a glaze at the point of contact when pressure, friction, and heat is applied to them; woods that are too hard resist wear; damp woods resist burning; decayed woods disintegrate under pressure. It follows that we must not use material that tends to glaze as, for example, western larch (tamarack), sweetgum, sourgum, pieces of pitch pine, and walnut. The wood should not be too hard, and it must be thoroughly dry when selected or, if damp, stored where it will dry before it is used. The wood must be solid seasoned wood because considerable pressure is involved in the friction method and material that is riddled with insect holes, or decayed, will go to pieces when pressure is applied.

The "best" wood to use for making fire by friction seems to depend upon which Indian tribe was observed and in which part of the country the people lived. Some of the many woods mentioned by earlier writers include cottonwood, poplar, aspen, poison oak, willow, ash, cypress, cedar, grape vine, buckeye, sage brush, white oak, linden (basswood), balsam fir, mulberry, and maple. There are many other species that could be included in this list so, in an emergency, do not pass over other kinds that are available provided they do not have the undesirable characteristics mentioned above.

Some Indians considered their "fire sticks" sacred and their ability to make fire with them a gift from "the Spirit That Moves in All Things." When they had made a set of fire sticks that worked well, they carried it from one camp to another, always keeping it dry in parfleches or rawhide cases. In some tribes it was believed that the fire spark "slept" only in certain kinds of trees, and only the roots of these were to be used in kindling a fire by friction.[17]

James Adair was an 18th century trader among primitive Indian tribes of what is presently the southeastern United States. For 40 years he lived with various tribes of this region carefully observing and recording their customs. In a fire making ceremony described by Adair the firemaker chose "a piece of dry poplar, willow, or white oak." ". . . having cut a hole, so as not to reach through it, he then sharpens another piece, and placing that with the hole between his knees, he drills it briskly for several minutes, till it begins to smoke — or, by rubbing two pieces together, for about a quarter of an hour, by friction he collects the hidden fire; which all of them reckon to immediately issue from the holy Spirit of fire."[18]

In the paragraph above, two different ways of making fire by friction are described by Adair, each of which uses only two pieces of wood. Specific details are lacking in the descriptions but, apparently, the first method is the ancient hand fire drill method. A flat piece of wood called the hearth or fireboard is cut to measure approximately 16" long, 3" wide, and 1" thick. With the point of a knife, a hole is cut in the board to a depth of ¼" or so, near the middle but 7/16" in from the edge facing the operator. A V-shaped notch, ¼" wide at the side of the board is cut so its apex is in the center — not the edge — of the hole in which the spindle is to turn. This notch is then cut to angle downward from the top side of the board to the bottom side.

The fire drill or spindle is a round stick 24" long that

The hearth or fireboard used in making fire with the fire drill (spindle), or the fire bow.

tapers in diameter from ½" at the upper end to ⅝" at the lower or contact end. This end is rounded so it will not slip out of the hole started in the fireboard; across it from one side of the rounded end to the other, cut a narrow shallow groove. The purpose of this groove is to collect the charred wood particles produced by friction and release them in the fireboard notch.

Good fire drills can also be made from the woody plant stalks of mullein, ragweed, and great burdock. Using a dry mullein stalk spindle and a red cedar fireboard, experienced fire makers can sometimes produce a live coal with one passage of their hands down the stalk, and elapsed time may be as little as two minutes. To do this, a stalk is required that is at least 4 - 6 feet long. As the upper end of the stalk tends to whip in the air after the hands have passed the half-way point, the operator must prevent this by cradling it in the crook formed by his shoulder and neck.

Using the material at hand, Indians of the deserts and plains bound together sections of dry yucca leaves to make fire drills. Leaves of the blue yucca (also called datil) attain a length of three feet, while those of the Mojave yucca grow to five feet in length. Stalks of the same plants also furnished good hearths for the drills.

There are good reasons for the foregoing dimensions of the fireboard and spindle but, even so, each dimension can be varied slightly provided the general proportions are kept. The good reasons? As the fire stick is rotated between the palms of the hands, first clockwise then counterclockwise, a downward pressure must be maintained to provide the necessary friction. This causes the hands to gradually move down the stick toward the fireboard. When the fireboard is reached, unless a second operator can take over, the hands must be quickly moved back to the top of the stick. At this point, the spindle stands still for a fraction of a second and heat loss occurs. To help eliminate this idle time, the stick is made longer than the one used with a fire bow, which will be described later, and it is tapered slightly to offer some resistance to the hands as they move downward against the taper. The stick diameter is kept relatively small because a small diameter stick will rotate faster and a greater number of times with each passage of the hands than would a stick of larger diameter. Also, the pressure at the point of contact will be concentrated in a smaller area. Fire drills recovered by archaeologists from the prehistoric cliff dwellings in Mesa Verde National Park, and which I examined at the Colorado Heritage Center Museum in Denver, were all noticeably small in diameter.

The center of the hole in the fireboard is located 7/16" from one edge so a small margin of wood (⅛") will remain after the ⅝" stick has worn and burned its way below the top surface of the board. You can see that if the stick is started too close to the edge of the board, too much of its contact surface would soon be outside the board. For the same reason, the notch is not made any wider than necessary. It is shaped so it flares downward to allow the charred dust to fall through rather than collect around the spindle end.

If you haven't already given up and quit reading this because it is too involved, please allow me to explain something. I know you are not likely to be carrying a ruler or a tape measure in the woods. The technical directions are given to provide you with precise instructions so when you are working and practicing at home you will know when you are doing everything right. In an emergency all measurements can be approximated. For example, to make this equipment in the woods I would first chop out two hardwood gluts (wedges), and using a rock for a sledge hammer, I would split out a rough board approximately 16" long by 3" wide, and 1" thick. Then I would whittle out a spindle about 24" long that tapered from about ⅝" to ½". I would whittle the tip at the large end so it would have a round contact surface, and across this end, from one side to the other, I would cut a narrow groove. Then, to locate the drill hole position on the fireboard, I would hold the stick vertically near one edge and sight from above along the side of the stick and reposition it until the edge appeared to be ⅛" in from the edge of the board. A vee slot, wider at the bottom than at the top could then be cut from the board edge to the center of the fireboard hole.

Chaz Rauch using a mullein stalk as a hand fire drill. Starting toward the top, the drill is whirled between his hands. As downward pressure is applied, his hands slowly move down the drill. This method is probably the hardest of the friction methods. More than one pass down the stalk may be necessary before fire is made.

To make fire with the drill, a small handful of good tinder is placed on the ground and the fireboard is positioned on top of it with its notch centered above the tinder. The board is held in place by the fire maker who kneels upon it with both knees as he rotates the spindle between the palms of his hands. As the end of the spindle turns rapidly in the fireboard hole the resultant friction and abrasion heats the wood while at the same time it removes tiny particles in the form of charred dust. Heat penetrating the fireboard causes the temperature at the point of contact to gradually increase until it reaches the combustion point, at which time the accumulated charred wood dust starts to smolder. When this small mound of smoldering dust is gently blown upon its color will change from dull red to bright red, at which time it is hot enough to ignite the tinder.

This is probably the most difficult of the fire-making

techniques described here; it is, however, a last ditch method to try after other methods have been ruled out for lack of equipment or material. Once started, don't be too easily discouraged but keep going and give it your best effort. After two minutes of continuous work, a small column of smoke may be noted, and after three minutes dark powder should start to accumulate. It may take eight minutes or more of hard work before a glowing ember is produced that is capable of starting a fire.

The second method described in the **Adair paragraph** appears to be that which has been labeled the fire plow method;[19] it is less complicated than the first method but, unfortunately, is just as difficult. Here again, only two pieces of wood are required. The first piece, the fireboard, is 14" long, 3" wide, and 1" thick. A groove 10" long, ⅜" wide, and ¼" deep is cut into its top surface. The second piece of wood is a round stick approximately 14" long and ¾" in diameter. About 1½" of the lower end is tapered to a rounded end that fits into the narrow groove of the fireboard. The operator rests one end of the board on a rock or log and allows the other end to contact the ground. The rounded end of the stick is placed in the groove, then, using both hands, the fire maker presses hard on the stick and moves it rapidly back and forth, from one end to the other, in the groove. Each round trip of the fire stick tears loose tiny particles of wood, and because the board is inclined, it collects at the lower end of the groove. When there is enough of this smoking powder to fill the depth and width of the groove it can be gently blown upon, then the glowing ember carefully transferred to a handful of good tinder and blown into a blaze.

It seems incredible that the fire bow, a perfect example of which was found in Egypt in King Tutankhamen's tomb, survives today and is used by some Eskimo, as well as by some Siberian and North American Indian tribes. Its use by isolated primitive people is perhaps more credible than the fact that even as recently as the nineteenth century fire by wood friction was used in the enlightened country of Great Britain to produce what they called "need fire" through which cattle were driven in the belief that it would save them from disease.[20]

Whether or not the fire bow was carried to this continent by migrating bands of hunters or was invented independently by North American natives is another of the mysteries shrouded by time. Its invention, however, marked an important advance in fire making techniques even though it wasn't adopted by all tribes who might have had knowledge of it. (You will recall that Ishi, the Yana Indian, was still using the hand fire drill in California as late as the year 1911.) Regardless of who invented it, the

"Hawk" demonstrates the proper use of the fire plow. Note the charred wood particles at the lower end of the grove.

168

"Hawk" demonstrating the fire bow method. Note left arm braced against knee.

fire bow affords the surest way of starting a fire by friction. The mechanical advantage of the bow, which must be used with a socket to support the upper end of the drill, lets us apply more pressure on the drill — therefore more friction — and at the same time gives us a degree of control that is lacking in the hand fire drill method. Fire making with the bow requires the use of four wood components, namely, fireboard, spindle, socket, and bow. A fifth item, a leather thong is needed to "string" the bow. With minor exceptions, the fireboard may be made the same as the one already described for use with the hand fire drill. The center of the starting hole should be located near the right-hand end of the board and ½" in from the side facing the operator. In this method the board is held in place with the left foot rather than with both knees as in the hand drill method.

Make the fire drill ¾" in diameter and only about 12" long. You will note that this drill is shorter in length and larger in diameter than the hand fire drill. The shorter length affords the operator better control and more leverage when using the bow than could be obtained with a long drill. Also, the bow drill is made larger in diameter because it must withstand greater side stress than is imposed on the hand fire drill. Taper about 1½" of the top (socket) end of the stick and whittle it to a round tip ⅜" in diameter. Taper 1" of the lower (contact) end and shape this end so it is round and about ½" in diameter. Cut a 1/16" wide groove across the rounded end from one side to the other. Incidentally, friction can be increased by placing a few grains of fine sand in the fire board hole before beginning to operate the drill. This is especialy helpful if the wood used tends to be the least bit gummy or resinous.

The upper end of the fire drill must be securely held while it is being rotated by the bow. Although this is the primary purpose of the drill socket, it also enables the operator to exert more pressure on the drill and thereby generates more heat and friction in the fireboard hole. Indians commonly used a cupped-out stone, a rounded piece of hardwood, or a clamshell to hold the top end of the stick.[21] The hole in the socket must be slightly larger than the upper end of the drill so it will not bind and at the same time not be so large as to allow the stick to shift positions in the socket. Walt "Grizz" Hayward of the American Mountain Men organization and a *companero* of many camps, recommends a half-round piece of soapstone that contains a small pit cut into its flat underside.[22] Some Indians embellished the socket by carving totemic figures in the hardwood surface. Even more elaborate ones were sometimes fashioned that contained a smooth piece of soapstone set in the socket hole. A smooth ideally shaped stone can occasionally be found, but an ordinary piece of hardwood will serve the purpose almost as well, although it is not as friction-free as soapstone and other minerals composed essentially of talc. After carving the socket piece, lubricate the socket hole with animal fat or grease from the camp skillet.

The fire bow bears little resemblance to a bow made to shoot arrows. For making fire we want a bow so rigid that with the "string" wrapped once around the spindle it will not slip when considerable force is exerted on the socket. Slippage of the string on the spindle occurs when the bow is too limber to permit of much tension, or when not enough tension is placed on the bow and string initially.

Go to the woods and select a curved tree limb that is about 1¼" in diameter and 30" long. A straight bow will do but a curved one will allow clearance between it, your knuckles, and the spindle while you are using it. Remove all bark from the wood and, if you wish to make it lighter and less cumbersome, whittle flats on the upper and lower sides of the piece you have selected. One-half inch from each end of the bow, drill a hole for the bow string, or thong, to pass through.

The cordage I have made from plant fibers and the inner bark of trees will not withstand the rough usage it is subjected to when used as a thong in the fire bow. The most durable thong is made from animal hide or from animal sinew. All animals, including we humans, have a bundle of sinews along each side of the backbone and in each leg. Leg sinew is much stronger than back sinew but sinew from the backs of larger animals is more suitable for our purpose because its strands are longer and require less piecing together and twining in order to convert them into fire bow cordage.

An excellent thong can be made from green hide, rawhide, or the tanned hide of a large animal. Cut a ½" wide strip from the hide and twist it so tightly that it appears to be round. Pass one end of the thong through a hole in the bow, cut a slit through the leather and slip it over the end of the bow. Push the other end of the thong through the hole in the opposite end of the bow, pull it tight and tie it securely.

Here in Kentucky the old timers swear by ground hog (woodchuck) leather for use as boot and shoe laces and for "banjer" heads. It is the strongest of the small animal skins but other kinds also make serviceable thongs. Of course, in order to obtain a long strip from a comparatively small skin you will have to cut a round piece, then starting at the outer edge, cut a spiral of leather ½" wide and long enough to be tightly twisted and fastened at both ends of the bow in the manner already described.

A tough long lasting thong can also be made from animal gut that has been emptied of its contents, cleaned, then twisted tightly to form a cord of round cross section. Incidentally, strings for fiddles and other musical instruments are made from animal intestines and on the market this material is called "catgut". Under survival conditions, a shoe or boot lace will serve as a bow thong, and a strip of leather cut from a belt is another good source. A thong for a bow can even be improvised from a long seam cut from the cloth fabric of a shirt or a pair of pants.

Using the fire bow is similar in one respect to using the hand drill, that is, after the fire maker determines that all pieces of equipment are as they should be and he starts the drill turning, he must keep it turning until a glowing ember is produced that is hot enough to start a blaze. The primary

difference in the two methods is that the fire bow enables the operator to apply more pressure and speed — therefore more friction — and in a shorter span of time, than can be achieved by either the fire plow or the hand fire drill method.

To prepare the bow and spindle for use, the thong is given one turn around the spindle. To do this, place the spindle alongside the thong, push one end of the spindle hard against the thong, then twist it under and over the thong. There is less likelihood of interference between the bow, the spindle, and the operator's hand if the spindle is mounted on the side of the string away from the bow. In other words, the spindle should be outside the "D"-shaped area formed by the bow and thong. If the spindle is inside this area, reverse the procedure and mount it correctly.

Hold the fireboard in position by kneeling on your right knee and placing your left foot on the board. To avoid strain and fatigue, lock your left arm around your knee while pressing down on the fire stick with the socket. Occasionally the stick may slip out of the hole in the board and be propelled a considerable distance by tension of the bow and thong. Retrieve it and resume work. As the depth of the hole increases, the spindle is less likely to slip. Use long steady strokes almost the full length of the 30" bow. As the wood powder produced by the drill changes color from brown to black and begins to smoke, increase pressure on the socket and spindle, then gradually increase the speed of the drill. Maintain this speed as long as possible or until the volume of smoke indicates that there is enough burning wood dust to produce a fire-making ember. With the point of your knife, gently push any glowing dust remaining in the fireboard notch onto the tinder under it and blow it into flame. If you don't succeed in making a fire by friction, either with the hand drill or the fire bow, yet you are confident you have given it a good try, don't search haphazardly for the reason. Stop and backtrack to discover where you made a wrong turn — check the kind of wood used and its condition; check all dimensions of the fireboard, spindle, and bow; if the thong is slipping, tighten and retie it. Making fire is a straightforward process but there is no good substitute for practice and experience. Given both of these, your technique will improve as will your physical condition and staying power.

The fire board is held in place with the left foot (top photo). Tinder is placed under the hole in the fire board. Twist the fire drill on the board using long steady strokes of the bow. When enough burning wood dust accumulates, blow it into a flame on the tinder (middle and bottom photos).

171

We should be thankful that there are a variety of ways to obtain fire, and with it, those indispensable twin benefits of heat and light. Without fire it would be impossible to survive for any great length of time. As a person who wants to continue to survive in the outdoors, I am sure you realize that it is not enough to learn just one method of firemaking, thereby making yourself totally dependent on that method. While travelling and camping in wilderness areas your ability to produce fire will be tested every time you are forced to cope with capricious weather and terrain, and the even more uncertain elements of material and equipment that may be available to you at any given time.

Before you read this article you may already have known more than one way to start a fire, but you now know several others. I say you "know" them but won't really know them until you try them and they become a part of yourself. Unless you are persistent, you may not actually be able to make a fire by some of these methods but you will have formed an evaluation of each one you try, and *that* will become a part of your permanent knowledge.

Another test of your skill in the woods pertains to your knowledge of wood and tinder. You should know which kinds make the best firewoods and which are best for making fire by friction. Knowing the best tinder to use and where to find it is also important. Regardless of where you live, you will discover several kinds of tinder that are superior to the others. Learn to select the best type of punk wood for making a charred cloth substitute and don't be content until you have used it to catch sparks and make a fire. Knowing these things for your home area is not enough. You should also make a point of learning the characteristics of various woods and tinders wherever you travel. If you do, you will one day realize that you have greatly increased your knowledge of woodcraft and reached a higher plateau in your understanding of nature.

In conclusion, I wish to thank Russell Sidebottom of Dillsboro, Indiana; Lee Wolf Abernathy of Big Sandy, Tennessee, and Ted Belue, Chaz Rauch, Ken Carsten, and Linda Horner of Murray, Kentucky. Their help with photographs, reference material, and advice is much appreciated.

FOOTNOTES

1 Noah Webster, *A Compendious Dictionary of the English Language,* (London, 1806), p. 311.

2 J. Evetts Haley, *Charles Goodnight Cowman and Plainsman,* (Norman, OK, 1949), p. 41.

3 Frederick Webb Hodge, ed., *Handbook of American Indians North of Mexico,* (Washington, D.C., 1907), p. 459.

4 Ascott R. Hope, *The Men of the Backwoods,* (New York, 1880), pp. 149-167.

5 Reubin G. Thwaites, ed., *Original Journals of the Lewis and Clark Expedition, 1804-1806),* (New York, 1969).

6 Morris Birkbeck, *Notes on a Journey in America,* (London, 1818), pp. 91-92.

7 George F. Ruxton, *Life in the Far West,* Glorieta, NM, 1972), p. 53.

8 J. R. Swanton, *The Indians of the Southeastern United States, Bulletin 137,* (Bureau of American Ethnology, 1946), p. 423.

9 Swanton, *The Indians of the Southeastern United States, Bulletin 137,* p. 425.

10 Carl P. Russell, *Firearms, Traps, & Tools of the Mountain Men,* (New York, 1967), p. 354.

11 John G. W. Dillin, *The Kentucky Rifle,* (York, Pa., 1959), pp. 57-58.

12 Haley, *Charles Goodnight Cowman and Plainsman,* p. 41.

13 Haley, *Charles goodnight Cowman and Plainsman,* p. 41.

14 Thwaites, ed., *Original Journals of the Lewis and Clark Expedition, 1804-1806,* Volume 7, p. 238.

15 Theodora Kroeber, *Ishi in Two Worlds,* (Berkley and Los Angeles, 1961).

16 Kroeber, *Ishi in Two Worlds,* pp. 184-185.

17 Thomas E. Mails, *The Mystic Warriors of the Plains,* (Garden City, NY, 1972), p. 536.

18 Samuel Cole Williams, ed., *Adair's History of the American Indians,* (Nashville, 1971), p. 111.

19 Williams, ed., *Adair's History of the American Indians,* p. 111.

20 Chas. Singer, E. J. Holmyard, and A. R. Hall, eds., *A History of Technology, Volume I,* (Oxford, 1955), pp. 220 & 224.

21 Mails, *The Mystic Warriors of the Plains,* p. 536.

22 Walter Hayward, *Using the Fire Drill* in *The Tomahawk and Long Rifle, Volume I, No. 5,* (1973), pp. 2-3.

Traveling Afoot & By Canoe

by Ralph "Two Shoots" Marcum

RALPH "TWO SHOOTS" MARCUM began shooting and making muzzle loaders more than 25 years ago. He was born and has lived his life in the hills of eastern Kentucky. Ralph made his first trip to the NMLRA National Matches in Friendship, Indiana in 1958 and hasn't missed attending either a spring or a fall shoot since then.

Marcum takes his muzzle loading seriously, especially in regard to hunting with the front loaders. His trophy room contains at least a dozen different species of game, all taken with a muzzle loader. He earned the name "Two Shoots" from making and shooting, almost exclusively, over/under swivel breech guns.

Ralph has written extensively for the NMLRA's publication, *Muzzle Blasts*. He is the Primitive Editor for *Muzzleloader* magazine with a regular column entitled "The Buckskinner's Way".

There are many interesting aspects about today's buckskinning game, but what we sometimes fail to realize is that the game as we play it today is a far cry from the real every day life of the early longhunter or mountain man. For in the day of the longhunter, any and all tasks or trips in the wilderness could be fraught with danger. But now when we recall this most picturesque era, many times we fail to comprehend the dangerous side of life of those early times. Nowadays nothing could be more enjoyable to a buckskinner than a trek or camp in the woods or on the plains, because all our attention can be paid to things like setting up camp or just appreciating the forest around us, with no need to post guard or be constantly on the alert.

Living here in the hills of eastern Kentucky, where it is still sparsely populated, I consider myself very fortunate in still being able to enjoy the woods and what they have to offer. As the county that I live in is almost in the center of the Daniel Boone National Forest, one can literally lose oneself in these hills for days on end, because nearly all of the old trails are still open to the public.

As for the buckskinner in most parts of our country, many times it takes some careful checking around to find suitable areas where one can "pack in" for a weekend. For what could be more enjoyable than packing or walking into a nice high alpine meadow in the west, or an overnight camp deep in a secluded part of the eastern forest and partaking of all that nature has to offer?

For those of you who haven't had a chance to attend a buckskin rendezvous in either the east or the west, let me tell you right here it's really something special to see buckskinners coming into camp either walking or on horseback, and even sometimes by canoe (when a rendezvous is held on or near a stream). For several years now on the first weekend in February each year at my cabin on the head-waters of the Rockcastle River I host what has come to be called "The Annual Freeze Arse' Rendezvous", which is open to all buckskinners from any club or group. This annual rendezvous can only be reached by walking or riding in, and as you might expect, it really separates the men from the boys. Sometimes this rendezvous has been really rough especially when the weather didn't cooperate. But as I always state in the notice or invitation to the rendezvous, that it definitely is not a camp for the timid, the frail, or the faint of heart, but rather for the hale and hearty individual, the likes of which first hunted, trapped and explored this beautiful land of ours.

Last year at this camp the weather was really rough with cold weather, light rain, and then snow on Saturday night. But the one thing that really made an impression on all of us, and the highlight of the whole thing, was Bud Shelboure and his friend actually traveling some 18 - 20 miles to the rendezvous by horseback and packhorses. Although Bud and his friend could have unloaded their horses and gear at my cabin, which is only a half mile or so from the rendezvous site, as the rest of us had done, they chose to ride in the 18 - 20 miles.

That was some sight with two riders in full mountain dress, carrying their trusty rifles, riding up the trail leading their pack animals. I'll tell you "them was shinin' times", especially when someone shouted, "Hey, look what's a coming up the trail", and the whole camp ran to get a better look. And, I think you will agree that a vision such as that, here in the 20th century, was indeed "a sight to see".

Modes of travel in the early days differed according to the geographic location. A mode of travel that was more prevalent in the east than in the west was that of travel on foot. The first longhunters who braved the eastern frontier in search of game, furs, and homes almost invariably did so on foot, due to the closed in brush and timber. But even here whenever possible the early hunter did bring along a packhorse for his gear, and to take back any game or furs that he may have taken. But again travel by foot was the easiest way to get from place to place. However, there is always a limit to how much gear one can carry even on a short trek or hunt, in which case some type of frame can be used to carry even a small amount of gear.

Most of the early packs were carried either slung over the shoulder or carried on the shoulders, and were patterned after the common Revolutionary War knapsacks. But as you might imagine, there were limitations due to their soft construction, both in how much could comfortably be carried and in their ability to withstand hard and constant use. The hunter who needed something more rugged, and a way to carry heavier loads had to resort to his

own ingenuity. By applying a little common sense, I think we can pretty well see what he probably came up with, since the two problems he had to overcome were something more durable and something that would hold more. This meant that he either needed some type of frame or container. No doubt the early hunter knew about and even used the large willow or white oak lath pack baskets which the Indians of the north had used for years. However, I am inclined to think that he possibly used some sort of pack-frame-like apparatus, not unlike our pack frames of today. I have no way of knowing this and would welcome more discussion and information on this from anyone who might shed more light on the subject.

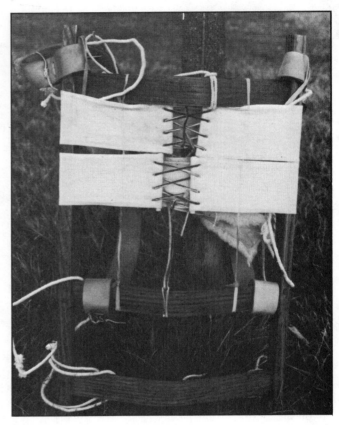

This simple pack frame, handmade by Larry Eisenhower of Boone, North Carolina, is an excellent way to carry your gear to a pack-in camp.

If the early frontiersman did make use of a type of pack frame, it could have been easily made from native woods at hand, namely hickory and white oak. It is relatively a simple matter to make up a very handy and serviceable frame of this kind, and when finished it closely resembles the common ladder back chair which has been in continual use since colonial times. These materials would include some good hardwood slats, a couple of uprights, some leather or canvas straps, and perhaps a small quantity of rawhide or sinew to hold the whole thing together. When finished, one had only to lash and tie his

A group of frontiersmen head into the forest carrying everything on their backs. The gear on this trek was carried in pack baskets, blanket rolls, haversacks, or on pack frames.

various belongings to the frame and he was ready to go. This type of frame allowed medium to heavy loads to be carried more easily and without undue fatigue. However, if you didn't care to go to the trouble of building such a frame with its uprights and slats, a regular wide board could be fitted with shoulder straps, thereby making a pack board instead of pack frame, which served the same purpose as the frame, but was somewhat heavier.

In order to keep articles or bedding dry on a pack frame it is always necessary to wrap the things you need to keep dry in waterproof canvas. This can be rather easily accomplished by first laying all your dry articles on your ground cloth, and wrapping up the whole thing. I suppose the pack basket might be called the lazy man's choice in selecting an apparatus for carrying his gear, because when breaking camp, all one needs to do is dump all his gear in, and maybe lash a canvas cover over the top and be on his way. Of course where a pack basket really comes into its own is in canoeing, which we will cover later in this discussion on travel by the early mountain man.

Some three or four years ago some local buckskinners, myself, and a couple of my American Mountain Men brothers started a club, which we now call the Kentucky Longhunters. When drawing up the rules, regulations, and primitive objectives, we also included that of walking a 44

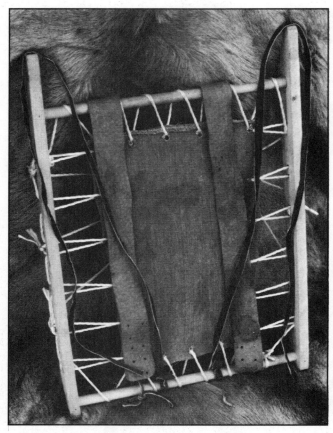

A pack frame as described in the text; made with four wooden pieces, a cloth back rest in the center, heavy cord, and leather shoulder straps.

The pack basket loaded up with gear for an extended stay in the woods. The leather bag mounted on the back of the basket contains the cooking gear.

mile section of the famous "Sheltowee" or Daniel Boone Trace, which meanders across the county where we live.

On this trek each of us carried all his eating, sleeping, and camping gear as well as his longrifle. And everyone chose to carry his gear on his pack frame, that each of us had made up especially for this trip. The following general directions might help you in making a very useful and sturdy pack frame.

The materials you will need include two uprights, approximately ⅜ x 2" x 20 inches long, a ¾ inch dowel rod from the local paint store, a ¾ inch wood bit, a hand drill, about 10 or 15 feet of strong cord or leather thongs, a piece of lower pants leg about 12 inches in length, and a couple of leather or canvas straps at least 2 inches wide and about 3 feet long for the shoulder straps.

First, a ¾ inch hole should be drilled in each end of the uprights in which will be fastened the lengths of ¾ inch dowel rod cross pieces. Then, between these holes, about an inch and a half apart, you will need to drill smaller holes of ¼ inch in diameter in which will go the cords or lacing. After you have joined the uprights and ¾ inch dowel rods by either gluing or pinning, you will now need to insert two 12 inch lengths of ¼ inch dowel rods or even pieces of a broken ramrod up into the length of pants leg you have cut off. Then by pulling the small lengths of ramrod to either side of the pants leg section and laying it inside the frame, you are now ready to start lacing the pants leg or back rest

in place, punching holes where needed. After drawing and redrawing out all the slack your frame is now ready for the fitting of the shoulder straps.

Another variation of the pants leg back rest would be that of using just a flat piece of leather or rawhide and lacing that in place. Rawhide works especially well, since it can be put in wet and when dried will really make for a good tight rest and frame. I mentioned the pants leg technique since good quality rawhide and sinew can be hard to come by and expensive too. After the whole thing is finished to your liking you can stain it to any desired color.

The essentials that each of us carried included a canvas ground cloth, a blanket, canteen, utensil kit, candles, a flint and steel and a tin cup for drinking and boiling water, with each man provisioning himself according to his needs in regard to food. The individual ground cloth that most of us carried was made from good heavy canvas and of a size

Traveling on foot was sometimes a necessity for the western frontiersman also. This painting, "Colorado Crossing" by David Wright, depicts a trapper in the Rockies with nothing but a gun, a pouch, and a buffalo robe slung over his shoulder.

that would double for a small lean-to type half shelter, as well as giving protection in case of rain. As with any group, each of us was in varying degree of physical fitness which really showed up the morning after the first day out. Some had failed to break in their moccasins properly, some got "charley horses", while some complained that they had brought too much food and gear, and promptly adjusted accordingly by actually throwing away some extra food and some gear. And some, whose pack frames and straps hadn't been adjusted properly, had to stop and re-adjust several times along the way.

The accompanying picture will give you some idea of what our "motley crew" looked like on the morning we started out. And unfortunately, or fortunately we might say, no one was on hand to take a picture of us at the end of our 44 mile trek. At any rate a good time was had by all and nearly all of us to a man, had to take another look at ourselves before considering ourselves real mountain men.

In getting back to the days of Bridger, Meek and Smith, about the worst thing that could happen to them, was to lose their horses. Such a predicament meant "heap much trouble", which could result in death by thirst or starvation, or maybe a slow painful death at the hands of the Indians who were past masters at all kinds of torture.

These old frontiersmen had to constantly be in top physical condition for just such a situation, as well as being able to endure the many common everyday ordeals that taxed both the mind and body to its limits. No doubt that just an average hunter or trapper of the fur trade era would stack up pretty doggone well even with today's top athletes. Old Colter did, when he outran all his Indian pursuers, literally running for his life, and barefooted at that!

I know that the 44 mile trek which I made really made me get on the ball and "shape up" after I returned, and I honestly thought I was in pretty good shape before the trip. We mentioned earlier about the longhunters bringing pack horses with them when they first came into Kentucky in the 1760s. However, it should be mentioned that even the few pack animals that they brought with them posed a problem when it was necessary to abandon the natural buffalo and Indian trails that led into and crisscrossed early Kentucky. Upon getting into good game or fur country the first order of the day was to set up a semi-permanent "station camp", as they called it, where the horses and furs were kept, while all hunting and trapping was done on foot, sometimes right under the very noses of the Indians who were always on the lookout for them. Even today in the still heavily wooded areas of the east it is almost impossible to get a horse across country due to the thick brush and timber. We can only surmise now how difficult it must have been back in Boone's time.

In summing up travel by foot, it might be said that it could be bad for either an early eastern or western hunter if he found himself on his own hook without his horse but probably much worse for the mountain man of the west.

Dave Poss, with pack frame, and Dave Wright, with smoothbore and haversack slung over his shoulder, prepare for a pack-in trek.

Taking a trip by canoe is a fine way to spend a primitive weekend or week in the wilderness.

Now after hitting the high places on travel by foot we naturally come around to another means of travel by both the easterner and westerner, that of travel by canoe. Another picturesque era would be that of the early French Voyaguer or the early mountain man in his quest for adventure or furs. We can almost see and hear the many unique sounds and sights that this early adventurer might encounter along one of the unspoiled virgin streams or rivers of the early 1800s.

This little bit of reminiscing, brings us to the conclusion that buckskinning and canoeing just naturally seem to go together. For what could be more enjoyable than shoving off down a wild, secluded and remote river and disappearing around that last bend into what seems to be another century and another world, especially if one has equipped himself with only the gear, accoutrements, and arms of the early mountain man. This means that in order to complete this journey back into time, that *all* semblance of the 20th century and all its luxuries must be left behind with not even one item to remind us later on the trip that we are travelers from another time.

I have been canoeing since the early sixties, and wouldn't even consider taking a canoe trip with anything but all authentic gear and arms. I first started on the buckskins and canoe idea about 1963 when I became acquainted with Hershel House the fine custom rifle maker from Morgantown, Kentucky, "Doc" Andy Baker, and my good friend Randy Cochran, from Cincinnati, Ohio. We all first met at a spring shoot at Friendship and a real lasting friendship among us began. Then at the following fall shoot in 1963 we began making plans for our first canoe trip, complete with skins and the whole bit. All of us had done some canoeing previous to this trip, but none of us had combined buckskinning with canoeing, as we were planning then. Needless to say, it was on that trip that we all became addicted to canoeing and buckskinning. And many, many more trips later we all still feel the same way. There's just nothing else to compare with it.

Along the way we have all learned many do's and don'ts regarding the use of the canoe and what it will and what it will not do. Mostly what it won't do! About the most important thing that can be said about canoeing is to get yourself a good partner and stay with him or her. The running and handling of any canoe is a very delicate matter, which means that those operating this most fragile of crafts must be on their toes each and every moment. Two men that understand each other and their canoe and work as a team are a joy to watch. While on the other hand two unskilled men in a canoe are both a comedy and a danger to themselves. In fact, about the only thing that is as funny as someone in a canoe for the first time, but much less dangerous, is one man trying to put up a tipi for the first time. There's definitely an art to it! It's an absolute fact that two men, used to each other in a canoe, can actually anticipate the next act or motion of their partner, which in rough water is a necessity. But, sooner or later, anyone who canoes regularly will turn over and "swamp".

This brings us to a discussion on the different types of canoes that are available to today's mountain men and buckskinners. Because unlike the early French Voyaguer or mountain man who used the birchbark or early wooden canoes almost exclusively, we of the 20th century are fortunate in having a rather wide variety of canoes to choose from. Although those that were available to the early hunter and explorer did serve the purpose for which they were intended, they were frail in construction, as compared to today's canoes. But before getting into the different types available to today's buckskinner, it should be mentioned that there are still a few old style birchbark canoes still being made by individuals around the country which should be number one on all of our want lists. However, the availability and price makes them prohibitive to many, unless we make them ourselves. For what could be more primitive and more rewarding than shoving off down a secluded stream in a birchbark canoe with all authentic gear into what can be another era and another world?

In getting back to canoes available to today's buckskinner, most fall into at least three categories. Since all canoes have the same basic shape, these categories are differentiated by the material from which they are made. These different materials include canvas, fiberglass, high impact plastic, and aluminum.

Up until fairly recently, in the last 25 years or so, the old standby of hunter, canoeist, and fisherman alike was the cedar framed canvas covered style made by companies such as "Old Town". These canoes were lightweight and maneuvered beautifully. However, due to their general construction of canvas stretched over a wooden framework they had their limitations as far as rough, hard use. The buckskinner of today would do well if he could "dig up" one of these old standbys. In fact, this style would be my second choice in a canoe from those available now.

The second category includes those made of fiberglass or high impact plastic. Their advantages would include very sturdy construction, quiet and easy maneuverability in the water, a pleasing selection of colors which will stay on, and flotation equipped.

The disadvantages might be a heavier weight than either aluminum or canvas, some brands which will actually break when hitting an obstruction and a general un-canoe like design which would only be noticed perhaps by the buckskinner.

However, there is one high impact plastic canoe made by the Coleman people that is really a fine canoe, especially their fifteen footer. It handles well, is relatively quiet, looks good and can be had in a choice of colors, and most important if it is moderately dented the dent can be just pushed right out with no apparent visible damage whatsoever. It definitely should be considered if you plan to traverse some really rough water.

The third group or category would be those canoes made from aluminum. The advantages would include lightweight, sturdy construction, facilities to keep them afloat even when filled with water, and moderate price tags.

The disadvantages would include being noisy to paddle, manuever and move around in, a finish that will not take and hold a painted finish well, and also one that will

Whether you're traveling by canoe or on foot, all blankets should be placed in the center of your ground cloth with all four sides neatly folded over and bound securely.

dent easily. However, there is one aluminum-magnesium model made by Sportspal that solves nearly all the above mentioned disadvantages with the possible exception of the last one.

This little "gem" of a canoe, just looks more like a canoe ought to, as shown in the accompanying picture. The Sportspal people have also solved the problem of noise, by covering every inch of the inside of the canoe with a durable ⅜ inch of styrofoam, which makes it as quiet as a whisper in the water, and with its nearly flat bottom and ample width it is one of the most sturdy canoes I have ever seen or used.

As you might imagine this is and has been my favorite water craft for some thirteen years now, and I would heartily recommend it to anyone looking for both dependability and style in a canoe.

The hunter who plans to actually hunt from a canoe is immediately confronted with at least two other decisions. Number one is whether to have a rifle or a shotgun along and the other is how to keep from ruining that favorite gun if you do overturn.

The first problem was the one foremost in my mind when I started canoe hunting several years ago. I quickly learned that a rifle just ain't the whole answer to all the hunting situations you will run into on a river. When the game is moving and you're moving, hitting anything consistently is pretty hopeless. I realized that you need something from both worlds, that is a rifle and a shotgun. But, since just one gun is difficult to manage in a canoe without the burden of an "extra" gun, I combined a shotgun and a rifle into one over/under swivel breech gun. With this .40 cal/20 gauge combination I was ready for most any small game as well as deer and bobcat.

With that gun I figured I had covered all the problems of a gun in a canoe until the day I was running the Rockcastle River near my home and swamped. I thought I had already learned all there was to know about canoeing. Boy, was I wrong. When I overturned I lost everything I had along (including the swivel breech) except my bullet pouch and powder horn. Luckily, my friend in the other canoe had some rope with him, so he tied the rope around his waist, waded out into the rapids, and retrieved my gun. It couldn't have been in the water more than 20 or 30 minutes, but that was plenty long enough for all sorts of bad things to start happening to my little jewel.

That incident led me to search for something that would prevent a gun from being completely ruined in an overturned canoe. This search led to the following procedure, which is the best protection for a canoe gun I know of.

This operation is really simple and can be done in a few minutes with a minimum of materials. Simply coat all inside areas such as under locks, inlays, buttplate, patch box, and all other places not covered by the outside finish, with plain old household paraffin wax. Cakes of this wax can be obtained at any hardware store. It can be applied with a regular cotton swab with a wire handle such as is used to apply liquid shoe polish.

Again, it goes without saying that you must cover every part where raw wood is exposed. First, melt a cake of paraffin wax in a small tin can. (It doesn't have to get too hot, but just hot enough to melt thoroughly.) The gun to be treated should be completely taken down. Keep the melted contents as close as possible to your work as the wax will cool and get hard quickly. When the swab cools too rapidly, just dip it in the melted wax on the stove and it's ready again for another part. The areas which need the paraffin most are underneath the butt, under the triggers and under the barrel. You now have merely to reassemble the rifle or shotgun and you're ready for canoeing.

I have found that a rifle with the wood waterproofed in this way can stay under water for at least a few minutes with no noticeable harm, that is if you disassemble your rifle immediately and dry it as thoroughly as possible. Needless to say, another thing that is a must in rough water or in any water for that matter, is the necessity of tying everything in securely. This goes doubly for a rifle, because even though you may have it waterproofed, there is still the danger of losing it if you should overturn. This can be guarded against by the use of a simple lanyard type thong tied either to the trigger guard or the wrist. Personally, I like to tie a thong all the way around the wrist and tie it really tight. In the event of a "swamping" in rough water, there will be considerable force and pressure on both the thong and the rifle. I like the thong to be of a length so that I can easily shoulder the piece as well as have plenty of room in loading it. In tying the rifle to the canoe and also in positioning it for quick and easy use, always do so, so that

the muzzle of the piece is away from your partner in the front or the back. I find it also a good idea to double tie your rifle so that in the event of overturning it will be securely lashed in at least two places, so that it will stay with the canoe and not fall out and be dragged along. In tying the rifle in these two places always use a simple bow knot so that you can release it quickly when game is sighted. However, a note of caution should be given here concerning the local game laws which may have laws against shooting or taking game from a canoe or boat.

One of the most important hints to be given in regard

When packing a canoe, tie the pack basket or pack securely to the canoe. If rawhide thongs are used, they should be tied tightly and checked regularly, because rawhide will stretch when wet.

Attach a lanyard from the canoe to your gun to keep both together in the event of a swamp. A long lanyard permits you to shoulder the gun for shooting. Check the game laws where you plan to canoe to make sure it's legal to shoot from a canoe.

The canoe can be utilized along with a piece of canvas to form an overnight shelter.

to preparing the rifle for firing even after it has had the wax treatment is that of "pegging the pan" if you are carrying a flintlock. By pegging the pan, I mean that you actually drive a small wooden peg solidly into the touch hole of the rifle. This is to insure that no moisture will enter into and wet and spoil the main charge, if the canoe should overturn. This small peg should be so made, and long enough, that it can easily be grasped and pulled from the touch hole before repriming and firing. I have found that a flint rifle so "pegged" can safely stay under water for a few minutes and then be taken out, reprimed and fired, providing that the ball and patch are a good tight fit. And anyone who has ever overturned with a flint rifle without pegging the pan will tell you that you really have a problem on your hands, with the only remedy usually being to actually pull the ball and clean out the wet and "gooey" charge.

If you are carrying a percussion, you can either "peg the nipple", or give the nipple and cap a good covering of candle or beeswax. With the flintlock, I find that dropping a few drops of melted candle wax around the "peg" in the pan further insures keeping the main charge dry.

The next article of importance that you may want to take precautions to keep dry is your bed clothing, for absolutely nothing on earth is half as bad as spending a cold night in damp blankets. In selecting blankets for either winter or summer canoeing, always select pure wool, if you can get it.

Wool has qualities which make it a good choice, not only because of its warmth but also because wool provides some warmth even when wet. The best way that I have found to keep blankets reasonably dry is to tie them up in a good heavy piece of sailcloth type canvas. A bundle tied and folded correctly really does a fine job of keeping those precious blankets fit for use on a cold night. This bundle too, must be tied in the canoe securely, with no chance of separating from the craft.

Another precaution that I have found that definitely makes for a better trip is that of having some sort of platform or rack in the bottom of your canoe to keep everything off the bottom and out of the water, which is bound to accumulate there either from the paddle or from a rainstorm. Some canoes come equipped with such a rack, but it is a relatively simple matter to make one to fit your individual canoe.

This brings us down to the night camp and its location, and I stress the word location. For more than once in my twenty or so years of canoeing, I found that picking the right place made the difference between a good enjoyable outing, and a trip of woe. It's just a plain fact that river waters change from high to low, which means that the first order of the evening after all the gear has been removed, is to securely tie the canoe up to some good solid, preferably green, mooring. Many times even if there is no rain where you are, there may have been a regular downpour somewhere upstream. And believe you me, it will get to your campsight in record time, especially if you haven't pitched your camp on high ground. This only happened to me once and that was enough. It's something else to try to grab all

184

your belongings in pitch darkness with the only warning being of some cold water silently creeping into your blankets with you. The closest man to the water on such an occasion will be the first to give the alarm and boy, will he sound off. I know, because I was the low water boy one dark night in June on the Rockcastle.

Most of us, instead of pitching a leanto or some other type shelter simply use our overturned canoe as a cover along with a piece of canvas which goes under us, then back up and around and then over towards the front of the upside down canoe. Such a camp when pitched right in regard to the wind and with a small fire in front of it makes for a comfortable camp for the night. But as I cautioned before, be sure you select a piece of ground that you think would be above the high water mark. You can usually tell where the last high water mark was by observing the debris which has lodged in nearby bushes or branches. Sometimes this high water mark may be several feet from the edge of the stream, but no matter, it's always better to have to walk a little farther to get your water, than have the water to come to you late at night. At least twice in my canoeing experience, I can remember having to try and overtake a canoe the next morning whose owner failed to tie it up properly the night before.

You who have ever silently moved down a secluded river just at dusk will appreciate the many beautiful and sometimes eerie night sounds that are heard. You have also noted that many animals, including deer, seem to have almost no fear of a silently moving object in the still of the evening. Instead of bounding off in their usual manner, many times they will just stand and stare at a canoe. The reason being, no doubt, that most danger usually comes from the bank rather than from the stream itself.

When canoeing in the fall of the year, when different game seasons are in, one can actually live "high on the hog" by living off the land. Many times on trips down the Rockcastle River, we have had such game as squirrel, rabbit, grouse, groundhog, and on one of our fall trips during deer season, a spike buck.

One of the most memorable and enjoyable canoe trips that I have taken was with my three old buckskinning buddies, Randy Cochran, Hershel House, and Doc Baker. It occurred back in the sixties on the Rockcastle River. I kept a journal on this trip and include it here with some brief notes on some of the entries.

RALPH MARCUM, HIS JOURNAL

Saturday Morning
Got off to a good start this morning. Two canoes, two men to each canoe. Think we have made about 3 miles so far. Will be glad when we pass the last homestead on this part of the river and leave civilization behind for a time. (Author's note: The place where we put in was near the headwaters of the Rockcastle where the first really good canoeing can be found. It is right at the edge of the Daniel Boone National Forest where private land ends and government land begins.)

Noon
Passed the last private land about 2 miles back. All feel relieved that we are now on our own and in the wilds. Have just finished our lunch of jerky, parched corn, black coffee and cornpone. Still haven't killed anything for supper. All will hunt harder now and be more alert. Getting ready to enter some really good hunting country. Did see three ducks high overhead a few minutes ago.

Mid-Afternoon
Stopped here at fine limestone spring, ate a few mouthfuls of parched corn. Randy killed the first game, a squirrel, with his smooth bore. He's over by the canoe gutting it. I killed a nice fat yearling groundhog. "Doc" had to finish it off, as it was a long shot for the 20 gauge barrel on my swivel and I didn't kill it dead the first shot. Problem of fresh meat now taken care of. Weather clear and sunny, but nippy. Everyone just resting, will take off in a few minutes for our night camp some 4 - 5 miles on.

Late Afternoon — Night Camp
Arrived here about 2 hours ago with sun still up. Made camp, brought in wood and cleaned game. Decided to roast the squirrel on a spit and cook the groundhog in Randy's big iron pot. Pot boiling now. Going now to spread bedding for the night.

All just finished supper, tasted fine. Just sitting around smoking our pipes and recalling the day's happenings. Was startled a few minutes ago by a wildcat's scream on the ridge above us. (Author's note: We camped that night at the famous "River Ford" which is mentioned many times in the journals and diaries of the early travelers of the Wilderness Road. It was one of the few places on the Rockcastle River, with its close in hills, that was really suitable for an overnight camp by the early travelers. In addition to this, it most always, even to this day, has an abundance of some type of grass or wild cane so treasured for the pack animals then. But even at its best, it did not always protect the early pioneers from deadly Indian attack because on leaving this relatively open area, the traveler was again plunged into the thick forest. Lastly, it was the last crossing before the river went into the somewhat rough rapids which begin just below here.)

Daybreak Sunday
Night uneventful except for bobcat chorus on ridge above us. All of us went hunting at daylight except "Doc"

While heading downriver, keep a sharp eye out for game. Animals don't seem to spook from canoes like they do from hunters on land.

who made the fire and coffee for us. Hershel and I each killed squirrels cutting hickory nuts. Randy got a shot at a red fox but distance too great for his critter getter. Cleaned the squirrels, fried them in bacon fat Randy brought. Everything tasted good. Right smart chill in the air. Will stop about two miles on down where I know there are usually some grouse. Will have to tie everything down good because of rough water ahead.

Mid-Morning

Stopped here awhile ago to grouse hunt some. Hershel stayed with canoes with his rifle. Us three took our smoothbores and went hunting. Doc finally killed one grouse, hard to hit. Hershel caught two good fish on crawdad tails while we were hunting. Picturebook kind of trip so far. Will keep grouse and fish for late supper at end of gorge. All eating a little parched corn and jerky for an early lunch. Going to rest awhile before shoving off. Four or five hours of hard paddling ahead. (Author's note: It was at the mouth of Lines Creek that we grouse hunted and rested for awhile before plunging into the really rough Rockcastle country. We tied everything in securely including our rifles. The rapids this far up are not really that bad, but the constant twisting and turning of the river here sometimes leads the inexperienced canoeist to panic. In fact, that's exactly what happened to me some years ago when I swamped near here and lost my swivel which I mentioned earlier.)

Night Camp

Got here about an hour ago, all worn out. Pretty trip but a busy one. No time to hunt or fish much. All attention toward keeping upright. Preparing supper now, frying fish in big iron skillet. Cornpone getting low, may have to use parched corn for bread. Going to get more wood now.

Just finished supper. Night cold and clear. Again recalling trip through the gorge area. Fire burning low, will probably let it go out again tonight. Will turn in as soon as this pipe is smoked out.

Monday Morning

All went hunting again this morning except Randy who stayed to make fire and coffee. All killed two squirrels and another groundhog. I got between it and its hole and done him in. Randy cleaning the squirrels now for breakfast. Will keep groundhog to roast over fire at noon. Cornbread all gone. Randy saw a deer wading in the shallows down river from our camp when he went to get water. He couldn't tell whether it was a buck or a doe. Going to break camp now. Have another half day's hard paddling.

With all the gear neatly stowed, it's time to shove off on the trek.

Noon Monday

Quartered up the groundhog for each man to roast. Built fire, made coffee and waited for fire to burn down to good roasting coals. Everyone hating to see the trip end. Vow to make this trip every year at this time. Good fellowship and good companions, the best. Fire about right for roasting. Will break camp after we rest awhile.

Monday Evening

Shoved off at about mid-day. Saw a beautiful red- dish colored whitetail buck cross in front of us just after moving out. May try him later this fall. I'm writing while Hershel is doing the paddling. Country still beautiful. Signs of civilization will be coming up shortly. Again, all wish trip could last much longer. Will be at pickup point in about an hour. (Author's note: It was here that our trip ended with a sort of sadness on all of our parts, because we had lived for a time as did our forefathers before us and all of us believed we managed to achieve some of the feeling and hardships that some of them had experienced. Even though nothing spectacular happened on the trip, it was still special to each of us.)

CONCLUSION

A whole book could be written on these subjects and I realize I've only scratched the surface, but I hope that I've whetted your appetite and made you want to get your own trek together. Whether you're on foot or in a canoe, I think you will all agree that an ordinary trip into the wilds becomes a special adventure when done using the gear and wearing the clothing of the longhunter or mountain man era.

Making Camp Gear

by George Glenn

IN 1950, 12 YEAR OLD GEORGE GLENN was given a Civil War Enfield by his father, who might have thought twice about the gift had he known his son would spend the next 34 years as a muzzleloader and buckskinner. Muzzleloading back in the '50s was sometimes lonely, and sources for supplies and equipment were a lot scarcer than they are today. Anyone who wanted authentic and reliable weapons, gear and equipment almost had to make it himself, and Glenn, like many others, fell into the habit of never buying what he could make. The growth of the muzzleloading industry has since reduced the need to make a lot of stuff, and it's often easier and less time-consuming to purchase what you need, but old habits die hard, and Glenn continues to make most of the things he needs.

In 1966 Glenn left the University of Illinois (where he received his Ph.D.) and moved across the Mississippi to join the theatre faculty at the University of Northern Iowa, where he is currently an Associate Professor of Theatre History. In 1974 he developed and taught what is believed to be the first college-level course in muzzleloading.

Glenn began writing for *Muzzleloader* in 1975, and joined *Muzzleloader's* editorial staff in 1976. His chapter on "The Lodge" was included in the first *Book of Buckskinning.* He is a member of The National Muzzle Loading Rifle Association and the North West Territorial Alliance.

Everyone who's ever gone to a rendezvous or stayed in a primitive camp for an extended period of time has felt the need for a few more "civilized" accoutrements than the bare minimum. On a primitive "pack-in" you find you can get along quite nicely with a blanket or two, a tarp, and a candle stub; but for a more permanent camp, some additional amenities come in handy.

This chapter will show you how to make a good many of the little extras that can make the difference between an adequate experience and a pleasurable one, whether you're on your own at a primitive walk-in, or staying a week at a large rendezvous. For convenience sake, the chapter will be divided into sections dealing with items made primarily from one kind of material or another: wood, willow and gourds, leather, horn and metal. Within each section I'll provide a list of basic tools and discuss basic construction techniques along with instructions for making a few items in each material group. Your own imagination and your own needs will probably suggest other projects that will employ the same methods and use the same tools and materials.

Where possible, I've indicated when an item was copied from or inspired from an original, since authenticity is an important consideration. I've also indicated the historic period of an item, since, although it's possible that a Colonial period item could continue to be used into the fur trade era, you wouldn't want to include an article from the 1830s in your Revolutionary War-period encampment.

The following instructions are meant as guides only, not as absolute strictures or rules that have to be followed. There's absolutely nothing wrong with making a museum-quality replica of anything, but it's not essential that you do so. What is wanted is a replica that is true to the style of the period, that's accurate in terms of materials used, and is recognizable as a one-of-a-kind, handcrafted item and not a mass-produced discount house special.

WOODEN EQUIPMENT

There are innumerable items, from plunder-boxes to candle-holders, that are useful around the camp (or cabin) that can be made from wood. We obviously can't deal with them all, but we discuss an example or two of a number of different items.

List of basic woodworking tools:
>hand saws (cross-cut, coping, hack, buck)
>hammer
>mallet
>chisels
>draw knife
>rasps and files
>screwdrivers
>power drill
>hand drill
>brace and bits
>squares
>clamps

Access to other power tools can be helpful:
>band saw
>table saw
>radial-arm saw
>drill press
>sanders

BOXES AND CHESTS

One of the most useful and prevalent items seen and used around the primitive camp is the wooden storage box or chest. There is a great variety of styles, shapes and kinds of wooden boxes and containers used for storing and transporting everything from clothing and camp gear to food and drink. Let's start by making my favorite simple "plunder-box" or "cassette."

This box is a flat-topped chest, made from standard dimensional lumber. Although the curved-top or "hump-

backed" style is perhaps better looking, I prefer the flat-topped model for two reasons: it's easier to make, and it's more convenient around the camp, since you can use it as a table or stool. You'll need the following materials to make a chest about two feet long, a foot deep and a foot and a half high. (See Figure 1.)

Materials:
A. Bottom (1) 1" x 12" x 24" clear white pine or #2 white pine (which will have a few knots) (NOTE: I suppose it's necessary to mention that a nominal 1" x 12" is really ¾" x 11¾"— be sure to take this into account when making your measurements.)
B. Ends (2) 1" x 12" x 11¾"
C. Sides (2) 1" x 12" x 26½"
D. Top Ends (2) 1" x 3" x 11¾"
E. Top Sides (2) 1"x3"x26½"
F. Top (5) 1" x 3" x 27" (This will give you a quarter-inch overlap.
G. 2 doz. #8 x 1" or #8 x 1¼" flat headed steel wood screws
H. 1 3' length ⅜" hardwood dowel
I. 2 brass "butterfly" hinges (Stanley's will do, but be sure you get some steel wood screws to replace the brass ones that come with the hinges.
J. 2 brass trunk handles (Stanley's — replace the screws that come with the handles.)
K. Sandpaper (various grits)
L. Wood stain and varnish or "Colonial Red" latex house paint.

Assembly:
1. Begin by assembling the two end pieces (B) to the bottom piece (A). (See Plate 1) Mark the three screw locations on each bottom piece and drill a pilot screw hole through the end pieces into the ends of the bottom piece. Then, since the screws will be hidden, with a ⅜" wood bit drill a counter-sunk hole for each screw to a depth of about half the width of the end pieces. (See Plate 1) Screw the end pieces to the bottom piece.
2. Fasten the side pieces (C) to the end and bottom pieces, using the same counter-sunk screw techniques. (See Plate 2).
3. Glue and clamp the top pieces together (or use 1 piece of 1x12). When gluing up boards, alternate them so that the grain of the wood runs in opposite directions from piece to piece. (See Figure 2). This evens out the stresses that can come from the clamping and possible warping of the boards. For additional strength, the boards can also be dowelled together. Stack the boards edge-up, and with a combination square mark the location of the holes you will drill for the dowel pegs. On these marks, mark the center of the board. This will be the locator for your drill holes. Drill your holes (use a ¼" or ⅜" wood bit), being careful to drill on the exact center and to keep your drill exactly perpendicular to the edge of the board. (A dowelling jig is extremely handy for this chore, if you have one or can borrow one. They cost about $30.00 if you

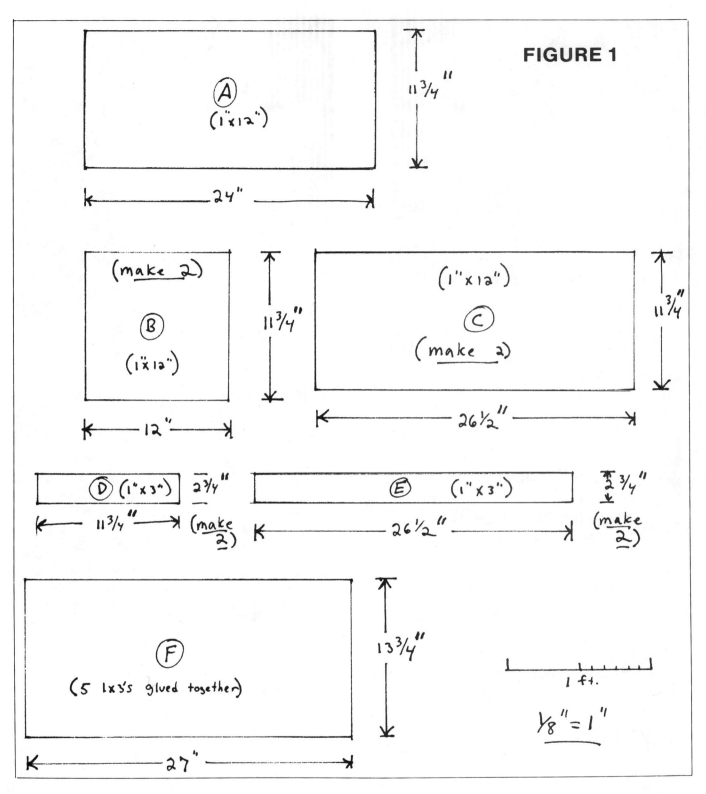

FIGURE 1

A (1"x12")

11³/₄"

24"

(make 2)

B (1"x12")

11³/₄"

12"

(1"x12")

C

(make 2)

11³/₄"

26½"

D (1"x3") 2³/₄"

11³/₄" (make 2)

E (1"x3") 2³/₄"

26½" (make 2)

F

(5 1x3's glued together)

13³/₄"

27"

1 ft.

⅛" = 1"

purchase one — I'd recommend purchase only if you expect to do a lot of dowelling.) Cut some ¼" or ⅜" dowels into the appropriate lengths (approx. 1½"), and file a small chamfer along the dowel to allow for glue expansion. Coat the dowels with glue, and with a mallet gently drive the dowel into the edge of the board. Tap the next board in place after gluing the edges. When all the boards are glued and dowelled,

apply your clamps, wiping away excess glue that's squeezed out when pressure is applied.

4. Assemble the top end and side pieces in the same manner as the lower end and side pieces. (See Plate 3).
5. Screw the top down on the assembled side pieces, again countersinking the screws. There will be about a quarter-inch overlap of the top. I like this, and my di-

PLATE 1: Attaching the ends of the box to the bottom. Note the countersunk screw holes.

PLATE 2: The sides screwed in place.

PLATE 3: The lid constructed. The screw holes are ready to be plugged.

PLATE 4: The screw holes plugged with dowel. The dowels are ready to be trimmed flush.

mensions planned for it. If you don't want an overlap, trim off the excess.

6. All your screws are countersunk well below the surface of the wood. Now is the time to hide the screws and make it appear as if your whole box is dowelled together without screws. Cut short lengths of ⅜" hardwood dowel, coat them with a little glue, and insert them into the screw holes. When the glue is dry,

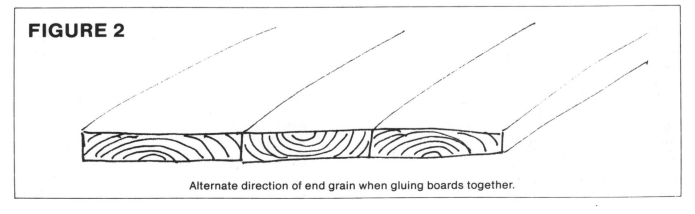

FIGURE 2

Alternate direction of end grain when gluing boards together.

cut them off flush with the surface. (See Plate 4.)

7. Sand all the exposed end cuts smooth. Sand all surfaces. As with any woodworking, remember that the quality of your final finish depends to a great extent on the care taken with the sanding of the wood surfaces. You can't expect to get a fine, smooth finish if you haven't sanded well.
8. Stain and varnish, or paint.
9. Hinge the top to the base. Attach the handles to the ends. Aside from greater strength, another reason for replacing the brass screws which come with the hinges and handles is a matter of authenticity; the steel screw is more authentic.

Your decision to stain or to paint is your own. If you like the look of wood, then use a stain and varnish finish. Historically, however, chests and trunks were painted and often decorated still further with handpainted or stenciled designs. Hudson's Bay Company "cassettes" were uniformly painted with "Spanish brown" paint (see the extant example in the Museum of the Fur Trade in Chadron, Nebraska), a color that is very similar to the modern dull-red "Colonial Red" exterior latex paints, which make a good substitute. If you use an exterior latex, it might be a good idea to give it a coat of protective varnish.

If you decide to stain, I'd recommend the use of an oil-based wiping stain, which doesn't cover up the grain of the wood like some varnish stains do. A technique that works well for me and that gives a good antique pine look is to paint on a coat of walnut oil stain, and almost immediately wipe it off (the longer you let it set before wiping, the darker the finish will be — and the kind of wood also affects the color). Practice on some scraps first if you're not sure how your stain will react to your wood. When the stain is dry, apply two or three coats of a good semi-gloss polyurethane varnish (which resists scarring and moisture), rubbing it down with fine steel wool between coats. For a very nice, handrubbed finish, rub the last coat down with linseed oil and powdered pumice or rottenstone. The technique is to take a rag and dip it first in the linseed oil, then in the powdered pumice (which adheres to the oily rag). Rub the finish with this, working in circular motions, and periodically polishing with a clean, dry flannel rag. You'll get a finish that looks like (and I guess really is) a hand-rubbed oil finish.

BOX AND CHEST VARIATIONS

This box design can be used as the basis for several useful variations. A Pennsylvania-style "blanket-chest" can be made by using a flat lid with no side or end thickness pieces. In this case, an edging of quarter-round or other commercial molding can be added to the edge of the lid and around the base of the box. Short legs can be added to keep the bottom off the ground. Legs can be carved or turned if you're handy with chisel and lathe, or you can use or modify commercial legs or turnings available at most lumber yards. Chests of this type were usually painted and decorated. To emulate the original Pennsylvania blanket and dower chests, the decoration could consist of typical rural Pennsylvania folk-art motifs.

An interior tray for small objects can easily be added to any chest style by simply building a smaller version of the trunk lid — one that will just fit inside the box. A ledge

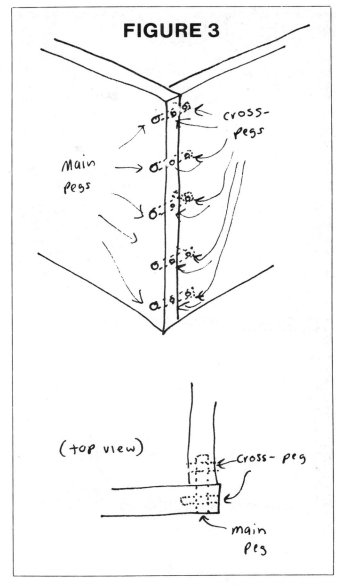

FIGURE 3

cross-pegs

Main pegs

(top view)

cross-peg

main peg

of quarter-round (with the flat side up) can be screwed or nailed to the inside of the body to form a lip on which the tray will rest.

The Museum of the Fur Trade has two original chests. One is a red-painted HBC cassette that is about 38" long, 21½" wide and 19½" high, with a slightly humped lid. The other is an iron-bound hump-backed Hudson's Bay Company ration box that is about 27" long, 16" wide and 15" high. It's painted green. (See the detailed plans in *Voyager's Sketchbook.*)

Boxes and chests like these can be made in a variety of sizes as well as styles. I find it convenient to use stock lumber, adjusting my dimensions to suit, rather than do a lot of gluing up of boards to get the required widths. Thus, I made a smaller version of my basic box for my son, using 1"x-10"s instead of 1"x12"s.

Further sophistication in construction (and more authenticity) can be obtained by using genuine pegged construction or by using dovetailed joints. The boxes can be held together quite well by dowelling and pegging (with glue) — a help here is to cross-peg to keep the joints from separating. (See Figure 3.) Cross-pegging isn't a difficult

194

procedure, and will produce a good looking and durable chest.

Dovetailing is a more complicated and advanced technique. In fact, unless you had more woodworking in high school than I did, I'd recommend that you stay with the simpler techniques, particularly if you plan to reproduce the original hand-cut dovetails. If you have access to a router with a dovetail attachment, dovetailing becomes a viable alternative, but you won't be able to reproduce the old hand-cut look.

ICE CHESTS

While most boxes and trunks will be used to hold the kinds of things they've always held, there is one variation which serves as a replacement for that modern necessity — the ice chest. Many buckskinners disguise their modern ice

PLATE 5: The "bottomless" ice chest cover; closed and with the lid raised, revealing the modern ice chest inside.

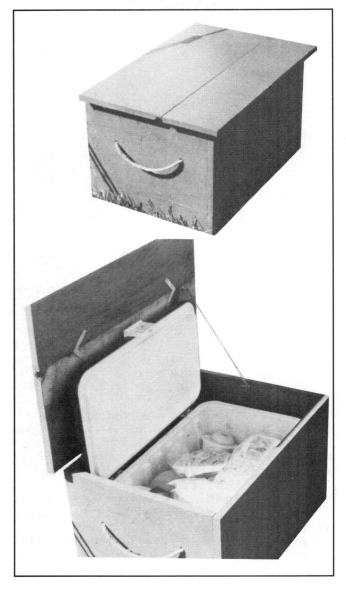

PLATE 6: A homemade ice chest of wood lined with styrofoam insulation.

chest by covering it up or keeping it out of sight, but there is an alternative. You can make your own.

There are two ways to go in making your own disguised ice chest. The simplest is to build a bottomless box that will hold your modern ice chest. Opening the lid of your wooden cover reveals the ice chest inside. (See Plate 5.) A little more complicated, but also more substantial version, is a box with a bottom that will hold your ice chest.

A different version is to build a box and line it with styrofoam. The sheet styrofoam can be cut to fit and glued in place with a wallboard cement like "Liquid Nails." You can even drill a drain hole in a corner or end of the box. Line the drain hole with a piece of tubing glued in place, and carve a plug or stopper. If you feel that one layer of styrofoam isn't enough, glue in a second thickness. Caulk the seams and apply a coat or two of styrofoam sealer; or omit the caulk and sealer, and the melted ice will simply seep out eliminating the need for a drain hole. (This may also eventually rot the wood.) (See Plate 6.) You'll find that an ice chest constructed like this will be heavier than a commercial modern ice chest, but that is not a great problem. Give your completed ice chest a coat or two of exterior house paint in a traditional old color, or use a weather-proof spar varnish for protection. (See also Plate 7.)

PLATE 7: A unique combination beer cooler/folding-back seat seen at a local rendezvous.

CAMP FURNITURE

Walk around any primitive rendezvous camp these days, and you'll see a great variety of camp chairs, tables, etc. Chairs or seats range in style from the rawhide-laced folding canoe chair to primitive looking chairs of wood slats. Many of these styles look "primitive," but there's

Camp furniture seen at modern rendezvous. Clockwise beginning above: Relaxing on the popular rawhide strung canoe chair; A folding collapsible table/stool; An authentic version of a popular early-to-mid 19th century furniture style (this chair is constructed from branches and twigs); A rugged primitive stool.

some question about their authenticity. More authentic would be the simple stools and trestle tables of the colonial or early 19th century periods. Not only are they authentic and relatively simple to make, but also they can be constructed at the campsite.

PRIMITIVE CAMP STOOL

All that's needed for a camp stool is a section of log split in half and three or four sections of a branch a couple of inches in diameter. You'll also need a brace and a 1" wood bit, a hatchet, axe or tomahawk (a draw knife comes in handy), a saw and a knife.

Cut a section of log to length — about 18". Split it in half lengthwise. With tomahawk and knife smooth the flat section; you don't want splinters! While you're at it, strip the bark off if you want. Now, with the brace and bit, drill three or four holes in the bottom (or rounded) part of the split log. These holes should be angled back and to the sides to give greater stability. Three legs will give you a more stable stool with less effort than will four, since the tripod doesn't have to have legs of equal length to sit steady. Bore the holes at least 2" deep. (See Figure 4.)

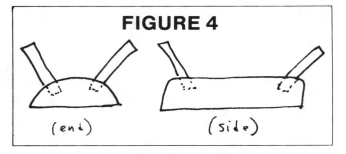

FIGURE 4

(end)   (side)

Next, with tomahawk, saw or knife, cut three or four branches a foot or so long (depending on how high you want the stool seat to be) and at least 2" in diameter. Carve a 1" diameter tenon on one end of each branch. This tenon should be at least 2" long, and should be a snug fit in the holes in the log section.

A more substantial join can be made if you've drilled

the sockets for the legs all the way through the log. Carve the socket ends of the legs long enough to project through the seat, and cut a slit in the end of the socket. (See Figure 5.) Now carve a wedge to fit the slot, and drive the wedge firmly into the slot after the leg has been inserted into the seat. (This type of wedge is called a "fox wedge". See Figure 5.) Trim the ends of the legs flush with the seat, pull your stool up to the campfire, stretch your legs out and relax.

WILLOW ROD BACK REST

One of the most comfortable of camp seats is the Indian willow rod back rest, or "lazy-back." The biggest problem you'll have constructing a couple of these (the Indians always made them in pairs) is gathering the necessary number of willow shoots, since you'll need 150-175 shoots for each back rest. Gather shoots that are straight for at least 3½ feet, and about ½" thick at the butt end.

Peel the bark from the shoots while they are still green; it's almost impossible to get the bark off after the shoots have dried. Bundle them tightly in several bundles, and let them dry.

Next, lay out a pattern to guide you in the marking and stringing together of the rods. The completed back rest will be a tapered mat about five feet long, three feet, six inches wide at the bottom, and two feet, six inches wide at the top. The willow rods are strung together on four cords run from top to bottom, spaced seven inches apart at the top and a foot apart at the bottom with 3" on either side. (See Figure 6.) Lay this pattern out with chalk on your basement or garage floor, or with strings and pegs on the ground.

Start the assembly by selecting a good straight round rod, trimming it to length, and drilling the four holes with an ⅛" drill bit. For cord, I'd recommend the same waxed 5-ply linen thread you'd use for saddle stitching (available at Tandy's) and a couple of egg-eye harness needles to pull it through the holes as you drill them. If you're insecure, or heavy, a stouter twine might work better. Measure out four lengths of cord about six feet long. Pass the end of each strand through each hole in your first rod, and tie them off. Lay the first rod on your base line on your pattern. Place

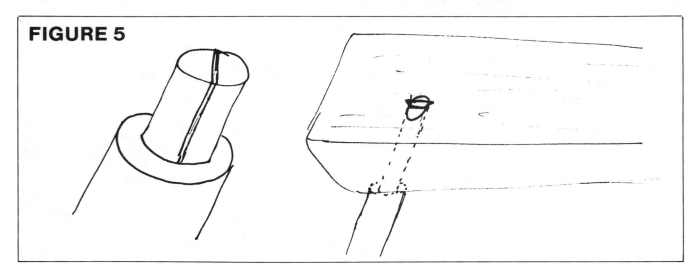

FIGURE 5

the next rod against it, alternating butt and tip as you go. Mark the position of the holes, drill, string, and so on. As you continue, keep pulling the rods up tight to one another. Continue marking, drilling, and stringing until you've reached the required length, and tie off the cords at the end.

Aside from decoration and a loop of buckskin at the top to hang the back rest from the willow rod tripod, the back rest is essentially complete at this point. Roll it up in a tight bundle to dry if you haven't already bundled and dried your rods.

After the rods are dry, the back rests can be painted. Examples in the Chicago Museum of Natural History, and at other museums I've visited, show that the decorations consist of six painted bands evenly spaced and extending about halfway down the back rest. Copying the design in the Chicago museum, I painted the top rod dark blue, followed by an unpainted section of eight rods (these could be painted yellow), followed by an eight-rod section, the first and eighth of which were painted blue, while the middle six were painted red. This is followed by another 8-rod unpainted (or yellow) section, then another (1) blue-(6) red- (1) blue section, and so on, until six bands altogether have been painted.

Finally, a loop of buckskin, 2½" wide and two feet long, is stitched to the front of the mat, the ends extending to the top rod of the second painted band (about 9-10"

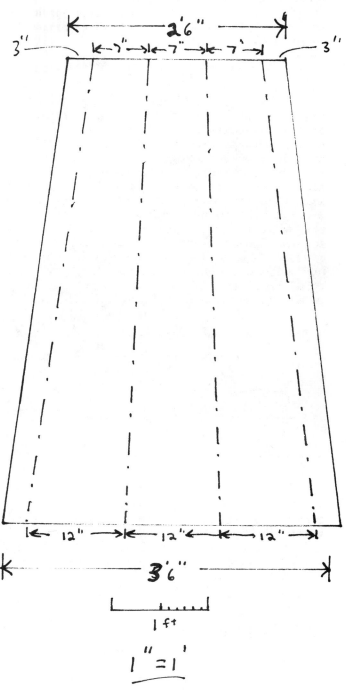

FIGURE 6

PLATE 8: The Sioux style willow rod "lazy back".

down from the top). Other decorations, such as horsehair "scalplocks" can be attached along the edges of the loop which can also be beaded or painted.

The tripod is constructed of light poles about an inch or two in diameter, and about five feet long. The Indians used pine saplings and either carved decorations in the bark or peeled and polished them. The tripod poles are lashed together near the top just as you'd tie the tripod poles of a tipi together. It's not a bad idea to sharpen the butts of the back rest poles, so that you can push them in the ground a ways to keep them from slipping away from you when you finally lean back to relax.

Properly cared for, lazy-backs will last a long time. I made mine in 1978, and they're still going strong. (See Plate 8.)

PLATE 9: Some plains tribes fashioned their back rests narrower than the Sioux style, and bound the edges with buckskin or red trade cloth.

FOLDING REVOLUTIONARY WAR CAMP COT

A comfortable place to rest your weary bones after a long day's activities at rendezvous or encampment is sometimes difficult to find. Despite the aesthetic pleasures to be derived from sleeping on a buffalo robe, the hard truth of the matter is that there are sometimes lumps and other hard, sharp things in the ground underneath it. Most of the time we can endure such privations (and even take a certain perverse pride in them), but the older I get the more I look for ways to sneak in a little more comfort.

I won't say anything about the piece of foam rubber I hide under my buffalo robe (I've seen plenty of you fellows doing the same thing), but I've always felt that a camp cot would be nice in damp weather. The only thing that stopped me from using one was the question: are they authentic? I'd always assumed they weren't (and modern ones obviously aren't), but in the *Collector's Illustrated Encyclopedia of the American Revolution,* I saw a photo of an original, authentic, folding Revolutionary War camp

cot. I had to have one. The following description is based on that original example, but I had to guess on the dimensions. I made it to fit me. I think if I were to make another one, I would make it narrower and lower (but not shorter). (See Plans, Figure 7.)

Materials:

    A & B (2) 2"x2"x7'3"
    F & G (2) 1"x12"x3'
    C (4) 2"x2"x3'
    D & E (2) 1"x4"x6'6"
    H & J (4) ¾" or 1" dowel x 12"
    ⅜" and ¼" dowel
    2 yards 54" heavy cotton canvas
    large carpet tacks or "wrought-head" tacks

The cot is really fairly simple in construction; as described, you'll notice that the only nails used in construction are those that hold the canvas in place. I'd also recommend doing as much of the finish sanding as possible on each piece before beginning construction — I didn't, and I wish I had.

A characteristic of this cot is the head and foot boards, which not only serve their usual function, but also help to hold the cot together. Two pegs are dowelled into each board so that they will swivel out of the way for transportation, and also fit into sockets drilled in each end of the side rails.

Begin construction by cutting the two side rails A & B. (I made mine long enough to give me a bed surface six and a half feet long.) Next, cut the four legs. These are a total of 34½" long which allows for the cutting of a 2" tenon on one end of each leg.

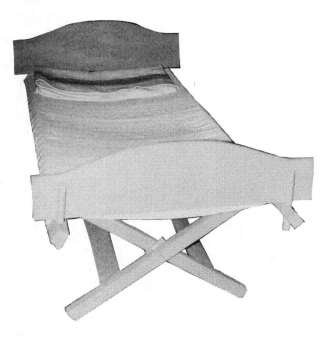

FIGURE 7

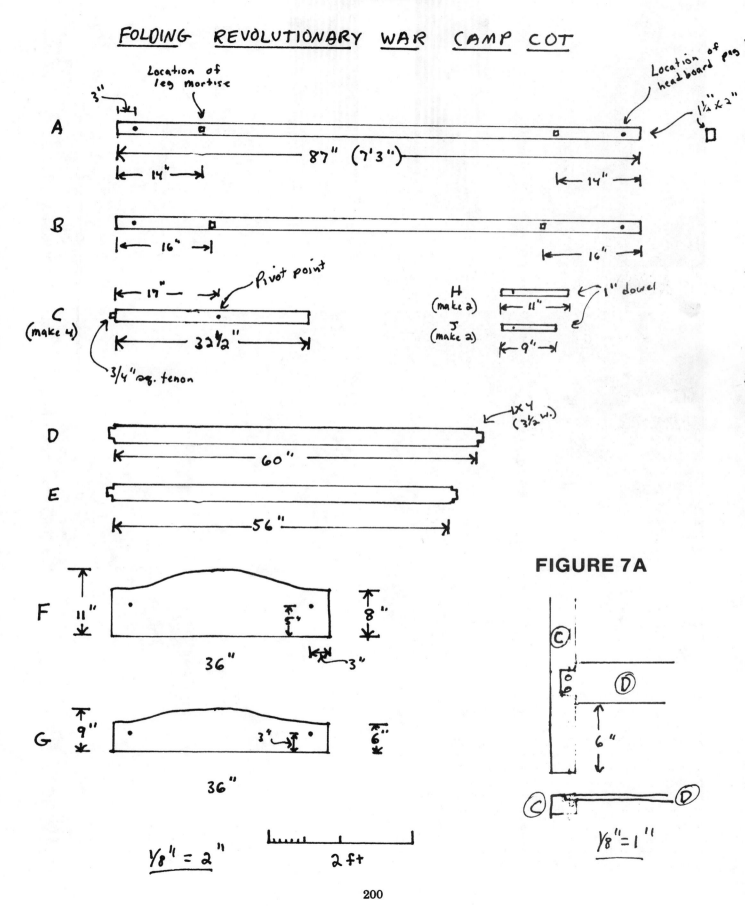

FOLDING REVOLUTIONARY WAR CAMP COT

Location of leg mortise

Location of headboard peg h...

3"

1×4

A

87" (7'3")

14"   14"

1½" × 2"

B

16"   16"

17"   pivot point

C
(make 4)

32½"

3/4" sq. tenon

H
(make 2)   1" dowel
11"
J
(make 2)
9"

1×4
(3½ w.)

D

60"

E

56"

F

11"   5"   8"

36"   3"

G

9"   3"   6"

36"

⅛" = 2"

2 ft

FIGURE 7A

C

D   6"

6"

C   D

⅛" = 1"

200

PLATE 9: After carefully marking the cot leg with a square, cut the tenon.

PLATE 10: Drilling the mortises in the cot rail. The corners will be squared off with a chisel.

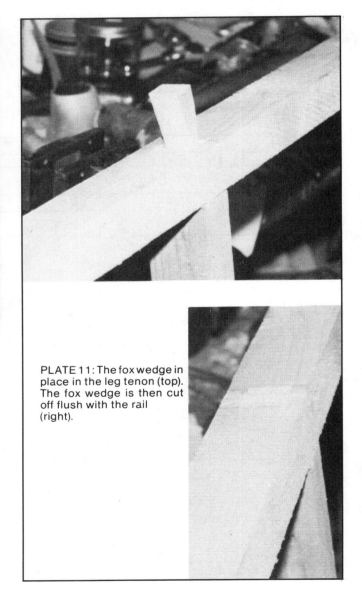

PLATE 11: The fox wedge in place in the leg tenon (top). The fox wedge is then cut off flush with the rail (right).

The tenons are cut to be an inch square and, in my case, 2" long (my 2x2s measured an actual 2"x1½"). The tenons are cut by marking them off with a square and carefully cutting down along the marks with a saw. (See Plate 9.) Next measure the rails for the position of the mortises. Note that these will not be the same distance apart in each rail, since one set of legs fits inside the other — this is so that they will criss-cross. In my cot, the distances were 14" from the end in "A", and 16" from each end in "B".

The mortise is fairly easy to make if the tenons are 1" square; simply drill a hole with a 1" bit and square the corners off with a wood chisel. (See Plate 10.) When per-

FIGURE 8

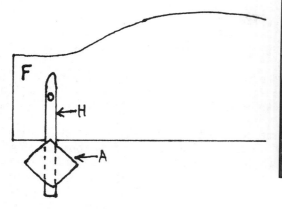

PLATE 13: The headboard in place.

PLATE 12: Laying out the pattern for the headboards on a 1"x12" board.

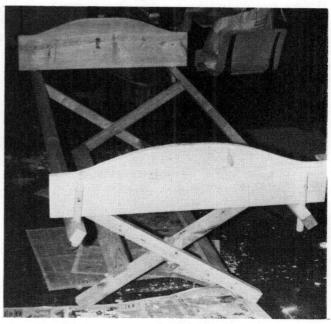

PLATE 14: The camp cot complete except for the canvas cover and the finishing.

manently inserting the tenons in the mortises, you can use just glue; but for a more substantial join, you can also use a "fox wedge". With your saw, cut a slit down the middle of each tenon. With plane, knife or draw-knife, make some wedges (1" wide). Insert the tenons into the mortises (with glue) and hammer the wedges into the slits cut to receive them. Cut off the excess wedge flush with the end of the mortise. (Plate 11.)

Next, attach the lower braces between legs. Cut the 1x4"s to length, and cut a 1" deep lap in each end. Cut a mortise to match in each leg (the braces will be flush with the front surface of the legs). See Figure 7-A for dimensions. Glue and peg in place.

Measure up each leg to the cross-point, and drill the hole for the cross-pin. (In my example, the distance was 17".) Insert the pins, and, if you wish, glue and dowel in place.

The basic framework is now constructed. Next, cut out the head and foot boards. (See Plate 12.) Measure for the headboard holes, mark, and drill. Notice that the hole goes through the side rail from corner to corner. (See Figure 8 and Plate 13.)

Attach the headboard pegs to the head and foot boards with ⅜" dowel. Glue the dowel in place in the boards, but leave the pegs free to swivel. Drill the pegs for

the dowel, and insert them on the glued-in-place dowels in the boards.

If you're going to stain or paint, now is the time to do it. (See Plate 14.) I decided to paint my cot a nice shade of "Concord Green" house paint I got from the paint store.

The next step is to prepare the canvas bed. I allowed a couple of layers of overlap on each side to allow for the wear of the canvas on the wood side rails. I also hemmed each end of the canvas. When done, mine measured 30" wide and 6'6" long. Tack it into place along each rail, spacing the tacks no more than a couple of inches apart. Now climb in and relax. Take a nap —you've earned it.

WILLOW ROD BED

An authentic tipi bed can be made using similar techniques to the willow rod back rests (see above), only in this instance the willow rod mat will not be tapered. Simply construct a mat that's about 2½ feet wide by as long as you need it (in my case about six and a half feet). It might be a good idea to use a heavier willow wand for this than you would for the "lazy back". To set up, drive four forked sticks into the ground at each corner of your bed (a little less than the width, a little longer than the length, and having cut two poles about seven feet long, place them in the forks of the branches to serve as side rails. Spread the mat on the side rails, and cover with your buffalo robe if you want to. This bed is comfortable, and has the advantage of getting you up off the ground. In cold weather, the space underneath can be filled with leaves or grass to serve as insulation.

BURL CUPS AND BOWLS

Burls are the lumps — large or small — which are sometimes found growing on the trunk and limbs of trees. They are a result of some former injury to the tree (analagous to scar tissue, I suspect). The wood has grown around the injury, sealing it off. The resultant knob can serve as the raw material for primitive cups and bowls and were so used by the pioneers and Indians. One characteristic of the burl is that the grain tends to be very twisted and dense, swirling around in interesting patterns.

The process begins by first locating a tree that has burls on it. Maples and walnut, as well as fruit trees were favorite sources in the past. The burl will be easier to work if it's green, but you don't want to damage a live tree any more than you can help. If you cut a burl from a live tree, be sure to doctor the wound with some kind of sealant —paint or pitch. The safest method is to cut your burl from a freshly downed tree. Just the other day, a neighbor down the street lost a large, old maple; and although I was too late to get a claim on it for firewood, Dave Williams and I were able to harvest a half-dozen good burls of various sizes with his chain saw.

Whether you use a chain saw or a buck saw, try to include some wood at the top or bottom of the burl. This wood can be used later for carving a handle. (See Plate 15.)

Traditionally, burls were hollowed out by placing coals from the fire in the middle of the burl, carving or gouging away the charred area, adding more coals, and so on. If you have a drill press, and the bark has been removed, you can drill out much of the interior (being careful not to drill too far). I found in working on a small cup-sized maple burl, that by using a wood carver's gouge and a rawhide mallet, I was able to hollow the burl out completely in about an hour without having to use fire or drill press. I suspect, by the way, that a propane torch could be used in the charring/carving process as well as coals.

I left the bark on during most of the carving process. I'm not sure it was necessary, but it did allow for a better grip during the carving. I removed the bark when I got near the final depth so that I wouldn't carve too far.

When working with green wood, there's always the danger of the finished item cracking or checking as it dries. When my cup was finished, I soaked it for a couple of days in pure mineral oil, and so far it hasn't shown any signs of checking. (See Plate 15.)

The cup or bowl can be left without a handle, or a handle can be carved from the excess wood. If there isn't any excess, a thong can be attached, or a twig or branch of the right configuration can be pegged to the burl to serve as a handle.

CAMP MIRRORS

PLATE 15: A completed maple burl cup resting on a larger maple burl ready to be worked.

Camp mirrors have always been a necessary camp item, particularly in the clean-shaven era of the 18th and early 19th centuries. Today mirrors are just as useful around the camp as shaving mirrors, and for the use of the ladies.

The *Collector's Illustrated Encyclopedia of the American Revolution* shows examples of several different types of camp mirrors ranging from mirrors in mitered frames, like picture frames, to a mirror that looks as though it's inlet into a mitered or rabbited recess. The Indians also had great need for mirrors and examples are known where the mirror was brass-tacked to a paddle-shaped board. This process is simple and requires only a carved wooden paddle, a mirror, and a few large-headed brass tacks. The tacks are inserted just alongside the mirror, and hold it in place the same way you'd thumbtack a photograph to a bulletin board. The only caution here is to pre-drill the holes in the wood for the tacks, otherwise you stand a good chance of breaking the mirror as you drive the tacks in with a hammer. A more sophisticated version would inlet the mirror until it's level with the surface of the board, and hold the mirror in place with the tacks.

BELLOWS

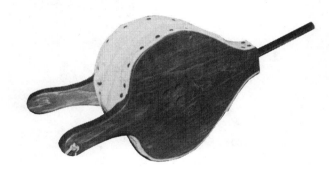

A handy item for camp or home is a bellows, and it's easy enough to make.

Materials:

(2) 1'x1"x8"
leather (scrap buckskin will do)
brass tacks
6" length of brass or copper tubing
carpet tacks or brads
muslin or scrap cloth for pattern
glue

Lay out the pattern on the boards, and cut it out with a coping saw or saber saw. (See Plate 16.)

Cut the neck off one piece (see Plate 17) and glue and clamp it to the other piece. When glue is dry, drill the hole for the nozzle. Cut an air hole or holes in one of the main pieces (see Plate 18), and loosely tack a piece of leather over it on the inside. This acts as a valve to allow the bellows to draw in fresh air. Cut a small piece of leather for use as a hinge, and tack it in place. (See Plate 19.) Tack fabric in place around the edges (see Plate 20), and trim flush. (See Plate 21.) Remove the fabric and use it as a pat-

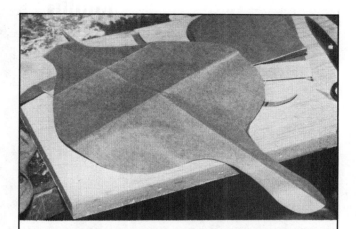

PLATE 16: Lay out the bellows on a piece of 1"x12". Then, to save time, tack two pieces of board together and cut out and shape both sides of the bellows at the same time.

PLATE 17: The nozzle end has been cut off and is being glued and clamped in place.

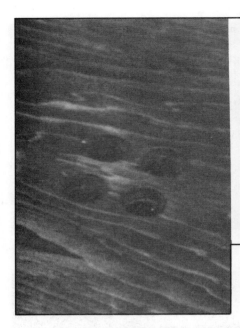

PLATE 18: The air intake holes in the main bellows piece (left). Note that the wood finishing is complete by this time. The nozzle hole has been drilled (right). When drilling the nozzle hole, clamp the bellows halves together and drill the hole an inch or so past the hinge line. This will insure that air gets to the nozzle. The leather valve has also been tacked in place over the air intake holes.

PLATE 19: The leather hinge tacked in place.

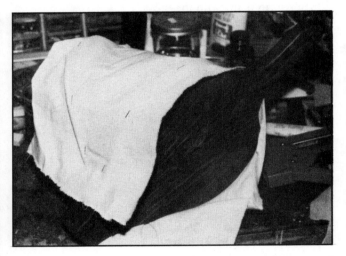

PLATE 20: Scrap muslin stapled in place to form the gusset pattern.

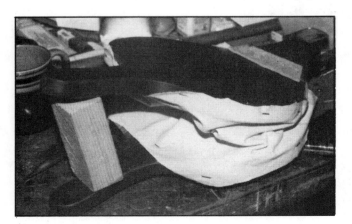

PLATE 21: The muslin pattern trimmed to shape.

FIGURE 9

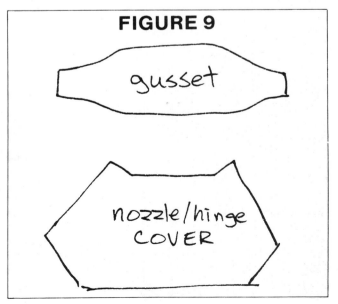

gusset

nozzle/hinge COVER

PLATE 22: The finished bellows.

tern for the leather. (See Figure 9.) Cut the leather out, enlarging the pattern by a half inch or so to allow for folding the leather under when tacking it in place. Sand, stain and finish the wood parts before attaching the leather. Tack the leather down with brass tacks, folding the edges under. Space the tacks fairly close together to minimize air leaks. Make a pattern for the piece that covers the nozzle area, and cut out a leather piece to match. Tack it in place. Glue the nozzle in place. (See Plate 22.) Start a fire.

CANDLE HOLDERS

PLATE 23: The completed two-candle standard.

A variety of authentic and primitive candle stands and lanterns can be made from wood. The following are based on actual examples from the book, *Colonial Lighting*. The first is a primitive, adjustable two-candle "floor lamp."

Materials:

> (1) ½ section of log
> (1) 4' section of 1" pole
> (1) 1"x3"x14" board
> (1) peg or section of dowel

Secure a half-section of log; either split it yourself, or do what I did and raid your woodpile (or your neighbor's). Strip off the back, and with tomahawk and/or draw knife smooth the flat side so that the section sits level and even.

PLATE 24: A close-up view of the two-candle adjustable arm.

Drill a 1" hole at least 2" into the center of the curved portion of the base.

Drill a series of ¼" or ⅜" holes in the section of a pole. Start about 3" from the top, and space the holes about three inches apart, running the series down for a couple of feet (the last hole should be about two feet above floor level).

Trim the piece of 1"x3" like the illustration (see Figure 10), and in the center drill a 1" hole. At either end, drill a ¾" hole (or candle-sized hole) partially through the board.

Insert the pole in the base, and the candle arm over the other end of the pole. Adjust the height of the candles by means of a peg or dowel in the appropriate hole. (See Plates 23 & 24.)

FIGURE 10

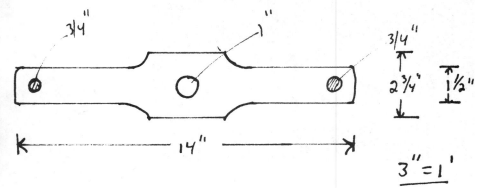

The original piece used a square upright, rather than a round pole, with a square socket chiselled into the base, and a wedge used to adjust the height of the candle arm. I think it's easier and quicker to use a round section of pole.

The base can be left behind if you're camping; simply sharpen the butt end of the pole and drive it into the ground. In either case, the overall height was planned for the relatively lower seats of the primitive camp. If you're planning to use it with "regular" height chairs, you might wish to make the upright pole a little taller.

A variant of this candle holder is also found in *Colonial Lighting*. It is the "Swing-arm single candle standard". The following directions deviate from the original only in that the base of the original was a flat slab, but we're going to use the other half of our split log. I also had to guess on the construction of the pins on which the swivel arms swivelled.

The materials and tools are similar for the double candle holder except that you'll need 3 pieces of 1"x2" instead of the single piece of 1"x3" for a candle holder.

The base and the upright are the same as for the double candle standard. The difference is in the swing-arm, here made of three pieces of 1"x2", each a foot or so long. Cut out each section (using a sabre saw or coping saw) according to the illustration. (See Figure 11.) In piece "C" you will drill a candle socket at one end and a ⅜" hole at the other. Piece "B" will have a ⅜" hole at each end, while piece "A" will have a ⅜" hole at one end and a 1" hole drilled at the other end. I also carved each piece into a "dog-bone" shape like the original.

Assemble the sections of the arm (C over B over A) by inserting a section of ⅜" dowel through each hole in the arm sections and securing it in place with a ¼" (or ⅛") dowel cross-drilled through each end. It might be a good idea to do your final sanding, staining and finishing before finally gluing or otherwise permanently securing these cross-pins in place. The tighter you can get the cross-pins to fit, the less "sag" there will be in the arm when it is fully

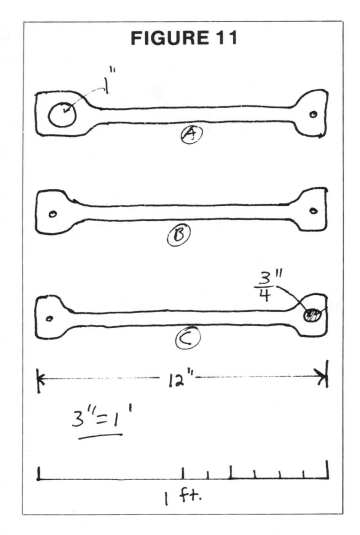

FIGURE 11

extended. When finished, place it on the upright, and adjust the arm to suit. (See Plate 25.)

PLATE 25: The extension arm in open and closed positions.

This is one way to relax on a lazy-back.

HORN EQUIPMENT

PLATE 26: Several easy-to-make horn items; salt horn, spoons, and two styles of cups.

Comparable in many ways to working with wood is making things out of horn. Most of us are fairly familiar with the process of making powder horns, but many other utilitarian and attractive items for the camp can be made from horn which was the "plastic" of the 18th and 19th centuries.

Generally speaking, horn can be cut, sawn, scraped, drilled, carved, and moulded into a number of items. Horn has the advantages of being lightweight, relatively unbreakable, easily shaped, and durable. In addition, it's waterproof; and thus makes a good container for gunpowder and other substances which benefit from staying dry.

Some of the techniques I will describe in the following section are some which I have devised myself (after some experimentation), taking my cue from hints gathered in reading the very little available information about early hornsmithing.

A SALT HORN

A good container for salt or other condiment can easily be made by sawing out a segment of horn and plugging both ends, using the same techniques as in making a powder horn. Begin with a raw horn, and square up the large end by cutting off the rough end with a hand saw or a band saw. Depending on the size of the horn, measure up two or three inches, and cut off the tip end.

Measure each opening, and cut a circle out of a scrap piece of 1" pine. Bevel the edges slightly. You don't have to cut the plug to match the contour of the horn. If your measurement is right and you haven't cut the plug too large, you'll be able to shape the horn into the perfect circle of the plug.

Here is where my technique differs from the traditional instructions for fitting powder horn plugs. We have always been told that at this stage in the construction process to boil the horn in water for some time, until the horn becomes pliable, and then force the plug into the softened end, and hold it in place until the horn dries, at which time the horn will hold its new shape. There are two other ways to soften the horn. One is simply to soak the horn in water overnight. The horn will be pliable and easily cut or shaped. (This is the easiest method of scraping a raw horn, by the way — soak it overnight, and you'll be amazed at how easily it can be scraped with a sharp knife.) The disadvantage with this method is that it takes longer for the horn to dry than it did to get it pliable; and it won't hold its final shape as well.

A better method is to simply apply heat. The old hornsmiths passed the horn through an open flame, and as the horn became flexible, they shaped it. The dangers

here are that too little heat won't allow the horn to bend, and too much will char the horn. (You'll find that the horn is sometime "toasted" a little as it is, but this can be steel-wooled away in the finishing.) I have found that putting the horn in the kitchen oven set at 300 or 350 degrees for a few minutes will render it flexible enough to bend easily and fairly severely, depending on the thickness of the horn, and without scorching. I haven't tried it in a microwave oven yet.

So, put your horn segment in the oven for a few minutes, and when it has softened, force the end plugs in about half-way. Take the horn out of the oven, and allow it to cool. You may find that the plugs are firmly fixed in place without any more work required on your part. If not, glue them in place with epoxy, and/or drill ⅛" holes around the base and glue in small pegs.

Next, saw off the excess plug material, and drill a small hole in the center of the completed horn. Carve a small plug for this hole. Your salt horn is basically complete, except for final finishing.

If you haven't yet scraped or sanded the horn, do so now. Finish up by going to ever finer grits of paper. I like to finish up with 400 grit paper, followed by 0000 steel wool and a coat of Johnson's Paste Wax. Your completed horn (see Plate 26) will be very similar to one shown in the *Collector's Illustrated Encyclopedia of the American Revolution* and you'll find that salt kept in it will never lump up, but will always stay dry and flow freely.

HORN CUPS

PLATE 27: The horn cup ready for the insertion of the base and final shaping and finishing.

209

A functional cup can be made by the same process used on the salt horn, except you glue in only one end plug. Sand the edges smooth, and scrape and sand the inside as well.

Another style of cup can be made by leaving a segment of horn that can be shaped into a handle. (See Plate 27.) Soften and scrape the horn inside and out, and cut a circular base plug (for all end plugs you may find it convenient to taper the plug a bit — this insures a tight fit. (See Plate 28.) The base plug can be circular — that is, you needn't worry about carving the plug to fit the contours of the horn, since you're able to shape the horn to the contours of the plug. Heat the horn in the oven, and when it is heated through, reach in and force the base plug in place. Grasp the handle segment with a pair of pliers or wooden tongs, and gently bend the handle to shape. Take care here to pre-shape the handle segment so that it is neither too thick and wide nor too thin and narrow. If it is too thick, it

PLATE 28: The base is in place, ready to be cut off flush with the bottom of the cup.

might not bend well. If it's too thin or narrow, it may not support the weight of the cup when filled with liquid. When you have the desired bend to the handle, remove the cup from the oven (maintaining the bend in the hot horn) and run it under cool water. As soon as the horn has cooled, it will hold the shape it has been given. (See Plate 26.) You may find that the base plug is fitted too firmly in place to remove (which is fine), but you may also find that a little epoxy will be needed to hold the plug in permanently. I like to drill and peg the base plug in, for cosmetic reasons if for nothing else. You'll also find that it's a good idea to do all

your final sanding and polishing before giving the horn the oven treatment.

HORN SPOONS

Many items can be made from horn that has been flattened into sheets. A band saw is handy here for sectioning the horn lengthwise, either in half if it is a narrow horn, or into more segments if it's larger. Either soak the segments until they are pliable and then clamp between a couple of boards until the horn has dried, or heat the horn and clamp. A handy gadget here is one that a friend of mine, Dave Williams and I have devised. We took a cheap pair of imitation "vice grip" pliers, and brazed a couple of steel plates to the jaws. These are very handy for flattening smaller segments of horn. The flattned horn can be made into horn combs, using either a band saw or a hack saw to cut the teeth or you can make another gadget, which we call "vice spoons", to make horn spoons.

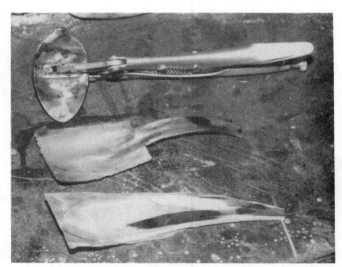

PLATE 29: Spoon mold and horn spoon blanks that have been pressed and are ready for trimming and final finishing.

We got a couple of stainless steel spoons from the hardware store, and brazed them to the jaws of the pliers. (See Plate 29.) Clamp a piece of paper in the spoons, and draw around them to give you a pattern for your spoon blank. Cut the blank, leaving the spoon end squared off at this point. (See Plate 29.) Now heat the blank in a 350 degree oven for a few minutes, reach in and pick up the blank with a pair of pliers or tongs, and insert the blank into the vice spoons. Squeeze gently, run under cold water (first giving a bend to the spoon handle if you wish), and you have a spoon. Trim the excess blank away around the bowl of the spoon, give a final polishing, and you're ready to eat. (See Plate 26.)

Many other little items can be made from horn, using these techniques, from real shoe horns to small containers of different types. I guess you could even make powder horns.

LEATHER EQUIPMENT

I really enjoy working with leather. It may be because my great-grandfather was a harness maker. At any rate, there is real satisfaction to be gained from making things from such a satisfying material. Leather can be cut, shaped, moulded, stitched, glued, and nailed to form a variety of useful and authentic items.

From other chapters, you're probably familiar with the techniques of working with garment leathers, buckskin and heavier moccasin weight soft leathers for footgear and shooting bags. Here, we're going to deal with the thicker, stiffer, vegetable-tanned "hard" leathers, like Tandy's "Oak Tanned" carving leathers. Some of the techniques are similar to those used in working with garment leathers, some are different. Some of the tools that are necessary (or handy) are also different. A basic list (all available at Tandy's) of tools and supplies might include:

1. awl
2. rawhide mallet
3. waxed linen thread
4. leather cutting shears (expensive, but worth it)
5. harness needles
6. skiver (to shave the thickness of the leather on the edges)
7. gouger
8. stitching-gauge wheel
9. edge slicker
10. stitching palm
11. stitching pony
12. knife (crooked knife will work fine)
13. metal straight edge (a wooden yardstick will do)
14. stripper
15. leather dye
16. beeswax
17. needle nose pliers
18. Barge's contact cement

The various thicknesses of leather are designated in ounces — the thickest usually available is 10 - 12 oz. For many projects a medium-weight 7 - 8 oz. might be preferable.

The general technique used for leatherwork of the type we will be employing consists of the following steps (regardless of the article to be constructed): (1) lay out the pattern on the flesh (rough) side of the leather; (2) cut out the pieces with shears or knife; (3) with an adjustable groover gouge out a stitching groove (to lower the stitches below the surface of the leather, protecting them from wear); (4) dye the pieces with Tandy's "Omega" leather dye, spraying it on rather than daubing it to insure a more even coverage; (5) apply a protective coating (Tandy's "Tan-Cote" is good); (6) with a stitching or pounce wheel, mark the stitch line (these wheels will indent the leather where each stitch should go); (7) depending on the thickness of the leather and the nature of the pieces to be stitched together, "skive" or thin the leather on the flesh side along the stitch line; (8) again, depending on the pieces to be stitched together, "baste" the pieces in place with contact cement (like Barge's cement); and (10) punch each hole with an awl.

A leather awl punches an elongated diamond-shaped hole. This should be aligned at an angle to the stitch line, to minimize the chance of the stitches tearing the leather.

Although the stitching awl is the traditional and preferred tool for punching stitching holes, I'd like to recommend a heretical technique that will horrify the traditionalists but will speed up your sewing. Instead of laboriously punching each stitch hole, use a *drill*. I chuck a small bit into my power drill or Dremel power tool and drill all the holes. An expert will be able to tell from the look that you haven't used a traditional technique, but if you don't want the hassle and blisters that a dull awl will cause, try pre-drilling your holes. (The size of the drill bit you use will depend on the size of your needles. Keep the holes as small as possible.)

The stitching technique is a two-needle process, using harness needles (which are relatively blunt, as needles go). Measure off a length of waxed thread equal to at least 2½ times the length of the line to be stitched (but never longer than you can conveniently reach while pulling stitches through). Attach a harness needle to each end of the thread. Pull one needle through the first hole, evening up the ends of the thread (like you were starting to lace your shoes); then pass both needles through the next hole from opposite sides. Each needle will go through the same hole. When you reach either the end of your stitch line, or the end of your thread, secure the stitching by back-stitching for two or three holes, and cut the loose ends off flush with the stitches. It is not necessary to tie a knot. Finally, after the stitching is completed, run over the stitches with the stitching wheel to "set" the stitches. Last, trim the edges even with a knife, dampen and/or redye them, and polish them with an "edge-slicker" or a rough piece of canvas.

THE LEATHER PORTMANTEAU

Travellers of the Colonial period and early 19th century used suitcases of leather called *portmanteaus*. These were not the oblong suitcases of today, but generally took an oval, round or hump-backed shape. They are relatively

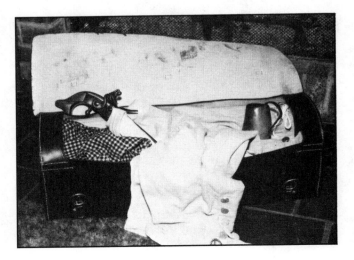

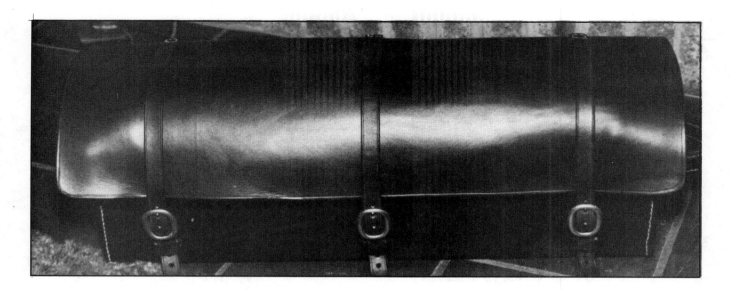

easy to make, and provide you with an authentic and good looking, as well as practical means of carrying and storing your rendezvous clothing and gear.

Let's begin by making a medium sized, hump-backed, flat-bottomed portmanteau.

Materials:

    10 sq. ft. of 10-12 oz. leather
    2 sq. ft. of 3-4 oz. leather
    ⅛" plywood or Masonite
    (3) 1" or ¾" brass harness buckles

Begin by laying out the pattern. (See Figure 12.) Cut out all the pieces, making sure that you keep the cuts vertical. "A", "E" and "D" are cut from the 10-12 oz. leather, "B" from the plywood or Masonite, and "C" from the 3-4 oz. leather. Straps "F" and "G" can be cut from a medium-weight leather (8 oz.) if you have it; otherwise from the 10-12 oz. (See Plates 30 & 31.)

Dye all the pieces (unless you don't mind if your con-trasting stitches are dyed the same color as the leather, and mark all the stitch lines ⅜" or so in from the edge (gouge the line and use the stitching wheel).

If you dampen the leather with a wet cloth, you can impress a decorative groove with the edge slicker ½" in along those edges on pieces "D", "E", "F", & "G" which are not stitched.

Assemble the pieces in the following order: (1) Skive the ends of the two "K" and "J" handle pieces to about half-thickness for a distance of a couple of inches. Apply contact cement to the flesh sides and glue the two pieces together. Punch the holes with an awl and stitch them together using the saddle-stitch. Mark the position of the ends on one of the "A" end pieces and glue and stitch in place (be careful not to get any glue on exposed surfaces):

(2) Spread contact cement on the flesh side of both "A" end pieces, and glue the plywood or Masonite "B" pieces in place. Coat them and the flesh side of the thin "C" inside end pieces with contact cement, and let dry.

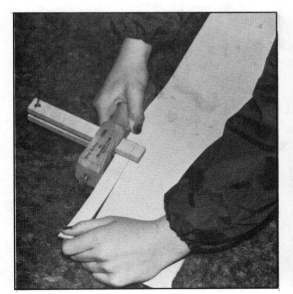

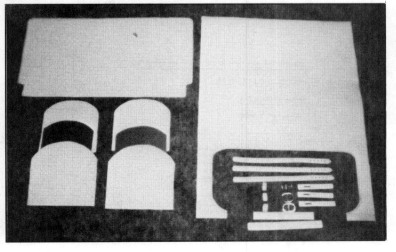

PLATE 30 (left): Cutting straps is made easier by using an adjustable stripping tool. PLATE 31 (below): The parts for the flat bottomed portmanteau laid out ready for dyeing and assembly.

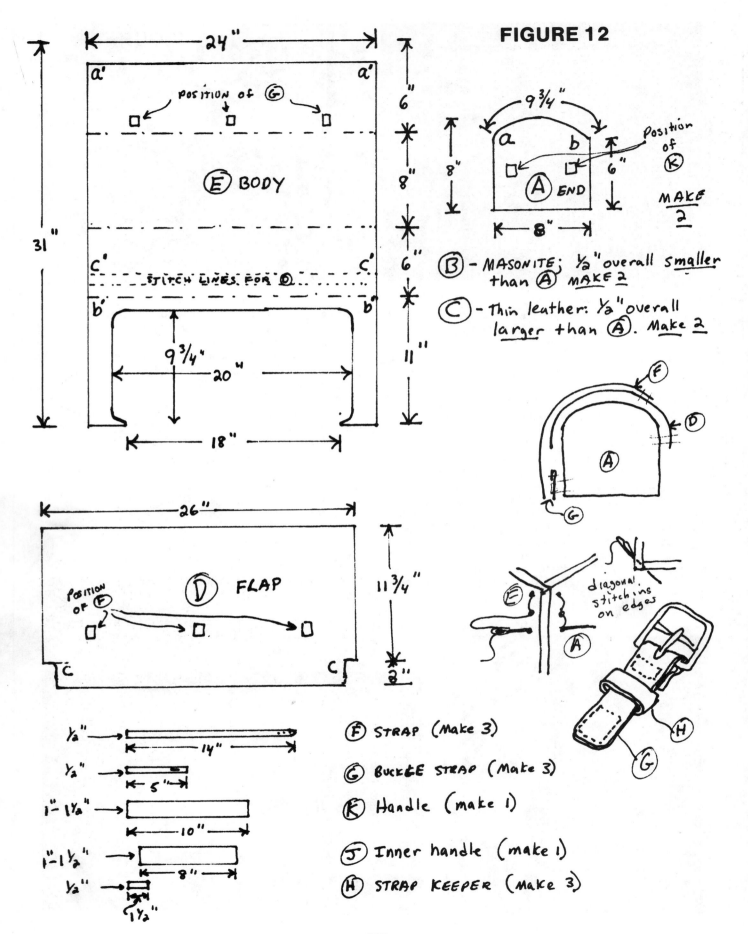

FIGURE 12

24"

a'   a'

POSITION OF Ⓖ

Ⓔ BODY

6"

8"

C'   C'
STITCH LINES FOR Ⓓ

6"

b'   b"

9¾"
20"

11"

18"

31"

9¾"

a   b

Ⓐ END

8"

8"

Position of Ⓚ

MAKE 2

Ⓑ - MASONITE; ½" overall smaller than Ⓐ MAKE 2

Ⓒ - Thin leather; ½" overall larger than Ⓐ. Make 2

Ⓕ
Ⓓ
Ⓐ
Ⓖ

26"

POSITION OF Ⓕ

Ⓓ FLAP

11¾"

C   C

3"

Ⓔ

diagonal stitching on edges

Ⓐ

Ⓗ

Ⓖ

½"
14"

½"
5"

1"-1½"
10"

1"-1½"
8"

½"
1½"

Ⓕ STRAP (Make 3)

Ⓖ BUCKLE STRAP (Make 3)

Ⓚ Handle (make 1)

Ⓙ Inner handle (make 1)

Ⓗ STRAP KEEPER (Make 3)

PLATE 32: A completed end-piece "sandwich".

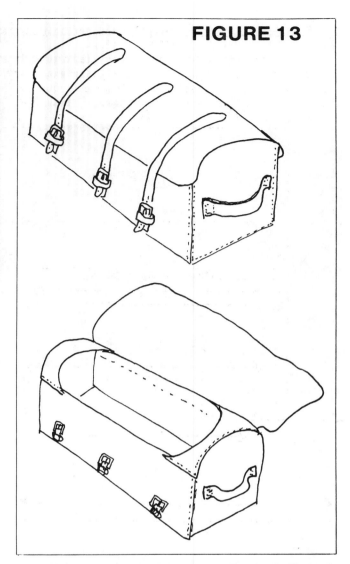

FIGURE 13

Soak the "C" pieces until they are pliable, and glue and form them to the previously glued-together "A" and "B" pieces. (See Plate 32.) Trim the edges of the "C" pieces to fit if necessary. Or, cut "A" from 12-14 oz. saddle skirting leather, and eliminate the lamination of "B" & "C".

(3) Stitch the buckles into the three "C" pieces and glue and stitch them into position on the main body piece, "E". Stitch the strap keepers together (see Figure 12) and stitch in place at the same time. (See Plate 33.) Glue and stitch the three straps ("F") in place on the flap "D".

(4) Glue and stitch "D" to "E". (See Plate 34.)

(5) Glue and stitch "E" to the end pieces "A". Overlap the edges of "E" on the "A" pieces (see Figure 12), and awl and stitch through at a diagonal (see Figure

PLATE 33 (below): Buckle strap, buckle, and strap keeper stitched in place on the main body piece (before folding). PLATE 34 (right): Ready to begin assembling the body to the end pieces.

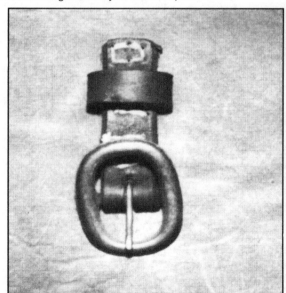

12). Start stitching by matching the corners and continuing around the end pieces. (See Figure 13.)

Another style of portmanteau is constructed with oval end pieces (the oval allows easier access than would a round cross-section). The construction technique is similar to our first portmanteau (see Figure 14), but it is a

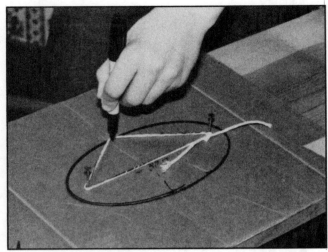

PLATE 35: Laying out an oval. The nails are 6⅛" apart; the loop of string is 15" in circumference. This results in an oval that is 8¼"x5¾" and 22¾" around.

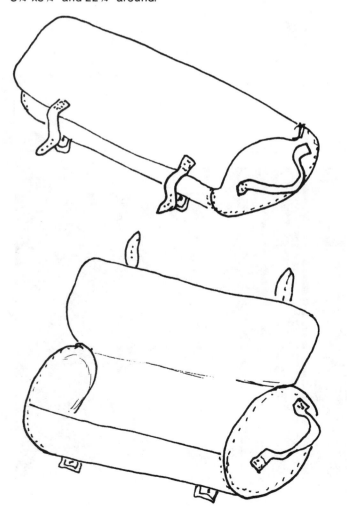

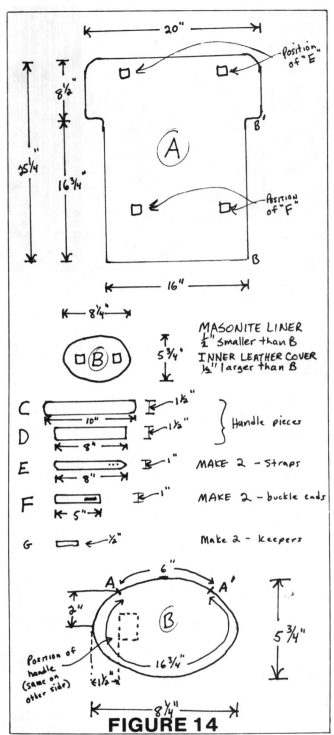

FIGURE 14

little smaller. It is assembled in the same order, with the exception that the flap and body are cut from a single piece of leather. The only problem in laying out a pattern is in inscribing the oval.

The oval pattern can be drawn by using two small nails, a loop of string, and a pencil. The string is looped around the nails and pencil, and the pencil is moved around against the tension of the loop, forming an oval. The problem is to determine how far apart the nails should be, and how long the loop of string should be. (See Plate 35.)

WALLETS & PURSES

Although hard money was scarce during the early years of our country's history, and paper money was often, literally, "not worth a Continental", there was still a need for some kind of container for bills, papers and coins. And, in our "pocket-plentiful" age, we are used to carrying bills, change, credit cards, licenses, etc. Our modern billfolds and purses, however, aren't really suitable for the rendezvous and encampment, nor does historic clothing always have the number of pockets we are used to. There are, however, authentic wallets and purses which are easy to construct. The following two designs are taken from examples in the *Collector's Illustrated Encyclopedia of the American Revolution:*

COLONIAL WALLET

This folding two-compartment wallet is sized for modern bills, and can be constructed from any thin leather, vegetable tanned (hard finish) or buckskin. It can be constructed with a cloth lining, as were the originals, or it can remain unlined.

Begin by laying out the pattern (see Figure 15) on your leather and lining material (use any scrap authentic material such as calico). Cut out the pieces. (See Plate 36.) Begin construction by sewing the flap pieces ("C") in posi-

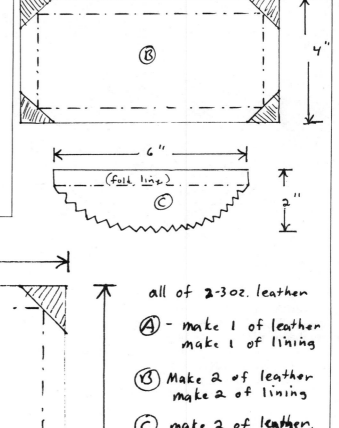

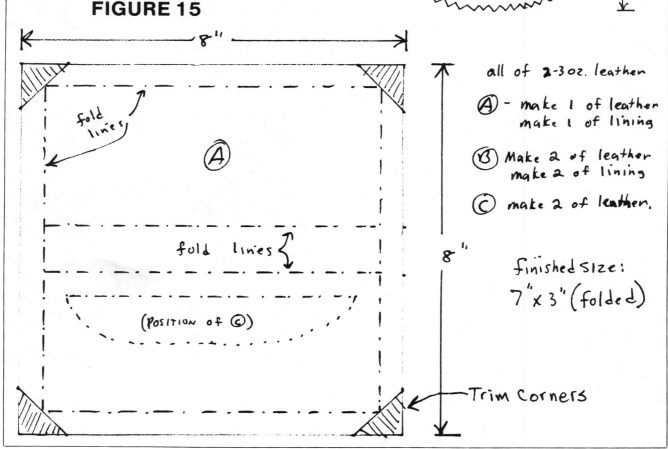

FIGURE 15

fold lines

Ⓐ

fold lines

(POSITION OF Ⓒ)

all of 2-3 oz. leather

Ⓐ – make 1 of leather
make 1 of lining

Ⓑ Make 2 of leather
make 2 of lining

Ⓒ make 2 of leather.

finished size:
7" x 3" (folded)

Trim Corners

PLATE 36: The pieces of the Colonial Wallet laid out and ready for assembly.

PLATE 37: The assembled wallet.

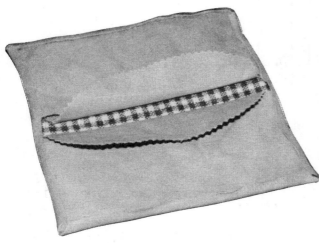

PLATE 38: The pieces of the Colonial Purse laid out.

tion on the lining or, if you don't mind your stitches showing, on the inside of "A". Glue the lining piece, with flaps stitched in place, on the flesh side of "A".

Glue the lining to the flesh side of both "B" pieces; fold and glue the edge down.

Position the "B" pieces on "A", fold "A" edges over (glue to keep in place), and stitch them down. (See Plate 37.)

COLONIAL PURSE

This two-compartment purse was a "uni-sex" design used by men and women. It also employs a unique flap closure. It is constructed from 3-4 oz. "oak tanned" leather, except for the closure, which is made from 10-12 oz. leather.

Begin by cutting out the pattern. (See Figure 16.) With the blade end of a folding tool and a straight edge, scribe the decorative lines on the grain side of the leather. Dampen the surface and run the folder back and forth several times on each line, embossing the line into the damp leather. Then dye and finish the leather. (See Plate 38.)

This purse is stitched inside out. Begin by gluing and folding in the ends of the main body, "A". Next, fold "A"

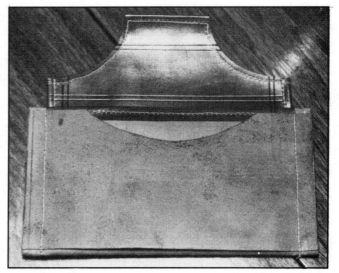

PLATE 39: The purse folded inside out and stitched along the sides.

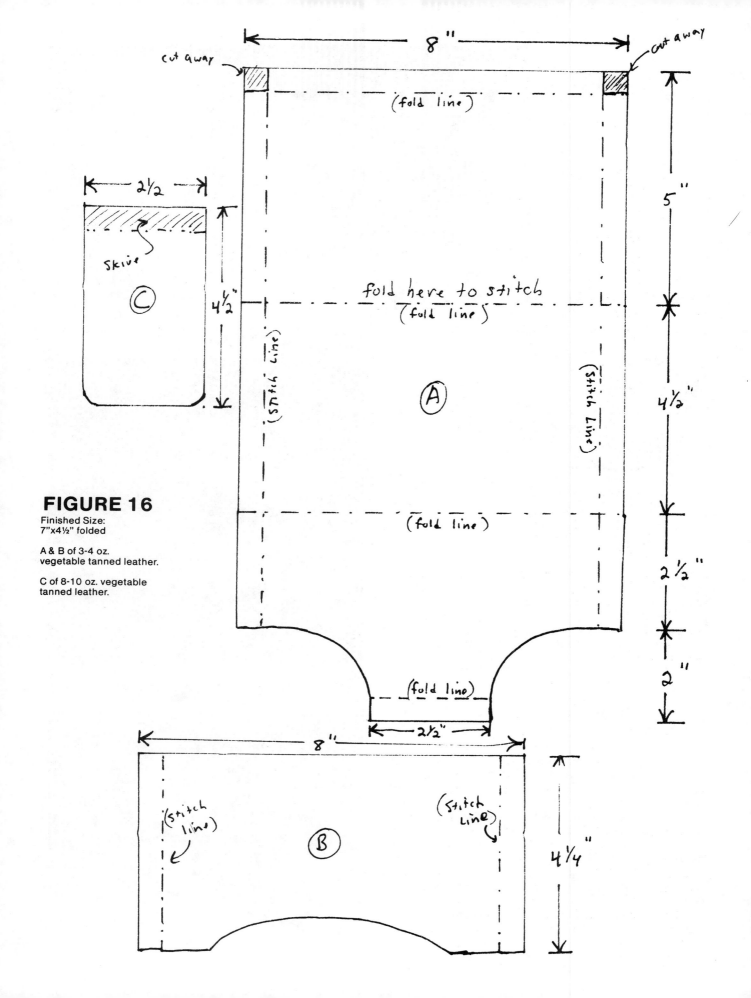

cut away

8"

cut away

(fold line)

2½

skive

C

4½"

fold here to stitch
(fold line)

(stitch line)

(stitch Line)

A

5"

4½"

FIGURE 16

Finished Size:
7"x4½" folded

A & B of 3-4 oz.
vegetable tanned leather.

C of 8-10 oz. vegetable
tanned leather.

(fold line)

2½"

2"

(fold line)

2½"

8"

(stitch line)

(stitch Line)

B

4¼"

FIGURE 17

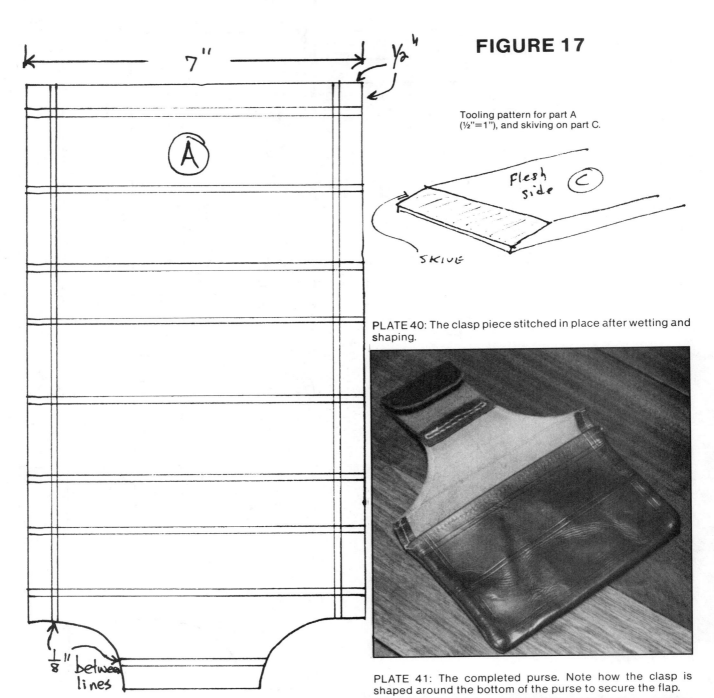

7"

½"

Ⓐ

⅛" between lines

Tooling pattern for part A
(½"=1"), and skiving on part C.

Flesh side Ⓒ

SKIVE

PLATE 40: The clasp piece stitched in place after wetting and shaping.

PLATE 41: The completed purse. Note how the clasp is shaped around the bottom of the purse to secure the flap.

with the grain side in, and lay "B" in position. Stitch the body together along the stitch lines. (See Plate 39.) Trim along the stitch line to within about ⅛" of the stitches. Turn the purse right side out. (It may help to dampen the leather along the seams to make it more flexible.)

Skive the end of "C", skiving on the flesh side. (See Figure 17.) Glue and stitch "C" to the flap of "A". (See Plate 40.) Next, thoroughly wet "C" and bend it so that it will wrap around the bottom of "A". (See Plate 41.) Clamp or otherwise secure and let dry. It will hold its shape when dry, and will serve as a clasp to hold the flap closed.

219

FRENCH COIN PURSE

Occasionally you'll find a kit which will be just what you want. This time, it's a new kit from Tandy's that costs about $3.00, and in half an hour makes up into a snap-clasp coin purse, very representative of the 19th century. There's really nothing to it. (See Plate 42.)

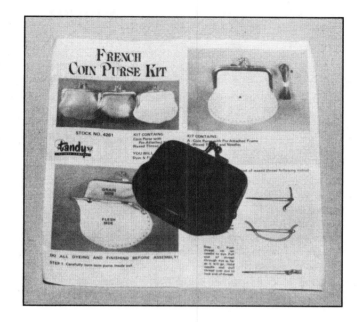

PLATE 42: Tandy's French Coin Purse Kit assembled.

RAWHIDE EQUIPMENT

The Colonists and frontiersmen weren't the only folks who made utilitarian containers from stiff leather. The Indians also made "suitcases" from their all purpose material, rawhide. Typical of the Indians' use of rawhide for containers is the parfleche, which is nothing more complicated than a rawhide envelope. (See Plate 43.)

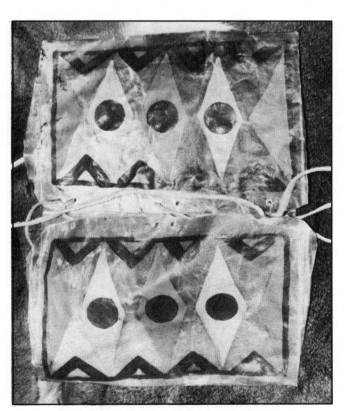

PLATE 43: A finished rawhide parfleche.

First, of course, you need to procure some rawhide. You can either make your own by scraping and de-hairing a hide and allowing it to dry on the stretching frame or by purchasing it. Homemade rawhide will likely be thicker than the rawhide from Tandy's, for example, but both are acceptable.

In either case, the rawhide needs to be prepared. Lay the rawhide on the ground or on a pad of several layers of newspaper or corrugated cardboard, and strike it many

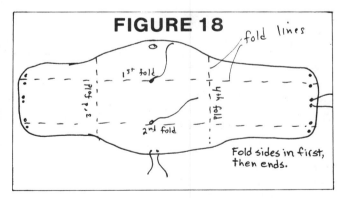

overlapping blows with the rounded back end of an axe or hatchet. This will whiten and somewhat soften the rawhide, making it easier to work. Lay out the pattern on the hide (see Figure 18) and cut it out, using leather shears, knife, or tin snips. Punch the holes as marked for the buckskin tie thongs. If you wish to decorate it in the Indian manner, now is the time to paint it. Finally, wet the parfleche, and fold it up, either tying or otherwise holding it in place until it dries. It will then hold its shape. Since the Indians always made two of every item, make another one while you're at it.

TOBACCO CANTEEN

Save your rawhide scraps, for they are useful either for stripping into laces or for making other small items, such as the tobacco canteen. These are useful little containers either for holding tobacco or lead balls, caps, etc.

Cut out two pieces as shown in the pattern (see Figure 19), and soak them well until soft and pliable. Stitch them together (using a single-needle whip stitch) with sinew, either real or artificial. While still wet, pack sand into the canteen to swell the body. Grease the wooden stopper (which you've carved in advance), and insert it into the neck of the canteen. As the canteen dries, remove and reinsert the plug several times to prevent the rawhide from shrinking around it. When it has dried, dump out the sand. Drop a couple of pebbles in the canteen and rattle them around to dislodge the sand that has stuck to the interior.

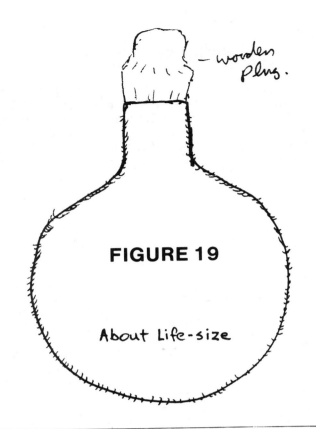

— wooden plug.

FIGURE 19

About Life-size

BAGS, POUCHES & PACKS

Buckskin and canvas can be used to make Indian style saddlebags (which can be hung from the tipi poles) and Revolutionary War knapsacks and packs.

SADDLEBAGS

Saddlebags were always made in pairs, each decorated the same. You can make them from buckskin, or from canvas. In either case, transfer the pattern (see Figure 20) to the flesh side of the buckskin or the wrong side of the fabric. Cut out the pieces, and stitch together inside out, right sides together. With the buckskin, stitch using wedge-pointed glovers' needles and artificial sinew or waxed linen thread. With the canvas, use a regular large sewing needle and a strong linen or cotton thread. For both, use the same whip stitch. The edges of the canvas bag flap will have to be hemmed, but the buckskin edge can be left "raw."

Attach the tie thongs (see Figure 20), decorate with bedwork or quillwork on buckskin and paint on the canvas bags, and you have decorative and practical additions to the furnishings of your lodge.

KNAPSACKS AND HAVERSACKS

Just as practical and authentic as the Indian saddlebags are the Revolutionary War knapsacks and haversacks, as illustrated in *Sketchbook '76*. The simplest is the basic haversack, which can be used as a pack, depending on how the straps are attached.

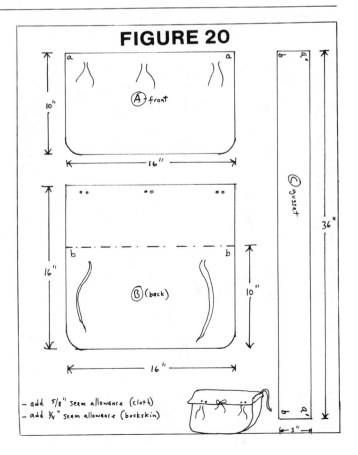

FIGURE 20

10"

ⓐ front

16"

16"

b   b

ⓑ (back)

10"

ⓒ gusset

36"

16"

— add ⅝" seam allowance (cloth)
— add ¼" seam allowance (buckskin)

3"

BASIC KNAPSACK

Make out of cotton or linen canvas with a good tight weave (no synthetic blends, please!). Cut out your pattern pieces (see Figure 21), and pin in place on your fabric. Cut

out the pieces. Straps can be constructed either by stitching together a tube and turning it inside out, or by stitching two pieces together. The latter is easier.

(1) Begin by pinning and stitching the straps in place: note the different possible locations, depending on whether you want to end up with a back pack, a knapsack, or an

FIGURE 21

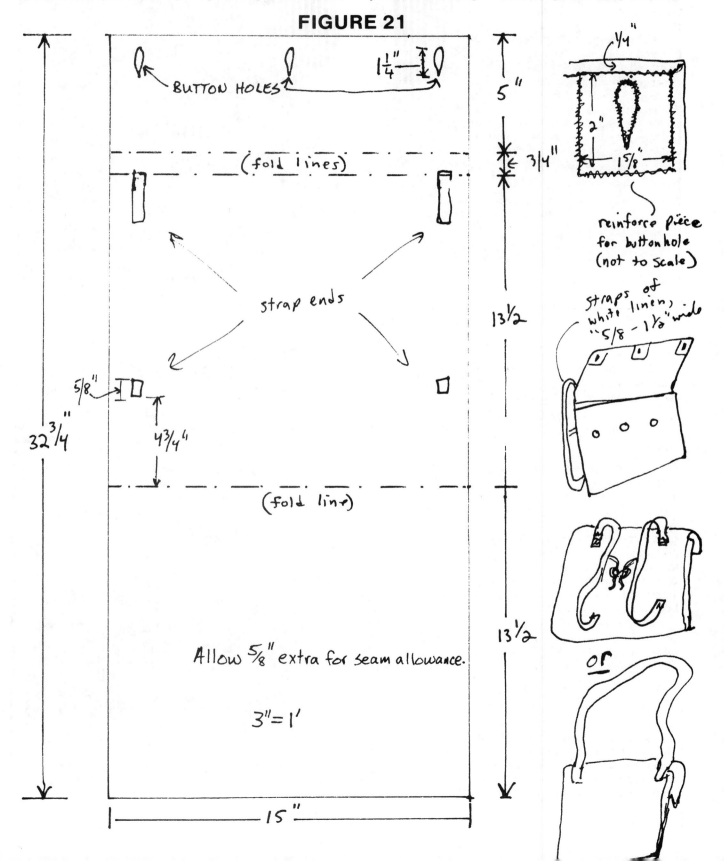

BUTTON HOLES

$1\frac{1}{4}$"

5"

3/4"

(fold lines)

$13\frac{1}{2}$

strap ends

5/8"

$32\frac{3}{4}$"

$4\frac{3}{4}$"

(fold line)

$13\frac{1}{2}$

Allow $\frac{5}{8}$" extra for seam allowance.

3" = 1'

15"

1/4"

2"

$1\frac{5}{8}$"

reinforce piece for button hole (not to scale)

straps of white linen, 5/8 - $1\frac{1}{8}$" wide

or

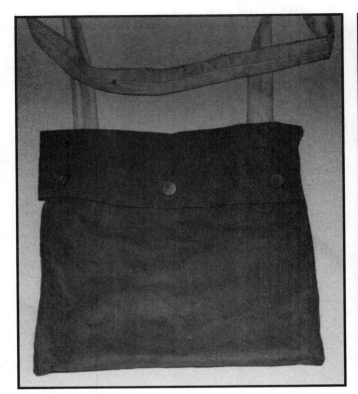
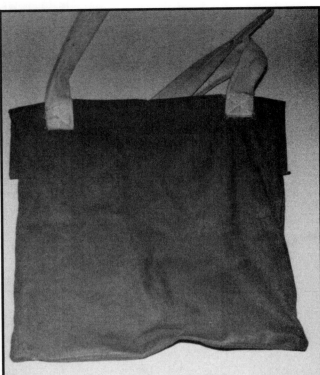

PLATE 44: Obverse and reverse of the Revolutionary War knapsack showing the position of the straps for the "over-the-shoulder" version.

over-the-shoulder haversack.

(2) Press and hem the raw edges.

(3) Stitch the buttonhole reinforcement pieces in place on the reverse side of the flap.

(4) Pin and stitch the bag together (inside out, right sides together), folding the hem over so that no raw edges will show.

(5) Cut and stitch the buttonholes (use a buttonholer on your machine if you have one; otherwise just whip stitch around the buttonhole.

(6) Attach pewter, brass, wood, or horn buttons.

You can leave the bag "in the white", or you can paint the exterior, which helps to weatherproof it (and is also authentic). The originals were painted with red ochre paint ("Spanish Brown"), but we can get much the same effect by painting with any "Colonial red" latex exterior house paint. If you plan to paint your knapsack, paint only the body, not the straps. You'll find it more convenient to paint what will be the exterior of the bag before you sew it together (otherwise you have to paint around the strap ends, for example). Use a "dry brush" technique; with the paint at either full strength or thinned somewhat with water. Dip your brush in the paint and squeeze most of the paint out on the edge of the can. Brush the paint into the fabric, using a criss-cross stroke, working it well into the fabric, but not "gooping" it on. The paint, when dry, will stiffen the fabric somewhat but not so much that you can't work with it, nor so much that it will crack. The advantage of the latex paint is that it is somewhat flexible and "stretchable". I have a painted haversack that I've used for years, and it has shown no sign of cracking or peeling. (See Plate 44.)

"NEW INVENTED KNAPSACK OF 1776"

This combination knapsack/haversack, as illustrated in *Sketchbook '76,* is fairly large, and is designed to hold many items. The original had a painted knapsack attached to an unpainted haversack, but you can also either leave the whole works unpainted or paint the entire body for additional protection. If you decide to paint any part, do it

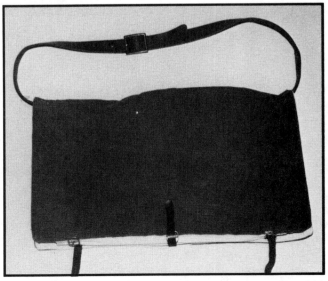

PLATE 45: The "New Invented" combination knapsack/haversack.

223

FIGURE 22

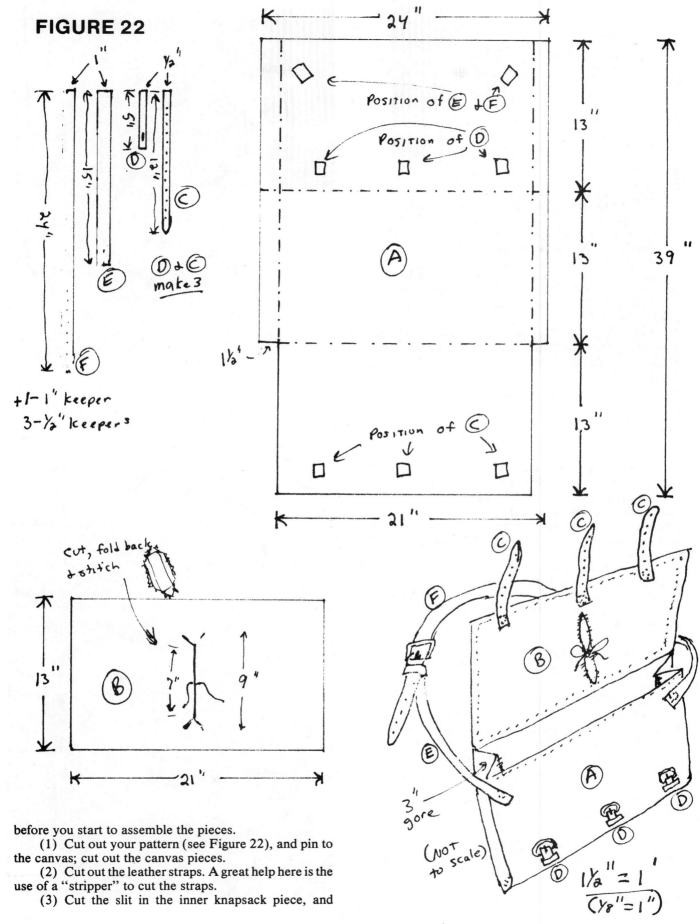

+1-1" keeper
3-½" keepers

Position of Ⓔ +Ⓕ
Position of Ⓓ
Position of Ⓒ

Ⓓ & Ⓒ
make 3

Ⓐ

Cut, fold back & stitch

Ⓑ

3" gore

(NOT to scale)

1½" = 1'
(⅛" = 1")

before you start to assemble the pieces.

(1) Cut out your pattern (see Figure 22), and pin to the canvas; cut out the canvas pieces.

(2) Cut out the leather straps. A great help here is the use of a "stripper" to cut the straps.

(3) Cut the slit in the inner knapsack piece, and

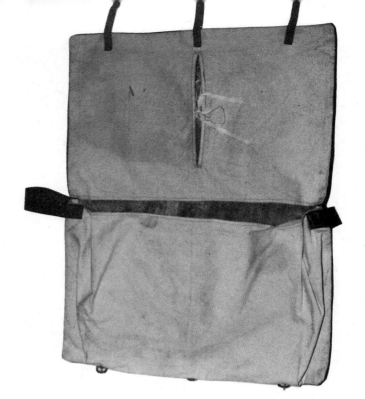

PLATE 46: The knapsack/
haversack open. Note the
inner pocket on the top flap.

hem it.

(4) Stitch the knapsack pieces together, hemming so that there are no raw edges.

(5) Using a saddle stitch (two needle), mark the location, glue and stitch the straps and buckle pieces together, and to the body of the bag, as indicated.

(6) Stitch the side seams of the haversack together, inside out (right sides together). Turn right-side out when completed. Tuck the gore in, and press to keep in place. (See Plates 45 & 46.)

Sketchbook '76 suggests that a blanket may have been carried between the folded halves of the bag. The bag was worn under the left arm, slung towards the back.

GOURD CONTAINERS

Gourds are grown these days primarily for their decorative properties in autumn "arrangements", but they are still capable of fulfilling the practical functions they provided in the past. Depending on the size and shape, gourds can be fashioned into many useful items, including canteens, jugs, dippers, cups, bowls and scoops, powder horns and ball flasks.

Before making anything, however, the gourd must be dried out. If it's fresh, start the drying process by scraping (gently) away the exterior "skin" or membrane. Then simply hang the gourd up and in a couple of days it will be dry enough to work.

GOURD CANTEEN

To make a gourd canteen or bottle, all you have to do is cut off the neck of the gourd, and with a stick or wire knock out all the seeds and dried membrane from inside the gourd. Devise some system for hanging or suspending the gourd, and perhaps carve a stopper from wood (or use the top of the neck itself reversed — see Plate 50).

Cups, dippers, scoops, and the like, can be made by cutting away the top half of the gourd (see Plates 47 & 48), and scraping away the seeds. For a handle use either the neck of the gourd or attach a wooden handle in place with glue, rawhide, sinew, wooden pegs, or whatever seems appropriate.

The cut off neck of the gourd can be used as a drinking cup.

225

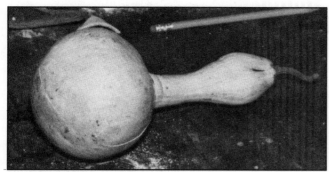

PLATE 47: A bottle gourd marked and ready to be cut open to form a dipper.

PLATE 48: All that needs to be done to finish the dipper is to scrape out the seeds and interior membrane. The other half can be used as a small bowl.

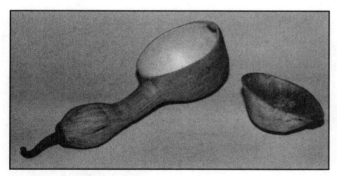

PLATE 49: Gourd dipper and burl cup.

PLATE 50: Water-bottle gourd. Note how the cut off neck has been inverted for use as a stopper.

PLATE 51 (left): A smaller water-bottle gourd or canteen.

IRON EQUIPMENT

Many useful camp items can be made from iron, if you can manage to acquire the necessary blacksmithing skills. I haven't, nor have I ever worked with tin which is another excellent source for numerous authentic camp items. Fortunately, one of the best blacksmithing buckskinners around lives in town so, I went to George Shimek in Waterloo, Iowa, to get the necessary information for this section of the chapter (I'm afraid I can't help you out if you want to be a tinsmith).

There are two items, according to George, that are essential to do decent blacksmithing — a forge and an anvil. George admits that it is possible to do some iron work with very minimal equipment, such as an acetylene torch for heat and something to pound on (like a hunk of railroad iron), but you can't expect totally satisfactory work.

It's best if you can get access to a real blacksmith's forge, but there are also expedients you can devise. A couple of years ago a friend of mine picked up an old hand-cranked bellows forge — a small one — at a farm sale, and you can keep your eyes open for that kind of deal. If that isn't possible, you can build up a forge, as George once did, by making a firebox in the backyard with loose brick, and liberating your spouse's hair dryer. Build up a box two or three bricks high, install some kind of metal tube running into the center of it. Attach the hair dryer to the other end of the tube, with the setting on "low" or "no heat" to supply the necessary augmented air supply. Alternatively, a barbeque grill bowl can be used, with the air pipe angled in to the bottom of the bowl. Some "how-to" books you can find will describe the making of a forge from an old brake drum. (See, for example, the *Reader's Digest Back to Basics*.)

Any of these methods will work, particularly if you're only interested in the occasional project. For fuel, nothing beats blacksmith's coal, which is a hard bituminous (don't use a soft bituminous or an anthracite — they have too many contaminants for the steel). Blacksmith's coal, George explained, is a low sulphur, high fusion coal, and produces the best heat.

As far as tools and equipment go, it is almost a necessity to have a good anvil — a minimum weight is 75 lbs. A good solid tree stump for a base is also needed. New anvils are expensive, so keep your eyes open at farm sales for a good used one. Hopefully, the anvil you find will have a hardy with it. The hardy is the wedge-shaped tool that fits into the hardy hole in the anvil. It's made from hardened steel, like a cold chisel, and is used to cut hot iron or steel to length. You'll need a good hammer, a 2-pound ball peen or blacksmith's cross peen hammer is best. In addition, while you're haunting sales and antique shops for an anvil, keep your eyes open for a good pair of blacksmith's tongs. A machinist's vise is also handy, and an adjustable end wrench (crescent wrench) is convenient to have.

Your raw material will be a mild steel; there really isn't any real wrought iron around anymore. What you'll be using mostly is hot rolled mild low carbon steel. Buy your steel in as close to the finished size of your project as possible, to save yourself a lot of forging.

Well, assuming that you have a forge, an anvil, a hammer, and some hot rolled mild steel, your first step is to build a proper fire. George starts with a handful of small kindling, and some torn up pieces of corrugated cardboard. Light the cardboard, and pile up the burning pieces; next add the kindling. When it's alight, add some coal (of course your blower is pushing air through your fire — but not at too rapid a rate). Add just enough coal to cover the wood. As it ignites and is burning well, add more coal. George claims that a good fire has a good depth of fire — at least six inches of burning coal at the air source. Finally, pile more coal on top, creating coke as the heat from the burning coal underneath "roasts" the coal on top. When you get a good pile of red coals in the middle, you're ready to begin. Once you have the fire going (and it took George only about five minutes to get his fire to this stage), you need to turn the air on only when you're heating a piece of steel.

A SIMPLE POKER

For his first sample, George decided to make a simple poker — a very handy implement for a camp fire. He started with a piece of ⅜" square bar stock, about 28" long. For this project you don't need tongs, since the piece is long enough that the heat from the end you're working won't make it to the end you're holding on to. George discourages the use of gloves at any time, since he believes it's safer to remember that you can be burned if you grab the wrong thing than to gain false confidence by wearing gloves, and then forget just once that you don't have them

PLATE 52: The end of the rod buried in the heart of the fire. Note that the fire is small but deep. Coal is heaped around the fire and raked into it as needed.

PLATE 53: The end of the poker, red-hot and ready for drawing out into a point.

PLATE 54: Drawing out the point of the poker. Note that the hammer hits square to the work.

PLATE 55: Starting the bend on the other end for the eye.

PLATE 56: Continuing the curve.

PLATE 57: Completing the curve on the anvil horn.

PLATE 58: Upsetting the eye to center it on the shaft of the poker.

on. But *do* wear safety glasses.

(1) Bury one end of the bar in the middle of your fire, and turn on the air. (See Plate 52.) The iron is ready to start to work when it reaches a nice bright orange color. Don't let it get too hot, particularly when working with small stock, or you may burn it. Shut the air off when you take the piece out of the fire.

(2) Move the bar to the anvil; with fairly light blows and the hammer face square to the work, hammer — or draw — the heated end out to a point. You may have to reheat the piece as you work it, since you can't work it if it cools too far. Don't try to do everything in one heat. (See Plates 53 & 54.)

(3) Let the pointed end cool down — don't quench it, or you run the risk of hardening the steel. Once it's cool enough to hold on to, heat up the other end so that you can forge an eye.

(4) Start forging the eye by hammering a curve in the stock over the edge of the anvil. (See Plate 55.) Reverse it, and continue to hammer it around. (See Plate 56.)

(5) Move to the horn of the anvil to complete the curve. (See Plate 57.) Keep the work straight.

(6) Reheat as necessary; then center the eye over the shaft of the poker by striking at the junction of the eye. (See Plate 58.)

PLATE 59: Putting a decorative twist in the handle.

(7) Let the work cool down, then heat the middle of the poker to a good bright orange, clamp in a vise, and with a crescent wrench, turn a decorative twist in the shaft. Brush off the scale that will form with a wire brush, let cool, and your poker is done. (See Plate 59.)

SMALL TONGS

A small pair of tongs can be handy around a camp fire, particularly to pick up a coal to light your after-dinner pipe. These small pipe tongs are basically the same in construction as the larger blacksmith's tongs. For these tongs. George chose a piece of ½" x ⅛" stock, about two feet long. You're going to make each half of the tongs at each end of the stock, so you don't have to use tongs to make tongs.

(1) Heat one end, place on the anvil, and hammer to draw down and round off one end of the flat stock — you're thickening it, basically. (See Plate 60.)

(2) Heat and draw down the other end to the same size.

(3) If you don't have a hardy, use a cold chisel to cut the forged ends off the main bar. Lay a piece of hardened

PLATE 60: Thickening up what will be the tong handle. Note the chalk mark indicating the eventual length.

PLATE 61: Cutting part way through the rod with a cold chisel. This can also be done on a hardy when the work is red hot. Note how the face of the anvil is protected by a steel plate against accidental marring.

steel on the anvil (so you won't inadvertently cut into the face of the anvil), and with hammer and cold chisel, cut part way through the stock 7" from the end. Do this with both ends. Finish the break by gripping it with a pair of pliers and bending or breaking it off. (See Plate 61.) If you have a hardy, this can be done hot on the hardy. Again, hammer the bar against the edge of the hardy, but only part way through; finish off by bending. (See Plate 62.) You can also hacksaw the piece off to length.

(4) Measure 1" from the cut-off end, mark with a center punch (see Plate 63), and drill a ⅛" hole for a rivet. Insert a ⅛" rivet and peen it down tightly (it'll loosen up as the tongs are worked). (Plates 64 & 65.)

(5) Return the riveted together pieces to the heat (the

PLATE 62: Completing the break.

PLATE 63: Center punching the position of the hinge rivet.

PLATE 64: The hinge rivet holes drilled and the rivet ready to be inserted.

flat end in the fire), and when hot enough, clamp in the vice. With the crescent wrench, make a 90° twist just ahead of the rivet. (See Plate 66.) Reheat, take back to the anvil, and give the jaws a little crimp, so that they don't come together absolutely flat. (See Plate 67.)

(6) Although we stopped here, you could reheat and forge the handles into a scissors-handle or bowed shape, or draw out and give a decorative twist to the handles, but it's not necessary.

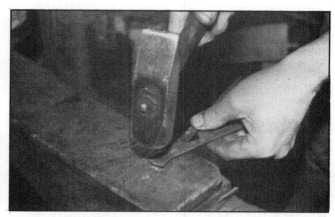

PLATE 65: Setting the rivet.

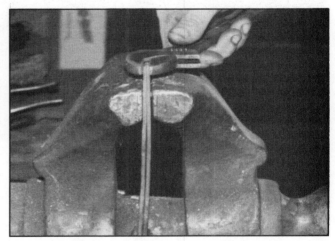

PLATE 66: Making the right-angle twist in the tong jaws.

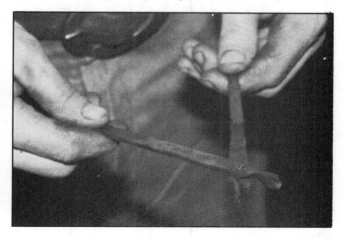

PLATE 67: The completed tongs.

CAMPFIRE FORK

This time George started out with ⅜" round stock, a couple of feet long.

(1) Heat one end, and on the anvil flatten it out for a distance of about 2 - 3 inches. (See Plate 68.)

(2) Let the end cool down and with a hacksaw, cut a slit down the 2" flattened length. Reheat, and split the ends apart on the edge of the anvil (see Plate 69), forming the start of two tines.

PLATE 68: Flattening out the end of the fork.

PLATE 69: After flattening, the end is split with a hacksaw, reheated, and split apart farther on the edge of the anvil. George is striking the opposite end with his hammer.

PLATE 70: Drawing out the tines to a point. Care must be taken in this step not to get the tines too hot or they will burn.

PLATE 71: Flattening out the tines on the face of the anvil.

231

PLATE 72: Bending the tines down over the horn.

PLATE 73: Flattening the tines so that they are in line with the handle.

(3) Heat and work one tine at a time. Heat carefully, so you don't burn up the work, which is easy to do when it gets this small. Draw each tine out to a point, making sure that each is the same length. (See Plate 70.)

(4) Heat both tines at the same time — very carefully — and hammer down over the horn to form the fork. (See Plates 71 & 72.) Make sure they're flat. (See Plate 73.)

(5) Wait for the fork end to cool, then heat and forge an eye in the opposite end as you did with the poker.

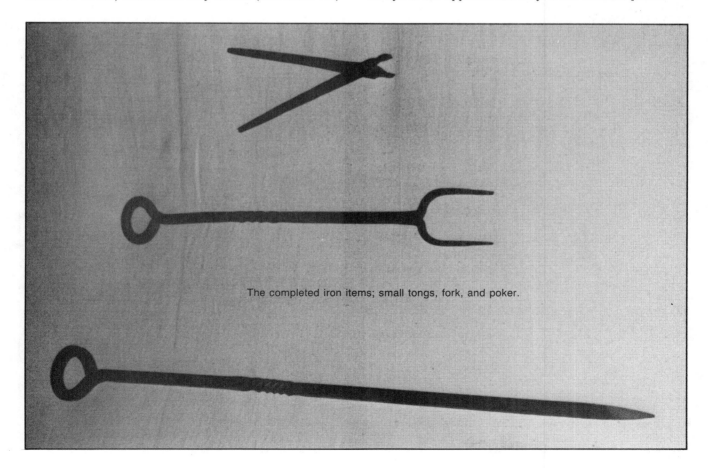

The completed iron items; small tongs, fork, and poker.

(6) A decorative twist can be added to round stock by first heating and forging a center portion square, then heating and twisting in the vice as with the poker. (See Plate 74.) The result will be a functional camp fork, that will even work in a backyard cookout over your barbeque grill.

A little imagination will suggest other things that can be hammered out just about as easily as the three pieces George demonstrated for me, including cross-bar and upright fire sets, and "S" hooks on which to hang your cooking pot; decorative hand wrought bales to replace the dull plain wire ones on your dutch oven; a stick-in-the-ground standard from which to hang a candle lantern; a tripod with an adjustable trammel hook to hang over the fire; a grill to set over the coals; and other long handled cooking tools such as a spoon or a spatula.

PLATE 74: You may put a decorative twist in the handle by squaring the middle portion and twisting it in the vise.

LEAN-TO

Once you've made all this, you'll probably find that storage is a problem, and you need an addition to your tipi or wall tent. Or, perhaps you really need a simple shelter that will fold up small enough to fit in the bottom of your pack basket. The answer to either need lies in the simple lean-to.

The simplest lean-to shelter is, I suspect, simply a blanket draped over a rope or stick; but it isn't hard to make a shelter that isn't much more complicated yet is a little more effective. I don't know about the authenticity of some lean-to designs. I do know that the "Baker" and "Whelan" style lean-tos being sold generally aren't much older in design than the 20th century. However, it isn't inconceivable that somebody much earlier devised a similar shelter — it's easy enough.

Start with heavy cotton or linen duck canvas. Don't use a synthetic blend — not only is it non-authentic, but should a spark get to it, it'll melt. The fabric I picked up was 60" wide, so many of my measurements are based on that. I also wanted to be able to stretch out full length, so determined that my lean-to should be 6'6" wide. My final pattern was a result of trial and error. (See Figure 23.)

I do most of my sewing on an old treadle machine I picked up almost by accident with a $3.00 bid at an auction. I find it invaluable for stitching heavy fabrics and the thinner leathers and buckskin. (And it also keeps me from wrecking my wife's machine.) (See Plate 75.)

I started out with the simplest design: a rectangle cloth. Since my fabric was 60" wide. the easiest thing was to stitch two 6'6" lengths together, which I did using a French seam (see Figure 23) which tends to be more waterproof than a simple overlap seam.

Next, all I had to do was add some ties and stake loops, and I'd have a basic lean-to. You can use pre-woven tape from the fabric store for loops and ties, or you can use fabric scraps and stitch your own, which is what I did, making them ¾" wide (2¼" strips tripled for strength). I attached five stake loops along the bottom edge, and two tie loops at the corners of the top edge. At 6'6" from the

PLATE 75: Did I just sew my fingers to the cloth? That old treadle machine will stitch through just about anything.

233

FIGURE 23

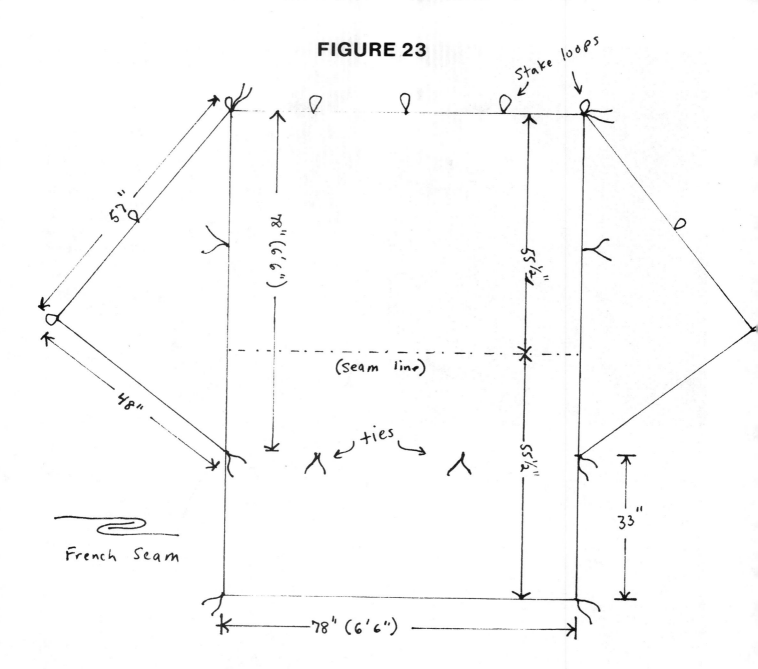

French Seam

(seam line)

ties

Stake loops

5"

48"

78" (6'6")

55½"

55½"

33"

78" (6'6")

bottom edge I added a line of eight ties — four on top and four at the same location underneath. I figured that with this arrangement I could either suspend the lean-to from a rope stretched between two trees or poles, or tie it to a horizontal pole underneath. This left me with a 33" front flap or awning. (Adding a third strip of fabric to the basic rectangle would have given me a flap that could reach all the way to the ground in front — I may do it someday.

So far, the lean-to is adequate, but additional protection from the weather can be obtained by adding side pieces. I did this by deciding that I wanted my lean-to to be at least 4' high in front, so using French seams, I added a triangular piece to each side that measured 4'x4'9"x6'6". I attached three stake loops along the bottom edge of the triangle (the 4'9" base). Then, in case I wanted to ever use an exterior framework of poles, I added two more ties halfway up the back. So far I've not used them, but it's comforting to know they're there for the time when I can't

find two trees the right distance apart and have to cut poles.

I finished the whole thing off by giving it a coat of commercial waterproofing which I picked up at our local tent and awning shop. I also cut and hemmed a rectangle of canvas for a ground cloth, and waterproofed it well. The whole thing easily folds up into a bundle small enough to fit in the bottom of a pack basket. Although I designed it as a one-man shelter, it was large enough for my 12-year-old son and me and all our gear on the last pack-in rendezvous we went to. (Plate 76.)

PLATE 76: Although designed as a one man lean-to, there was enough room for my son and me on a walk-in rendezvous.

A lean-to like the one described is perfect for carrying into a secluded camp or as a supplementary shelter along with a larger lodge at rendezvous.

KITS

Although everything we've made in this chapter was made "from scratch", except the French coin purse, don't overlook the possibility of finding a kit that will make your job easier. You still have the problem of determining authenticity and quality, but those aside, there's no reason why a kit may not serve your purpose. Tedd Cash, for example, has a very nice candle lantern kit, and I've seen ads lately for a canoe chair kit. Tandy Leather has kits that can be used "as is" or modified. There are a number of firms offering furniture kits, and some of them will do as is, or can be modified to make them more suitable for a primitive camp.

CONCLUSION

Well, that's about it. I hope you find something useful in these suggestions. Most of this stuff is pretty basic, but even if you find nothing here that you can use, at least I hope that your imagination is triggered, and you realize that almost everything you need you can make given the tools, material and patience. Let's end this chapter with a list of some of the sources for ideas and materials that I turned to in preparing this chapter. You'll find further information and ideas in them.

Sources:

Buckskin Report, The, Big Timber, MT: The Buckskin Press, Inc.

Early American Life

Foxfire Book, The, (several volumes)

Graham-Barber, Lynda, *The Kit Furniture Book,* New York: Pantheon Books, 1982.

Hanson, James A. and Kathryn J. Wilson, *The Mountain Man Sketchbook, Vol. I* and *Vol. II,* Canyon, TX: The Fur Press, 1976.

Hanson, James A., *The Voyageur's Sketchbook,* Chadron, NE: The Fur Press, 1981.

Hayward, Arthur H., *Colonial Lighting,* Boston: B. J. Brimmer Company, 1923.

Hunt, W. Ben, *The Complete How-To Book of Indiancraft,* New York: Collier Books, 1973.

Klinger, Robert L. and Richard A. Wilder, *Sketchbook '76,* Arlington, VA: R. L. Klinger, 1968.

Laubin, Reginald and Gladys, *The Indian Tipi: Its History, Construction, and Use,* New York: Ballantine Books, 1971.

Make It With Leather, Fort Worth, TX: Tandy

Muzzle Blasts, Friendship, IN: National Muzzle Loading Rifle Association.

Muzzleloader, Texarkana, TX: Rebel Publishing Co., Inc.

Mack, Norman, ed., *Reader's Digest Back to Basics: How to Learn and Enjoy Traditional American Skills,* Pleasantville, NY: The Reader's Digest Association, Inc., 1981.

Miller, Robert W., *Pictorial Guide to Early American Tools and Implements,* Des Moines, IA: Wallace-Homestead Book Co., 1980.

Neumann, George C. and Frank J. Kravic, *Collector's Illustrated Encyclopedia of the American Revolution,* Harrisburg, PA: Stackpole Books, 1975.

Peterson, Harold L., *The Book of the Continental Soldier,* Harrisburg, PA: Stackpole Press, 1968.

Schneider, Richard C., *Crafts of the North American Indians: A Craftsman's Manual,* New York: Van Nostrand Reinhold Co., 1972.

Sloane, Eric, *ABC Book of Early Americans,* New York: Doubleday & Co., 1963.

Sloane, Eric, *A Museum of Early American Tools,* New York: Funk & Wagnalls, 1964.

Sloane, Eric, *A Reverence for Wood,* New York: Ballantine Books, 1974.

Underhill, Roy, *The Woodwright's Shop: A Practical Guide to Traditional Woodcraft,* Chapel Hill: The University of North Carolina Press, 1981.

Wilson, Kathryn and James A. Hanson, *Feminine Fur Trade Fashions 1800-1840,* Canyon, TX: The Fur Press, 1976.

Gun Tune-Up & Care

by J. W. "Doc" Carlson

J. W. "DOC" CARLSON HAS BEEN BUCKSKIN-NING for more than 35 years. He started into the sport before it was a sport. Buckskinning at that time wasn't "cool", merely weird or eccentric.

About 15 years ago, his hobby of tinkering with muzzle loading and modern guns grew to the place that it became a business. Doc's veterinary practice, from whence comes his nickname, was relegated to a limited practice. He is a full time, working gunsmith who operates Upper Missouri Trading Company in Crofton, Nebraska with his wife, De. In addition to handling a full line of muzzle loading guns and accessories, Upper Missouri manufactures many parts and accessories used in muzzle loading.

Carlson is on the board of directors of both the NRA and the NMLRA and chairs the Black Powder Committee of the NRA. He also serves the Association of Importers and Manufacturers for Muzzleloading as a member of its board of directors. Doc's services to muzzle loading include providing expert testimony in product liability cases involving muzzle loading.

As Technical Editor for *Muzzleloader* magazine, Carlson writes a regular column entitled "Doc's RX". He also writes the new product reviews for the official NMLRA magazine, *Muzzle Blasts*. His chapter, "How to Get Started", was included in *The Book of Buckskinning*.

Doc and De Carlson attend as many buckskinning events around the country as his schedule permits. Both have several state and regional championships to their credit in both rifle and pistol events.

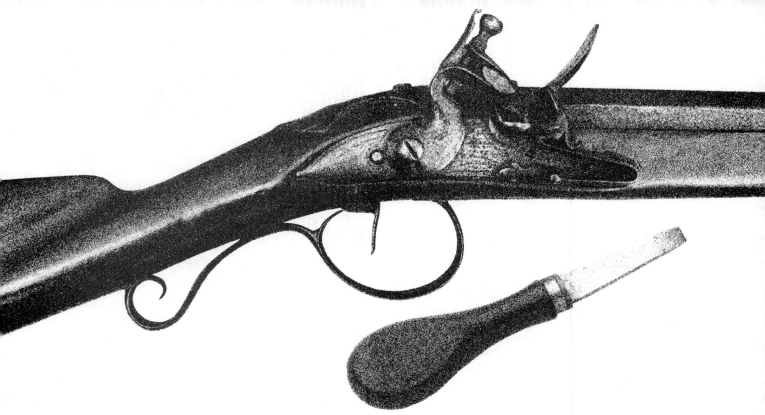

THERE'S one thing that all muzzle loading shooters have in common. One thing that all, regardless of race, creed, etc., must have to join the shooters' ranks. They must all either own, or have access to, a muzzle loading firearm. This is the most basic part of the sport and, at the same time, probably the most complicated. Guns come in all shapes and sizes and, sorry to say, in all classes of quality also. The muzzle loading arm is a pretty simple mechanism, reduced to its basics. But, because of this simplicity, each part must function correctly and in harmony with the other parts for the whole to give quality performance.

Suppose you are in the market for a rifle. Let's take a look at some of the decisions that you will have to make. You'll want something that will do well for target shooting, plinking, hunting and will look right if carried with a buckskin outfit.

First, what ignition system? Some of this decision will depend on the period of American history that appeals to you. Assuming that you are going to use this rifle in your buckskinning hobby, the era of time that you are using as a model for your outfit will have a lot to do with the ignition system and the style of rifle that you'll want. Obviously, if you are using the Eastern Long Hunter as your model, you don't want a half stock percussion gun. The historical issue aside, which is best? The percussion form of ignition was invented for a reason. It's an overall more reliable form of ignition. Even the most dyed in the wool flint shooter will usually agree to that. A percussion lock can be of medium quality and still work well enough to do its job reliably. Not so with the flintlock. The flintlock, to be reliable, must be of good quality, well designed and maintained, and treated with care and respect. Rain and damp weather, while giving the percussion shooter problems, will nearly put the flint shooter out of business. We'll get into some of the ways to keep everything dry and shooting a little later on. One other consideration in the ignition department is cost.

Usually percussion guns are cheaper over the counter, and there is much more selection available among commercially made guns. Percussion is more reliable and more popular, flintlock is more romantic or "buckskinnish", if you will.

Caliber is another decision you'll have to make. If you plan to use your rifle for hunting, what kind of game? Naturally you shouldn't plan to hunt squirrels with a .54 caliber, neither will you hunt deer with a .36. The smaller calibers are easier to handle on the target range, usually, but they fall behind for hunting of deer sized animals. A .45 caliber is a good middle ground. It's accurate enough for target, recoil is mild, and it is adequate for deer sized animals, if shots are kept 75 yards or less. The other two calibers seen most often are .50 and .54, both of which are good hunting calibers. They do well on target also but the recoil begins to pick up a little. This can be a very real consideration at a two or three day shoot where many shots are fired.

Overall style of the gun and stock configuration will, again, be dictated by the period of time that you are dealing with. There is, however, some overlap of time periods. Keep in mind that earlier guns were used in the later periods of our history. The people of the period had preferences for the older styles, or maybe, in some cases couldn't afford the latest and used what they had.

Kit or completed gun? If you have normal manual dexterity, there is no reason that you can't build one of the commercial kits on the market. They are, for the most part, well designed and are relatively easy to put together. You can save some money buying the kit over the made up gun and it gives you a chance to "individualize" your gun a little. It won't look so much like everybody else's. On the other hand, the completed gun is ready to go. No hassles. Just load it and you are shooting the same afternoon.

Well, with all those decisions made, or at least, in the thinking stage, let's go shopping and see what you want to pay particular attention to in buying a gun.

First, look at the overall quality — by this I mean, how does the wood fit the metal? How is the finish applied — is it even and smooth? Look for sloppy workmanship. While some leeway is allowed in production guns, there shouldn't be any gaps in inletting. The butt plate should fit well. If there is a patch or cap box, it should be well inletted with no gaps and should work easily. Remember you will be trying to get the lid open in all kinds of weather and conditions. Therefore, if the latch defies your attempts to open it in the store, it isn't going to get any easier in the field. The trigger guard must be of a design that is comfortable for you. Plenty of room for your finger to enter and contact the trigger. I prefer a smooth type of guard with no finger rests or other projections. This is only personal preference and I really have no real problem either way. I just don't think that the finger rest type trigger guards are comfortable — at least to my hand. You may think otherwise. Try several styles and see what feels right to you.

Check out the ramrod. Does it come out of the ferrules easily and yet, is it tight enough that it won't fall out every time the muzzle of the rifle is pointed down? Is the ramrod big enough for the job that it will be called on to do? Many guns around have very small, skinny ramrods. If the gun is in a large caliber, they just won't take the forces required to seat a bullet, especially if the bore is fouled from shooting. Look carefully at the grain in the ramrod. It should run the length of the rod, pretty much. Beware of cross grain. The rod should be hickory. This resists breakage and doesn't have the tendency to shear off on an angle and go through your hand when pushing on it. The rod should be fitted with brass ends that will fit the curve of the bullet and they should be drilled and tapped to take cleaning jags and ball pulling screws. Most guns on the market are deficient in the ramrod department. You'll probably have to make a replacement in order to have a good one. Just be sure that the ferrules and hole in the stock are large enough to carry a good rod. For .45 calibers 5/16" rod size is about minimum, ⅜" is plenty small for the larger calibers, .50 and over.

While you are looking at the ramrod, check the barrel. Barrel evaluation is something that is difficult for the beginner and not much easier for the so-called expert. It's pretty difficult to look at a barrel and tell very much about it. You can check to see that the rifling seems to be even and fairly deep. The crown on the end of the barrel should be even and centered. The rifling that you can see should be smooth, not cut up with a lot of tool marks and scoring.

Take a little time with the lock. The hammer should fit the nipple. That is, the nose of the hammer should contact

A great deal can be told about the condition of a barrel by checking the muzzle. Note whether crown is even and condition of rifling. Notice the sloppy fit of the forend cap of this kit-made gun.

the top of the nipple evenly for good ignition. The mainspring should be stiff enough to give good resistance to cocking the hammer. It shouldn't feel "soft" or "limp wristed". It shouldn't be so strong that it will batter the nipple, though. Try cocking several and you'll get a feel for it. Don't ever drop the hammer on an unprotected nipple! That's a real no-no. You'll give gun sales people grey hairs and brand yourself as a real "know-nothing". Pull the trigger and ease the hammer down.

When a good lock is cocked, the clicks, as the sear drops into the notches on the tumbler, should sound sharp and clear. Try the sear engagement on both half cock and full cock. The half cock notch must hold against any attempt to pull the trigger, within reason. Obviously, you don't want to break the trigger off trying to get the sear to come out of the half cock position, but it should set firmly and safely into the notch. If it doesn't, some major lock work is indicated and, on a new gun, this would indicate that something is pretty sloppy somewhere. This would be a good gun to pass up. The full cock notch should hold firmly, also. Pushing on the hammer shouldn't allow the sear to jump out of the notch. It should pull fairly easy with the trigger, however. Naturally a heavy pull requirement to trip the hammer isn't going to help accuracy any. Some roughness is to be expected, however. Most production guns have pretty heavy pulls out of the box. They take a bit of stoning to smooth them and give a good, clean, crisp

One thing all black powder shooters have in common is the owning and shooting of muzzle loaders. Top: A group of buckskinners hold a blanket shoot at the Mid-America Rendezvous. Left: A buckskinner touches off a round at a local shoot.

pull. If the gun has a set trigger, and most do, the roughness becomes less important as the kick off of the set trigger will overcome all but the heaviest pulls.

If the gun is a flintlock the problems are multiplied. All that was said about caplocks pertains to flints, except, of course, the nipple to hammer fit. Look at the overall fit and finish of the flintlock. Remember a flintlock must be of better quality, overall, than a caplock to give reliable ignition. Make sure that the frizzen fits the pan well, that it will snap closed firmly and with authority, and that it also snaps forward to clear the pan well. I wouldn't buy a flintlock without snapping it with flint to see how well it sparks. Now, this doesn't mean that you will go into a store and snap every flintlock in the place. But, when your mind is pretty well made up and you have decided on the gun you wish to buy, snap it a time or two before closing the deal. Most clerks will allow this. Check the position of the touch hole. It should be in the center of the pan, centered on a line through the top of the pan. If it is clear down at the bottom of the pan, ignition will be slowed while the powder burns down to the hole. If too high, the flash of the priming powder may not ignite the main charge.

Now, shoulder the rifle. Check to see if the butt plate fits well, and how the length is. Try to visualize the rifle

240

during recoil. Is the top of the comb going to raise into your cheekbone? Check the sights — they should be clear, clean and not too coarse. That is, the rear notch shouldn't be too wide or the front sight too thick for good alignment at longer ranges — remember the sight will be bigger in relation to the target the further out the target is.

A major consideration should be who made the piece. Is it a commercial job? If so, who made it? Is it one of the known manufacturers who has a good reputation? It is probably better for the beginner to stay with known manufacturers. Use the reputation of the company to help you make up for the deficiencies in your judgement of what is good or not. If you are pretty knowledgeable as to what it takes to make a quality gun, then you can probably take a chance on some of the lesser known manufacturers. By and large, the guns on the market are reasonaby well made and safe, however, there are exceptions. Knowing the manufacturer can be a big help in sidestepping some of these exceptions.

By the same token, a reputable dealer whom you know and have confidence in, is pretty good insurance against being "taken". A good dealer has his reputation to think of and certainly won't sell you something that you will be unhappy with.

What about buying a hand built rifle? Well, most of what has been said above applies. Who made the lock and barrel? Are they well known competent manufacturers? The overall workmanship of the piece will tell you a lot, if you don't know the maker of the gun. A gun built from one of the well-known kits can't be hurt too much other than cosmetic appearance. The best bet on something like this is to get the advice and counsel of someone who has some experience and whose opinion of muzzle loading arms you trust.

Any used gun, be it home built or manufactured, will have a few clues to its condition. Check the end of the barrel. Look at the muzzle. If the muzzle shows wear, rust or pitting, you can bet the inside of the barrel will look the same. If the overall appearance of the gun shows a lot of abuse and lack of care, again the barrel will probably look the same. Honest wear is a different thing — we're talking about frank abuse such as rust, beat up stock wood and the like. Usually a person who is careless about the outside of the gun will be the same with the lock and barrel innards. If the sights are clearly off center, maybe there's a problem with getting the gun to shoot on target. It's tough to beat a session at the range to find out how good a gun is. Unless you are interested in a wall hanger only, and few buckskinners are, there's no reason to buy a rifle that won't shoot well. Obviously you won't be able to test fire new guns,

usually, but used ones, especially those bought from an individual, should always be shot first. Another trick that can be done in store or wherever, is to take a ramrod with a tight fitting patch on the end and "feel" the barrel. Gently push the rod down the barrel and "feel" the bore as you do. You'll pick up roughness or tight spots easily with this method. Roughness indicates either poorly machined rifling or rust pitting. A barrel with tight and loose spots just won't shoot well, usually. Don't confuse a "choked" barrel with an uneven bore, however. Many barrels, especially custom type, are a bit tighter at the muzzle. This is done for ease of loading and accuracy. Whether it helps accuracy or not is open to argument, some say yes, some no. The choke or muzzle constriction must be even and in the very end of the muzzle. The rest of the barrel should be smooth and even in size.

Well, suppose that you have all the above behind you. You have a rifle. Now you'd like to tune it up, clean it up and make it something that you will be proud of at rendezvous. Most production guns and kits are made of good basic parts but there are things on all of them that can be improved with a little careful work. The necessity of holding price down to an affordable level makes it impossible for a production gun to have a lot of hand polishing and fitting done to it. Too much labor will be incorporated in the price. This is what makes a finely made custom type gun so expensive. Well, let's see what the average buckskinner can do to "slick up" his (or her) favorite gun a bit.

TUNING THE LOCK

Probably the first place most gun owners start with a tune-up is the most obvious — the lock. It's also the easiest part of the gun to foul up badly with a little bit of poorly planned or executed tinkering. The relationships of one part to another in a gun lock are very important. Many times the obvious cure for a fault isn't the correct one and will, in fact, make the condition worse. A good example of this is sear notches. While it looks as if a bit of polishing and stoning is in order, it may be the angle of the notches that is at fault and the stoning will merely aggravate the problem.

All locks have certain parts in common. The internal parts, that is, the ones behind the lock plate, hidden in the wood, are pretty much the same in all locks, be they flint or percussion. They'll consist of a tumbler which extends through the lock plate and carries the hammer, a sear, which engages notches on the tumbler and holds the hammer at half and full cock positions, a bridle, which fits over the tumbler and sear to give them support, a mainspring, which bears on the tumbler and gives the hammer its impetus, and a sear spring which forces the sear into the notches on the tumbler. Some locks, especially cheaper ones, dispense with the bridle. Bridle-less locks have been made for centuries, so the practice is not new. The bridle was an improvement that was invented sometime during the muzzle loading period and was used on the better locks of the time. The earlier locks and cheaper, less precise locks were made without, and such is the case today. A bridle-less lock is hard to tune to a good trigger pull and, especially in the case of flintlocks, difficult to tune for a clean crisp action.

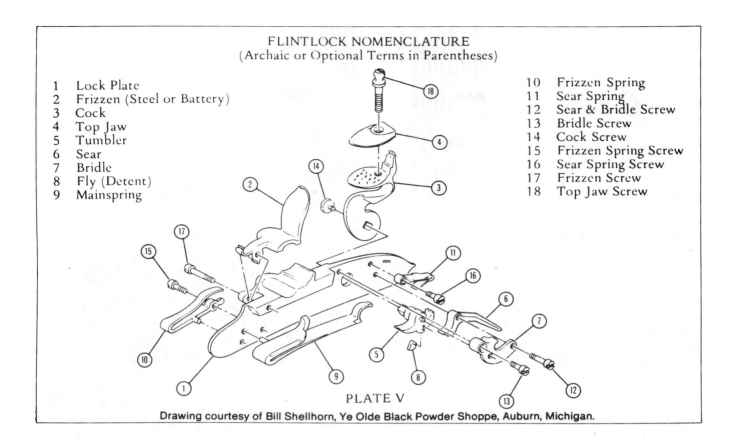

FLINTLOCK NOMENCLATURE
(Archaic or Optional Terms in Parentheses)

1 Lock Plate
2 Frizzen (Steel or Battery)
3 Cock
4 Top Jaw
5 Tumbler
6 Sear
7 Bridle
8 Fly (Detent)
9 Mainspring

10 Frizzen Spring
11 Sear Spring
12 Sear & Bridle Screw
13 Bridle Screw
14 Cock Screw
15 Frizzen Spring Screw
16 Sear Spring Screw
17 Frizzen Screw
18 Top Jaw Screw

PLATE V

Drawing courtesy of Bill Shellhorn, Ye Olde Black Powder Shoppe, Auburn, Michigan.

Let's tackle the toughest part first. The tumbler. Check the fit between the hammer and tumbler. It should be tight. The hammer should not wiggle on the tumbler square. Put the lock at half cock and see if the hammer can be moved forward and backward. How about side to side? Take out the hammer or cock screw that holds the hammer on the square (or in some cases hexagon) shaft of the tumbler. The hammer should have to be tapped off, it should be

that tight. Usually the shank is tapered a bit where it fits into the hammer so that it will pop off easily with a light tap on a punch set in the screw hole. Be sure that the punch clears the sides of the hole easily or you may foul up the threads. Support the lock in your hand and tap the punch lightly. If it doesn't release the hammer, the mainspring, sear spring, bridle and sear should all be removed, the lock plate supported close to the tumbler all around, and the

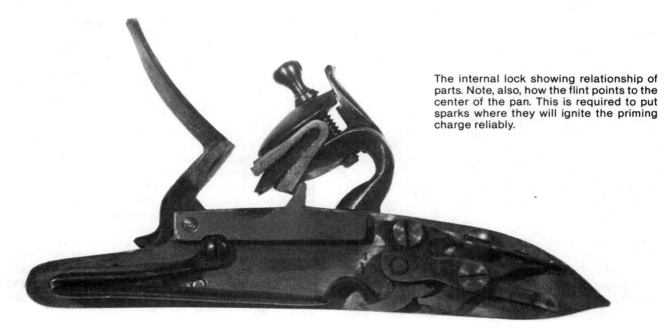

The internal lock showing relationship of parts. Note, also, how the flint points to the center of the pan. This is required to put sparks where they will ignite the priming charge reliably.

242

A punch that will fit in the tumbler screw hole should always be used to tap the tumbler shaft out of the hammer. This protects the threads from damage.

If the hammer hole is much oversize, a small chisel can be used to upset metal into the hole.

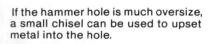

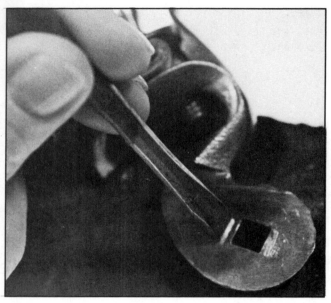

A small ball peen hammer can be used to tighten the hammer on the tumbler shaft.

hammer tapped free. If it is this tight, you probably have little problem with a loose hammer.

With the hammer off, lay it on a solid surface and tap the back side, around the tumbler hole, with a small ball peen hammer. The idea is to upset a bit of metal into the square hole for the tumbler. Don't tap right at the edge of the hole. Upset metal from further back and the repair will last. If the fit is very loose, you may have to use a chisel and make impressions parallel to the sides of the hole to move enough metal into the hole area. Go slowly. It's surprising how little tapping it sometimes takes to tighten up the hammer-tumbler fit. This is a good place to issue a warning — don't make a practice of taking the hammer off the tumbler. Once everything is tight and the tumbler is "tuned" leave it alone. The more that the hammer is removed, the more likely for looseness and wiggle to develop. This is especially true if the above tightening exercise has been done.

With the sides of the tumbler shank fitted, are there still gaps at the corners? If so, these can be helped with the judicious use of a center punch or a caping chisel, which is merely a very narrow cold chisel. Work the corners in slightly, again fitting often. You should end up with a firm, press fit between tumbler and hammer.

Now, with the lock assembled, check the half cock notch on the tumbler. The hammer should stand at half cock, just off the nipple for a percussion outfit and with the flint just clear of the frizzen face for a lock of flintlock persuasion. The sear nose should enter the half cock notch under a slight hook so that the sear can't be disengaged

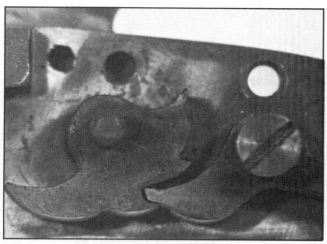

The nose of the sear should enter the half cock notch solidly.

The relationship of sear to full cock notch.

easily by the trigger pull. In other words, the lock shouldn't trip from the half cock position when the trigger is pulled. If it does, the half cock notch must be deepened. Do this very carefully. It is very easy to go too far and either destroy the notch altogether or get it too deep so that the hammer goes too far forward. If the notch is too deep to start with and the hammer goes too far forward, the lock is best given to a muzzle loading gunsmith to repair. This will take a bit more correction than the average home craftsman can handle with limited tools. The tumbler will either have to be replaced or built up by welding and the notch recut.

The full cock notch in the tumbler must be clean and sharp, well polished and the sear nose must fit it closely in

Use a very hard Arkansas stone to polish the sear nose and full cock notch. Be very careful to keep the angles of both flat and true. Be certain that the stone isn't "rocked" back and forth. This will produce a curved surface that won't make contact smoothly.

order to have a clean, crisp trigger pull. Anything else will give a soft, mushy pull. Or, as has been said, a bad trigger pull is like a house with a spoiled kid in residence — it has a little creep in it. The full cock notch should be in line with the axis of the tumbler. That is, a line drawn through the pivot center of the tumbler. The sear should pivot cleanly out of the notch with no tendency to force the tumbler back against the mainspring. Beware of getting the full cock notch tipped the other way also. If this is the case the sear nose won't hold in the notch and the lock won't stay cocked. If any polishing is done on the sear nose and tumbler notch, great care must be exercised so that these angles are not changed. If the angles are wrong to start with and the trigger pull is hard and creepy, recut the tumbler notch to correspond with a line drawn through the pivot axis of the tumbler. Make it absolutely flat and true and polish well. Then true up the sear nose to match it. Don't go from one to the other and back. This will usually make things worse instead of better. Beware of shortening the sear nose so that the hammer moves too far forward on half cock. You should end up with a clean let off but the notch must be deep enough so that the sear stays in the notch with no chance of slipping out and firing the gun when you don't expect it to. This can make you very unpopular on the firing line or in the hunting field. Sear nose and tumbler notches are something that shouldn't be worked on unless, 1. they need it and 2. you understand exactly what you are doing. In other words, if it isn't broken, don't fix it!

Often times, a hard trigger pull can be traced to a poorly fitting sear spring. The tip of the sear spring should bear right behind the pivot screw on the sear. If it is further back, the trigger must overcome more resistance and the pull is increased. If the point of the spring is too far back, the spring can be replaced with one longer or the spring can be pivoted further down. This will entail recutting the slot for the retainer bar on the sear spring. This is done with a cold chisel or caping chisel. Metal is pushed from the bottom side of the slot and upset into the slot itself to move the sear spring down until the tip moves forward on the sear. This is best done very carefully with the final position of the sear spring carefully marked. Measure three or four times and cut once, as the carpenters say.

Many locks have a detent or fly in the tumbler. This is a small pivoting piece that is pushed out of the way by the sear when entering the half cock notch and is snapped forward as the sear enters the full cock notch. The fly then

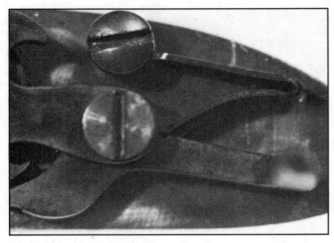

Note where tip of sear spring bears on the sear — further back will make for a hard trigger pull.

A small chisel can be used to move the sear spring slot to pivot the sear spring up or down.

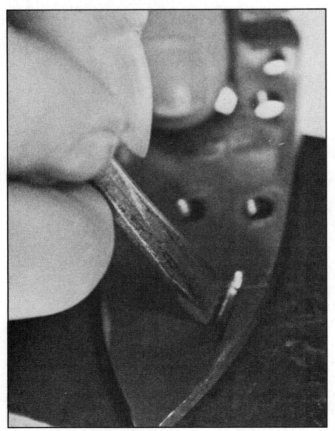

Always use a spring vise when removing or replacing springs.

A substitute spring vise can be made using a parallel clamp with a piece of metal under the main arm of the spring to support it and spread the force.

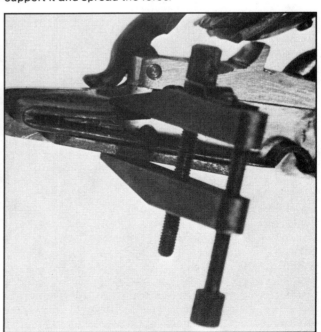

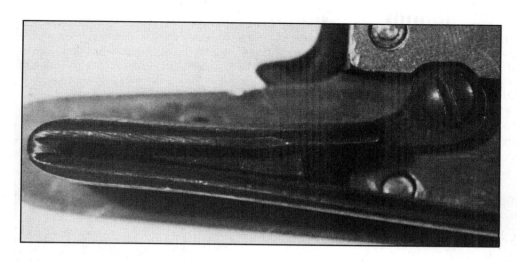

A wedge put in at the bend of the spring will sometimes strengthen it.

rides ahead of the sear nose as the tumbler is released from full cock. It blocks the sear nose from entering the half cock notch as the tumbler pivots and the hammer comes forward. The purpose is to keep the sear from catching the half cock notch as the lock is fired. It is required with most of the double throw, double set triggers that are in use today. If it doesn't function as it should, the problem can usually be discerned if the lock is functioned slowly with the mainspring out. Usually a very slight polishing will cure most problems with a fly. If it is too short to do its job, replacement is the only answer. Again, be sure that you understand what needs to be done before working on a fly.

The lock plate can be polished with very fine emery paper, 600 grit, wrapped on a flat piece of hardwood. This helps cut friction and makes the lock function cleanly.

The mainspring of a lock is all important. It must be strong enough to make the hammer function as it should, firing the cap or striking sparks from the frizzen, and at the same time, not be so heavy as to make trigger pull too hard or stress parts of the lock unnecessarily. The bearing surface on the tumbler should be polished, both on tumbler and mainspring. The spring shouldn't rub against the lock plate. If it does sometimes a careful grinding on the lockplate side of the spring will help. Do this carefully. If much is taken off it can throw the spring out of balance and ruin it. If the spring is too weak, which is more often the case, it can sometimes be helped by the addition of a wedge. This is merely a piece of soft steel or brass that is filed to wedge tightly in the bent end of the spring when the hammer is full down. This wedge adds stress to the spring as the hammer is cocked and will often bring the spring up to a strength where it will do its job. If this doesn't work, a new spring is in order. Because of the uneven stresses applied to the spring by this wedging method of repair, the mainspring may well break in use. Really not much loss as a weak mainspring is of little use except to help in selling the gun to some poor unknowledgeable soul. If a coil spring lock, the spring can sometimes be strengthened by stretching it to a greater length and replacing it in the lock.

A mainspring that is too strong can be weakened by carefully grinding off metal from the lower arm. This is a very tricky operation, more an art than a science, and a spring can be easily ruined. Be very careful to remove metal evenly, retaining the "buggy whip" or "fishing rod" taper to the spring. Without this tapering shape it won't flex evenly and cleanly.

Never, repeat never, remove the mainspring from a lock without a properly fitting mainspring vise. Pliers and the like can slip at a bad time and the spring will be broken. The mainspring vise flexes the spring much the same as it is flexed in the lock. Pliers and vise grips do not and can cause uneven stresses and the spring will often break. More mainsprings are broken by mishandling than ever break in use. If a mainspring vise isn't available, a reasonable replacement can be made from a parallel clamp of proper size with a flat piece of steel added to one jaw to give support to the bottom arm during clamping. A slot cut in a flat piece of steel can also be used to remove and replace a mainspring. This method can't be used to flex the spring, however, merely to hold it once flexed.

The fit of the bridle should be such that it gives support to the tumbler pivot and the sear screw without binding. It should fit up against the tumbler and sear so that there is little tendency of either to wobble. If the bridle binds, it should be shimmed to give more room for the tumbler or some can be filed off the inside flat of the bridle where it rubs the tumbler to give this clearance. If the fit is sloppy, the stud that bears against the lockplate can be taken down slightly to tighten up the fit.

Sometimes a lock will be found which has a bridle that is off center with the tumbler pivot. This will cause the pivot to bind when the hammer is moved. This is easy to see when the lock is functioned with the mainspring out. Usually the only cure for this, short of a new bridle, is to enlarge the hole in the bridle where the pivot rides. This isn't conducive to a tightly functioning lock, but it is the only answer in many cases. It's better than having the lock bind.

The stop on the tumbler should contact the bridle at the same time the hammer is stopped by either the nipple, or a stop on the hammer itself hitting the lockplate top, in the case of the flintlock. This tends to distribute the shock over the entire lock rather than having the hammer or tumbler take it all.

The bridle, sear and tumbler must be hard to resist wear. Many of the alterations that we have talked about will have to be done on a soft part. If the part is hard, and if it must be altered, it can be heated to a bright red color and buried in something that will insulate it and allow it to cool slowly. Lime is used by many. Ashes are very good. I have used a very dry sand or even fine dirt, if dry. Anything that will hold the heat in for a time will work. Usually a lock that is well hardened will need very little work besides some judicious polishing. More often the lock parts will be too soft and most of the problems will be traceable to this. Hardening of parts isn't a particularly difficult chore. You must have a source of heat that will bring the part to a bright cherry red. Dull red won't get it. It has to be bright. The best method to use is case hardening. The only thing in steel that will harden is carbon. Case hardening merely cooks carbon into the surface of the steel. When steel is heated to a bright cherry red it will absorb carbon, albeit slowly. The longer it is held at temperature with the case hardening compound in contact with it, the deeper the hardened layer. The part is heated, rolled in the compound to give it a good coating and brought up to cherry red. It is held here for a minute or so and then rerolled in the compound. The compound will melt as the proper heat is reached and attention must be given to the areas that you want hard such as the sear notches in the tumbler and the sear nose. Keep cooking and rolling for three or four times and then quench in water or 10 weight oil. I prefer water. If you use oil, do it outside as it will catch fire occasionally. The hardening compound will crack as it hits the water and it can spatter so protective goggles and long sleeves with gloves are a must. I use a case hardener put out by Upper Missouri Trading Company but there are many on the market. Kasenit is a common trade name. Properly used, these compounds will impart a hard layer over the softer metal underneath. This gives wear protection with a softer core to withstand repeated shocks, an ideal situation for lock parts. If the lock parts are of high carbon steel, the above treatment could make them too hard and brittle. If you have doubts about the steel content of the parts, they can be put in an oven at 500°F. for a half hour or so to take out some of the stress. If parts are of a high carbon steel this step will help preclude breakage.

With the lock assembled and in the gun, check how the hammer hits the nipple or frizzen. The hammer nose should be centered on the nipple as it hits. If a flintlock, the hammer should move in a centered plane with the frizzen. If this isn't the case the hammer can be bent to bring it into position. This can be done cold but a hammer will occasionally break. It's best done with the part heated to a dull red. Measure carefully just how much the hammer must be moved and in what direction. Clamp the bottom portion in a vise and heat the neck of the hammer to a dull red color. Use a solid jaw wrench (I use a crescent type) adjusted to fit the upper part of the hammer. Carefully twist or bend, as the case may be, the hammer into the proper configuration. Make a mark on the vise so that you know exactly how much to move everything. Try to do it in one

To case harden a frizzen (or any part), heap the case hardener on the frizzen (above) before heating. Then heat it to cherry red (below). Three or four applications are usually necessary. Quench the part in water or light oil.

bend, whether you do it hot or cold. Too much back and forth bending will weaken the hammer. Let the hammer cool slowly; don't quench it. This may harden it and induce breakage later in use.

If we are dealing with a flintlock, they are a special breed. The geometry of a flintlock, the relationship of each part to the others, would fill a fair sized book. As you are stuck with the lock that is on the gun and not building a lock, let's look at a couple of things that you can do to get better ignition out of this cranky machine.

Without doubt the biggest cause of poor ignition is a frizzen that is too soft. There are two ways to fix this. First, and easiest, is to case harden the frizzen. This is done the same way that the internal lock parts are hardened, with particular attention being paid to the face of the frizzen. Really soak the hardening compound into the frizzen face. Do this several times and quench. Put it in the lock and try it. If it still is too soft (which is doubtful if the hardening was done right), the next step is to half sole the frizzen face. Many older guns are found with this having been done so it's certainly not a modern invention. To do this, a piece of good, high carbon steel, such as a saw blade or file, is heated to cherry red and packed in ashes or whatever to hold in the heat and anneal the steel. When it is cool and soft, this piece of steel is fitted to the frizzen face. It is shaped so that it fits very closely. The thickness is worked down so that the frizzen isn't thickened appreciably by the addition of the piece. Some can be taken off the frizzen also. After fitting, the piece of steel is heated cherry red and quenched in water. This will make it glass hard. Now clean the face of the frizzen and the piece of steel. Tin the frizzen face with solder and flux the matching steel half sole. Put the steel in place on the frizzen and heat, from the frizzen side, until the solder just flows. This will do two things — it will stick the steel to the frizzen and it will draw the steel just a bit and make it soft enough for the flint to knock sparks from it. The sparks created when the flint strikes the frizzen are the result of small pieces of steel being sliced off the frizzen face. These heat to white hot, due to the friction of being cut off. Rarely a frizzen will be found that is so

hard that the flint can't cut any metal off. If this is the case, then heat the blade of the frizzen until colors just begin to appear, replace in the lock and try it. If still too hard, reheat and bring a little more color into the steel. This will usually cure the hardness.

The frizzen should snap open smartly when hit by the flint and should close tightly over the pan. If there is trouble here, it can be helped by fitting the frizzen to the pan and checking the action between the frizzen and its contact with the frizzen spring. The point of contact can be reshaped, if necessary, for a snappy action both ways. Any filing on the pan to improve fit must be done very carefully. It's easy to overdo it. Use inletting black on the frizzen to show the high spots on the pan. Take off very little each time until little or no light can be seen between frizzen and pan.

The flint should strike the frizzen no lower than half way down from the tip. If it is hitting too low, sometimes the frizzen can be heated cherry red and bent back just a little. It will then have to be rehardened. The flint should point directly into the pan when the hammer is in full down position. If you do anything with either the frizzen or hammer, think awhile about the change in relationships brought about by what you are about to do. Sometimes just turning the flint over in the jaws of the hammer will accomplish the same end. Flintlocks are funny critters and seem to take a certain amount of witchcraft to make them function reliably. They are, by the way, probably the most

The touch hole on this rifle was too high for consistent, reliable ignition. The original touch hole has been tapped and plugged. The new touch hole was drilled just below it, centered and level with the top plane of the pan.

authentic type of lock for a pre-1840 rendezvous. I doubt if there were a lot of percussion guns on the frontier this early.

Now, suppose the touch hole is out of place. We noted before that the touch hole should be in the center of the pan, on a line that follows the top plane of the pan. If the hole is too far down in the pan, ignition will be slowed — if too high ignition will be sporadic, at best. Moving a touch hole isn't too much of a problem. The hole should be enlarged and tapped. The size of the tap isn't important, although smaller is usually better. Take a screw of the proper size, tin it well with solder and turn it into the threaded hole. This should be done with the breech plug out so you can see into the barrel. Drive in the screw until it just shows in the bore. Cut it off on the outside and heat the barrel until the solder melts and takes — holding the screw firmly in place. Now slide a round piece of steel into the barrel and support the screw inside the barrel with it. Peen the screw on the outside of the barrel well. This will swell the screw in the hole and bind it even tighter. Dress the screw off flush on both the inside and outside of the barrel and mark the location of the new touch hole. Center punch the spot and drill a new touch hole. I would drill the hole with a #3 drill and tap ¼ x 28 for a touch hole liner. This will give better ignition than the standard 3/32" touch hole as it is tapered from the inside and allows the powder charge to be much closer to the priming powder in the pan. Drill carefully. You might want to drill a pilot hole of ⅛" or so to help guide the bigger #3 drill. Don't let the drill move into your old, plugged hole and ruin all your work. Usually barrels are soft enough that the drill will cut the screw and barrel about the same and won't have a tendency to wander.

Before leaving flintlocks, we probably should mention the material that is available for half soling frizzens. It is called by many names but it amounts to an iron/magnesium compound that will throw very hot, large sparks when struck by a sharp object, such as a flint. It is fitted to the frizzen face much the same as any other half soling material but it is usually attached with epoxy or the like. It can be riveted on also. It won't take solder, so another method of attachment is required. This stuff really does throw sparks. It will throw sparks that will literally burn holes in your shirt sleeves when shooting a flint rifle using it. It usually won't be allowed at rendezvous as it is far from authentic, being a "space age" material. I don't like the stuff as a full half sole on a frizzen. It's just too much of a good thing. It throws many more sparks than are needed for good ignition. I'm not sure I want all that fire that close to my eyes either. One use that I have found for it is to take a spare frizzen, make a hack saw cut across the face about ⅛" above the heel where it fits against the pan, and set a small piece of the material into the cut. Epoxy it in place and peen it well then smooth it to match the rest of the frizzen face. The frizzen will have to be softened, the cut made, then rehardened before installing the piece of material. What this does is give a very hot spark right at the bottom of the hammer fall and drops it right into the pan. I specified a spare frizzen because it shouldn't be used in matches or at rendezvous. But for hunting, when an entire trip may hang on a shot on a damp day, it has merit. Something to consider anyway.

This might be a good spot to go into the knapping of flints. For any flint lock to work efficiently the flint must be sharp. If it is to do its job of slicing off thin bits of metal from the frizzen, the edge must be sharp and well supported. As the lock is fired time after time, small bits and pieces of flint are broken from the edge and it becomes dull. How many shots can be fired before this occurs will depend upon the lock itself and the quality of the flint. With some locks, as the flint dulls it can be merely turned over in the jaws and it will resharpen itself as it is used. Usually, however, the edge must be "knapped" or sharpened. There are several ways of doing this. First, the gun should be unloaded, if possible. If it can't be fired, empty the pan and be very careful where both the muzzle of the gun and the touch hole

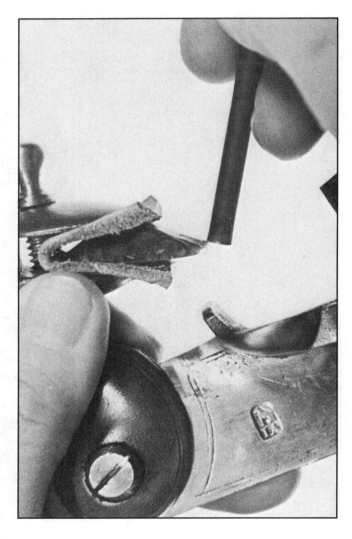

point while working on the flint. It is very possible to knock a spark loose during knapping and have it fire the gun. Naturally the muzzle is dangerous in this situation, but the touch hole will also spew out hot gas and powder fragments if it fires. An eye could be easily lost if this small volcano was directed towards your face. Being careful is easier than healing. If the gun is loaded, it is safer to take the flint out of the hammer jaws and knap it away from the gun. Or replace the flint with a sharp one and knap the dull one in the hammer jaws when the gun has been fired.

Knapping merely involves striking downward from the top of the flint right at the edge. This will break a small flake off the bottom side of the edge portion leaving a sharp edge exposed. This can be done free hand with a small hammer type instrument or the back of a knife or with a small punch to direct the force of the blow. The punch type arrangement works better as it is more controllable. The tip of the punch can be positioned right at the edge and then tapped with a small hammer or even a rock. It is very easy to control the amount of flint that is chipped off, using this method. The idea is to take off a very small amount all along the edge until it is sharp.

Another method to be used on an unloaded rifle only, is to lower the heel of the frizzen against the top edge of the flint and push down on the frizzen until it flakes off a small amount of chips from the underside of the edge. This works quite well with a little practice but, again, must be done with an unloaded gun only. The reason should be obvious — it is easy to strike a spark and fire the piece using this method of sharpening.

Three methods of knapping a flint. Preceding page: Knapping with a small punch. Left: Knapping with the type of knapper that was issued to Revolutionary War troops. The edge is set on the flint and the top is struck with the back of a knife, a small hammer, or the like. Right: Using the heel of the frizzen to knap a flint. The frizzen is pushed against the edge of the flint.

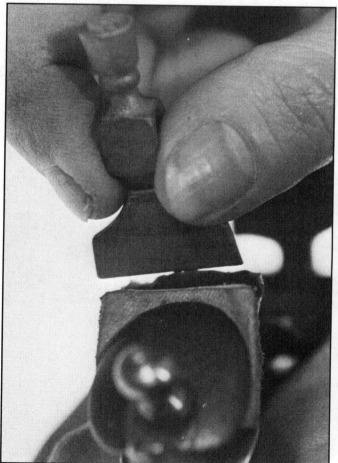 

With the lock properly tuned, ignition should be nearly instantaneous. This greatly increases accuracy and shooting pleasure.

TUNING TRIGGERS

A great many shortcomings in lock let off can be side stepped by the use of a set trigger, which is why so many of the production guns use them. Most are of pretty good design and function well. Most have screw adjustments so they can be set as light as you wish. Hardening and stoning the engagements of the set trigger are about the same as work on a lock. The same principles apply. The rear, or kick off trigger, should fly up on being released, hit the sear knocking it out of engagement and drop back enough so that the sear is not held out of engagement. This is where the fly we talked about earlier comes into play. It keeps the sear from dropping into the half cock notch. If the lock won't cock unless the trigger is set, a bit of metal may be taken off of the tip of the trigger mainspring so that the kick off trigger isn't held so high. This will allow the lock to be cocked and fired by the use of the front trigger alone, if desired. Occasionally a trigger unit will be found that is designed to work only set. That is, the sear is held out of engagement unless the trigger is set. The trigger must be set before cocking the gun. These are seldom found on production guns although there are a few around that use them.

Sometimes a trigger unit will be found that is set too high in the stock so that it blocks the sear action. This is usually found on kit guns. The cure here is to shim the trigger unit by putting thin pieces of wood under it until it works freely. The wood shims are then glued in place.

For a gun with a single trigger, if there is a lot of slack and play in the trigger, it can be inletted deeper into the wood to take out some of the slack, or the blade of the trigger where it contacts the sear bar can be built up by welding. The slack really doesn't hurt anything once you become used to it, if the lock has a good let off. The slack is caused by an appreciable distance between the top of the trigger blade and the sear bar on the lock. There must be a little bit of clearance so that the sear isn't blocked from going into the half cock notch, but the distance shouldn't be so great that there is a noticeable amount of trigger take up before the sear bar is acted upon.

Three types of triggers. Top: Standard single trigger. Middle: A double throw set trigger. The front trigger will fire the lock either set or unset. A fly in the tumbler is needed for this type of trigger to function properly. Bottom: A single action set trigger. The rear trigger kicks up and holds the sear out of engagement unless the trigger is set.

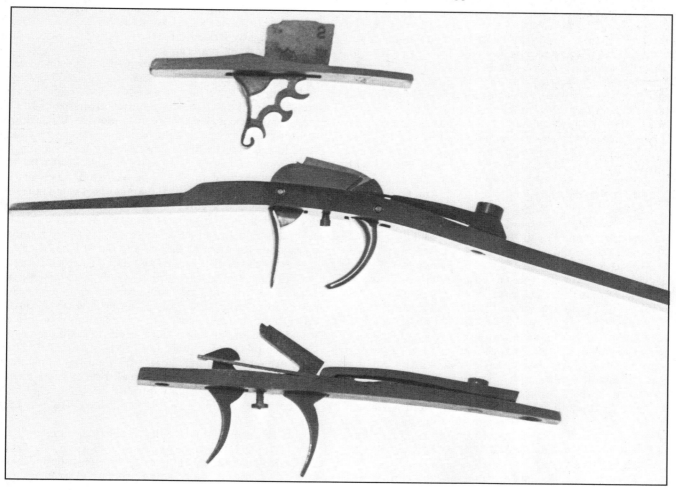

STOCK WORK

The next thing that I'm about to recommend may cause some raised eyebrows. The average production rifle is pretty sloppy in barrel fit in the stock. Probably the single most helpful thing that can be done to the average rifle, accuracy-wise, is to glass bed the barrel. This is easily done and is not noticeable, if properly done. It seals the barrel channel and beds the barrel for an even pressure throughout. Probably more important, it greatly strengthens the forend wood, reducing the chance of splitting or breaking. There are many bedding compounds on the market. I prefer one called Brownell's Accra-glas, but there are others. The Accra-glas is available in a gel that is very easy to use.

The first step in bedding your barrel is to take it out of the stock and remove the lock. Inspect the barrel and fill any dovetails or under cuts with modeling clay so that the glass can't get into them and lock the barrel into the stock. The breech area must be bedded well also, so if your gun has a hook type breech, take the tang portion out of the stock and do the modeling clay bit with any under cuts on it also. Paint the barrel, breech, tang, barrel keys and any other metal that will come in contact with the epoxy with a good coat of the release agent that comes with the bedding kit. Paste floor wax will also work just as well, maybe better. The secret is to fill any under cuts and put a good coat of release on everything. Give the outside of the stock a good coat of floor wax everywhere that the epoxy might touch, except where you want it to stick. Look over the barrel channel and see that the epoxy won't leak into the ramrod hole. If there are any holes that it could go through, plug them or cover them with paper. The barrel channel isn't waxed, by the way; you want the epoxy to stick there. Mix up the bedding compound, according to directions and add coloring agent to make it pretty dark. Put a good coat of the stuff in the barrel channel. You want the barrel to force bedding compound out all around it as it is seated. If the gun is a hook breech type, put the tang in place first and tighten the screws down. The screws were coated with release agent, weren't they? Now put in the barrel and push it down into the bedding compound. Push it clear down and put in the barrel retaining pins or keys or whatever holds it in. The bedding compound will squeeze out of all the cracks and crannies as the barrel is pushed down. This is why you coated the outside of the stock with wax. It will help get the stuff off when it has set up without sanding the stock again. If you are going to refinish the stock anyway it's not as important. Let the compound set up until it is just a little rubbery, almost hard. Then tap out the pins, keys or whatever, and tap the barrel upward out of the stock. If everything was well covered with release agent, it should come out fairly easily. The reason to remove it now is in case you missed any undercuts. If the stuff is a bit soft, you can still get the barrel out. It has to be hard enough to hold its shape, however. After the barrel and tang are removed, replace them and let the material set up hard. Clean off what has gotten on the wood and sand or file down the edges of the barrel channel smooth and flush. The resulting job shouldn't be noticeable and will really give you a skin tight fit between barrel and stock.

What if you followed directions and now can't get the barrel out of the stock? It happens. You either didn't get everything coated with release agent or you were a little sloppy in getting all the holes and undercuts filled with clay. You now have a one piece rifle. All is not lost. Epoxy will weaken if heated. Take a piece of steel that will just about fit the bore of the barrel. Heat it until it is just too hot to hold and slide it into the bore down to the breech. This will heat the barrel and, at about the temperature of boiling water, the epoxy should weaken enough so that you can get it out. This little trick might save you having to build another stock.

REFINISHING

Something that will improve the looks of the usual production gun is a refinish job. Most of these guns look pretty much alike. A little work can turn them into a good authentic looking rifle. Finishes can be taken off with one of the many finish removers on the market. Cracks and breaks in the wood can be glued with one of the two part epoxies that are available. The secret to this is to clean the crack or break well, keep oil and grease out of it, and work the epoxy deep into the break. Clamp the parts together very tightly. Plan out your clamping operation before you add the epoxy to the wood. If you are careful a very strong, almost invisible repair can be made, especially if the stock is refinished.

Most of the production stocks are too light colored, as they come from the factory. After the finish is removed and the wood lightly sanded, stain the wood to your taste with a good water stain, preferably.

As you are sanding the stock, you might want to clean up some of the lines, if they need it. Be careful that you don't round or "blur" any sharp edges. Don't sand flats on round parts, like the forend, or round off sharp edges, like the edge of the cheek piece and lock mortice. Use a dowel to wrap the sandpaper around to help you keep everything straight and clean in these areas. Always use something to back your sandpaper. Use heavy leather or felt for the rounded areas and something hard, like a dowel or flat piece of hard wood, for the flat areas. This can be the difference between a good looking gun and one that just doesn't make it. Many guns that you'll see that just don't seem to look right will often have too many things rounded on them giving them a "fuzzy" and out of focus look.

After the stock is sanded and stained, use a mixture of ½ turpentine and ½ spar varnish. Really soak this into the wood. This will seal it very well and fill the pores. This will save considerable time in building up a good oil finish. After the spar varnish coat is dry, sand it lightly to smooth it and add another thin coat, if needed, to fill the pores. Continue this until a good, level base is achieved. Then hand rub on several light coats of True-oil or some other linseed oil base finish, rubbing well between coats with very fine steel wool. A very durable, good looking finish can be achieved this way that won't look like a factory job.

If you think that you really want to individualize your rifle, Reinhart Fajen of Warsaw, Missouri and Otter Creek Rifle Works of Vergennes, Vermont, supply semi-inletted stocks for many of the production guns around.

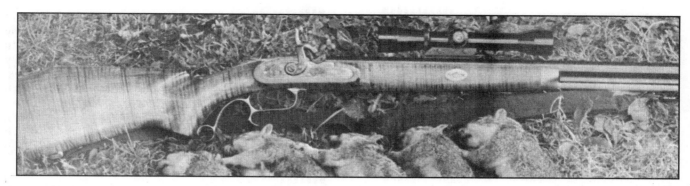

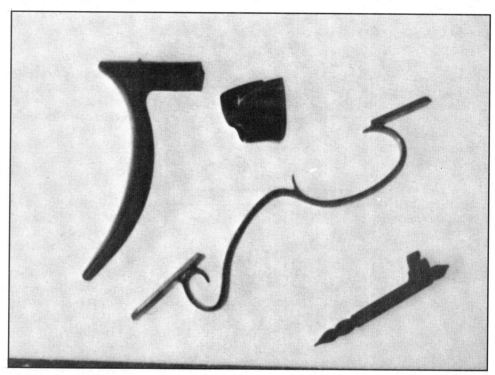

A couple of changes you can make in a production rifle to improve its looks. Top: A curley maple stock by Reinhart Fajen. This stock is obviously not authentic to the mountain man period. It is shown here to show the figure in the wood. Stocks of more traditional design are available for many of the production rifles. Right: A conversion kit offered by the Hawken Shop for Thompson/Center Hawken rifles. Many people like to replace the brass hardware with the more authentic iron set.

Fajen stocks are almost totally finished and are available in various grades of wood. The Otter Creek stocks have a cast off built into them that makes them come up to the shoulder very nicely. A cast off means that the butt of the stock is bent away from the shooter's face slightly to make shouldering the gun more natural.

If your gun has a blued finish to the metal, the look can be very much improved by removing the blue with a commercial blue remover and browning the steel. The various cold browning solutions available are easy to use and most anyone can get a good job with a little care. My preference is Plum Brown, put out by Birchwood Casey, but there are others that will work as well. I like to heat the parts to be browned after degreasing them with alcohol or the like. A propane torch can be used for heating. Bring the temperature up until the browning solution dries immediately when wiped on. It shouldn't sizzle but should dry immediately. After degreasing, handle the parts with cotton gloves or

wire hooks so that you don't get finger grease on them. Oil is the enemy of browning solutions. Heat the steel and rub on the solution. Keep heating and rubbing until the depth of brown that you want is achieved. If you get a spot that won't take and stays bright, merely keep heating and rubbing and it will eventually go brown. Browning greatly improves the looks of a rendezvous rifle, or pistol.

There are also companies that specialize in replacement parts for some of the production guns. These parts will interchange with the factory stock fittings and give the gun a totally different look. One such company is The Hawken Shop in St. Louis, Missouri. They put out a line of steel stock fittings that will make the Thompson/Center rifles more closely resemble the original Hawken rifles of yesteryear.

There are probably as many ways of individualizing a gun as there are folks doing it. Wrapping with wet rawhide in the wrist area or in the forend area are methods that will

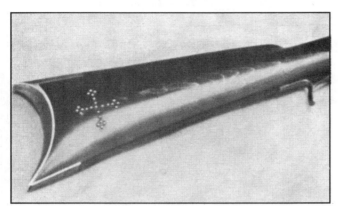

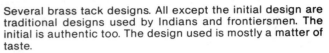

Several brass tack designs. All except the initial design are traditional designs used by Indians and frontiersmen. The initial is authentic too. The design used is mostly a matter of taste.

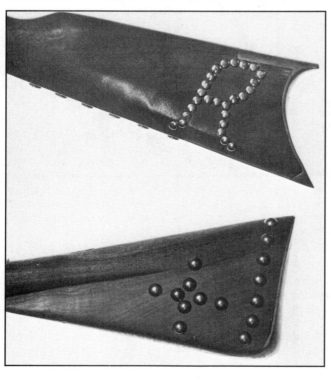

wood also. Most gunstocks are pretty hard and a small pilot hole will greatly facilitate driving the tacks in the proper place with no bending of the tacks or splitting of the wood, especially in the forearm area.

SIGHTS

Well, let's look at a few things that might help you hit something. First and foremost is sights. Good ones are a thing of beauty and a joy forever while bad ones are impossible to work with. First, if you have any choice in the matter, be sure the rear sight is at the proper distance from your eye for you to focus on it easily. This distance varies from person to person. Generally, those of us over forty have our rear sight further up the barrel than the kids. We don't focus as close as we once did. Naturally, open sights only. Most all rendezvous will not allow anything but open, nonadjustable sights. Adjustable open rear sights can be used usually if they are sealed with wax or something so that they can't be adjusted during the matches.

Everyone has their sight preferences. Some like one shape, some another. One man's meat is another's poison, as the saying goes. The traditional type of sight is a rear sight of whatever shape with a very fine "V" notch in it and a very narrow front blade. These sights are fine if your eyes are very good and the light is right. They leave something to be desired, however, for all but ideal conditions. Probably the most common is a front sight with a bed or round top on a narrower post coupled with a rear sight with a "U" type notch to match. This sight is easy to see for most of us, and is a very good hunting sight. For target work the "partridge" type sighting system is preferred by many. This is a post type front matched with a rear using a square notch. The rear notch is matched in width to the front post so that, when viewed by the shooter, there will be a very narrow band of light showing on each side of the front sight when centered in the rear notch. By making sure that both bands of light are equal, sight alignment is assured. If the front sight isn't too wide, good target accuracy can be achieved with this type of sight.

The shape of the rear sight, other than the notch, is a matter of traditional looks, whim, ingenuity or merely personal preference. All type of shapes were common on

add to the looks of a gun, if well done. Brass tacks in the stock will add to the overall picture, also. Tacks should be added with some design in mind, rather than just haphazardly. Stick with traditional designs. Look in a few books and see what the originals had in the way of design and patterns. Initials and the like usually don't look all that "right" but, if it makes you happy, go ahead. Usually tack jobs that look bad are the result of too many rather than too few. Small holes are best drilled to guide the tack into the

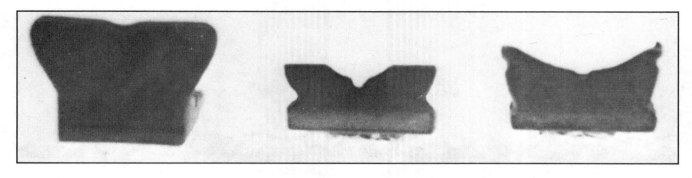

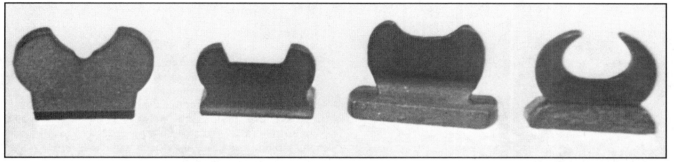

Reproduction sights available from most black powder suppliers. Top: Rear sights for Pennsylvania style rifles. Bottom: Rear sights (semi-buckhorn and buckhorn style) commonly used on 19th century plains rifles.

original rifles and the same is true on the reproductions we see today. Buckhorn type rear sights are very popular. These are, as the name implies, a sight that has two "horns" that project above the notch area and sweep towards the center, much like ram's horns. They can be merely small projections or can almost meet in the center. They are designated semi- or full-buckhorn sights, depending upon the sweep of the horns and how close they come to meeting. This type of sight isn't a bad idea for a hunting sight, as it will allow fast line up for close snapshots. The front sight can be caught quickly between the "horns" and will be close enough for a quick shot at a fast moving, close in deer or other game animal.

Many original rifles are seen that have the sights very low and close to the barrel and a lot of replicas follow suit. This is an advantage in heavy brush as they aren't so likely to catch on weeds, twigs and the like, however, the big disadvantage is that heat waves off the broad expanse of the barrel will distort the sight picture. This can really become a problem as the barrel warms from shooting or merely in the suns rays on a warm day. The other extreme begins to look like an Olympic type modern rifle. Something in the range of a sighting plane ¼ inch or so above the barrel is workable from the heat wave standpoint and still doesn't look out of place.

Sights are a very individual matter. A lot depends upon your style of shooting, type of gun, your eyes and just your preference. Try different guns and sight systems whenever shooters congregate. Don't be too quick to change from something that works for you. Sight selection takes time. Eventually you'll find the system that works best for you.

RAMRODS

Most of the off-the-shelf guns that one can buy have ramrods that are woefully inadequate for today's type of shooting. Original guns often have a very thin ramrod when compared to the bore, and many reproduction guns copy this drawback. Generally speaking, the old timers didn't shoot as tight a patch/ball combination as we do today. Therefore they didn't need short starters and heavy ramrods as we do. Rarely do you see a short starter in old original accoutrements. Even with the looser patch/ball combination, we often see references in older manuscripts and diaries to a "wiping stick". This was a larger, longer ramrod that was carried in the bore of the rifle and taken out before shooting. Occasionally we will see a reference to someone shooting without pulling the wiping stick—that must have been a very attention getting action. Recoil at least, would have been spectacular. At any rate, the issue ramrod on many guns can stand replacement.

A good ramrod should be as large as the under barrel ferrules will take. The ferrule size, unless you plan to change them, will dictate the diameter of the rod. If possible the rod should be just a bit under bore size. The larger the better. I never broke a ramrod because it was too big. It should have a threaded end that will take a cleaning jag of the proper size or the rod should have a cleaning jag permanently attached. Suppliers have both types available. A bullet puller that will thread into the rod is also a necessity. The rod should be as long as practicable. It can stick out past the end of the barrel, when in the ferrules, but this

should be held to a minimum. It's pretty easy to hook the protruding end and break the rod. Sometimes the rod hole in the stock isn't deep enough to hold a rod that is long enough to reach to the face of the breech plug. In this case, you have little choice. The rod will have to protrude from the ferrules. The rod must be long enough to reach to the breech plug face and still have enough of its length out of the barrel to get hold of.

Rods carried with the rifle should be of hickory. Most commercially available ramrods are hickory and have a minimum of cross grain. Ideally the grain in a ramrod should run from tip to tip, all grain parallel. In actual practice, given modern manufacturing methods, the grain will run pretty much end to end with some run out. This is alright as long as the cross grain doesn't occur in a fairly short area. Then the rod could shear off along the grain when force is applied as in seating a bullet. What this sharp end could do to a hand that was pushing hard when it let go takes very little imagination.

Most rods that one purchases will be bent to some extent. This is not a problem as all hickory will take a set or warp in storage. As long as the bend or warp is gradual and not sharp and kinky, it will straighten in the ferrules. A small amount of warp is good as it helps hold the rod in the ferrules and precludes loss.

The very best hickory that can be obtained is a hand split rod. These are split from blocks of wood and the grain runs end to end perfectly. They are very flexible and extremely hard to break. They are usually found in ¾" square splits and must be carefully worked down to a round cross section. These make the very best rods but are hard to find. Occasionally someone at shoots or rendezvous will be selling these. I have never seen them listed by muzzle loading suppliers although some may carry them. The second best rod is a commercial hickory rod that has been tempered. This is done by soaking the rod in kerosene for several weeks. The kerosene will eventually penetrate to the center of the rod and will make it very flexible and tough. This can be done yourself, using a plastic pipe with both ends capped. The rods are put in, the pipe filled with kerosene, and with a top cap on, the whole works is set away for some time, usually three to six weeks. As a rod is used, replace it and you'll always have some rods that are well soaked and usable when you need them. The rod can be left in the kerosene for long periods of time with no bad effects that I know of. Obviously, don't use this type of rod to stir your campfire.

A work rod or old time wiping stick should be made up for use at the range or in the hunting field. This rod should be made up like the regular rod but can be longer and bigger for ease of use. It should be nearly bore size and have fittings on both ends for ball pullers and jags. The ends should be glued on and cross pinned so they will resist pulling off during rough use, such as pulling that bullet you forgot to put powder behind. This work rod can also be one of the steel rods that are on the market and available from muzzle loading suppliers. Steel rods are actually easier on the bore than wood. Hard to believe, but consider this, wood can become impregnated with dirt and grit, making it a pretty fair substitute for sand paper. Steel is less likely to pick up this grit and, therefore, will have less wearing effect on the bore. So, don't be afraid to use a steel rod. They've been used for several hundred years.

LOADING & CLEANING

Let's take a fast look at load workup. This is merely a guide. The various books on the market on basic muzzle loading go into this much deeper and should be consulted. One of the best is the Lyman Black Powder Handbook. There are many pages of tables listing loads, velocities and, more important, pressures generated by the loads. This will serve as a guide in developing loads, while we'll take a quick overview.

As a rule of thumb, calibers over .45 should be loaded with FFg granulation black powder and those under .45 should use FFFg. This is a pretty good place to start with load work up. However, you may find that some guns seem to prefer FFFg even in the larger calibers, such as .50 or .54. I have a .54 caliber that performs better with FFFg. It fouls less and I seem to get better accuracy. If you use FFFg in larger calibers, keep in mind that pressures increase with the same loading weight-wise as FFg. It is best to drop your charge by 10% or more and work up gradually until the best accuracy is reached.

For a starting load for a new rifle, use the recommended loading of the manufacturer in the instruction manual. This is, by far, the best procedure. If the manual is unavailable or nonexistent, use a load of 1½ times the caliber, in grains, for calibers .45 and over and about ¾ the caliber, in grains, for those under .45. This would be, for example, 75 grains for a .50 caliber and 30 grains for a .40 caliber. These are merely starting loads and the most accurate loads will probably vary from this. It takes experimentation. Work up or down in small increments until you find that magic, very accurate load. Usually the most accurate load will be relatively mild. A very heavy load is usually not very accurate. So there is little to be gained by using heavy, hard kicking loads in your favorite rifle. It merely abuses both you and the gun.

Patch/ball combinations must be tight enough to seal the bore with a minimum of gas leakage. Here again the best practice is to use the manufacturer's recommended loadings. I prefer a fairly heavy patch, in the .015" range for calibers .45 and above with the ball selected for a good fit and ease of loading. I use .010" patching for calibers under .45. This will give a fit that loads easily and is accurate enough for most of my shooting. The target shooters will often use a ball of bore size and patch it .010"

Painting by David Wright

Wiping the bore between shots is a good way to keep the fouling soft and somewhat cleaned out during a match. It usually results in better accuracy.

or so. This fit is tight enough that the bullet must be started with a small mallet. In my view this is too tight for the rendezvous, load from the pouch situation, or for hunting. You'll have to make your own decision on this. It's a matter of what you want — top accuracy or ease of loading.

Many shooters run a damp patch down the barrel after each shot. This cleans the barrel so that the bore is the same shot to shot, and also kills any sparks that may be smoldering in the barrel. It's a good practice from a safety and accuracy standpoint. Other shooters will fire several shots between wiping. Again, you will develop your own preference with experience. I would recommend the practice of wiping between shots to start with.

After the day's shooting is done the messy, disagreeable job of cleaning must be done. This is probably the one thing that most folks dislike about muzzle loading. It really doesn't have to be such a bad job. My method is this — first swab the bore with a couple or three patches well saturated with a good black powder solvent. Use something that is water soluble. Put your finger over the nipple or touch hole and pour the bore full of water. Pour this out. Do this several times until clean water is draining out. Now take another solvent-saturated patch and wipe the bore again. If this patch looks pretty clean, proceed with drying the bore with several patches and oil it well. If the solvent patch is dirty, go the water route again. This will be plenty good enough for day to day cleaning.

For longer storage, it's best to use one of the tube flush accessories on the market. These replace the nipple with a tube that can be put in a container of water and the water pumped in and out of the barrel by a tight fitting jag and patch on your ramrod. This can also be done by removing the barrel and putting the breech end in a container of water. Tube flush accessories for flintlocks are now on the market also. These use rubber gaskets for a positive seal and make cleaning simple and not so messy. Usually flint guns clean quite well using the wet patch method as they don't have the long flash channel that many percussion guns do and there is less chance of ignition problems due to fouling accumulating in the flash channel.

Another method of really cleaning out the last vestige of fouling is to pour hydrogen peroxide down the barrel and allow it to really boil out the powder residue. This must be done carefully and isn't recommended for every day cleaning as peroxide is an oxidizing agent and will induce rust formation in the bore if it isn't very well oiled after using this type of cleaning. It is a good method to use before extended storage or once or twice a season to really get the bore clean.

How well you must clean each day will depend upon the amount of shooting you do and your climate. Naturally, if the gun will be put away for some time before the next shooting session it must be cleaned better than if it will be used the next day. Also if your climate is very humid and damp, you must be more careful with cleaning so that rust doesn't form in the barrel. In dryer areas there is less chance of rust forming in the short term.

Very little is written about how the old timers cleaned their guns. It was such a common thing that it never occurred to anyone to write down exactly how they did it in the field. From what can be gleaned from diaries and the like, I think that water was the solvent used most of the time. Oil was used to prevent rust or, failing a supply of that, natural greases such as tallow, sperm oil or whale oil were commonly used. There is more in diaries from the eastern portion of our country about cleaning than the western. Again, I'm sure this is because, in the dry, arid west, you can get away with being less meticulous in cleaning than in the more humid, damp east. I do find that the damp patch method of cleaning does suffice on a day to day basis, in most areas and climates. I think our forefathers used much the same method — after all, they used their guns almost every day.

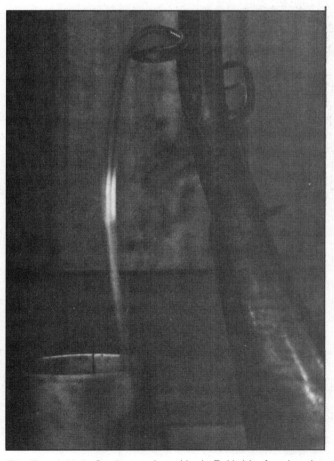

The Touch Hole Sealer produced by L. R. Hobbs for cleaning flintlock guns.

DEALING WITH WATER

"Watch yore topknot" and "Keep yore powder dry" were two commonly heard admonitions during the muzzle loading era. The former often depended upon the latter. Keeping water out of a muzzle loading gun, be it flint or percussion, was a problem then and is now. Percussion guns are somewhat easier. Usually a leather cover over the lock area made of well greased leather is sufficient to keep a percussion outfit functional in damp weather. This is assuming that the gun is clean of fouling. Black powder fouling draws moisture and, because of this, it is almost impossible to keep a fouled gun shooting in rain or very damp conditions. A tight fitting cap on the nipple helps and the seal can be helped some by the addition of tallow or a like grease over the cap. Be careful not to get the tallow inside the cap as it will "kill" the chemical that fires the cap. Be very careful of synthetic, "space age" greases and oils for the same reason. They tend to penetrate under the cap and dampen the fulminate igniter charge.

Flintlock guns should also use the "cow's knee" lock cover device to keep moisture from the lock area. The edge of the pan can be coated with tallow and the frizzen lowered to seal the priming charge from the damp. Again, this works fairly well if the gun isn't fouled. If it is, ignition will often be slow, if at all, in spite of your best efforts. There are some new products on the market that can be mixed with priming powder to waterproof it. They do work and are well worth a look for hunting situations. Most dealers in black powder supplies will carry one of the various brands.

The lock cover or "cow's knee" is an easy accessory to make. It was originally made of a portion of skin from a cow that covered the hock of the back leg. This gave a tent-like shape to the piece of skin, hence the name "cow's knee". These can be made from most any kind of oiled leather sewed down one side to make a triangular shape that will fit over the lock. The pattern should be made of paper first to get the shape and fit right, then transferred to leather. There should be a thong that goes under the stock to hold it in place on the lock and it should be easily removable. A thong tied to the trigger guard will prevent loss when the cover is removed and dropped hurriedly during a hunting situation.

CONCLUSION

Your rifle, pistol, shotgun or whatever is the focal point of your hobby and, in the case of the buckskinner, the focal point of your dress. It sets the period of your dress recreation and the general theme. In this chapter we've

Homemade "cow's knee". This one is buttoned under the stock using a brass button. A thong tie will work as well. It must be fast and easy to get off in a hunting situation.

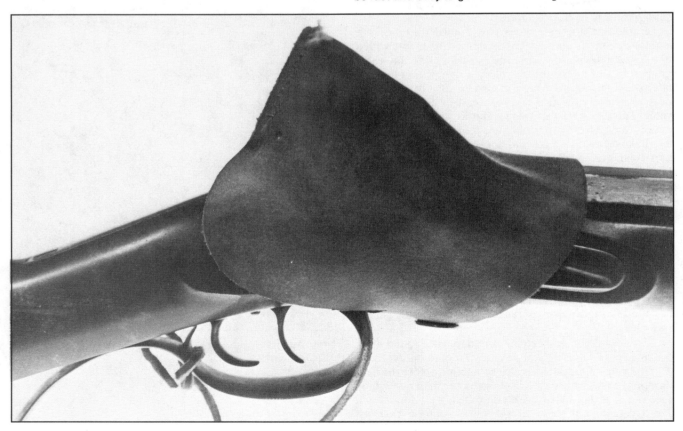

touched on a few of the facets of decoration and care of your firearm. You can think up many more as you follow this trail of the buckskinner. You'll never be totally satisfied with either your gun or costume. You'll probably own many of both during your buckskinning life. Each will be a little better. This is progress. Just don't get so far into progress that you reinvent the cartridge! Let's keep it reasonably traditional. Good luck and watch yore topknot!